THE ACTS OF THE APOSTLES
1 Corinthians, Galatians & Ephesians

FOR CCEA A LEVEL

2nd EDITION

COLOURPOINT EDUCATIONAL

Juliana Gilbride
Updated by Paula McCullough

© Juliana Gilbride, Paula McCullough and Colourpoint Creative Ltd 2008, 2017

ISBN: 978-1-78073-109-4

Second Edition
Second Impression, 2018

Layout and design: April Sky Design
Printed by: W&G Baird Ltd, Antrim

Cover picture: iStockPhoto

All rights reserved. No part of this publication may be reproduced, stored in a retrieval system or transmitted in any form or by any means, electronic, mechanical, photocopying, scanning, recording or otherwise, without the prior written permission of the copyright owners and publisher of this book.

Colourpoint Educational
An imprint of Colourpoint Creative Ltd
Colourpoint House
Jubilee Business Park
21 Jubilee Road
Newtownards
County Down
Northern Ireland
BT23 4YH

Tel: 028 9182 0505
Fax: 028 9182 1900
E-mail: sales@colourpoint.co.uk
Web site: www.colourpointeducational.com

The authors

Juliana Gilbride

Juliana Gilbride, B.Ed (Hons), M.Ed, is the Principal Examiner for AS Religious Studies (Acts of the Apostles) for CCEA.

She has over fifteen years experience of teaching 'A' Level Religious Studies. She lives with her family, Martin, Tom and Kate in Shercock, County Cavan.

*In memory of
Pierce Gilbride*

Paula McCullough

Paula McCullough has 28 years experience of teaching in Northern Ireland and examining at GCSE, AS and A2 level. She is currently head of the Religious Education Department at Methodist College Belfast and also teaches Learning for Life and Work.

Contents

An Introduction to the Acts of the Apostles

1. The Context of Acts
   Section 1: The Background to the Acts of the Apostles 5
   Section 2: The Characteristics of the Early Christian Community 47

2. The Beginning of the Church
   Section 1: Early Events in Jerusalem 64
   Section 2: The Missionary Activity of Peter and John 86

3. The Growth and Expansion of the Church
   Section 1: The Role of Stephen and Philip 99
   Section 2: The Role of Peter 123

4. Paul the Apostle
   Section 1: Paul's Conversion and Missionary Journeys 134
   Section 2: Paul's Speeches 166

Themes in Selected Letters of St Paul

5. Paul's Letter to the Galatians
   Section 1: The social and historical context of the letter 181
   Section 2: Paul's Teaching to the Galatians 190

6. Paul's First Letter to the Corinthians
   Section 1: The Issues Arising in Corinth 204
   Section 2: Christian moral living 215

7. Paul's Letter to the Ephesians
   Section 1: The Background to the Letter 243
   Section 2: The Main Themes of Ephesians 249

8. Synoptic Assessment 278

Bibliography 307

Glossary 315

Index 319

Publisher's Note: This book has been through a rigorous quality assurance process by an independent person experienced in the CCEA specification prior to publication. It has been written to help students preparing for the AS/A2 Religious Studies specification from CCEA. While Colourpoint Educational, the author and the quality assurance person have taken every care in its production, we are not able to guarantee that the book is completely error-free. Additionally, while the book has been written to closely match the CCEA specification, it is the responsibility of each candidate to satisfy themselves that they have fully met the requirements of the CCEA specification prior to sitting an exam set by that body. For this reason, and because specifications change with time, we strongly advise every candidate to avail of a qualified teacher and to check the contents of the most recent specification for themselves prior to the exam. Colourpoint Creative Ltd therefore cannot be held responsible for any errors or omissions in this book or any consequences thereof.

1

The Context of Acts

Section 1:
The Background to the Acts of the Apostles

INTRODUCTION: THE CONTEXT OF ACTS

The book of 'The Acts of the Apostles' is an attempt to set out the early history of Christianity in an orderly way. It is regarded by most scholars as a sequel to Luke's Gospel, which tells the story of the life and work of Jesus. Acts continues the story, describing how Christianity spread rapidly until it reached Rome, the centre of the ancient world. Packer (1966, p2) points out that the title, 'The Acts of the Apostles', is strange for a book that says nothing at all about the majority of the apostles. It focuses mainly on Peter and Paul, providing some insight into the contribution to the spread of Christianity of individuals like Stephen and Philip. Lake and Lake (1938, p67) comment that the value of Acts "is that it affords us a unique series of glimpses into the beginnings of Christianity. It is not a complete or a perfectly connected story, but our whole knowledge of the founding of the Greek-speaking church depends on it."

Christianity began in Galilee in Palestine in the first century AD following the death and resurrection of Jesus. The first followers of Jesus, who were all Jews, began a movement or sect within Judaism with Christ as the central figure. The word 'sect', as we know it, implies separation. However, the Greek translation means 'choice', and before AD70 (the Fall of Jerusalem), there was a great variety of parties within Judaism, each laying stress on particular aspects of their religion (Guy, 1969, p6), which Jews could choose to follow. The only condition was an insistence on loyalty to the belief in one God (monotheism) and to the Jewish way of life.

The movement was called 'the sect of the Nazarenes' (Acts 24:5; 24:14; 28:22). While we would assume that the term 'Nazarene' derives from Nazareth, Jesus' home town, most other Jews in the first century would have taken it to mean 'observant people' or people who observe a certain way of life (Bruce, 1958, p70), as the word is derived from a root that means 'to observe'.

Almost immediately, one of the other Jewish parties, the Sadducees, were antagonistic towards the Nazarenes. The Sadducees strongly opposed belief in the resurrection, and unsuccessful attempts were made to suppress the movement in its early days. However, it was too popular and even priests and members of the Sanhedrin (Jewish Council) were drawn to it. Most members of the party of the Pharisees could find little fault with the Nazarenes and regarded them as pious Jews who observed the Law. While the belief that Jesus was the Messiah would have been looked upon as absurd, the fact that it was based on Jesus' resurrection would have been viewed as 'a sign of grace' (Bruce, 1958, p72).

The sect of the Nazarenes appealed mainly to the ordinary people because of its simple message of forgiveness. Acts tells us that from Galilee the movement reached Jerusalem and flourished. Many converts were made when the apostles preached that Jesus was the long-awaited Messiah who was crucified, rose again and ascended into heaven. The movement spread through Judea and Samaria and, following the death of Stephen (Acts 6–8; 11:19), it extended to Syrian Antioch. Initially the movement consisted of Jews alone, but gradually Greek-speaking Jews and Gentiles were accepted.

As a result, the sect of the Nazarenes came to see itself as a new religion, separate from Judaism, although the term 'Christianity' was not used until after New Testament times.

Jerusalem evolved as the centre of the Jewish branch of the movement, while Antioch became the centre for Gentile Christians. From Antioch, Christianity spread through predominantly Gentile cities in Asia Minor and Greece until its eventual arrival in Rome.

Factors helping the spread of Christianity

When writing his letter to the Galatians, Paul stated that God chose exactly the right time to send his son: "But when the time had fully come, God sent his son" (Gal 4:4). Bruce argues that "politically and religiously the world was ready for the gospel at that time as it had not been before" (Bruce, 1958, p24). In the fifty years before 145 BC, the Romans had spread their empire over most of the known world. This led to relative peace and stability and also resulted in another benefit: good communications. The Romans had a reputation for building excellent roads, some of which survive today. Travel was safe and efficient, which helped the early Christians with their evangelising.

Greek culture and the widespread use of the Greek language was another factor that helped to provide the right conditions for the spread of the new religion. The official language of the Roman Empire was Latin, but most people spoke Greek. Green (1993; 2002, p13) comments that "it is interesting to note that St Paul addresses high-ranking Roman officials in Greek, not Latin, and to notice the centurion's surprise that Paul, an oriental Jew, should speak Greek, the cultured language of the world, not Latin (Acts 21:37ff)."

Against this background of peace and unity was a growing discontentment with the contemporary religions and philosophies. Bruce (1958, p24) notes that "the greater part of the civilised world was politically united, but the old classical religions were bankrupt." According to Green, "it is not surprising to find a growing dissatisfaction in Greek thought with the worship of many Gods with human characteristics" (1993; 2002, p14). Some Gentiles, known as 'God-fearers', were attracted to the monotheism of Judaism, but religion was tied too closely to one nation to have widespread appeal. During this period, the mystery religions were growing in popularity. These cults tried to satisfy a craving for salvation and the hope for immortality; they are another factor that favoured the spread of Christianity.

In conclusion, Green notes: "In the years between AD33 and 64 a new movement was born. In those thirty years it got sufficient growth and credibility to become the largest religion the world has ever seen and to change the lives of hundreds of millions of people" (1993; 2002, p7).

THE STRUCTURE OF ACTS

The book of Acts covers a vast amount of information giving us a chronological record of events in the church in the first century. However, it is fragmentary in places. For example, sometimes one verse will cover many miles (Ch 18:22) or sometimes no detail is given of a visit (Ch 19:1), while other events are described in great detail (Ch 15). It is difficult, therefore, to analyse the way the book has been structured by the author. Different theories have emerged, which, as you will see later, are linked to the purpose of the book.

Theories on the structure of Acts

1. The structure of Acts can be viewed in three parts, based on the pattern of Jesus' command in Acts 1:8, which involved the gospel spreading to:

    … Jerusalem (Ch 1–7).

    … Judea and Samaria (Ch 8–12).

    … Rome, the centre of the world (Ch 13–28).

2. Another possible division of Acts is into two parts, explained by the parallel between the ministries of Peter and Paul:

... Peter (centred in Jerusalem) Ch 1–12.

... Paul (centred in Antioch) Ch 13–28.

Guy (1969, p9) explains that chapters 1–12 deal with the church in Palestine and Syria – how it spread from Jerusalem to Samaria, Joppa, Caesarea, Damascus and Antioch, with Peter as one of the main characters. Chapters 13–28 tell of the church in the Gentile world, with Paul as the leading character. Luke "relates the journeys to Cyprus and Asia Minor, to Macedonia and Greece, and how Paul was arrested in Jerusalem, held prisoner at Caesarea and eventually taken to Rome." (Guy, 1969, p9). An outline of the parallels between the ministries of Peter and Paul is set out below:

Peter's Ministry	Paul's Ministry
Missionary to Jews	Missionary to Gentiles
Jerusalem	Antioch and Gentile world
Speech at Pentecost (Ch 2)	Speech at Pisidian Antioch (Ch 13)
Healing of Lame Man (Ch 3)	Healing of Lame man (Ch 14)
Judgement of Ananias and Sapphira (Ch 5)	Judgement of Elymas (Ch 13)
Escape from jail in Jerusalem (Ch 12)	Escape from jail in Phillipi (Ch 16)
Raising of Dorcas from the dead (Ch 9)	Raising of Eutychus from the dead (Ch 20)

This division of Acts acknowledges the importance of the work of bringing the gospel to the Jews (by Peter) and the Gentiles (by Paul). However, it does not take into account material in Acts that has nothing to do with Peter or Paul.

3. Parallels have also been made between the structure of Luke's Gospel and Acts, which of course is based on the theory that Luke was the author of both. Smith (1988, np) points out that:
    - both acknowledge the importance of Jerusalem.
    - both are arranged in the form of journeys.
    - both end with accounts of trials.
    - in both there is the pattern of rejection of Jesus and his teaching by the religious authorities.

4. Short summaries that occur at intervals throughout the book are another feature of the book of Acts:

Summary Reference	Events
Ch 2:42–47	The lifestyle of the believers
Ch 4:32f	The use of possessions
Ch 5:12	Signs attributed to the apostles
Ch 9:31; 16:5	Progress up to that point
Ch 5:42; 15:35	Teaching and preaching
Ch 6:7, 12:24; 19:20	Expansion of the church as the Word of God

5. A special feature of Acts is the 'we' passages, which indicate that the author was present at the events. This has led some to regard the structure of Acts as influenced by Luke's travel diary.

6. Finally, there are certain similar phrases used in Acts based around the term 'The Word of God', which may influence the structure of the book. These phrases comment on further expansion of the church:

Reference	Phrases	Expansion of church
Ch 6:7	The Word of God increased	After the appointment of 'The Seven' to support the apostles
Ch 12:24	The Word of God grew and multiplied	After Antioch has become an important centre for mission, and when the church at Jerusalem is experiencing problems
Ch 19:20	The Word of the Lord grew and prevailed mightily	After the success of Paul's missionary journeys

Outline of the book of Acts (for AS Level study)

Main Events	Detail	Reference
The beginning of the church	Prologue Jesus' initiation of the church's mission The Pentecost event The first preaching of the gospel (Pentecost speech) First summary of the life of the Early Church	Ch 1:1–2 Ch 1:3–11 Ch 2:1–13 Ch 2:14–42 Ch 2:43–47
The church and the Jewish Authorities	The healing of the lame man and Peter's explanation The arrest of Peter and John Prayer for boldness Second summary of the life of the Early Church Ananias and Sapphira Growth of the church Second arrest of apostles	Ch 3:1–26 Ch 4:1–22 Ch 4:23–31 Ch 4:32–37 Ch 5:1–11 Ch 5:12–16 Ch 5:17–42
The church starts to grow	The Appointment of the Seven Stephen's speech and martyrdom The evangelising activity of Philip Paul's conversion Paul begins to preach	Ch 6:1–7 Ch 6:8–8:1 Ch 8:4–25 & Ch 8:26–40 Ch 9:1–19a Ch 9:19b–31
The start of the Gentile mission	Peter's miracles The conversion of Cornelius The church at Antioch The imprisonment and escape of Peter	Ch 9:32–43 Ch 10:1–11:18 Ch 11:19–30 Ch 12:1–25
The First Missionary Journey	Cyprus, Pisidian Antioch, Iconium, Lystra	Ch 13:1–14:28
The Second Missionary Journey	Derbe, Lystra, Macedonia, Thessalonica, Berea, Athens, Corinth	Ch 15:36–18:22
The Third Missionary Journey	Caesarea, Antioch, Ephesus, Miletus	Ch 18:23–21:17

WHO WROTE THE BOOK OF ACTS?

It is generally accepted that Luke's Gospel and Acts were written by the same man, but neither the Gospel nor Acts actually claims this to be Luke. Tradition names the author as Luke, "the beloved physician" (Col 4:14) and a co-worker of Paul (Philemon 1:24 and 2 Tim 4:11), although his name is in fact only mentioned three times in the New Testament. Barclay feels that it is obvious that Luke was a doctor because he instinctively uses medical words (1955, pxiv). However, Banks highlights the view of Cadbury that the language used does not require a medical author since it is found also in the language of non-medical authors (2006, p14).

We can also work out from Colossians 4:11 that Luke was a Gentile. The verse concludes with a list of greetings from Jews and a new list begins in verse 12. The natural conclusion is that this is a list of Gentiles. Luke is mentioned in this list, and if we accept that he is the author of Acts, then the fact remains that he is the only Gentile author in the New Testament. Banks (2006, p12) also points to Acts 1:19, in which the author refers to "their language" when speaking of the Aramaic spoken by the residents of Jerusalem. The quality of the author's Greek, the general lack of Semitic (Jewish) words and the universalism found in Luke–Acts also imply that he is a Gentile (Banks, p12).

There are two types of evidence to support the argument that Luke is the author of both pieces of work. The first type of evidence we will look at is 'external' evidence, meaning that it is found 'apart from' or outside Luke's Gospel and Acts. The second type of evidence is 'internal' evidence, so called because we look inside the Gospel and Acts for clues to the authorship.

External evidence

1. Packer (1966, p2) points out that as early as the end of the second century AD the tradition of the church held that Luke wrote Acts. Irenaeus was an early Christian writer who lived in the second century. He held that Acts was written by Luke and he was supported by other early Christian writers, for example Clement of Alexandria (AD150–215) and Tertullian (AD160–225).

2. In the early days of Christianity the New Testament did not exist in the form that we have it today. Rather it developed over a long period of time, with some books being rejected from the final 'Canon of Scripture', which closed in the fourth century. However, some earlier evidence of a compilation of New Testament books exists. Around AD170, a list of New Testament books was collected known as 'the Muratorian Fragment'. The 'Acts of all of the Apostles' is one of the books included on this list, naming Luke as the author.

3. Another piece of evidence is found in a preface to the third Gospel, written at about the same time, called 'the anti-Marcionite prologue'. In it Luke is named as the author of Acts as well as of the Gospel.

Internal evidence

1. Luke's Gospel and Acts can be looked upon as a two-volume work. Acts continues the story at the point at which the Gospel finishes. Freed (2005, p4) points to Acts 1:1, which indicates that Luke intended the second volume to complement the first. This argument is further supported by Guy, who comments that "the end of the Gospel overlaps with the beginning of Acts" (1969, p6) and Barrett, who adds that "the end of the story of Jesus is the church; and the story of Jesus is the beginning of the church" (1961, p57ff). Furthermore, both Luke's Gospel and Acts were addressed to the same man, Theophilus.

2. Acts is written using mainly the third person pronoun (He did this; they went to), a style that suggests the author was not present at the events he is recording. However, there are four passages in Acts (16:10–17; 20:5–15; 21:1–18; 27:1–28) where the pronoun changes from the third person to the first person (I did this; We went to). These are referred to as the 'we' passages because it is obvious that the author was present at these events. These passages can be described as eye-witness accounts and were written like a travel diary record. "In these passages we find more exact notes of place and times than in other parts of the book. The natural conclusion is that the writer was himself present at these points" (Guy, 1969, p14).

3. Freed also points out that "common vocabulary, similarities in literary style, and some of the same religious beliefs also support the views of common authorship" (2005, p14). Longenecker agrees, adding that "stylistically and structurally, the Gospel of Luke and the Acts of the Apostles are so closely related that they have to be assigned to the same author" (1995, p238).

TASK

Rather than trying to work out who the author was, work backwards and use the method of elimination. In other words, who could the author NOT have been? For example, if you were writing a diary account of a day spent with friends it might read as follows:

> "Tom, Kate, Amy and I drove down to the beach yesterday. It was a really hot day and we ran into Jon and Sam at the café so we all went for coffee and had a right laugh."

> Who wrote this account about the day at the beach? Well, we know it wasn't Tom, Kate, Amy, Jon or Sam because they are mentioned. It must have been someone else.

In Paul's letters he mentions nine travelling companions: Aristarchus, Crescens, Demas, Justus, Luke, Mark, Timothy, Titus and Trophimus (Hewitt, 1964, p22). The author of Acts has to be one of them. Using the 'we' passages from Acts (see below), work out who the author could NOT have been by matching the names of Paul's travelling companions from these passages to those mentioned in his letters:

'We' passage	Paul's companions
Ch 16:10–17	
Ch 20:4–15	Sopater, Aristarchus, Secundus, Gaius, Tychicus, Trophimus and Timothy
Ch 21:1–18	Philip, Mnason, James
Ch 27:1–28:16	

Who does this leave as a possible author?

- *Crescens, Demas, Justus, Luke, Mark or Titus*
  From Acts and the letters we know that Mark was no longer a travelling companion (Acts 15:36–41) and Demas had deserted him (2 Timothy 4:10). This reduces the possible list to the following:
- *Crescens, Justus, Luke or Titus*
  Crescens and Justus had very little contact with Paul, so they can be dismissed, leaving us with:
- *Luke or Titus*
  Titus is not mentioned in Acts or in any church traditions, and so we are left with:
- *Luke*
  Luke was not an original eyewitness or disciple of Jesus. He was a professional who researched his information and compiled his document under the inspiration of the Holy Spirit. In Colossians 4:14 Luke is described as "the beloved physician and friend" of Paul. He was with Paul during his imprisonment in Rome (Philemon 1:23–24), which is also a period covered by the last 'we' passage. Lewis (1960, p20) argues that the author was one who reached Rome with Paul and did not leave him.

Challenges to the traditional authorship of Acts

The evidence presented in this section has given support for the traditional view of the authorship of Acts:

- The author of Luke's Gospel also wrote Acts as a two-volume work.
- The name of Luke is given to this person.
- He is thought to be a Gentile doctor and a travelling companion of Paul.
- He was an eyewitness to many of the incidents described in Acts.

However, critical views of the authorship of Acts challenge these conclusions, claiming that both books were the work of an anonymous writer. This person was not an eyewitness, but used written sources already in existence, including the 'we' passages. According to Brown (1977, pp267–268), scholarly opinion is currently evenly divided on the issue of whether Luke's Gospel and Acts were written by Luke the Doctor.

Other modern scholars have questioned whether all the letters attributed to Paul are his own authentic writing. Collins (2004, p4) claims that most contemporary scholars do not accept 2 Timothy as a genuine letter of Paul. The author of Colossians as Paul is similarly held in question by some. These letters provided some of the evidence for the traditional view of authorship. 2 Timothy 4:11 suggests that Luke is Paul's companion: "Only Luke is with me", while Colossians 4:14 refers to "our dear friend Luke, the Doctor". This raises the difficulty that if these letters are not the work of Paul, it cannot be assumed that Luke and Paul are travelling companions.

Finally, there are differences between Acts and Paul's letters that have raised doubts as to whether Luke was a friend of Paul. It seems as if he did not have access to some of his letters, as shown by the following discrepancies:

- Following Paul's conversion in Acts, he visits Jerusalem to meet with Peter and the other apostles (Acts 9: 26–30). However, the sequence of events is different in Galatians, where Paul writes, "I did not go up to Jerusalem to see those who were apostles before I was, but I went immediately into Arabia and later returned to Damascus" (Gal 1:17).

- Speaking in tongues appears to have a different meaning in Acts than it does in 1 Corinthians. Peterson (2009, p13) comments that "the other tongues on this occasion were unintelligible languages different from their own, not the sort of tongues mentioned in 1 Corinthians 12–14, which could only be understood if someone interpreted".

- In Acts, Paul appears to have a different attitude towards Jewish rituals than in the letters. He has Timothy circumcised (Acts 16:3) and is willing to take part in discharging a vow in the Temple (Acts 21:24). However, in Galatians, Paul gets angry with Peter for refusing table fellowship with Gentile Christians (Gal 2:12).

Conclusion

Gasque (1988, p179) concludes that if Luke did not write the third Gospel and Acts, it is difficult to explain how the tradition connecting his name with these documents ever arose, since he is otherwise an insignificant figure in the Early Church. Lewis agrees, adding that "tradition can be quite unreliable, but in this instance, where authorship is ascribed to a comparatively unimportant person in the Early Church, it carries more weight since the tendency is always to attach works of such religious value to great names" (1960, p20).

Although the external evidence unanimously identifies Luke as the author of Acts, the internal evidence is inconclusive (2006, p14). However, throughout this book for the sake of convenience the author will be referred to as Luke.

PRACTICE ESSAY QUESTION
Writing essays for AS Level

Your course is assessed through writing essays. For each module, you will have an exam requiring two essays to be written in 1 hour 20 minutes. Each essay will be in two parts: for part (a) you must demonstrate knowledge and understanding; for part (b) you will be required to analyse and evaluate aspects of, and approaches to, religion and belief. Part (a) and Part (b) are each worth 50% of the marks so they should be of a similar length.

Question from CCEA's Specimen Assessment Materials

(a) Discuss the main arguments for the authorship of Acts. [25 marks]

Your answer could make reference to the following points:
- The traditional view that Luke is the author of both Luke's Gospel and Acts; he was most likely a friend and travelling companion of Paul.
- A discussion of the internal evidence for authorship: the similarities between Luke and Acts.

- A discussion of external evidence for authorship: reference to early church fathers, such as Irenaeus, Tertullian and Clement of Alexandria.
- The evidence offered by the 'we' passages.

(b) Comment on the view that the issue of who wrote Acts is unimportant. Justify your answer. [25 marks]

Your answer could make reference to the following points:
- With ancient texts there can often be uncertainty as to the original author and with many texts the author remains unknown.
- There are many more important questions concerning the background of Acts than authorship, for example, the purpose of Acts as a historical narrative, an apology for Christianity or a defence for Paul's trial.
- A discussion of authorship takes into account the relation of the work to other books in the New Testament, such as the synoptic Gospels.
- Fuller meaning is given to the questions of purpose and characteristics when authorship is considered as important background.

WHEN WAS ACTS WRITTEN?

The dating of the book of Acts is not a foregone conclusion. Three dates have been suggested by scholars, which differ by almost as much as forty years. There is an early date, around AD63; an intermediate date, around AD75; and a late date, around AD98.

Early date – around AD63

There are several factors that contribute towards the argument for an early date:

1. Abrupt ending of Acts

The book of Acts finishes rather suddenly with an account of Paul reaching Rome and being held under house arrest for two years (Acts 28:30). Luke does not record the death of Paul, which happened during the reign of the emperor Nero (AD54–68), probably around AD65. Therefore it can be argued that Acts must have been written before Paul's death, because otherwise Luke would have recorded it.

However, it is not clear whether Luke finishes his account with Paul alive and well in Rome because events had caught up with the time of writing or because he had taken the story as far as he wanted it to go. Marshall (1980, p47) believes that Luke's purpose in writing Acts was to show how the gospel reached Rome, rather than to tell Paul's life story; therefore the question of when Paul's death took place remains open. Streeter even suggests that Acts might be renamed 'The Road to Rome' (1924, p532). Guthrie (1961, p357) points out that some scholars believe that Luke knew of Paul's death, and agrees with Marshall that it was no part of his purpose to close with this because it would draw too much attention towards Paul and away from the progress of the gospel. Another possibility is that Luke planned to write a third volume to tell the rest of the story, including the death of Paul (Guthrie, p358). However, if this were the case then surely a better breaking-off point should have been possible between the end of Acts and the start of the 'third volume', similar to the smoothness of the break between Luke and Acts.

Guy (1969, p18) believes that "it is more probable that Luke ended the Acts in this way in order to emphasise that even in the imperial city Paul was allowed to teach and receive visitors, showing that the Roman authorities were tolerant towards him and his message even when he was a prisoner". Hanson (1967, pp212–230) even suggests that Luke omitted to mention Paul's death because everyone already knew about it.

Bruce (1988, p11) comments that the fact that Paul's death is not mentioned in Acts is not a decisive argument for the dating of the book. It may even be that the outcome of Paul's trial is not mentioned because Luke himself died before he could finish writing the book (Lietzman, 1950, p78). But Bruce (1988, p11) believes that Luke probably finished his book exactly as he intended to do.

2. Positive attitude towards Romans

Another point supporting the early date concerns the positive attitude that Acts reveals towards the Romans. It can be argued that Acts must have been written before the atrocities of the emperor Nero's persecution of the Christians (AD64). Harnack (1911, cited in Barclay, 1955) points out that "the generally optimistic and hopeful atmosphere of Acts would have been impossible any time after the Neronian persecution". When we look at Revelation 17:1–6, for example, we see Rome portrayed as "the scarlet woman drunk with the blood of saints and martyrs", a very different picture to that reflected in the book of Acts.

3. Dominant issues in Acts

Acts focuses on issues that were dominant in the church before AD70, for example, the admission of Gentiles into the church, Jewish-Gentile relations within the church, and arguments over food laws. After Jerusalem was destroyed in AD70, such matters became less important as the church became predominantly Gentile. This observation supports an early date.

4. Theological outlook of Acts

The theological outlook of Acts reflects primitive or very early Christianity. Primitive titles are used, for example, to describe Jesus ('Christ', 'Son of Man', 'Servant of God'); and Luke uses the term 'disciples' to describe Christians, which is not a feature of Paul's letters.

5. Paul's letters

Paul wrote thirteen letters to the churches he founded and yet Acts does not offer any knowledge of their existence. It is possible that Paul's letters were not collated and issued until the end of the first century. It may even have been the heroic picture of Paul in Acts that led to the collection of his letters in the first place (Barclay, 1955, p246).

One great difficulty with the early date is raised by Guy (1969, p18), who points out that Luke used Mark's Gospel when writing his own. The probable date for Mark is AD65–70, shortly after the death of Paul, which means that Acts must have been written after that time. This will be discussed further in the next section on an 'intermediate date'.

Intermediate date – around AD75

Given that Luke wrote a Gospel as well as Acts, it is useful to consider the dates of both pieces of work together to get a more accurate picture.

Most scholars agree that Luke based his Gospel on Mark's Gospel, which is usually dated after AD70 – the year Jerusalem fell to the Romans. They base their argument on the fact that Luke seems to see in this event the fulfilment of a prophecy made in Mark Ch 13. These scholars tend to be in agreement that such a prediction could not have been written before the event took place. If Mark's Gospel was written after AD70, it would have to have been in general circulation before Luke could use it. Therefore it has been suggested that Luke wrote his Gospel around AD72, followed by Acts around AD75.

The fall of Jerusalem is foretold in the gospels of Matthew, Mark and Luke:

Matthew 24:15f
"So when you see standing in the holy place 'the abomination that causes desolation' spoken of through the prophet Daniel ..."

Mark 13:14
'When you see 'the abomination that causes desolation' standing where it does not belong – let the reader understand – then let those who are in Judea flee to the mountains".

Luke 21:20f
"But when you see Jerusalem being surrounded by armies, you will know that its desolation is near".

In Matthew and Mark there is a prophecy, based on a saying in Daniel. However, this is not the case in Luke. Instead there appears to be a description of a historical event that has already taken place. Matthew and Mark's version tends to hint at some desolate sacrilege, whereas Luke speaks plainly of surrounding armies. The argument is that Matthew and Mark wrote before the event happened, whereas Luke wrote after it. Therefore Luke's Gospel, and subsequently Acts, must have been written after AD70.

However, this then raises the question of why Luke did not mention an event as important as the fall of Jerusalem (AD70), or have anything to say about the martyrdom of James in AD62 or the martyrdom of Peter and Paul. Guthrie (1961, p356) suggests that the destiny of Jerusalem would perhaps not have appeared as tragic to the Christian Church as it would to the Jewish people. This may be why Luke did not mention the event. However, du Plessis (1998) argues that Jewish Christians in Jerusalem could not have been unaffected by the fall. He regards the failure of Luke to mention it as a reason to doubt whether the events had yet happened.

Another point, which we have already touched on, concerns the attitude of the Romans towards Christianity in Acts. Would the favourable attitude presented in Acts be realistic after Nero's persecution in AD64, when many Christians were tortured and put to death?

Finally, if Luke wrote around AD75, why did he not use Paul's letters? Guy (1969, p19) points out that Paul's letters would not have been collected together by that time and circulated extensively. So they would not have been available to Luke, especially if he was writing in Rome, because most of the letters had been sent to churches in Asia Minor or Greece and were probably collected at Ephesus.

A late date – around AD98

Some scholars believe that in writing Acts Luke has carefully considered all aspects of his story to present it in a meaningful way, rather than simply recording a mere chronicle of events. Marshall comments that "it is arguable that a writer cannot do this successfully unless he stands at some distance from the events so that he can see them in perspective" (1980, p47). This gives some support to the argument for a late date, although there are other significant points to consider:

1. In the writing of Acts, Luke used the work of a Jewish historian, Josephus of Alexandria. This work, 'Antiquities of the Jews', was published in AD96. Therefore it is argued that Acts was probably written shortly after this, around AD98. However, it should also be noted that by AD98 Paul's letters would have been well circulated and at Luke's disposal. If Luke was prepared to use the work of a Jewish historian, then he would definitely have used the work of Paul, the man who dominates much of the story of Acts.
2. Another factor against the suggestion of a late date is that Acts does not reflect the interests and outlook of the church at that time. There is no mention, for example, of the sacraments, the development of the three-fold ministry or apostolic succession – issues that were of utmost importance to the church in the second century. Moreover, there is no mention in Acts of the death of James (AD62) and that of Peter, who was martyred in Nero's persecution.
3. Finally, it is important to take into consideration Luke's own life-span, which is difficult to estimate. Guthrie argues that "it would certainly not be impossible for Luke to have written Acts any time up to about AD85 but it could hardly have been much later" (1961, p356).

Conclusion

The question of when exactly Acts was written remains unanswered. Acts gives no information of events in Paul's life after his two years in Rome, and yet at the same time the book gives the impression that the author is looking back on events with a sense of reflection. Bruce (1988, p13) believes that the writing of Luke–Acts took place over an extended period of time and that the story was brought to an end at a significant point, that being "the completion of the process of bringing the gospel to Rome."

TASK

a) Explain the reasons for the various proposed dates for the book of Acts.

Your answer should include some of the following:
- Internal and external evidence for the dating of the Acts of the Apostles – early (circa AD63), middle (c AD75) and late (c AD98) dating options explored.
- The views of modern scholarship regarding dating.

b) Explore the claim that the relationship between Paul and the author of Acts is central to the dating of Acts. Justify your answer. (This question should be answered after completion of Chapter 1.)

An exploration of the claim may include, for example:
- Information on the authorship of Acts and implications regarding the dating of the text.
- The link between the writer of Acts and Paul's travelling companion 'Luke'.
- Controversy regarding the travel diary/'we' passages.

THE PURPOSE OF ACTS

In determining the purpose of Acts (that is, why it was written), Marshall (1980, pp18–19) comments that we are dealing with the second part of a two-volume work. Luke tells the story of Jesus (in his Gospel) and the story of the beginning of the church (in Acts), which together form the basis of the Christian Church. Bruce (1998, p6) points out that the two parts, for all their stylistic differences, make up an integral whole, with one coherent purpose.

> "Many have undertaken to draw up an account of the things that have been fulfilled among us, just as they were handed down to us by those who from the first were eyewitnesses and servants of the word. Therefore, since I myself have carefully investigated everything from the beginning, it seemed good also to me to write an orderly account for you, most excellent Theophilus, so that you may know the certainty of the things you have been taught." (Luke 1:1–4)

The strong link between the two books is further highlighted by Neil (1973), who points out that "it is thus not without significance that he tells the story of the Ascension twice; once at the end of his Gospel and again at the beginning of Acts". However, the question of why Luke wrote this companion to his Gospel, and what the two-volume work was meant to achieve, is one that has produced a variety of responses.

Acts as a history book

Marshall (1980, p17) comments that most people approach Acts as "the history book of the early church". As a piece of history, it traces the Ascension of Jesus and the story of the beginning and spread of Christianity from Jerusalem, through Asia Minor, Macedonia and Greece until the arrival of the gospel in Rome, the centre of the world at that time. Stott (1990, p23) adds that Luke was well qualified to write such a history, for "he was an educated doctor, a travelling companion of Paul, and had resided in Palestine for at least two years."

As well as being a historian, it has been suggested that Luke was writing more as a preacher and as such was selective. The history Luke presents is not simply a chronological record of everything that happened from one day to the next. He is forced to be selective of events due to the broad range of his subject, so it is written in such a way as to highlight significant moments and events. Furthermore, as an ancient writer, Luke would have written on a papyrus roll, which would have only been about 9 m/30 ft long, just enough to hold Acts as we know it. Such circumstances would also have been factors in his reasons for being selective. Guthrie agrees, adding that "Luke intended his work to be regarded as historical, but not in the sense of a dry chronicle of events" (1961, p349). There is much we would like to know, of which Luke is silent. Guthrie wonders if this is due to Luke's desire to write about Paul as soon as possible.

On the other hand, there are those who argue that the church never suspected it would have a history (Fuller, 1966, p123). After all, most early Christians believed that Jesus' return (*Parousia*) would be in their own lifetime. What would be the point of writing anything down if the world was going to end? Dibelius had earlier made this point, commenting that:

> "To write down the history of the oldest community, to give an account of its difficulties and conflicts, to describe its spread to Rome and to tell how the way was prepared for the reception of the Gentile, and of the obdurate refusal on the part of the Jews – all this could not have

seemed an obviously necessary undertaking to those Christians who were waiting for the end of the world, and who had neither inclination nor ability for literary work." (1956, p103)

A Work of literature

Luke uses impressive language and a certain style, which suggests that Acts was written to attract an educated audience. The style used by Luke is that of the Greek Old Testament (the Septuagint), which may be an indication that he regarded the history he was recording as sacred (Marshall, 1980, p18). It is probable that Luke believed he was recording events that were the fulfilment of Old Testament prophecies and that his purpose was to convince the educated in society of the validity of Christianity. Bruce argues that:

> "At any time in this period a work which gave an intelligent history of the rise and progress of Christianity, and at the same time gave a reasoned reply to popular calumnies against it, was sure of a reception among the intelligent reading public – or rather listening public – of Rome, of whom Theophilus was probably a representative." (1988, p11)

Haenchen (1971, cited in Guthrie, p353) sees Acts as an edifying piece of literature, in which the author uses literary means to make the events memorable to his readers. Hunter (1945, p79) describes Luke as "a literary artist" commenting that Acts "abounds in memorable narratives" such as:
- Stephen's martyrdom 6–7
- Paul and Barnabas at Lystra 14
- Paul and Silas in prison at Philippi 16
- The riot in the theatre at Ephesus 19
- Paul's defence before Agrippa 26
- The storm and shipwreck on the journey to Rome 27

To promote universalism

However, others believe that Luke was writing to a wider audience, that is, rich and poor, educated and uneducated, Jew and Gentile. Scholars point to the roll call of countries in Acts 2:9–11 as a sign that the gospel was for everyone. As previously mentioned, both Luke's Gospel and Acts are dedicated to Theophilus (Luke 1:1; Acts 1:1), which is a Gentile name. It can be argued, therefore, that its purpose was to show that the gospel was for Gentiles as well as for Jews. This idea is known as 'universalism', because it shows that Christianity is for everyone. Hewitt (1964, p20) supports this view, pointing out that in Acts Christianity gradually embraces Gentiles, as Stephen, Philip, Peter and finally Paul include them in its baptism.

Some scholars (Hunter, 1945, p77) believe that Luke's main purpose was to describe the breaking down of the barriers between Jew and Gentile as the church moved outwards in the power of the Spirit from Jerusalem to Rome. Lewis (1960, p16) argues that Luke writes with an eye on Rome as the destination of the gospel, which is his concern in both his books. In his gospel he tells how Jesus brought the Good News to the Jews. In Acts he tells how the gospel travelled from Jews to Gentiles, and from Jerusalem to Rome.

Lewis (1960, p20) comments that "Luke is not out to write a biography of Paul in Acts, any more than he was out to write a biography of Jesus in his Gospel."

The gospel of the Spirit

Some scholars believe that for Luke it was important to acknowledge the divine activity behind the events in the Early Church, and therefore his work places great emphasis on the work of the Holy Spirit. Bruce (1988, p13) comments that "Luke wishes to make it clear that the progress of this faith was no mere product of human planning; it was directed by divine agency." Scott agrees, arguing that this progress happened "through the energy of the Spirit" (1932, p95). Guthrie therefore points out that "it is not inappropriate that this book has been called the Acts of the Holy Spirit" (1961, p350).

However, Willimon argues that "it would be a mistake to infer that Acts features the Holy Spirit the way that the Gospel features Jesus" (1988, pp8–9), commenting that there are great portions of Acts where the Spirit is not mentioned or only mentioned in passing. For example, the Holy Spirit is mentioned most often in the first half of Acts and there are eleven chapters where he is not mentioned at all.

An apology

Many scholars see in Acts an apologetic purpose. Banks (2017, p100) explains that the term 'apology' comes from the Greek 'apologia', meaning 'defence'. So an apology may be a speech or piece of writing that defends Christianity against attack. When the Christian Church began, opposition came from the Jews only and Christians were left well alone by the Romans. The Romans initially regarded Christianity as a branch of Judaism, which allowed it to have the status of '*religio licita*' (legal religion). Judaism was tolerated by the Romans because, as Banks explains, "it was an ancient and national religion which Rome had the good political sense not to confront" (2017, p28).

However, once the Roman authorities realised that the Christians were different from the Jews, they no longer extended the same freedom to the church and persecution was inevitable.

Acts can be regarded as an apologetic work in two ways: firstly, in defending Christianity against Jewish attack; and secondly, in defending Christianity against Roman attack.

1. An apology to the Jews

Luke stresses the close connections between Christianity and Judaism, which may be an attempt to convince Jewish readers of the validity of Christianity. Some examples of this include:

Reference	Example
2:17–21; 2:25–28; 2:30; 2:34–35; 3:22–23; 4:11 (some examples among many)	Appeal to Old Testament prophecy (Jewish Scriptures)
16:3 23:6 18:18; 21:17–26 15	Christian observance of Jewish ceremonial requirements: • Timothy circumcised • Paul's claim to be a Pharisee • Paul's vow • James' insistence on relationship between Judaism and Christian procedures at Council of Jerusalem

2. An apology to the Romans

Acts can be perceived even more as an apologetic work in its presentation of the relationship between the Christians and the Roman authorities. Guy comments that in Acts the Romans were either favourably inclined towards Christianity, adopting a lenient attitude, or "exhibited the official attitude of cold indifference" (1969, p12) towards it. Perhaps Luke presented the Romans in this light in an attempt to establish Christianity, like Judaism, as one of the accepted religions in the Roman Empire. Bruce comments that in general there was a widespread suspicion that Christianity was, "a subversive movement, a menace to imperial law and order" (1988, p8), and Luke himself wrote that "people everywhere are talking against this sect" (Acts 28:22). Stott (1990, p26) states that Luke produced evidence to show that Christianity was harmless, innocent and lawful, and he argues that Luke was deeply concerned about the attitude of the Roman authorities towards Christianity, going out of his way to show how the Romans were impartial in relation to Christians (1990, p26). Hunter (1945, p74) agrees and regards this as deliberate on the part of Luke, who is eager to vindicate Christianity in the eyes of his Gentile readers, to convince them that it was no threat to the '*pax Romana*' (peace), as its enemies were insinuating. It is significant to note that almost a quarter of the book is taken up with Paul's trials, through which Luke is "at pains to present Paul as a loyal and law-abiding Jew" (1988, p10).

The following table gives examples from Acts of the attitude of the Romans towards Christianity:

Reference	Example
Acts 10	The conversion of the Roman centurion, Cornelius
Acts 13	Sergius Paulus is presented as being very favourable towards the gospel message
Acts 16	In Philippi the magistrates apologised to Paul
Acts 18	Gallio had no interest in the religious concerns that formed the basis of the Jewish charges against Paul
Acts 19	At Ephesus the city secretary was very reasonable, declaring Paul and his friends to be innocent; the Asiarchs were friendly to Paul
Acts 26	Agrippa and Festus agreed that Paul could have been released if he had not made an appeal to the Emperor

Willimon adds some doubt to the theory that Acts was an apology to the Romans, pointing out that much of it "would be unintelligible to pagan Romans" (1988, p9). It is difficult to imagine that a Roman official like Felix would take the time to read Acts just to learn about Christianity.

A defence for Paul's trial

This is based on the idea that Paul's trial is in progress and Luke is preparing a detailed account of the background and nature of Christianity for Theophilus, a high-ranking Roman official who may have influence over the outcome of the trial (Williams, p15ff). However, some scholars (Barrett, cited in Guthrie, 1961, p350) consider it far-fetched, if not absurd, that a book such as Acts would have the power to dispel the suspicions of someone like Emperor Nero. Also, Lewis (1960, p15) argues that much of Acts is concerned with Jesus' continuing deeds through his Holy Spirit, which suggests that Luke "is addressing a wider public than just Theophilus".

A theological purpose

It has been suggested that Luke had theological concerns at the forefront of his mind in writing the book of Acts. Williams (1975, pp24–25), for example, comments that Acts revealed the triumph of Christianity in a hostile world. Therefore the spread of Christianity from Jerusalem to Rome can be argued to have theological significance.

Marshall (1980, pp18–19) insists that Luke is both historian and theologian, and that as a theologian he was concerned that his message about Jesus and the Early Church should be based upon reliable history. Hunter agrees, commenting that "Luke may also claim to be a theologian in his own right, and no mere historian" (1945, p78). His is a theology of salvation, with Jesus as Saviour, the exalted Lord, in whose name the forgiveness of sins is offered to men. This salvation is for Gentiles as well as Jews; and it is the apostles' task to confirm it, build up the church and carry the gospel to the ends of the earth.

To mend the split between the followers of Peter and Paul

Acts can be regarded as an attempt to minimise the split between the followers of Peter and Paul. Baur (in Gasque's, translation, 1975, p326) came up with a theory that the Early Church was split into two camps: those who supported original Jewish Christianity represented by Peter; and those who supported Gentile Christianity, represented by Paul. He argued that Acts was an attempt to deny the hostility between Peter and Paul. Stott (1990, p28) points out that most scholars think Baur took this theory too far. Stott regards Luke as "a peacemaker in the church", who wanted to show that the apostles Peter, James and Paul were in fundamental agreement about the gospel. He adds that "the reconciliation between the leading apostles was real, not fictitious".

However, from reading Acts it is obvious that the real split was between James and Paul, with Peter caught up in the middle of it. Further insight into this can be gleaned from reading the following: Acts 11:1–18, Acts 21:17–26 and Galatians 2:11–14. According to Paul, it was James who intimidated Peter about associating with the uncircumcised.

Conclusion

While many suggestions have been put forward for the purpose of Acts, it is important to keep in mind Luke's own statement of the purpose of his writing, that is, "to confirm the Christian message by providing a reliable account of its beginnings (Banks, 2006, p25). All other purposes should take second place.

TASK

a) Explain the various reasons suggested for the purpose of Acts.

Your answer should include knowledge and understanding of some of the following:
- A range of purposes: apologetic, missionary, evangelical, historical, etc.

b) Explore in particular the claim that the author of Acts has a special interest in the acceptance of Gentiles into the church. Justify your answer.

An exploration of the claim should include:
- Identification of the needs of Luke's audience and the context in which Luke wrote.
- Specific textual examples concerning the acceptance of Gentiles into the church.
- Identification of other interests shared by Luke, for example, concern for the poor and oppressed.

c) Comment on the claim that the purpose of Acts was to give an account of the growth of the church. Justify your answer.

Your answer should include an exploration of the following examples:
- A defence of the claim showing the progress from Jerusalem to Rome.
- Other purposes: a continuation of Luke, for Theophilus, legal defence, apologetic, a defence of Christianity before Rome, a second volume.

d) Explore the claim that it was important for Luke that the gospel message reached Rome.

An exploration of the claim should include some of the following:
- A defence of the claim showing the progress throughout the book from Jerusalem to Rome with examples from the text.
- Comment on Acts 1:8 as a theme for the book.
- Paul's determination to reach Rome.
- Comment on the ending of the book.

THE CHARACTERISTICS OF ACTS
The characteristics of Acts are the main features that are prominent in the book. If we approach Acts thematically, it may be easier to distinguish certain characteristics that dominate its pages, for example 'Universalism', 'Role of the Holy Spirit' or 'Theology'. The main characteristics are described below, although some will be explored in more detail later in this book.

The place of Acts in the New Testament
It is significant that in the canonical order (that is, the chronological order of the books in the New Testament), Acts has been placed between the Gospels and the letters. Hunter comments that it "is the link which holds together the Gospels and the rest of the New Testament" (1945, p80), and it certainly connects the accounts of Jesus with the apostolic correspondence that follows. In many ways, the letters are not fully understood until they are read alongside the book of Acts. Acts reveals the main trends in the development of Christianity, making a vital contribution to an understanding of the relationship between the teaching of Jesus and the apostolic doctrine (Guthrie, 1961, p351).

Universalism
The fact that Christianity is for everyone and not just the Jews is a major theme in Acts. For example, in chapter 15, there is an account of a debate at the Council of Jerusalem concerning the terms through which Gentiles could be admitted into the membership of the church. Many Gentiles, who knew little of Jewish traditions, accepted the gospel message and were baptised. However, Jewish Christians were alarmed because they felt that all new members should be circumcised and instructed in the Law of Moses. The decision made at the Council, that Gentiles need not be circumcised to become Christians, broke huge barriers and led to a greater spread of the faith.

Role of divine control and guidance
The events that occur in the life of the church in Acts are seen to be brought about by the will and power of God, and as such are a fulfilment of Old Testament Scripture (Marshall, 1980, p24). The following table gives some examples of this:

Reference	Fulfilment of Prophecy
2:17–21	the outpouring of the Holy Spirit
13:47	the mission to the Gentiles
15:16–18	the acceptance of the Gentiles into the church
28:25–27	the refusal of the Jews to accept the gospel

Such events, as listed in the table, would not have been possible without God's power, which is primarily seen through the work and influence of the Holy Spirit. Luke describes the continuing work of Christ in the church through the power of the Spirit. Guthrie (1961) comments that God is seen to be as active in the early Christian community through the Spirit's power as he had been in the life of Jesus (13:2; 15:28; 16:6). Marshall (1980, p24) agrees; however, he points out that while sometimes the Spirit directed the church, at other times angels spoke to Christian missionaries (5:18–20; 8:26; 27:23) or messages were mediated by prophets (11:28; 20:11f), and on one occasion the Lord himself appeared to his servants (18:9; 23:11).

Primitive church life and worship
Acts does not give a detailed account of early church worship, but we do find a general impression of church life. Christians are seen to be spiritual and moral individuals. The church was united, as reflected by a communal lifestyle, regardless of significant differences of opinion. There is an obvious element of joyfulness among these early believers, although there were problems that Luke did not shy away from reporting. For example, the story of Ananias and Sapphira shows a moral lapse that was not tolerated.

Theology
Drane (1986, p240) regards much of the theology in Acts as having a far less sophisticated character than the theology either of Paul or of the church later in the first century. It is possible to detect a form of primitive theology in the many speeches recorded in Acts. For example, the titles ascribed to Jesus in the speeches in Acts are a valuable guide to the early development of Christology (the study of the person of Christ).

Look at the following references from Acts and complete the table, listing the primitive terms used to describe Jesus, the Christians and the church:

Terms	Reference in Acts	Equivalent in Acts
Jesus	Acts 2:36; 3:20; 4:27	The Messiah/Christ
	Acts 3:13, 26; 4:25–30	The Servant of God
	Acts 2:36	Lord
		Prince of Life
		Saviour
		The Righteous One
	Acts 7:36	The Son of Man
Christians	Acts 6:1–7; 9:25–26	Disciples
The church	Acts 9:2; 19:9, 23; 24:14, 22	The Way

Marshall (1980, p23) is another scholar who regards Luke's writings as having theological significance. He argues that Luke brings out this significance in the way he tells the story of the church. This view is supported by Fernando (1998, p23), who highlights some evidence from the text of Acts to stress Luke's concern with theology. For example, the results of the ministry in Derbe during the First Missionary Journey produced "a large number of disciples" (14:21), and yet there is only a single sentence about Paul's work there. On the other hand, the ministry in Athens produced only "a few" converts (17:34), but takes up nineteen verses. The argument is that Luke selected material because of the value it had in promoting theology that was important to him.

Kerygma (early Christian preaching)

Although Acts is not intended to be a theological or doctrinal book, it does provide insight into the elements of early Christian preaching, which Dodd (1944, p7ff) has called '*kerygma*'. Marshall points out that the main message proclaimed in Acts "is expounded in a series of public addresses scattered throughout the book" (1980, p25). The content of this message contains essential truths about Jesus. An outline is provided overleaf:

The *Kerygma* of the Early Church'	References in Acts
• Old Testament prophecies have been fulfilled with the coming of Jesus the Messiah	2:30; 3:19, 24; 10:43; 26:6–7
• God anointed Jesus as Messiah at his baptism	10:38
• After his baptism, Jesus began his ministry in Galilee	10:37
• Jesus' ministry is characterised by good deeds and miracles through the power of God	2:22; 10:38
• Jesus the Messiah was crucified according to God's purpose	2:23; 3:13–15, 18; 4:11; 10:39; 26:23
• He was raised from the dead and appeared to his disciples	2:24, 31–32; 3:15, 26; 10:40–41; 17:31; 26:23
• He was exalted to the right hand of God and given the name Lord	2:25–28, 33–36; 3:13; 10:36
• He gave the Holy Spirit to begin the new Christian community	1:8; 2:14–18, 38–39; 10:44–47
• He will come again to judge	3:20–21; 10:42; 17:31
• Everyone who hears the message of salvation should repent and be baptised	2:21, 38; 3:19; 10:43, 47–48; 17:30

Focus on Peter and Paul

One of the most striking features about Acts is that it has so much to say about the work of Peter and Paul and yet says so little about the work of the other apostles. Nothing is said, for example, about the Christian mission in Alexandria, the second city of the Roman Empire, inhabited by as many as a million Jews. Luke chooses not to record every expansion of the church but is instead selective, and as a result Acts is dominated by Peter and Paul.

In chapters 1–12 Peter is the main focus as the narrative moves from Jerusalem to Antioch. He takes the lead before and after the dramatic events at Pentecost. It is Peter who commands the lame man at the Temple gate to walk in Jesus' name; and twice he defends the church before the Sanhedrin. Peter is not afraid of confrontation and condemns Ananias and Sapphira for lying to God; he also confronts Simon the Sorcerer in Samaria. And such is Peter's presence that his very shadow heals the sick.

Then from chapter 13 to the end, the missionary activity of Paul becomes the main focus of attention. He is introduced dramatically as an enemy of the faith at Stephen's death in chapter 7, which stands in great contrast to his conversion in chapter 9. Scholars have pointed out that several of the features of Peter's ministry are repeated. (Refer to table in 'Structure' section, p8) Both men heal cripples. Both heal people by strange means. Both encounter sorcerers. Both are miraculously released from prison. Perhaps these parallels are drawn to suggest that Paul was just as much an apostle as Peter. The narrative at the end of Acts (chapter 20 onwards) centres almost totally on Paul and shows him moving inevitably towards Rome, but with courageous determination.

TASK

a) Describe the main characteristics of the book of Acts.

Your answer should include knowledge and understanding of some of the suggested characteristics of Acts, for example:
- Emphasis on the geographical spread of the gospel.
- The message of the gospel.
- Emphasis on the Holy Spirit.
- The Jewish response to the gospel/Gentile inclusion.
- Focus on Peter and Paul.
- Relations with Roman authorities.

b) Explore the claim that the main characteristic is a record of the early Christian message (*Kerygma*).

Exploration may include some of the following points:
- The recognition that the *kerygma* is one of the focuses in the book of Acts, with examples from speeches studied at AS level.
- Arguments concerning the importance of other characteristics, for example the Role of the Holy Spirit.
- A personal evaluation of which characteristic is most important.

THE 'WE' PASSAGES

The 'we' passages have already been mentioned in the previous section as part of the discussion on the internal evidence for the authorship of Acts. These sections of Acts, written in the first person (we did this, we went to) are also important when considering the date, reliability and sources of Acts.

The value of a historical work depends upon the quality of the sources used to write it. The more reliable the sources used in writing, the more valuable the end result should be. Therefore, in determining the origin and reliability of the sources used by Luke, we are really asking 'where exactly did he get his information from?'

However, this is not as straightforward as it sounds. Hanson (1967, p48, 50) points out that "it is very difficult indeed to reconstruct, or even tentatively to identify, Luke's sources for the book of Acts." Johnson agrees, pointing out that unlike his Gospel, "Luke apparently had no overall guide for his extended narrative" (1992, p3). Lewis feels that "when we come to Acts we are helpless, so scholars are still speculating and disagreeing about Luke's sources" (1960, p103). However, it is certain that Luke relied on various sources, which can be divided into two main types:

Primary Sources – Luke's own experiences of events.

Secondary Sources – The experience of others passed on to Luke.

Acts 1–15 (secondary source material)

As well as having direct experience of some of the events, the author of the 'we' passages would have met significant people who could give him valuable insight into other events for which he was not present. Hunter (1945, p74) argues that this could have been through the three great centres of early Christianity: Jerusalem, Caesarea and Antioch. For example, it appears that the author of Acts was at one time a companion of Paul (Acts 16:10). "Beyond a doubt Luke's friendship with Paul would bring him into touch with all the great men of all the Churches and all their records and stories would be at his disposal" (Barclay, 1953; 1955, pxix). As Paul's travelling companion, Luke would have had immediate access to the information recorded in: 9:1–31; 11:25–30; 12:25; 17: 28–31. Guthrie (1961, p389) also points out that it is known from Colossians 4:10–14 that Luke was with Mark and could certainly have obtained useful information from him regarding the early growth of the church. Stott (1990, p22) agrees, adding that Mark may have kept a written account. Acts 12:12 refers to a prayer meeting in the house of Mark's mother, so it is reasonable to assume that this home was a regular meeting place for Christians. Mark would certainly have been familiar with much, if not all of the events preceding the Council of Jerusalem (Guthrie, 1961, p389). Therefore, as one who knew Mark and was a travelling companion with Paul, Luke was certainly in a position to write a reliable account of the growth of the Early Church.

Acts 16–28 (containing some primary source material and secondary source material)

Johnson points out that in this section "the information available to Luke seems to have been both more substantial and reliable" (1992, p4). There are a number of passages written in the first person (I, we), which are known as the 'we' passages. The implication is that Luke was present at some of the events that he has recorded. Such access to first-hand evidence would mean that the 'we' passages are very valuable as sources.

It is significant that the 'we' passages occur when a sea journey is undertaken. Did Luke sail with Paul and keep a travel journal which he later included when writing Acts?

Possible explanations for the 'we' passages:

There are four main arguments:

1. The most obvious reason for the use of 'We' is that the author wishes to show that in the events described in these passages he was one of Paul's travelling companions. At these points in the narrative, Luke is producing a first-hand account. It may be called a literary device to distinguish between primary and secondary sources of information. This view is supported by the uniformity of style and language with the rest of the book. Peterson comments that "Luke draws attention to his own eyewitness material by casting it in the first person plural" (2009, p7).

2. The 'We' sections form whole or part of the author's own personal diary. Where appropriate in Acts, he quoted the relevant portions, retaining the first person as in the original entry. However, this view is possibly less likely than the first, as Luke would not use travel jottings, which were probably not intended for publication in their original form, without adapting them first.

3. The author of Acts was not an eyewitness but used someone else's diary or travel notes, which he incorporated into his own text without alteration – not even changing the first person. Porter (2001, pp10–46) argues that the author of Acts had access to a previously written

source, using the first person, that was not his own. However, many scholars feel that this suggestion is even less likely than the second – another author would not have retained the 'We' form, particularly without giving any indication of the identity of the person speaking.

4. The only other possibility is that the use of 'We' is no indication of an eyewitness, but is used as a literary device to give the impression of authenticity. However, if this were the case, then why is the device not used more often in Acts? Also, a greater impression of authenticity would surely be given if a name had been given to the fictional writer. Scholars generally regard this as the least likely of the four suggestions. Witherington claims that "no one has yet produced telling evidence from ancient historical documents that such 'we' passages in these sorts of historiographical works were ever added purely for verisimilitude or as a veiled claim to be using a source written by another" (2001, p23).

There is general agreement that the author of the rest of the book and the 'We' sections is one and the same person. This reinforces the view that Luke is an accurate and reliable writer who has "carefully investigated everything from the beginning" and is attempting to "write an orderly account" (Luke 1: 3). As Peterson writes: "Although some have doubted the authenticity of the 'we' passages, most scholars view these as evidence of the author's participation in the events recorded" (2009, p7).

The 'we' passages and the date of Acts

A view held by many scholars is that these sections show that the author of Acts (Luke) was present on some of the sea voyages with Paul. Luke could be using his travel diary or simply reverting to the first person to show that he was present. It is generally accepted that Paul's missionary journeys took place between AD49 and AD57. This means the author could not be present on the voyages and writing Acts in the second century, which leaves either of the earlier dates as a possibility. If, however, the 'we' passages are taken to be Luke using another person's records, then the late date is still possible.

THE HISTORICAL RELIABILITY OF ACTS

Introduction

The book of Acts has faced some severe criticism regarding its historical accuracy and reliability. For example, the Tübingen School (Munck, 1986, cited in McCann, 2003, p2, online) regarded Acts as a piece of propaganda literature, written in the early second century and considered unreliable as a historical document. They argued that Acts was written mainly for the edification of the church, and its author was a theologian who manipulated the historical facts to suit his purpose, even inventing material when it suited him (Hunter, 1945, p77).

It has been suggested that historians in ancient times were tempted to write from their own biased agenda and therefore should not be trusted to give an accurate historical account. However, the most reliable ancient writers were careful to accurately present the facts in the same way as practised by modern historians. Carson, Moo & Morris (1992) give the examples of Polybius, Lucian and Thucydides as ancient historians who were concerned to present facts as accurately as possible and who disapproved of exaggeration. McCann (2003, p2, online) believes that Luke deserves to be placed among these ancient historians and only differs from today's historians because he does not present every historical detail but is deliberately selective, choosing to concentrate on events relevant to the growth of the church. At times it may seem that Luke got his facts mixed up, especially where he is relating events that happened long before he himself came to the scene, but to suggest that Luke made up history to suit his theological purpose is to question his trustworthiness and integrity.

Perhaps a compromise can be reached by regarding Luke as both a historian and a theologian; in other words, he was a man who composed his book on the basis of real history, but used the historical facts to preach the gospel of salvation through Christ (Hunter, 1945, p77).

The original purpose of Luke's work

Although we have already looked at the purpose of Acts, it might be useful to consider Luke's original purpose for writing his gospel (Luke 1:1–4). As pointed out by Fernando, "the prologue of the Gospel of Luke, which applies to Acts as well, indicates that Luke intended to write an account that was historically accurate (Luke 1:1–4)" (1998, p23). Therefore, it is generally agreed amongst scholars that Luke's intention to be accurate extended to Acts as well as his Gospel (Stott, 1990, p22).

Relationship between Acts and Paul's letters

Scholars, such as Haenchen (1971, pp462–468), who question the historical reliability of the book of Acts, point to the discrepancies between the account of the Council of Jerusalem in Acts 15 and the writing of Paul in Galatians 2. While Luke provides a simple account of the Council in Acts 15, difficulties arise when Luke's account is compared with what appears to be the same event in Galatians (Bruce, 1988, pp282ff). For example, in Galatians Paul is speaking about his second visit to Jerusalem after his conversion, but in Acts Luke says that it was his third visit. Another difference is that the conference in Galatians is held in private, whereas the meeting in Acts 15 is held publicly, before the Jerusalem Church. Bruce (1988, p282) argues that the differences arise because the authors are in fact speaking about two entirely different events. Wainwright (1965, p175) supports Bruce in these differences and feels that Galatians 2:1–10 has actually more in common with Acts 11:27–30, than with Acts 15.

However, if we put the differences between the above texts to one side, it is possible to consider other examples in Acts that support the idea that Luke was an accurate historian:

- Luke gives correct details regarding Paul. Paul reveals that he was trained as a Pharisee (Phil 3:5; Gal 1:14) and Luke tells us that Paul was trained under Gamaliel, one of the most important Pharisees of the day (22:3).
- In Paul's own letters he claims to belong to the tribe of Benjamin (Rom 11:1; Phil 3:5), and Luke tells us that Paul's name was 'Saul' (7:58), which is the name of the most distinguished member of the tribe of Benjamin.
- Paul mentions that he persecuted Christians (Gal. 1:13) and Luke comments that Paul had put Christians to death (Acts 8:1) (Powell, 1991, p89).

Archaeological evidence

The reliability of Acts is supported by Luke's attention to detail, which Bruce (1989) argues proves to be accurate in the field of archaeology. Hunter (1945, p78) agrees and points to Ramsay's archaeological digging in Asia Minor at the beginning of the 20th century, where a study of inscriptions showed how accurate Luke actually was regarding certain terminology. Bruce (1988) regards Acts as "a masterpiece of historical accuracy", because Luke shows himself to be correct every time. McCann (2003, online) provides evidence of this accuracy through a discussion of details of titles, groups of officials, names, descriptions of customs and practices, and other historical events. Each of these will be explored in turn:

1. Titles

McCann (2003, online) explains how titles used in Acts to describe various authorities have proven to be correct. Luke always uses the right word to describe Roman administrators, and sometimes uses words that would only be familiar to people living in certain cities (Drane, 1986, p240). For example, McDowell (1991, p111) points out that some scholars assume that Luke's use of the term 'politarchs', which was a title for civil authorities in Thessalonica (17:6), was inaccurate, since the word was not known to exist in classical literature. However, recent discoveries have shown Luke to be perfectly accurate in his use of this word, since around nineteen inscriptions were discovered that use the title, five of which are used in specific reference to Thessalonica (McDowell, 1991, p111).

The title 'chief man' is also an accurate description used by Luke to describe the Roman governor, Publius, of Malta, which was the island where Paul was shipwrecked (28:7, studied at A2). Bruce (1989, p499) comments that this official title has been archaeologically verified by the discovery of two Maltese inscriptions, one in Greek and the other in Latin.

Drane (1986, p240) provides further evidence of Luke's precision. In Acts 13:7–8 and 18:12 Sergius Paulus and Gallio are correctly designated 'proconsuls'; Philippi is accurately described as a Roman colony, ruled by 'praetors'. This unusual word has been discovered on inscriptions, showing that it was a colloquial term used in Philippi itself (Acts 16:12, 20–22). Guy (1969, p9) comments that such evidence proves the writer of Acts to be trustworthy. Hunter agrees, adding that Luke "never wittingly played fast and loose with his historical facts" (1945, p78).

2. Names

Acts refers to individuals by name and is correct in describing their positions in society: Achaia was a Senatorial province from 27 BC to AD15, and then from AD44 onwards (Bruce, 1943, p82). In Acts 18:12–16 the proconsul of Achaia, Gallio, is named, which is supported by a letter written by the Emperor Claudius where he indicated that Gallio must have become Proconsul of Achaia in AD51 (Unger, 1982, p245). It is significant to note that Luke, like Claudius, accurately calls Gallio 'proconsul of Achaia' and not 'of Greece', which was a departure from Luke's usual custom of calling countries by their general title.

3. Events

McCann (2003, p2, online) describes how Luke is also accurate in describing events in the world at that time. Luke mentions Agabus' prophecy of a great famine extending throughout the world being fulfilled in the days of Claudius Caesar (11:27-30). This has proven to be a historically correct reference when compared with other ancient writings. The historian Suetonius spoke of frequent famines during the reign of Claudius (AD41-54), Eusebius mentioned famine in Greece, and Tacitus made reference to two famines in Rome at this particular time.

4. Geography

Luke is seen to be correct in his knowledge of geographical locations (Cadbury, 1924, cited in Hunter, 1945, p78). Cadbury offers the following examples from Acts:

- Perga in Pamphylia (13:13).
- Phillipi, a city of the first rank in that district of Macedonia, and a Roman colony (16:12).
- Fair Havens in Crete, "not far from the town of Lasea" (27:8).
- Phoenix, a Cretan harbour exposed south-west and north-west (27:12).

5. Religious customs and practices

Acts has also claimed to be reliable concerning common religious practices and ideas in the Roman world. Luke describes the popular longing for a "way of salvation" (26:17, 30) which often manifested itself in polytheism and mystery religions. For example, at Lystra (14:11) and Malta (28:6), he highlights the belief that the gods sometimes descended to earth, and in Ephesus he speaks of the worshippers of Artemis, venerated by "all Asia" (19:27).

Similarly, in Athens Luke's main character, Paul, makes reference to the intellectual curiosity and 'religiosity' of the Athenians (Acts 17:22), which has been backed up by other ancient writers (Thompson, p389). Luke goes on to describe (Acts 17:23) an idol that bore the inscription "to an unknown god". Pausanias, who visited Athens in AD150, also mentions in his book, Description of Greece, that there were "altars of the gods named unknown" (Unger, p238).

Luke also provides information on the influence of sorcery in New Testament times. He describes the influence of sorcerers at Samaria (8:9ff) and at Cyprus (13:6ff), the sorcerers with their magical parchments (14:19) and the strolling exorcists who tried the names of any gods or spirits that might prove useful (14:13) (McCann, 2003, p2, online).

6. Trade
Archaeology has shown Acts to be accurate in its references to trade. In Acts 16:11–15 Luke records how Paul and his companions speak with some local women at Philippi, including Lydia, who is described as "a purple merchant from the city of Thyatira". Thyatira was a city in the ancient kingdom of 'Lydia', a place that was popular for the manufacturing of purple dyes extracted from the juice of the madder root (Bruce, 1988, p311). In support of this, there is evidence to show that the trading in purple dye was common in Philippi at this time (Bruce, 1988, p311).

Conclusion
Luke had, of course, his limitations and it is important not to expect modern standards of historical accuracy, based on critical research, to be found in Acts. His outlook was that of the first century and his purpose in writing Acts would have had a degree of influence upon his writing. It is true that his information is lacking in places and some of the historical references are doubtful. For example, Guy (1969, p11) is one among many scholars who point out that Luke's treatment of Paul differs from the Paul found in Paul's letters. When we compare his narrative with references in Paul's letters, we see that there are many gaps, which may contradict the generally positive evaluation of Luke's trustworthiness as a historian.

However, on the whole, the book of Acts may be relied upon as an accurate history of Christianity in its first half-century. Luke, as an eyewitness and travelling companion of Paul, was openly committed to providing an accurate and trustworthy historical account of early Christianity. McCann (2003, p2, online) concludes that it was his ability to do this that led to Ramsay's conclusion that "Luke is a historian of the first rank [who] should be placed along with the very greatest of historians" (Ramsey, 1915, p222).

TASK

a) Consider how far the author of Acts attempted to write a true history of the beginnings of the Christian Church. Justify your answer.

Your answer should include an evaluation of some of the following:
- The purpose(s) of the text – Acts as a historical and/or an apologetic/theological text.
- The detailed establishment of the church, its early growth and development.
- The significance of the 'we' passages.
- Luke's honest description of strengths and weaknesses.
- Evidence of Luke's reliability beyond the New Testament.

b) Explore the view that the author of Acts skilfully tells the story of the Early Church and its growth. Justify your answer.

Your answer should explore some of the following:
- Luke's writing skill, structure, accuracy, dramatic story telling, clear message, reliability.
- Luke's ability to describe early Christian faith (speeches), dependence on the Holy Spirit, miracles, Christian practices and lifestyle.
- The expansion of the gospel from Jerusalem to Rome, Acts 1:8.
- Other interests that Luke may have had.

TASK

Research/Revision – PowerPoint Presentation

In groups of three or four choose one of the topics from this chapter as a revision topic. Using the information from this book, and from other scholars (refer to in-text citations for suitable references), present the main arguments in a PowerPoint Presentation to the rest of your class.
- Include an evaluation of some scholars' opinions.
- Conclude your presentation with a thought provoking question for the class to consider, which might inspire a lively debate.

OTHER ASPECTS OF HUMAN EXPERIENCE

Part of the questions in Section B of the AS examination paper requires an exploration of the ways in which the taught course can relate to other aspects of human experience. The following themes are listed in the specification:
- the role of the sacred text for the religious believer in any age.
- perennial issues surrounding religious belief, life and practice.
- characteristics and relevance of the charismatic and Pentecostal movements.
- the debate about the relevance of miracles in strengthening religious faith.
- defending religious belief and practice in a hostile world.
- evangelism in a multi-cultural, multi-religious, pluralistic and secular age.
- the importance and relevance of mission for the spread of religious belief.
- the challenge of religious witness in any age.

It should be noted that while each of these themes relates to a specific section on the specification, these ideas can be explored in relation to any topic.

Candidates may explore connections to alternative religions, spiritual and moral teachings, values, beliefs and practices. The connections that candidates make can have either/or both historical and contemporary contexts.

By definition it is not possible or indeed desirable to provide a prescriptive, exhaustive 'list' of other aspects of human experience to which the taught course can be applied. By its very nature this element of the exam is 'open' to whatever meaningful connections candidates can themselves make. The information below is intended merely to provide stimulus for further ideas or discussion on how some aspects of the taught course might be applied to some other aspects of experience.

How to prepare for the human experience element of the AS Examination

- Keep in mind that the connections you make should move beyond the taught course while still relating to content studied.
- They should give you an opportunity for exploration, discussion and critical analysis, rather than being limited to simple comparative statements.
- Keep up to date with current affairs. Read newspapers and church publications for the latest on current events, as well as on issues that are being debated within the church and religious groups.
- Use the internet. It is a good idea to keep a file of resources and ideas you can use later.
- Take time at the end of every chapter to think about what you could do. Discuss with other members of your class.

OTHER ASPECTS OF HUMAN EXPERIENCE

The role of the sacred text for the religious believer in any age

This section on the background to Acts raises many questions, including a consideration of its purpose, characteristics and reliability. This human experience theme develops on these ideas and looks at some of the wider aspects of the role of sacred texts.

To refer to a text as 'sacred' implies that it is worthy of respect and set aside for worship. A sacred text is regarded as infallible and therefore a source of truth and authority. Some sacred texts are seen as the unchanging word of God, whereas others are revised by later generations. There are also different ways of interpreting sacred texts, whether literal, symbolic or both.

The Bible as the Word of God

For Christians, the Bible is the Word of God:

> "All scripture is God-breathed and is useful for teaching, rebuking, correcting and training in righteousness, so that the man of God may be thoroughly equipped for every good work." (2 Timothy 3: 16–17).

Sometimes the Bible quotes the direct words of God. For example, Exodus Ch 20, containing the Ten Commandments, opens with the phrase "And God spoke all these words". When writing to the Corinthians, Paul recognised that he was giving commandments from God: "What I am writing to you is the Lord's command" (1 Corinthians 14: 37). John also writes that his teaching came from God and that to reject it was to reject God (1 John 4:6). The parts of the Bible that are not given as the direct words of God are believed to be the work of ordinary men and women writing under the direct inspiration of God; therefore, they are recording what God wants written down.

The Catholic interpretation of scripture is to be found in the *Catechism of the Catholic Church*, Part 1, Article 3. For example, "God is the author of Sacred Scripture because he inspired its human authors; he acts in them and by means of them. He thus gives assurance that their writings teach without error his saving truth."

A literal versus a symbolic interpretation of Bible texts
Christians are agreed that the Bible is God's Word, although there are differences of opinion as to the exact interpretation of some texts. Some Christians believe that everything in the Bible is literally, scientifically and historically true, but by the middle of the last century many Christians had come to a different view. While many stories in the Bible are historically accurate and should be taken literally, there is a range of literature within the Bible, including allegory and parable, which was never meant to be regarded as science or history.

An example is the Genesis account of the creation of the world. Creationists hold a literal belief in the six calendar days of creation as described in the Bible and therefore reject the theory of evolution. However, many Christians believe the language used in the Bible's account of creation may be symbolic, yet contains the absolute truth that the universe exists because of God. When the earth began, God was in control and he continues to control how the world is evolving.

The importance of sacred texts in other world religions
In Judaism, the primary text is the Hebrew Bible, known to Jews as the Tanakh. It consists of three sections, Torah (The Law contained in the first five books), the Nevi'im (the Prophets) and the Ketuvim (Writings). According to Jewish tradition, the Torah was dictated to Moses by God on

Mount Sinai. It is the foundation of Jewish religious life, containing the Ten Commandments and 613 other instructions from God.

The Qur'an is the sacred book of Islam. Muslims believe it contains the final word of God given to Muhammad by the Angel Jibril (Gabriel). This divine revelation took place over a period of 22 years, beginning in 610 AD. Muslims believe that, where possible, the Qur'an should be read in its original language of Arabic. For Muslims, the Qur'an covers every aspect of life, including worship, food, clothes and laws for society.

TASK

1. Use the internet for further research on this theme. You could investigate:
   - The role of a sacred text (or texts) in a world religion of your choice.
   - How sacred texts are used in worship, for example, where the text is placed, whether there are any preparations needed before the text is used and the language the text is written in.
   - The content of sacred texts, for example, spiritual teachings, laws to govern society and personal conduct.

2. Discuss the following questions in small groups:
   - If the Bible is accepted as the Word of God, does this mean that everything in the Bible is relevant for Christians today?
   - Should some of the teachings in the Bible be revised to reflect modern values or would this undermine the status of the Bible as God's word?
   - Do you agree with a literal or symbolic interpretation of the Genesis account of creation?

Section 2:
The Characteristics of the Early Christian Community

CHURCH LIFE AND ORGANISATION

The references concerning church life and organisation required to be explored for the purpose of the AS level examination are:
- The fellowship of the believers 2:42–47.
- The believers share their possessions 4:32–47.
- The choosing of the seven 6:1–7.

In this section, for your own interest, reference may be made to other parts of Acts that give further insight into the nature of church life and organisation.

Who belonged to the church?

The members of the first group of believers, who waited in Jerusalem for the coming of the Holy Spirit at Pentecost, consisted of the apostles (1:13) and many others including women and relatives of Jesus. Guthrie believes that "there is significance in the special mention of women in the company of believers. This at once shows the Christian company to be distinct from their environment, since few in the ancient world assigned value to women for their own sake" (1961, p109). The Early Church clearly held the same attitude towards women that Jesus had shown, recognising that men and women are on an equal footing through the gospel.

Entry into the church was through repentance of sin, faith in Christ, baptism and receiving the Holy Spirit. Infant baptism was not a feature in the book of Acts. Instead baptism was performed on "consenting adults who had confessed their sins and acknowledged Jesus as Lord" (Hewitt, 1964, p201). The bestowal of the gift of the Holy Spirit *usually* followed through the laying on of hands. In Jerusalem on the Day of Pentecost 3,000 people became Christians. Luke tells us how the Lord continued to add to that number daily.

Two events changed the locality (originally Jerusalem) of membership of the church.
1. The martyrdom of Stephen and James, the son of Zebedee, led to the dispersion of the early Christians throughout other parts of Judea, into nearby Syria and further, perhaps even to Rome (for example, Priscilla and Aquila).
2. The conversion of Saul, the main persecutor of the church. Paul began his ministry in Antioch, preaching not only to Jews in the synagogues

but also to Gentiles. More often than not, the Gentiles were more receptive to Paul's preaching than the Jews (Acts 13:47–48, 15:3, 16:13; 17:12). After the Council of Jerusalem, Gentiles soon outnumbered Jews as Christians.

Church life
The fellowship of the believers 2:42–47

In Acts 2:43–47 Luke presents "an ideal picture of this new community, rejoicing in the forgiveness of sins and the gift of the Spirit" (Bruce, 1988, p73). Bruce comments that "the apostolic fellowship found expression in a number of practical ways" (1988, p73).

Four ways are specifically mentioned – the apostles' teaching, the fellowship, the breaking of bread and the prayers – all painting a picture of an aspect of early church life.

1. The apostles' teaching

"They devoted themselves to the Apostles teaching"

The Christian community relied on apostolic teaching, realising that just because they had received the Spirit, he was not the only teacher they needed. Barclay (1955, p25) insists that the word used for 'teaching' or 'doctrine' in verse 42 is not passive; it is active. This conjures up a picture of the believers actively seeking guidance and instruction in their new Christian lives. One of the methods of teaching used by the apostles with the new community may have been the exposition of Old Testament prophecies, that is, study and explanation of the meaning of the prophesies.

2. The fellowship

"They devoted themselves to the fellowship"

The Greek word for 'fellowship' is *koinonia*; it comes from *koinos*, which means 'common'. It shows that the first Christians shared together and that this fellowship was in God – Father, Son and Holy Spirit. As they were also Jews, they continued to meet and worship in the Temple in Jerusalem (Acts 2: 46; 3:1; 21: 20–26) and in the synagogues.

3. The breaking of bread

"They devoted themselves … to the breaking of bread …"

The fellowship of the early Christians was expressed not only in caring for each other, but in corporate worship too. Guthrie (1961, p735) explains that this was carried out through "worship in the Temple and common meals in the Christians' homes". The worship of the Early Church was both formal and informal, for it took place both in the Temple Courts and in their homes. The worship of the Early Church was joyful and reverent.

Worship included times for the breaking of bread (Acts 2:42–47). Acts gives no indication of how the Lord's Supper was observed, but there is no doubt that the earliest Christians saw at once the need to observe it (Guthrie, 1961, p735). In a closely knit community it may have been a daily celebration at the main meal of the day. In the early days the breaking of bread does seem to have taken place before, during, or at the end of an ordinary meal (the *agape*). The practice of eating together as a group was common and was clearly motivated by concern for the physical needs of each believer. (The breaking of bread and *agape* later came to be carried out separately.)

Further insight into the celebration of the Lord's Supper is given in Acts 20, where Luke describes events at Troas. A farewell meeting was held on the first day of the week (20:7), suggesting that the Christians were already regarding Sunday as the day for worship.

4. Prayer

> "… and to prayer."

The early Christians knew that they could not meet life in their own strength and that they did not need to do so (Barclay, 1955, p26). Prayer was very important both for the individual believer and for the Christian community as a whole. Bruce comments that while the community's prayers would follow Jewish models – we know that the apostles also attended the Jewish prayer services in the temple (3: 1) – the content of those prayers would be enriched because of the Christ-event (Bruce, 1988, p73).

5. Sharing

> "*Selling their possessions and goods, they gave to anyone as he had need*".

The believers share their possessions (Ch 4:32–37)

Bruce (1988, p101) points out that one of the chief means of linking the Christian groups planted all over the Eastern Mediterranean world was the practice of mutual aid. This practice was based on the example at the start of Acts where Luke describes the believers sharing their possessions. Barclay (1955, p26) explains how the early Christians had an intense feeling of responsibility for each other, resulting in the sharing of possessions. "They never forgot that someone was hungry, that someone had not enough and that all must help … it seemed to be unthinkable that anyone of them could have too much whilst another had too little. This awoke a real desire to share all that they had" (Guthrie, 1961, p735).

Hewitt (1964, p56) describes this as an "experiment in communism" and believes it arose out of the belief that Jesus was going to return very soon (the *Parousia*). However, it must be pointed out that it was a voluntary communism of goods in which all shared and none went short.

In practical terms it seems that there was a common fund set up for individual needs. Believers could voluntarily sell their property to contribute to the fund. It was not something imposed by the leaders of the church. For example, when Peter rebuked Ananias, he told him that it was his own decision whether he contributed his money or not (5:4).

Even more important was the strong social concern the believers had for each other. Special provision was made for widows (6:1), which caused some dispute between the Hebrews and the Hellenists and led to the appointment of the seven. Clearly there was a sense of responsibility among the believers towards those of their members who were socially deprived. After all, a large number of the first believers were drawn from the lower levels of society, "which would have imposed on the Christians a common need to take some sort of concerted action" (Guthrie, 1961, p735).

Church organisation

The word 'church' (Greek *ekklesia*), which literally means 'an assembly', appears for the first time in Acts 5:11. Unlike the use of the word today, 'church' does not refer to a building anywhere in the New Testament (Guy, 1969, pp31–32). Instead, it is associated with the group of believers in Christ, that is, the people.

When the church began its life in Jerusalem, it was led by a group of apostles, who guided it in the power and wisdom of the Holy Spirit. "That was the government with which the church was born. There were no elders, no deacons, no bishops… Governmental structure and administrative organisation developed as the need for these arose" (Boer, 1976, p27). As there were no buildings, the structure of the church was based on the house-church. Christians met in the home, often that of women such as Lydia (Acts 16:14–15, 40) in Philippi and Chloe in Corinth (1 Cor 1:11). Here they prayed and shared in the breaking of bread.

For a long time Christianity was considered to be just another Jewish sect and so it existed as a group within Judaism. Therefore the Christian community continued its Jewish connections and practices, such as worshipping in the Temple (Guthrie, 1961, p734). There is also evidence that

Christianity was influenced by some of the Jewish models of organisation. However, Acts gives us little insight into the 'offices' of the church such as the role of apostle, elder or deacon. As a result, it is necessary to read between the lines to try to come up with a picture of what their organisation was like.

Apostle

The office of apostle was obviously of great importance, probably because Jesus himself had appointed the twelve. The qualifications for an apostle (1:21–22) were that he must have been with Jesus since his baptism by John and been a witness of the resurrection. The term 'apostle' is derived from a Greek verb meaning 'send forth' and means a messenger (Guy, 1969, p22). In the Early Church an apostle was a special kind of disciple or follower.

Kirk (1975, pp249–264), however, believes that while the twelve were apostles, this does not exhaust the term, and it could also be applied to others. He argues that the New Testament idea of apostle is a person who is sent by Jesus to proclaim the gospel and to plant churches. Guy (1969, p22) agrees, pointing out that later in Acts we find others named as apostles, "so the designation was not confined to the twelve." For example, Paul and Barnabas are twice referred to as apostles (14:4; 14), although Luke does seem to draw a distinction between them and the Jerusalem apostles (15:2).

Deacon
The choosing of the Seven (Ch 6:1–7)
"As the church grew it began to encounter all the problems of an organisation and an institution" (Barclay, 1955, p50). Acts 6:1–7 describes how a second group within the Christian community was installed when trouble arose over the daily distribution to widows. "The seven men chosen for this task were to be men of good repute and full of the Holy Spirit and wisdom, although their task was essentially practical" (Guthrie, 1961, p740). Bruce elaborates that they were to be "competent in administration" (1988, p121).

Bruce points out, however, that "their activity was by no means confined to this" (1988, p122). Two of the men chosen, Stephen and Philip, were also very involved in the preaching ministry. "The choice was made after prayer, and confirmed by the usual method employed amongst Jews and in ordinations ever since, namely by the laying on of hands" (Lewis, 1960, p35). While the seven are not specifically described in Acts as 'deacons', their function seems to be similar to the later office of deacons. They were appointed to serve a particular need which was tedious but nevertheless important. Lewis (1960, p35) argues that as the word 'deacon' itself comes from a Greek word meaning 'to serve, or minister to', it remains a suitable title in view of the task given to the first seven elected to the office.

Elder

A third office – that of elder – came into being in the Early Church, and has remained until the present day. However, there is no record of its origin in the New Testament. Later offices, such as that of the bishop, grew out of the office of elder. The earliest reference to elders in Acts (11:30) speaks of the poor brethren in Jerusalem, and how aid was sent to the elders there by Barnabas and Saul. This reference assumes the existence of elders as a known and established fact. Boer (1976, p28) suggests that it is possible that the separate meetings for worship that the believers in Jerusalem began to hold after Pentecost were patterned on the Jewish synagogue. In the synagogue the elder, who was next to the rulers in authority, occupied a prominent place. It may also be that the older members of the Christian community were automatically looked upon as the leaders, and after that the office of elder was either elective or appointive. Neil (1973, p102) suggests that they would have been charged with the oversight of worship, discipline, administration and instruction, more or less along the lines of the "rulers of the synagogue."

There are various references to elders in the church in the rest of Acts. In Acts 14, Luke describes how, at the end of the first missionary journey, Paul and Barnabas backtracked through each of the towns they had visited, to strengthen the disciples and encourage them to remain true to the faith (14:22). Paul and Barnabas are also reported to have appointed elders in churches they had established. These elders "would be local leaders among the Christians, responsible for the church during the absence of the missionaries" (Guy, 1969, p56). Later in Acts, mention is made of elders in the Ephesian Church (20:17). Elsewhere in the New Testament (1 Timothy 5:17; Titus 1:5; James 5:14; 1 Peter 5:1, 5) there is further evidence of the existence of elders.

Other offices

Acts 13:1–2 speaks of two further groups, "prophets" and "teachers" (1 Cor 12:28), whose functions differed. Prophets (Acts 11:27–28; 13:1) were not attached to any one local church, so they wandered from place to place, "listening for the word of God then taking that word to their fellow men" (Barclay, 1955, p96).They shared with the apostle "the place of pre-eminence in the church" (Hewitt, 1964, p206). Teachers (Acts 18.26), on the other hand, were placed in local churches and it was their duty to instruct those who joined the church, and to explain and reinforce the truth that was already possessed.

Other groups mentioned in Acts are miracle workers, healers, helpers and administrators, and evangelists. An evangelist was one who held no office but possessed a gift for proclaiming the gospel and, like the prophet, moved from place to place (21:8).

Why does the book of Acts tell us so little about church organisation?

Christians in the early days believed that the end of the world was imminent (1 Thes 1:10, 2:19, 3:13, 4:17) and so they were urged by Paul to live in such a way that they be ready for the end (1 Thes 5:6–22). It appears that clerical functions were to a large degree fulfilled by men who had been specially endowed for this purpose by the Holy Spirit (6:1–7).

TASK

Class discussion: 'No branch of the Christian Church today can claim to reproduce in its present practice or structures the church that Luke describes in Acts'.

TASK

a) **Examine the main features of church life and organisation in the Early Church in Acts.**

- Church life includes an exploration of fellowship, teaching, breaking of bread, prayer and sharing.
- Organisation includes the roles of Apostle, Deacon and Elder.

b) **Comment on the claim that as the church developed it has lost its sense of mission.**

- This answer requires a look at other aspects of human experience. You might find it helpful to look at how the church developed during the first three centuries (Banks, R (2017). *The Early Church: 3rd Edition*). Compare how the role of the Holy Spirit took a step into the shadows as the church reacted against movements such as Montanism. Look at the role that the Holy Spirit has on guiding the church today. Have positions of authority taken over from spontaneity?

THE NEED FOR DISCIPLINE IN THE CHURCH

Ananias and Sapphira (Ch 5:1-11)

In 5:11 the word "church" is used for the first time in the book of Acts to describe the community of believers.

This story has been described as both a "chilling tale" (Dillon, 1990, p738) and "a sordid episode" (Stott, 1990, p109). It might well have been left out of the book of Acts because it reveals that even in the Early Church there were imperfect Christians (Barclay, 1955, p42). By including this account, Luke shows us how honest he was in his writing, which supports the historical accuracy of Acts discussed in Chapter 1 of this book.

Luke describes how a married couple tried to deceive the apostles by claiming to have made a much greater financial sacrifice for the church than they actually had. Ananias and Sapphira sold property and gave part of the proceeds to a voluntary common fund established by the apostles (Guy, 1969, p31). In itself this action of only giving part of the money to the church was not wrong. However, they pretended to have given all the money from the sale to the apostles. Perhaps before the sale Ananias and Sapphira had entered into some kind of contract to give the church the total amount raised (Stott, 1990, p109). Their sin was one of deception. It was not that they withheld part of their property but that they lied about it and sought credit for having given their all (Lewis, 1960, p33).

Perhaps they wanted to look good in front of the other believers. Bruce (1988, p105) suggests they did it to gain a reputation for being more generous than they actually were. Another suggestion is that Ananias and Sapphira might have noticed how well thought of Barnabas was when he sold his property for the church. They may even have been jealous of his popularity (Gutzke, 1966, p63).

Peter seems to be able to read minds, as he knows he is being lied to. Perhaps he had "the power of spiritual insight" (Marshall, 1980, pp111-112). He is clear in stating that the money was not the issue (v 4); the lie was (v 5). Ananias immediately dropped dead, which many scholars regard as divine judgment for his sin (Marshall, 1980, p112). However, it is important to note that there is no reference to any such death sentence in Peter's words. Peter had only intended to rebuke Ananias for his awful sin, and hope for repentance. He was probably as shocked as anyone that Ananias dropped dead before his eyes. Could it have been the result of a heart attack due to the shock of being exposed as a liar? The lie was to the Holy Spirit himself (Packer, 1966, p43).

Ananias was buried immediately. Bruce (1988, p106) points out that burial in that climate quickly followed death. Sapphira is presented as being oblivious three hours later to what has happened. Peter's action may be regarded as being insensitive, for instead of telling her of the death of her husband, he tackled her about her deception. Sapphira was given the chance to tell the truth (v 8), although some scholars see this as merely encouraging her to implicate herself in the lie. Her only hope was to admit the truth of the matter. When she failed to do so, it was plain that she would suffer the fate of her husband. She, too, collapses to the ground and dies. While this might seem too much of a coincidence for some, it must be remembered that she suffered a double shock – that of being found out and of being told of her husband's death. Marshall comments that "this double punishment deeply affected both the Christians and everybody who heard of it" (1980, p113). Fernando (1998, p197) comments that those who witnessed their deaths must have been surprised to see Peter, not a rich man, rebuking the rich giver of a large contribution.

The hypocrisy of Ananias and Sapphira was not allowed to spread, for God's judgement fell on them (Guy, 1969, p31). Many are shocked by the severity of God's judgement resulting in their deaths, and have questioned Peter's ethics in not giving them an opportunity for repentance and in not telling Sapphira of her husband's death. Browne points out that we cannot imagine Christ acting towards sinners as Peter is here represented as doing (1925, pp83–84). Jesus' reaction to Judas, whose sin was a thousand times worse, is certainly not on this level. However, it should be taken into account that he was not handing out a curse of death to either Ananias or Sapphira. They died because God, not Peter, wanted it to happen. Paul's letter to the Hebrews tells us that while God is infinite love and has tremendous patience, there is also a judgment of God – and it is a fearful thing to fall into the hands of God. Knox (cited in Haenchen, 1971, p237) adds that some even hope that the story is fictitious. If you check 'Google', you will find a number of interesting discussions on this issue.

TASK

a) Give an account of the story of Ananias and Sapphira.

- Common fund.
- Deception of Ananias and Sapphira.

- The reason for their sin.
- Peter's spiritual insight.
- Death of the couple and surrounding discussion.
- The significance of Luke including this story in his book.

b) Evaluate the claim that God's judgement on Ananias and Sapphira was too severe.
- Christ's message of forgiveness.
- Peter's neglect in not telling Sapphira in a sensitive manner that her husband was dead.
- Discussion concerning whether or not this is a true story.

THE ROLE OF MIRACLES IN AIDING THE SPREAD OF THE GOSPEL

What is a miracle?

From Wikipedia, the free encyclopaedia:

> "The word miracle, comes from the old Latin word *miraculum* meaning 'something wonderful'. It describes divine intervention by God in the world by which the ordinary course of nature is overruled, suspended, or changed. Although many religious texts and people confirm witnessing or prophesying various events which they refer to as 'miraculous', it is disputed whether miracles are scientifically confirmed. People in different faiths have varying definitions of the word 'miracle'. In everyday usage, 'miracle' may also refer to any statistically unlikely but beneficial event (such as the survival of a natural disaster) or even to anything which is regarded as 'wonderful' regardless of its likelihood, such as birth." (www.wikipedia.org/wiki/Miracles)

Miracles in Acts (the references to be studied for AS examination are in bold)		
Peter's miracles	3:1–10 5:12–16 9:33–34 9:40	**Healing of the lame man at Beautiful Gate*** **General miracles – Peter's shadow*** Healing of Aeneas at Lydda Raising of Tabitha to life at Joppa

Paul's miracles	13:11 14:10 **16:16–37** 19:12 20:9–10 28:5 28:8	Striking blind of Elymas the sorcerer at Paphos Healing of lame man at Lystra **Casting out evil spirit from girl at Philippi/escapes prison*** Many healed through contact with aprons and handkerchiefs Raising Eutychus to life at Troas Not being affected by snake bite in Malta Healing of Publius' father
Other	2:43 **4:23–31** 6:8 8:6	Apostles performing miracles **Prayer for miracles (below)** Stephen performing miracles Philip performing miracles

* Further commentary on three out of the four references are covered in this book on pages 88 (lame man), 80 (Peter's shadow) and 151 (Paul in prison).

Luke records the miracles in Acts as a natural succession to those of the Gospels (Hewitt, 1964, pp255–256). They are a key part of the ministry and mission of the church in Acts. Like the gift of powerful speech, we see how miracles had an effect on those who witnessed them. A miraculous event can be described as a time when something happened that challenged what was natural in the eyes of the people. For example, it was not natural that a man who had been lame from birth could suddenly walk or that people could be healed through the contact of an apron that had touched Paul. Such events were accompanied by a verbal explanation of God's power working through the Holy Spirit. Note how Peter explains (Acts 3:11–26) that it was through the power of Jesus' name that the lame man was healed, not through Peter himself. The effect of this healing was that "all the people were astonished and came running to them" (3:11). Then Peter seized the opportunity to declare the gospel. Clearly the miracle helped to attract the crowd. This had a knock-on effect, for the subsequent arrest of Peter and John then led to their witness before the Sanhedrin.

Prayer for miracles (Ch 4:23–31)

This prayer comes after the release of Peter and John from prison, following their arrest by the Sanhedrin after the healing of the lame man in Acts Ch 3. Peter and John returned to where the other believers were and told them of their experience before the Sanhedrin. Bruce (1988, p98) explains how "the whole company resorted to prayer". They specifically prayed for courage to speak boldly and to proclaim the gospel without fear. There is a clear understanding of a connection between the power of miracles alongside preaching the gospel (v 29–30). They asked for God to give his approval of their witness by "granting further mighty works of healing and similar signs and wonders through the same name which had cured the lame man" (Bruce, 1988, p99).

"Once again the Spirit came to the company with shattering power" (Guy, 1969, p31). The place shook as if there were an earthquake, showing God's approval and assurance that their prayer would be answered. Marshall regards this as "indicating a divine response to prayer" (1980, p107). It was God's way of saying that he was present and would answer the prayer (Fernando, 1998, p170). Bruce (1988, p100) comments on how "the Holy Spirit filled them all and sent them forth to proclaim the good news with renewed confidence".

TASK

a) **Using examples, describe the different types of miracles in Acts.**
- Direct healing miracles – Peter and the lame man.
- Indirect healing miracles – Peter's shadow; Paul's contact with aprons and handkerchiefs.
- Nature miracles – earthquake at Philippi.
- Exorcisms.
- Raising from the dead – Tabitha.

b) **Give an account of how miracles in Acts aided the spread of the gospel.**
- Usually followed by preaching.
- Attracted large crowds.
- Led to conversions.

Give examples from Acts to support these.

c) **Comment on the claim that 'the author of Acts records miracles as a central part of the ministry of the church.'**
- Number of miracles scattered throughout Acts.
- Various believers carried out miracles, not just the Twelve.
- A sign of the Holy Spirit.

Give examples from Acts to support these.

d) **Evaluate the view that miracles belong exclusively to the period of the Early Church.**
   - Explore the view that some people feel that miracles do not happen today versus those who believe that there is still a place for them.
   - Argument that routine operations carried out by doctors today would have been regarded as miraculous in New Testament times.
   - Use examples from other aspects of human experience, for example Lourdes or healing rallies.
   - Discuss the validity of miracles today.

OTHER ASPECTS OF HUMAN EXPERIENCE

Perennial issues surrounding religious belief, life and practice

This theme is linked to some of the issues faced by the first Christian community and examines how they continued to be important for the Early Church. It is important to remember that the examples given here can also be applied to other sections on the specification. A further question for consideration is to what extent these issues remain relevant for Christians today.

Discipline

Even in the early and enthusiastic days there was a combination of good and bad in the church. Stott believes that the incident involving Ananias and Sapphira teaches the necessity of church discipline, commenting that the church has tended to alternate in this area "between extreme severity (disciplining members for the most trivial offences) and extreme laxity (exercising no discipline at all, even for the most serious offences)" (1990, p112).

Research some answers to the following questions:
   a) How did the church deal with sin then?
   b) How does it deal with sin now?

Penance
Another aspect of human experience you could research is that of the development of penance in the Early Church (See Banks, R (2017). *The Early Church: 3rd Edition*).
   a) What were the advantages and disadvantages of such a system?
   b) How is the Sacrament of Reconciliation celebrated in the Catholic Church today?
   c) Research the term to 'fence the table' in the Presbyterian Church. What does this mean regarding those who have sinned?

Money
Something that arises from the deceit of Ananias and Sapphira is the use of church funds. In the church today scandals over how funds are misused are common. Christian workers may be tempted in the following ways:
- To receive financial help by pretending to need more money than they actually do.
- Accepting more funds than are actually needed for a project.
- Letting funds be used for something other than what the money was given for.
- Allowing themselves unnecessary expenses, for example expensive lunches.
- Avoiding tax.

Avoiding such temptations can be helped by being accountable to someone about the use of money. This means keeping someone else informed about all financial dealings. If a Christian does give in to the temptation, being accountable to someone can help them to make a determined effort to avoid similar temptation in the future.

Read 1 Cor 5:5 and Matt 18:15–17.
   a) What advice do Jesus and Paul give concerning someone who sins?
   b) How relevant is this advice for Christians today?

How necessary is the role of an important leader?
According to the Catholic Church, Peter went on to found the church at Rome and became the bishop of Rome or the first Pope. This means that all succeeding bishops of Rome automatically became the leader and focus of the Christian Church.

Other denominations, while not having a leader who is deemed to be infallible (regarding pronouncements on matters of faith or morals), also have a type of leader to represent the people. For example, the Presbyterian Church has a moderator who is elected once a year.

Beyond the church, schools have principals, businesses have managers, etc. Once in these positions, these people are given respect whether they deserve it or not. Most of the time, leaders of various organisations are successful due to hard work, skill and determination. However, sometimes they fail and the organisation falls apart.

a) See if you can find examples of successful leadership and of failed leadership, religious or secular.
b) Use the examples to illustrate the importance of strong leadership in the church, linking your response to the leadership of Peter in the Early Church.

Church organisation in the first two centuries
References:
- Boer, H (1976). *A Short History of the Early Church*. Grand Rapids, MI: William B. Eerdmans Publishing Company.
- Banks, R (2017). *The Early Church: 3rd Edition*. Newtownards: Colourpoint.

Thirty years after Christ's death, both Peter and Paul were dead (martyred AD64 in Rome). A further thirty years on, the *Parousia* was no longer thought of as being imminent (1 and 2 Timothy; Titus). Towards the end of the first century, a more structured ministry emerged in some of the churches: presbyters/bishops (including one regarded as the 'first among equals') and deacons.

Acts, the letters of Paul, Clement's letter to the Corinthians, (AD96) and Ignatius of Antioch's letters to the seven churches written on his way to Rome (AD107) enable us to discover a reasonably accurate account of how church life developed in the New Testament and beyond.

o Using the suggesting reading, explore how church organisation developed in the first three centuries, making comparisons with the early days.

The role of women in 'Montanism'

Montanism arose in Phrygia (modern central Turkey) in AD156. It was a movement that emphasised the work of the Holy Spirit. It was called after Montanus, who had previously been a pagan priest before becoming a Christian. He was joined by two women, Maximilla and Priscilla, who had left their husbands to help him. Initially they worked within the umbrella of the Catholic Church, but soon their teachings were regarded as heretical and they were forced to set themselves up as a separate organisation.

Banks (see reference below) describes it as a "charismatic movement in the sense that it encouraged the involvement of all believers, including females, and the use of spiritual gifts in church life".

a) Find out why the church was opposed to Montanism (Refer to Banks, R (2017). *The Early Church: 3rd Edition*. Newtownards: Colourpoint Books)

b) In your opinion, was there anything of value in Montanism that the church lost for being so opposed to it?

BY THE END OF THIS CHAPTER YOU SHOULD BE ABLE TO:

- demonstrate knowledge and understanding of, and critically evaluate the background to the Acts of the Apostles, including:
  - internal and external evidence for the authorship of Acts;
  - the arguments for an early, intermediate and late date;
  - the purpose of Acts;
  - the characteristics of Acts;
  - the 'we' passages;
  - challenges to the traditional authorship and historical accuracy of Acts; and
  - the social and historical context of Acts; and
- demonstrate knowledge and understanding of, and critically evaluate the characteristics of the early Christian community, including:
  - church life and organisation, focusing on the church as a fellowship of believers (2:42–47, 4:23–37);
  - the need for discipline in the church (5:1–11); and
  - the role of miracles in aiding the spread of the Gospel (3:1–10, 4:23–31, 5:12–16, 16:16–37).

The Beginnings of the Church

Section 1:
Early Events in Jerusalem

JESUS' INITIATION OF THE CHURCH'S MISSION (CH 1:1–11)

In this chapter, we see that Jesus himself makes significant preparations prior to the founding of the church, which begins with Pentecost as described in Acts Ch 2. The detail described by Luke in Acts Ch 1 reinforces the importance of the events that lay ahead.

Jesus' initiation of the church's mission is important because it sets the scene for the rest of the story in the book of Acts. Within this section, vital 'behind the scenes' work takes place as preparation for both the Day of Pentecost and the events that follow in the growth of the church. Chapter 1 of Acts deals with two matters: Jesus' contact with his apostles prior to his Ascension; and the choosing of Matthias to fill the vacancy among the 'Twelve', caused by Judas' betrayal and death.

Prologue (Ch 1:1–3)

As mentioned in the last chapter, there is much speculation among scholars concerning the identity of 'Theophilus'. Bruce (1988, p29) comments that it has been suggested that he was not an individual, as the name 'Theophilus' means 'dear to God' and could refer to the Christian reader in general. However, most scholars feel that the use of "most excellent Theophilus" indicates that Luke was probably addressing one man, who was someone of high rank. Hewitt (1964, p22) mentions that Theophilus was the secret Christian name of Flavius Clemens, cousin and heir of the Emperor Domitian. It is known that his wife admired the Christian faith and that he himself was an enquirer. Flavius Clemens was put to death by Domitian in AD96.

Bruce (1988, p29), however, argues that it "is quite probable that Theophilus was a representative member of the intelligent middle-class public at Rome whom Luke wished to win over to a less prejudiced and more favourable opinion of Christianity than that which was current among them".

It is implied that Acts was to be an account of all that Jesus would continue to do and teach through the power of the Holy Spirit. The use of the term 'apostles' refers to the twelve men Jesus had chosen earlier in his ministry (excluding Judas). They would be the ones entrusted with the task of founding the Christian Church (v 2). Luke directs our attention to how they were given "decisive proof" (Stott, 1990, p35) that Jesus was alive. Over forty days between the Resurrection and Ascension, he appeared on various occasions to the apostles "in a manner that could leave no doubt in their minds that he was really alive again, risen from the dead" (Bruce, 1988, p31).

Jesus not only appeared to them, but he also spoke about the Kingdom of God; Dodd (1936, pp46–47) explains that the Kingdom of God "is conceived as coming in the events of the life, death and resurrection of Jesus, and to proclaim these facts, in their proper setting, is to preach the gospel of the Kingdom of God". Jesus also ate with his apostles, which highlights that he was not a spirit but a human that could be touched. Bruce (1988, p34) adds that Jesus would have no personal need of food, but would have taken it to convince the apostles that he was really with them and was not a 'phantom'. Marshall (1978, pp124–126) comments that it may even have been communion that he shared with them. Stott (1990, p35) concludes that such experience of the risen Lord was an indispensable qualification of an apostle, which explains why Paul and James could be apostles.

Commission (Ch 1:4–8)
Jesus instructed the apostles to stay in Jerusalem until the Father (God) fulfilled his promise of giving the Holy Spirit to them. Bruce (1988, p34) comments that this promise was foreshadowed by the ministry of John the Baptist (Luke 3:16). John baptised with water, but "the new baptism is to be something more than water, it is to be baptism into a source of power" (Hewitt, 1964, p29).

The Jewish belief was that the promised Messiah would build up God's Kingdom here on earth. Hewitt (1964, p34) comments that even the disciples, who had received instruction on the true nature of the Kingdom of God, at the last moment still clung to their Jewish beliefs and evidently hoped to see the Kingdom of God realised in the restoration of Israel's national independence (Bruce, 1988, p35). Their question in verse 6 concerning the time of the restoration of the Kingdom suggests that they still regarded the Messiah's work as unfinished. Jesus did not directly say 'no', but rather he directed their attention to the task that lay ahead; they were commissioned to proclaim the good news of God's grace in Christ (Bruce, 1988, p36) and act as witnesses to Christ from Jerusalem to the end of the earth (Marshall, 1980, p59). The dates and times are irrelevant, as they are the Father's business, not theirs (Packer, 1966, p22). Bruce comments that "instead of the political power which had once been the object of their ambitions, a power far greater and nobler would be theirs. When the Holy Spirit came upon them, Jesus assured them, they would be vested with heavenly power …" (1988, p36).

The Ascension (Ch 1:9–11)

In Luke's Gospel the impression is given that the Ascension took place on the same day as the resurrection. In Acts, however, Luke states that the Ascension took place forty days after the resurrection. Hewitt (1964, p29) comments that this tradition of forty days, when Jesus appeared to the disciples on various occasions in places as far apart as Galilee and Emmaus, is regarded as more valid. Bruce (1988, p37) comments that during the forty day period Jesus was not 'earth-bound', meaning that he was not trapped on the earth. Rather, he believes that Jesus paid visits to the disciples from "that eternal order to which his 'body of glory' now belonged".

Marshall (1980, p59) comments that Luke alone describes the Ascension of Jesus as a visible event. In answering the question regarding what the disciples actually saw, Hewitt (1964, p29) admits that it is impossible to know. He argues that with our concept of the universe it is difficult to imagine Jesus 'going up' to heaven. Our understanding of heaven is that it is not a geographical location 'up there', but rather 'it is a condition of the Spirit'. Barclay (1953, 1955, p6) points out the importance of the Ascension, suggesting that there would have been something quite wrong if the resurrection appearances had just slowly faded out. Guy (1969, p21) suggests the possibility that the idea of a bodily ascension was introduced and the whole scene constructed by Luke to express a fitting conclusion to Jesus' human life and his work on earth. Marshall (1980, p60), however, argues that the fact of the Ascension is firmly attested elsewhere (1 Tim 3:16; 1 Pet 3:21f), and he adds that it is best not to interpret the story over-literally. Rather, it is wise to concentrate on the symbolism of 'ascension', which expresses the way in which the physical presence of Jesus left this world, to be replaced by his spiritual presence.

The two white-robed men who appear are angelic messengers. In asking the disciples why they are staring into the sky, the angels are really prompting them to get a move on; they have a command to follow and, having witnessed the Ascension, they now have the assurance that just as it was possible for Jesus to ascend into heaven, "so he would return in the same way" (Marshall, 1980, p62). This is called the Second Coming of Christ, or the *Parousia*, and is fundamental to the belief of the Christian Church. Bruce (1988, p39) argues that from Luke's perspective, the *Parousia* would not happen immediately. Stott (1990, p35) agrees, pointing out that much of the Early Church's life and thought was influenced by the mistaken belief that Jesus would return in the near future. The apostles' immediate duty was straightforward: they had to wait in Jerusalem until they received the Holy Spirit. So they returned to the city.

TASK

Class Discussion: Did the Ascension really happen? What do you think? Organise into two groups, one 'For' and the other 'Against'.

TASK

a) Comment on the claim that the events that took place prior to Pentecost were significant in preparing the disciples for the coming of the Holy Spirit.

Your answer may include some of the following:
- How the disciples were given decisive proof that Jesus was alive.
- Jesus spoke to them about the Kingdom of God.
- The anticipation of the coming of the Holy Spirit and the significance of the promised baptism compared to John's baptism.
- How the disciples witnessed the ascension and the significance of this event.
- The significance of replacing Judas in keeping the number of apostles as twelve.

THE EVENTS ON THE DAY OF PENTECOST
Pentecost event (Ch 2:1–13)

Pentecost, the Jewish festival celebrating the wheat harvest, means 'fiftieth', and is so called because it fell fifty days after Passover. (Another name for Pentecost is the 'Feast of Weeks'.) The Passover was celebrated in the middle of April, with Pentecost falling in June, a time when travelling conditions were at their best. As a result, there was a very international crowd in Jerusalem at the time of Pentecost. The Law stated that on the Day of Pentecost no one should work (Leviticus 23:21; Numbers 28:26), so there would naturally be more people out and about than usual.

The disciples were sitting together when suddenly the room was filled with what seemed "like wind". Bruce (1988, p50) comments that the wind was understood as symbolising the Spirit of God, which had come upon the disciples in power. John the Baptist had spoken of how one greater than he would carry out a baptism with wind and fire (Luke 3:16–17). In the Old Testament, fire represented the divine presence (Exodus 3:2–5). Similarly, fire played a part on this occasion, with what appeared to be tongues of fire resting on the head of each of the disciples. Marshall comments that "with these outward signs came the Holy Spirit as an inward, invisible reality" (1980, p69). The possible connection between the "tongues of fire" and the "other tongues" that the disciples began to utter has been pointed out by some scholars (Bruce, 1988, p41).

Glossolalia

Glossolalia comes from the Greek term *'glossa'*, or 'tongue', used in the New Testament and referring to 'speaking in tongues'. This means a 'language miracle', where a person is able to speak under the inspiration of the Holy Spirit and, in divine ecstasy, utters words over which he has no control or understanding.

There is considerable debate over the nature of glossolalia in the New Testament. The difficulty lies in how to compare Acts Ch 2 with 1 Corinthians Ch 14, which seem to describe two different things. It appears that the tongues of Acts Ch 2 are understood by the foreign visitors (2:5f), while the tongues of 1 Corinthians Ch 14 cannot be understood without the spiritual gift of interpretation (1 Cor 12:10, 28–30; 14:2–19), implying that tongues are unintelligible speech. It was uttered in a speech that no one could understand until someone with the spiritual gift of interpretation explained what had been said.

Acts 2

Hewitt (1964, p41) points out that there are three possibilities for what is meant by speaking in tongues on the Day of Pentecost:

1. A literal interpretation where the disciples were blessed with the ability of speaking in foreign languages without the effort of having to learn them. However, in this case an accusation of drunkenness would have been unlikely.

2. The use of common languages. Barclay (1955, p15) and Guy (1969, p24) point out that to speak in foreign languages at Pentecost was unnecessary. The crowd was made up of Jews, proselytes and God-fearers (that is, Gentiles who had accepted the Jewish religion and way of life). Only two languages, Greek and Aramaic, would be necessary for a crowd like that to understand what was being said. Hewitt, however, adds that simple Galileans such as the disciples would hardly have had the opportunity to travel outside their province and would not be likely to speak Greek. Therefore, it is argued that 'other languages' in fact really meant 'languages other than Hebrew'.
3. The use of ecstatic speech or 'glossolalia' (see definition above). Guy (1969, p24) argues that glossolalia does sometimes include foreign words, which the speaker has heard and forgotten but which come from the unconscious under the stress of excitement. Some of those present may have thought that the speech of the disciples, unintelligible to them, was in someone else's language.

1 Corinthians 12–14

1 Corinthians 12–14 gives no impression that tongues can be translated through a natural knowledge of the language. They can only be understood spiritually through the spiritual gift of interpretation (1 Cor 12:10). Bruce (1988, p52) comments that it was a spiritual gift that was highly valued in the Corinthian Church.

Chapter 14 deals with the issue of tongues in the context of a potentially chaotic worship service. Many of the Corinthians favoured public expressions of tongues and ecstatic behaviour, which was bound to provoke confusion and ridicule from visitors not aware of spiritual matters (14:23). "Paul acknowledges that the Corinthian glossolalia is a genuine gift of the Holy Spirit, but deprecates the undue importance which some members of the church at Corinth attach to it" (Bruce, 1988, p52). He responds by favouring the intelligible forms of inspired speech such as prophecy for the public worship service (14:2–4, 17–18, 21–24). The unintelligible forms of inspired speech, such as tongues, are directed to God alone and serve to edify the individual speaking. Paul allows tongues to be expressed in public, but only if accompanied by a spiritual interpretation, the responsibility of which is laid on the shoulders of the speaker (14:14–27). The chief purpose in public worship is to serve the edification of the church (14:26).

The primary function of tongues for Paul in 1 Corinthians 14 seems to be for private prayer, while prophecy is for the public (14:18–19). In other words, tongues are for self-edification before God as one gives thanks to God "with the spirit" (14:3, 14–15, 18).

How can these two descriptions of speaking tongues be reconciled?

1. Some explain the difference by pointing out the international nature of the audience of Acts Ch 2 compared to the provincial nature of the congregation in Corinth. The difference in audience between the two texts could explain why the tongues were understood naturally in Acts Ch 2, while they required a spiritual interpretation in 1 Corinthians Ch 12–14 (12:10).
2. Acts 2:6 states that each "one" heard "them", possibly implying that each person in the audience heard Jesus' followers speak in his or her language. Were the tongues of Pentecost unintelligible glossolalia that were accompanied by a miracle of hearing in which each person heard the Christians speak in his or her particular language (v 6, 8, 11)? Stott (1990, p67) objects to this, pointing to evidence from v 4 – they "began to speak in other tongues as the Spirit enabled them".
3. Different outlook between Luke and Paul: Luke seems to allow for tongues to have a public sign value that is not prominent in Paul. For Luke, tongues were a sign of the universal reach of the Spirit's witness. In Acts 2, the God of Israel is revealed in the languages of the nations – the sacred language is heard in the Gentile tongues of the nations. Similarly, the explicit reference to tongues at the Gentile reception of the Spirit is not without significance (10:46). Luke's point is clear: the Spirit has been poured out upon all flesh in a way that mends divisions and brings about unity.

TASK

a) Give an account of the coming of the Holy Spirit at Pentecost.

Your answer could include some of the following:
- Establishing the context: Pentecost, Jerusalem.
- Outline of the events in the upper room.
- The events in the street and the allegations of the crowd.
- Peter's speech (*kerygma*, Joel, the Psalms).
- The response of the crowd and the significance of the events.
- Explanation of points of interest or debate.

b) **Comment on the claim that the author of Acts has confused "speaking in tongues" with speaking in foreign languages.**

Your answer could include a discussion of some of the following:
- Suggested possibilities of what was meant by speaking in tongues on the Day of Pentecost.
- Comparison of Acts 2 with 1 Corinthians 12–14.
- Personal opinion supported by reasonable evidence from the New Testament.

c) **Discuss the view that if the Pentecost event had not taken place the church as we know it would not exist today. (This question requires knowledge of other aspects of human experience.)**

Your discussion may include some of the following:
- How the Holy Spirit changed the disciples.
- The immediate significance of the event for the life of the Early Church.
- The gift of the Holy Spirit in enabling the disciples to carry out Acts 1:8; the witness of the believers as a result.
- The growth of the church from the Day of Pentecost until Paul took the gospel to Rome.
- The expansion of Christianity in the first four centuries until Constantine made it the official religion of the Empire.
- Why Christianity appealed to all members of society and continues to do so today.

The role of the Holy Spirit in the emerging church

The book of Acts is saturated by the presence and power of the Holy Spirit. The Spirit is repeatedly mentioned, "on average just over twice in each chapter" (Hull, 1967, p11), prompting a number of scholars to comment that it should have been called 'The Gospel of the Holy Spirit' (Ehrhardt, 1969, p129; Barclay, 1955, p46) or 'The Acts of the Holy Spirit' (Bengel, 1742, repr 1862, p389). "For Luke, everything that happens in the life of the Church from the beginning to the end of his story is in one way or another controlled, inspired and furthered by the Holy Spirit" (Neil, 1973, p70). The Spirit's previous activity in Jesus is replicated on a wider scale through the believers. Luke gives us a practical demonstration of this through the lives of key people such as Peter, Philip, Stephen and Paul. However, he never loses sight of the fact that the Holy Spirit is the true centre of the story.

The coming of the Spirit at Pentecost

Between Jesus' resurrection and Ascension, Jesus taught his disciples more about the Kingdom of God, telling them to wait in Jerusalem for the gift of the Holy Spirit. Clearly the Spirit's coming, which happened on the Day of Pentecost, did not come to them unprepared (Marshall, 1980, pp347–369).

As you will recall, Peter, in his speech at Pentecost, reminded his audience that in the Old Testament scriptures God had promised he would "pour out" his Spirit on all people and all nations in the last days (2:17–18, 33; 10:45). This promise "of the Father" (Acts 1:4) reveals God to be the primary giver of the Spirit. It was accompanied by unusual physical phenomena – a sound like a "mighty wind" and "tongues like fire" (Acts 2:2–3) – reminiscent of the wind and fire which, in John the Baptist's preaching, were to be the instruments of the Coming One's purifying ministry (Luke 3:16–17).

The Pentecost event was unique because it signified the beginning of the age of the church. God's people, described by Neil (1973, p71) as "ordinary men and women", became the spirit-filled body of Christ. The extraordinary signs of wind and fire were unique to this initial experience, since they are not repeated in Acts. Although the Holy Spirit would continue to be given, the outpouring would never again signify the inauguration of a new era.

Repentance and baptism

On the Day of Pentecost, Peter was able to proclaim the gospel with a new understanding: "Repent and be baptised, every one of you, in the name of Jesus Christ for the forgiveness of your sins. And you will receive the gift of the Holy Spirit" (Acts 2:38). The Spirit convicts and leads people to repentance of sin and faith in Jesus Christ. Bruce (1988, p69) describes such repentance as "a complete change of heart". The Spirit comes on all people, who repent and believe, not just on some individuals for certain purposes, as happened in the Old Testament (2:17). By the end of the day of Pentecost, receiving the Spirit was not confined to the apostles and their companions; many more enjoyed the heavenly gift. The Jews initially thought this meant all Jewish people, but they eventually realised it meant all people, regardless of religious background, race, age, sex or social standing (2:38–39; 15:8–9; 19:5–6).

Repentance was linked to baptism. On the Day of Pentecost about three thousand people repented of their sins, were baptised, and received the Spirit, making them members of a new community. John, who baptised with water, claimed to be the forerunner of one greater than himself, who would baptise with the Holy Spirit. It might have been expected therefore that baptism in water would now become obsolete. This did not happen and believers in Jesus continued to be baptised in water. Bruce explains: "Baptism in the spirit is an inward work; baptism in water now becomes an external token" (1988, p70). Their water baptism was a sign that they belonged to God, and was accompanied (not replaced) by the baptism in the Spirit.

When was the Holy Spirit received?
1. At baptism
From the events of the Day of Pentecost, we can see that a convert receives the gift of the Spirit at baptism (2:28). Lampe (1951, p76) believes that this was the normal practice.

2. After baptism, through the laying on of apostolic hands
Those who became believers on the Day of Pentecost clearly received the Spirit as soon as they were baptised in Jesus' name. However, when Philip baptised the Samaritan converts, including Simon Magus, they did not receive the Spirit there and then (Acts 8:12–13). On hearing the news of Philip's evangelism in Samaria, the leaders of the mother church sent Peter and John to see what was going on. They were pleased with what they found, but they discovered that something was missing. The Samaritan converts had not received the Spirit, so they prayed for them, laid their hands on them, and then the Samaritans received the Holy Spirit (Acts 8:14–17).

Luke does not explain the time lapse on this occasion between the Samaritans believing in Jesus and their receiving the Spirit. The most natural explanation of the interval is that when at last the Spirit fell on the Samaritan believers, they received assurance from the authoritative leaders of the church that they were no longer outcasts, but were full members of the people of God in the new age. It is obvious that the Samaritans' reception of the Spirit was accompanied by the same audible signs (speaking in tongues) that the believers had manifested at Pentecost.

It should be noted that there are three occasions when the Spirit is imparted by the laying on of hands:
1. The conversion of the Samaritans as described above (8:12–17).
   Bruce (1988, p169) comments that there is no suggestion here that the believers' reception of the Spirit was conditional on their having apostolic hands laid upon them.
2. The conversion of Saul of Tarsus (9:17–19). It was Ananias who laid hands on Paul, and he was not an apostle.
3. The disciples whom Paul found at Ephesus (19:1–7). Paul was not an original apostle.

Lampe (1951, p76) believes that these three exceptions have special importance and so are different.

3. Before baptism

Shortly after the events at Samaria, under the unmistakable guidance of the Holy Spirit, Peter went to visit Cornelius, the Roman centurion, in Caesarea, taking six believers along as witnesses. On his arrival he explained to Cornelius that he had never entered a Gentile house before or taken food at a Gentile table, but that God had taught him not to look on anyone as "common or unclean." Then he related the gospel story to Cornelius, from John the Baptist's ministry to Jesus' death and resurrection, concluding that through Jesus – crucified and risen – forgiveness of sins was available to every believer (Acts 10:34–43).

Peter had barely finished speaking when the Holy Spirit fell on those present, the experience being accompanied by the same outward signs as at Pentecost. Both Peter and the six men he had taken along with him were stunned at what they saw and heard. Here were Gentiles "speaking in tongues and praising God." God had clearly shown his approval by sending his Spirit on them. Peter had no option but to go along with this act of God: "Can anyone keep these people from being baptised with water? They have received the Holy Spirit just as we have." So he ordered them to be baptised in the name of Jesus Christ (Acts 10:44–48).

SUMMARY

In Acts the reception of the Spirit could take place:
- immediately after the confessing of faith in Christ and submitting to baptism in his name, for example, on the Day of Pentecost the believers in Jerusalem received the Spirit immediately after they were baptised.
- with the laying on of apostolic hands, a considerable time after the exercise of faith and submission to baptism, for example, the believers in Samaria, although 'baptised into the name of the Lord Jesus', did not receive the Spirit until apostles laid hands on them.
- before baptism and without the laying on of hands. At Caesarea the Gentiles received the Spirit as they listened to Peter preaching. Peter realised their conversion was genuine and then they were baptised.

> - after baptism, in the name of Jesus with the laying on of hands, in the experience of some who had to a certain extent become disciples of Jesus already.
>
> Clearly there was no set pattern to how the Spirit was received. What is important is not the sequence of these stages in becoming a Christian, but their presence.

How was the Spirit active in the Christian community?

1. In individual lives

The first Christians thought of the Holy Spirit in terms of an invisible but divine power, clearly marked by its effect on the life of the recipient. The impact of the Spirit left the individual (or onlooker) in no doubt that a significant change had taken place in him as a result of a divine power. In Acts the most mentioned manifestations of the Spirit are inspired speech, speaking in tongues, prophecy and praise. The Spirit encouraged, strengthened and even comforted individual believers (9:31). Although the term 'comforted' is not directly used in Acts, it is surely implied that the Holy Spirit comforted Stephen (7:55) and Paul (23:11, 27:23). Neil (1973, p89) also points out that more often than not it was the "uncomfortable" comfort that the Spirit provided, pushing the believers "forward into uncharted and intimidating waters with only their faith to sustain them", turning them into missionaries and proclaimers of the good news (Acts 1:8) (Stott, 1990, pp29–45).

2. In Christian fellowship

Becoming a Christian was not a solitary experience. Drane (1986, p393) comments that they "were bound together as a group not by the fact that they all belonged to the same organisation but because they were all inspired by the same Holy Spirit". The Spirit united them into a fellowship that could not be paralleled in any other group. "Acts presents a vibrant community that was passionate about mission, with members caring for each other, pursuing holiness, and dealing with matters that affected its unity" (Fernando, 1998, p123). The invisible fruit of the Spirit's activity is the '*koinonia*', the unity and fellowship of Christians, manifested in a number of ways, not least in their sharing of goods. According to Hewitt (1964, p232), both Paul and Luke obviously believed fellowship to be the creation of the Holy Spirit. It was a two-way sharing; together they shared Christ and through Christ they shared with each other.

3. As a guide/instructor

Through the Spirit, Jesus exercised his authority over his followers. One of Luke's purposes in writing Acts is to show that the Holy Spirit initiated and guided the activities of the church, especially concerning mission. This theme is regularly repeated in Acts, where we read of instances in which the church or individuals follow a certain course or adopt a certain policy through the guidance of the Spirit.

TASK

In Acts, Luke shows us how each of the key apostolic leaders depended on the Holy Spirit for guidance or instructions. Complete the following table of examples (some of it has been done for you):

	The Holy Spirit as a Guide
	Enables Jesus to give instructions to the apostles
1:2	
1:7–8	
	Directs new developments in the church regarding the spread of the gospel
8:26, 29	Willimon (1988, p72) comments that in being obedient to the Spirit, preachers like Philip find themselves in the oddest of situations with the most surprising sorts of people: Following the conversion of the Ethiopian, Philip was sped northward by the Spirit on another mission, in a manner comparable to the experiences of Elijah and Ezekiel (Ezek 3:14 & 8:3).
9:17–18	
10:19–20	
13:1–3	Drane (1986, p392) believes that this sense of dependence on the Spirit's guidance is perhaps the main characteristic of Paul's work, both in the stories of the Acts and in his own writings. What do these verses tell us? When the church at Antioch in Syria sent Paul and Barnabas off as missionaries, it was acting on the instructions of the Holy Spirit, who spoke directly to the congregation through certain Spirit-filled individuals within it.
	Gives wisdom about problems within the church
6:1–6	

	Leads and guides the decisions and actions of the Christian leaders
15:28	One of the occasions in Acts when the Christian community exhibits a strong awareness of the Spirit's centrality in its life comes to light in the letter sent to the Christians in Syria and Cilicia by the Council of Jerusalem. As you will not study the proceedings of the Council of Jerusalem until A2 level, some explanation might be useful at this point. The decision made by the Council of Jerusalem was introduced in the letter with the words, "It seemed good to the Holy Spirit and to us"; that is, "The Holy Spirit has decided, and so have we" (Acts 15:28). The spontaneity and matter-of-factness of this declaration stresses the church's role as "the vehicle of the Spirit" (Bruce, 1988, p298). The apostles and elders do not try to explain why the decision was primarily the Holy Spirit's and only secondarily theirs. They were so conscious "of being possessed and controlled by the Spirit that he was given prior mention as chief author of their decision" (Bruce, 1988, p298).
16:6–7	
19:2–7	
20:22–23	
Prohibits, compels and warns, often by visions	
16:6	
16:6–10	He directs the course of Paul and his companions, as he had previously done for Philip (Acts 8:29) and Peter (Acts 10:19–20), indicating which routes they must avoid and which they must follow (Acts 16:6–10).
20:22–23	

4. Prophecy

The Spirit who spoke through the Old Testament prophets continued to speak in the church, through prophets of the new age. Prophecy could be a form of ecstatic speech of the Spirit, which differed from glossolalia in that it was intelligible to the hearer. Prediction of coming events formed part of the prophet's function but a prophet's greatest contribution in the Early Church was preaching, which was inspired by the Holy Spirit.

For example, through the prophet Agabus, the Spirit foretold the great famine of Claudius' day, enabling the church of Antioch to take steps to provide for their fellow believers in Jerusalem (Acts 11:27–30). And it was probably through one of the prophets in the church of Antioch that the Spirit gave directions for the release of Barnabas and Saul for the special work for which he had called them (Acts 13:1–2).

5. To discipline/purify the church

The power of the Holy Spirit in the Early Church is underlined in another way in the incidents involving Ananias and Sapphira (Acts 5:1–11) and Elymas (13:9–11). Ananias and Sapphira tried to deceive the church by acquiring credit for being more generous than they actually were. The Christian community was so closely identified with the Spirit that a lie told to the church was a lie told to the Spirit. The Holy Spirit gave Peter insight as to what Ananias and Sapphira had done and gave him authority to deal with them. When Ananias and Sapphira realised the enormity of their actions, that they were guilty of such a serious offence against the Holy Spirit, they were so appalled that one after another they fell down dead.

When the sorcerer Elymas opposed the missionaries (13:9–11) on the first missionary journey, Paul was forced to rebuke him because of his negative influence upon the proconsul. Note how Luke points out that Paul was "filled with the Holy Spirit" for this task (v 9) (Fernando, 1998, p376), evidence that the Holy Spirit acted as a purifying agent, stamping out corruption.

Resisting the Spirit

God's bestowal of his Spirit is his response to genuine faith. The withholding of faith, especially on the part of those who have heard his voice, is seen as resistance to the Spirit, and there is no deadlier sin than this. In the Old Testament those who did not pay heed to the prophets were in effect resisting the Spirit who spoke through them, and the consequences for them were disastrous. Similarly in the Early Church, those who continually refused to accept Jesus had no hope of repentance or salvation. This is the point of Stephen's charge: "You are just like your fathers: You always resist the Holy Spirit!" (Acts 7:51). The same point is made by Paul at Pisidian Antioch: "Look, you scoffers, wonder and perish, for I am going to do something in your days that you would never believe, even if someone told you" (Acts 13:41). Paul makes this point again at the end of Acts when he applies the warning of Isaiah 6:9–10 about "unhearing ears and unseeing eyes" to the leaders of the Roman Jews: "The Holy Spirit spoke the truth to your forefathers when he said through Isaiah the prophet: 'Go to this people …'" (Acts 28:25–28).

6. In mission

Bruner observes that in Acts the Holy Spirit is Jesus at work "in continuation of his ministry" (1970, pp156–157). The main emphasis of the work of the Spirit was mission. The apostles were to play a full part in this mission, and they would be empowered to do so when the Spirit came upon them: "you shall be my witnesses ... to the end of the earth" (Acts 1:8). Boer (1976, p71) describes how the Spirit restlessly drives the church to witness. The gospel would be heard in Jerusalem, in Judea and Samaria, and to the end of the earth, revealing the Holy Spirit as the principal actor in the drama of the expanding church (Barclay, 1955, p13).

TASK

Copy and complete the table below, which highlights the methods used by the Spirit to spread the gospel:

The Spirit used various means to carry out the church's mission

Testimony, story and the proclaimed word	Acts 2:14, 36; 3:12–26; 5:32; 7:2–53; 8:4; 13:16–41; 18:5; 19:10	
Trances	Acts 10:19	
Prophets	Acts 11:28	
Worship services	Acts 13:2	The Holy Spirit sent this message, probably through one of the prophets.
Church councils	Acts 15:28	
Inner constraint	Acts 16:7	

Through these means, the Spirit was active in making the mission of Jesus universal (Green, 1975). In other words, salvation was available for Jews and Gentiles alike. For example, after Peter's preaching at Caesarea, Gentile evangelisation was approved and promoted. Not only that but it was marked by the spontaneous outpouring of the Spirit, as spontaneous as the initial outpouring on the Day of Pentecost.

The Holy Spirit told the apostles what to say in their preaching (1:8; 2:4; 4:8, 31; 11:24; 13:9, 52) and gave them the boldness to say it. During his ministry, Jesus had told his disciples not to be concerned about the form of words they should use when called to account in a court of law – the Holy Spirit would tell them what to say (Luke 21:15). Just as the Spirit had spoken through David and the prophets in ancient Israel (1:16; 4:25; 28:25), so he now gave power, courage and boldness to preach and witness (2:14; 4:8; 6:10; 7:1–53; 8:4–5).

The apostles experienced the significance of this assurance the first time that they were challenged by the Jewish authorities in Jerusalem. Fernando (1998, p152) comments that "this is one of several instances in Acts where God's servants are filled with the Holy Spirit in order to face a special challenge" (see 4:31; 7:55 and 13:9). Another is the healing of a lame man in the temple precincts, which led to the arrest of Peter and John. When they were brought before the chief priests they were asked on whose authority had they acted? Peter, then "filled with the Holy Spirit", replied that the lame man had been healed by the power of the crucified and risen Jesus.

Another example of a courageous speaker is Stephen, who is described as "a man full of faith and the Holy Spirit". It was the Spirit who enabled him to speak before the Synagogue of the Freedmen[1], giving him such "inspired wisdom" (Fernando, 1998, p245) that when he spoke "they could not refute him" (Acts 6:10).

7. Giving power to perform miracles

Miracles were impossible without the work of the Holy Spirit. Through the Spirit's power, Peter performed miracles to such an extent that many hoped his shadow would fall on them so that they would be healed.

Similarly, throughout Paul's journeys the Holy Spirit's presence and activity are evident in Paul's acts of healing and exorcism. Paul, too, was held in such high regard that handkerchiefs and aprons that touched him were taken to the sick (19:12). However, it is important to bear in mind that God was the one who carried out these miracles through the power of the Holy Spirit, not Peter's shadow, or belongings that had come in contact with Paul.

8. Appointed for a task

Seven men were appointed to take charge of the common fund to needy members of the community. The qualifications laid down for them were that they should be "of good repute, full of the Spirit and of wisdom" (Acts 6:3). One of them, Stephen, is especially singled out as "a man full of faith and of the Holy Spirit." He showed these qualities when he was challenged by his opponents who "could not withstand the wisdom and the Spirit with which he spoke." When they accused him of blasphemy before the Sanhedrin, his defence speech filled them with such rage that his execution inevitably followed. Luke describes how, full of the Holy Spirit, he gazed into heaven and said, "Behold, I see the heavens opened, and the Son of man standing at the right hand of God" (Acts 7:55–56).

---

1   The Freedmen were Jews who had been taken prisoner by the Romans but later given their freedom.

Guthrie (1961, p740) adds that in Acts 20:28, in Paul's address to the Ephesian elders, he reminds them that the Holy Spirit has made them guardians of the flock, to feed it. "This suggests that Paul accepts as a matter of course that elders were appointed by the Holy Spirit."

Conclusion

Acts leaves us in no doubt that the church was essentially a community of the Spirit. It was controlled and directed by the Spirit and this had an important bearing on the function of the ministry (Guthrie, 1961, p733) and on the spread of the gospel to Rome. Throughout Acts the Spirit is shown to be as important a character as Stephen, Peter and even Paul, giving support for the idea that the book could have been called 'The Gospel of the Holy Spirit'.

TASK

a) Describe the ways in which the Holy Spirit is presented in Acts.

- How the Spirit is received.
- The Spirit in individual lives and in the community.
- How the Spirit guides, disciplines, inspires and motivates.

b) Explain the importance of the Holy Spirit in the outreach of the Early Church. Give examples from Acts.

- As a motivator.
- Boldness to preach.
- Encourages through opposition.
- Guides.

c) Evaluate the claim that 'The Gospel of the Holy Spirit' is a more appropriate title for the book of Acts.

- Do you think the Spirit is as important a character as Peter and Paul, etc? Could the mission have happened without the Spirit? Discuss using examples from Acts.

OTHER ASPECTS OF HUMAN EXPERIENCE

Characteristics and relevance of the charismatic and Pentecostal movements

A key incident in this section is the coming of the Holy Spirit on the Day of Pentecost. On that day, the most prominent gift of the Spirit was speaking in other tongues. However, in Paul's letters, other gifts are described, such as healing and prophesying. The charismatic and Pentecostal movements emphasise the work of the Holy Spirit and a direct experience of God through gifts such as speaking in tongues and healing. This theme for human experience examines the role played by these movements in the Christian Church today.

A brief history of the charismatic movement

The Charismatic movement is one of the fastest-growing branches of the church today. Throughout the history of the church, there have been 'revivals' or special times when God has sent his spirit to empower the church. The result is that many people become Christians, as seen in the 1859 revival in Northern Ireland. It is said that there were over 100,000 converts to Christianity and many new churches had to be built to accommodate this massive increase.

In 1906, there was a revival at the Azusa Street Mission in Los Angeles, which is thought to be the start of the charismatic/Pentecostal movement. It was here that people claimed to have been "baptised by the Holy Spirit" in a similar way to the Apostles on the Day of Pentecost. The people who attended these meetings witnessed speaking in tongues and miracles of healing and their enthusiasm spread throughout America. By the 1970s, this unique way of worshipping had spread to Europe, resulting in a number of new denominations. The movement takes its name from two Greek words, *charis* meaning 'grace' and *mata* meaning 'gifts'. *Charismata* therefore emphasises the gifts of the Holy Spirit as a sign of the presence of God's spirit. Charismatic Christians maintain that the signs of the Holy Spirit given to the Early Church can still be experienced by Christians today.

The relevance of the Pentecostal/charismatic movement:
- Christians who worship in this way believe that their movement is returning to a type of worship that has much in common with the

church of the New Testament. Faith in God is to be experienced, often in a dramatic way, not something that depends on rituals or actions.
- Pentecostal worship is lively and dynamic, often with spirited singing, dancing and movement, such as waving hands and arms in praise. Worshippers believe they are being driven by the power of God within them.
- Pentecostal churches stress the importance of a conversion experience, which fills the believer with the Holy Spirit. This helps a person to live a truly Christian life.

Catholic Charismatic Renewal

This is a movement within the Catholic Church that has had an impact both locally and globally for over 50 years. It involves aspects of both Catholic and charismatic worship and emphasises the importance of having a personal relationship with Jesus. The movement works locally at parish level through prayer groups held outside of Mass. At these meetings, worshippers might express the gifts of the spirit through prophesy, healing and speaking in tongues.

The CCR has an important role to play in the work for Christian unity, as it is strengthening relationships with Protestant, Pentecostal and independent church groups. Pope Francis is a great proponent of this type of spirituality and has stated that Baptism in the Holy Spirit is for the whole church. He is keen to meet, to pray and work together with leaders in other denominations with a view to building strong personal relationships.

The Sacrament of Confirmation

In the Catholic Church, this sacrament involves the anointing of participants by the Holy Spirit. The Christian teaching of the Holy Trinity is that God is present in three persons, Father, Son and Holy Spirit. The Holy Spirit is the guide and helper that Jesus promised to send to his apostles, who came to them on the day of Pentecost. The Catholic Church teaches that at confirmation, the gifts of the Spirit are given to a believer as at the first Pentecost. It is the final sacrament of initiation into the Catholic Church, where the bishop or priest prays that the person being confirmed will receive the Holy Spirit and his seven gifts. These gifts are wisdom, knowledge, understanding, courage, right judgement, reverence and wonder and awe in God's presence.

TASK

1. Read the following article:

How the Pentecostal movement is changing the Christian church

Pentecostal and Charismatic churches all share a belief that, following conversion to Christianity, there is then a second experience that comes later where the believer is "filled with the Holy Spirit", an event which manifests itself in the receipt of spiritual gifts such as prophecy, healing prayer or the ability to speak in tongues.

The word 'Charismatic' is derived from the Greek word for 'gift' and reflects this belief. The word 'Pentecostal' refers to the event described in the book of Acts, known as Pentecost, where the Holy Spirit was first given to Jesus' followers.

The World Christian Database estimates that globally there are 584 million Pentecostal Christians, which is about a quarter of all Christians. It is one of the most rapidly growing forms of Christianity in the world.

More locally, only about 1% (15,000) of Northern Ireland's population said that they attended Pentecostal churches in the 2011 census, but that number is growing, as evidenced by the increasing number of such churches in the province. Pentecostal churches tend to be independent: not affiliated to the traditional denominations or even to other Pentecostal churches.

Worship services in such churches tends to be dominated by loud, band-based music. Green Pastures Church in Ballymena, for example, has an auditorium that can seat 1000 people with a large band, stage lighting and screens that display the words of the songs, verses from the Bible or other visual aids for the person speaking. The purpose of this style is to attract people who have no previous church experience, and who may be put off by the more traditional style of worship found elsewhere.

Pastor Owen Crane of Life Church in Belfast says "Everything we're trying to do on a Sunday morning or Sunday evenings is trying to engage with an unchurched audience."

However, some independent churches have found that their structure can make them more susceptible to problems or scandals, because power is concentrated in a small number of leaders.

Speaking on BBC Radio Ulster in 2013, Professor Drew Gibson from Union Theological College in Belfast said: "Any structure in which there is a pyramid with one person at the top is a very dangerous structure. Those groups where there were problems either fell apart or developed accountability structures where it wasn't one person at the top but a corporate leadership."

Nevertheless, the movement is growing and it is likely that more such churches will appear in the years ahead.

Discuss these questions in small groups:
1. The headline claims that the Pentecostal movement is changing the church. Do you agree with this statement?

   What are some of the ways in which Pentecostal worship is different to a more 'traditional' style of worship? What are some of the possible advantages of worshipping in this way?

   Do you think that churches today should try to be more like the church in the New Testament?

2. Does the Holy Spirit still play a vital role in churches today? In your answer research some of the following areas:
   - The Pentecostal movement.
   - Attitudes to gifts of the spirit in churches today.

Section 2:
The Missionary Activity of Peter and John

PETER'S SPEECH ON THE DAY OF PENTECOST (CH 2:14-41)

Joel's prophecy (Ch 2:14-21)

Whatever the ecstatic utterances were, they achieved the purpose of drawing a crowd, which Peter took advantage of in giving his first speech. He begins with a denial of the charge of drunkenness: it is only nine o' clock in the morning, much too early for them to have been able to drink in excess. Hewitt (1964, p45) also points out that the Law did not allow a Jew to eat or drink before the first hour of prayer (9.00 am). The men were not full of wine, but of the Holy Spirit, as had been prophesied by the prophet Joel.

Peter continues commenting that with the Spirit's coming the last days have come. Stott (1990, p73) argues that the age of the Spirit stretches between the two comings of Christ. God's Spirit will be poured out on all flesh, "irrespective of their outward status, and people would prophesy, through 'visions, dreams and by word of mouth'" (Bruce, 1988, p61). This can be considered as a "long day of opportunity, during which the gospel of salvation will be preached throughout the world" (Stott, 1990, p75).

On first reading verses 19-20, it may seem difficult to understand. Stott (1990, p74) suggests the possibility that these predictions are upheavals of nature which began on Good Friday. On that day the sun darkened during the early afternoon and the paschal full moon may well have risen blood-red in the sky as a result of the darkening of the sun (Bruce, 1988, p62). The prophecy concludes with a promise that whoever appeals to the Lord for help will be saved, which Christians regard as an appeal for salvation in the name of Jesus.

The Resurrection of Jesus proclaimed (Ch 2:22-28)

Bruce (1988, p63) comments that Peter now takes up his main theme, which is the proclamation of Jesus as Lord and Messiah. He directs his speech to the "men of Israel," that is, the Jews. He immediately focuses on Jesus, who had been marked out by God for them through the various miracles and signs that God had performed publicly through him (Marshall, 1980, p74). Instead of treating Jesus as a man of God, the Jews put him to death by crucifixion. "Lawless men" refers to the Romans who carried out the death sentence, but it is the Jews who are considered to be responsible. Bruce (1988, p64) adds that at this point Peter is addressing the people of Jerusalem, and not the visitors.

However, all this was part of God's plan that the Messiah should suffer. Marshall comments that "here we have the paradox of divine predestination and human free will in its strongest form" (1980, p75).

> ### TASK
>
> Find out the meaning of 'paradox' and 'predestination' and explain the meaning of Marshall's comment in your own words.

Jesus' sentence and death were reversed by God's intervention in raising him from the dead. God raised him because it was not possible for death to hold him. Bertram (cited in Fernando, 1998) comments that "the abyss can no longer hold the Redeemer than a pregnant woman can hold the child in her body". To confirm his claim, Peter now uses an Old Testament prophecy, Psalm 16:8–11, which is regarded as a statement by David about the Messiah (v 25–28). Peter argues that the words of this prophecy cannot refer to David, for he did not rise from the dead. Therefore, the passage must be referring to Jesus, David's descendant. Jesus is therefore the expected Messiah.

Jesus: Lord and Messiah (Ch 2:29–36)
David knew that God had promised that one of his descendants would sit on his throne (see Ps 132:11). Peter therefore claims that what was prophesied has been fulfilled in Jesus: the Messiah had risen from the dead. Having established that Jesus, as the Messiah, must rise from the dead, Peter can now go on to give the explanation of the pouring out of the Spirit (Marshall, 1980, p78): that Jesus received the Holy Spirit from the Father and had now poured that Spirit out on his followers.

Call to repentance (Ch 2:37–41)
Peter's preaching was successful in stirring the consciences of his listeners. If Jesus was the Messiah, then the guilt they were feeling over their treatment of him was vast. In panic, it seems, they asked what they should do. Peter told them to repent and be baptised in Jesus' name. Stott (1990, p78) describes this as humiliating for them: firstly, because Jews regarded baptism as necessary only for Gentile converts who wished to become proselytes; and secondly, because they would be submitting to baptism in the name of the very person they had previously rejected. It would certainly be a public token of their genuine repentance and faith.

In return, they would not only receive forgiveness of sins but also the gift of the Holy Spirit – the gift which had been bestowed on the apostles themselves only a few hours before (Bruce, 1988, p69). This promise was for them and the generations that followed, for those far off such as the dispersion Jews and for everyone called by God. "Through the apostolic witness Jesus thus acquired more followers in one day than in the whole of his public ministry" (Bruce, 1988, p73).

Summary of Peter's speech at Pentecost:
- Charge of drunkenness denied – the apostles are full of the Holy Spirit; prophesied by Joel.
- Jesus was killed by the Jews.
- Jesus was raised from the dead. The resurrection of one of David's descendants was foretold in Ps 16:8–11 and Ps 89:4.
- Jesus is the descendant to which the prophecy applies.
- Jesus is ascended into heaven and given the promise of the Holy Spirit.
- Jesus has now poured out the Holy Spirit. The gift of tongues is evidence of this.
- Psalm 110 speaks of the reign of a Messiah – Jesus is shown to be that Messiah.
- The challenge is to repent of sin and accept Jesus.

FOCUS ON TEACHING AND MIRACLES

The healing of the lame man (Ch 3:1–10)
Dillon (1990, p735) comments that this first miracle story in Acts has a clear connection with Acts 2:43, which speaks of the various wonders and signs carried out by the disciples. It is noticeable that by acting "in the name of Jesus" Peter is able to perform similar miracles to those performed by Jesus in the gospels. Marshall (1980, p86) regards this as an example of the continuity between the ministry of Jesus and the witness of the church.

The story begins with the description of a man being carried by his friends to be set down at the entrance to the Temple. Many scholars suggest that this was probably the Nicanor Gate, which separated the court of women and the court of Gentiles. As people would have been on their way to worship, this was an ideal place to beg, particularly as the giving of alms was an exceptionally meritorious act in the Jewish religion (Marshall, 1980, p86).

Luke begins by referring to the apostle John (presumably the son of Zebedee) as accompanying Peter. However, John plays no active role in the story. He remains the silent partner, which is similar to the other occasion where his name appears (8:14–17). It has been suggested that Luke referred to two apostles witnessing together for legal purposes (Dillon, 1990, p735). He was following the biblical pattern that two witnesses are needed to establish a matter (Numbers 35:30; Deuteronomy 17:6; 19:15; Matthew 18:15f; 1 Timothy 5:19).

Peter's speech in Solomon's Colonnade (Ch 3:11–26)

The healed man kept close to Peter and John as something like a stampede of people ran towards them, amazed at what had happened. Peter seized the opportunity to explain the gospel to them, directing their attention towards Jesus, the power behind the miracle. The apostles never regarded themselves as the sources of power but only as the channels of power (Barclay, 1955, p30).

Many features of this speech are similar to the speech at Pentecost. However, Tannehill (1994, p58) feels they are complementary rather than repetitive. "The most remarkable feature of Peter's second sermon, as of his first, is its Christ-centredness. He directed the crowd's attention away from both the healed cripple and the apostles to the Christ" (Stott, 1990, p92). The speech thus gives additional teaching about the person of Jesus, describing him as God's servant, the Holy and Righteous One, the Author of life and the prophet like Moses. It can be summarised as follows:

- The miracle had happened due to the power of God; the same God who had revealed himself to Abraham, Isaac and Jacob. In other words, the God that they, the Jews, worshipped.
- This same God had glorified his *servant* Jesus.
- They, the Jews, had denied Jesus – "*the Holy and Righteous One*" – before Pilate and instead they had asked for Barabbas, a murderer, to be released. Dillon (1990, p735) comments that no distinction is made between participants in Jesus' execution and any others.
- They had killed Jesus, "*the Author of Life*", and God had raised him from the dead.
- It was through faith in Jesus' name that the lame man had been healed. Hewitt (1964, p49) comments that in using the 'name' of Jesus, Peter was following a tradition. A name personified the character and nature of a person. To speak Jesus' name was to call upon the power and authority of Jesus to perform the miracle.

Packer comments that the list of titles (see previous italics) given to Jesus impresses upon the crowd the messianic nature of his mission.

Marshall (1980, p95) comments that Peter now moves into the specifically evangelistic part of the speech:

- What the Jews and their leaders had done was due to ignorance. Bruce (1988, p83) comments that "they did not realise that Jesus of Nazareth was their divinely sent Saviour." Peter was not interested in bringing an accusation against the Jews for their crime. Instead, he hoped they would act on the message of salvation, which God had given them. This implies that their action could be forgiven.
- However, in reality, the Jews' action of killing Jesus had in fact fulfilled God's plan, foretold by the prophets, that Christ should suffer.
- The Jews now have the opportunity to repent and be forgiven of their sins.
- Jesus was the Jews' Messiah and he would return at the *Parousia*, although this would not happen immediately.
- Moses had spoken of a prophet that God would send (Deut 18:15–19; Lev 23:29); a second Moses was the general consensus among the Jews. Peter here assumes that Jesus is this prophet.
- All of the Old Testament prophets, from Samuel onwards, had been concerned about the end times, which were the events that were occurring.
- These promises made by the prophets were made for the Jews.
- Jesus had been raised to bless the audience by turning them away from their sin.

TASK

a) Give an account of the healing of the lame man as described in the early chapters of Acts.

- First miracle story in Acts.
- Links to Ch 2:43.
- Continuity of Jesus' mission.
- Background to the lame man.
- Significance of where it happened in terms of being witnessed.
- Healing in the name of Jesus.
- Peter's lack of prejudice against a beggar.
- Peter's speech.

> b) **Explore the relevance of miracles for religious believers. Justify your answer.**
> - Consideration of different types of miracle, for example, nature, physical and spiritual.
> - The place of faith healers, centres for healing, prayer and the anointing of the sick in various traditions.
> - The observation that miracles are not an everyday occurrence and can be seen as God at work in the world.
> - Arguments surrounding the validity of miracles.

Many Healed (Ch 5: 12–16)

Luke gives another summary, presenting the church as having a powerful healing ministry (Marshall, 1980, p114). It seems the unbelieving Jews left the Christians alone as they met together in Solomon's Colonnade. Bruce (1988, p109) suggests that the death of Ananias and Sapphira had scared off all but the totally committed Christians. They realised that "the awesome power of the Spirit that judges also demands commitment and responsibility" (Polhill, 1973, p164). Despite some being deterred, many became Christians and others looked for healing of their sickness from Peter. Packer comments that the power of the Spirit is again apparent, working through Peter as the leader (1966, p46). His reputation for healing was so exceptional that people believed even his shadow could heal them. This notion that shadows had magical powers was a common belief at that time (van der Horst, cited in Marshall, 1980, pp204–212). Fernando (1998, p210) comments that this is the closest we have in the Bible to a modern-day healing campaign.

THE APOSTLES' ATTITUDE TOWARDS OPPOSITION

Opposition to Peter's evangelism (Ch 4:1–22)

This is one of the times when one of the followers is filled with the Holy Spirit (v 8) in order to be equipped for a special challenge. See also 4:31; 7:55; 13:9.

Marshall (1980, p86) comments that the witness of the first Christians brought them into conflict with the Jewish leaders. These leaders, from the party of the Sadducees, would have been responsible for public order in the Temple. They tried to keep on friendly terms with the Romans to keep their own wealth and power. They knew that while the Roman government was very tolerant regarding Judaism, it was merciless if there was any public disorder (Barclay, 1955, p34).

As Sadducees, they would reject the belief in the resurrection. So they not only saw the apostles "as agitators but as heretics" (Stott, 1990, p95). They arrested Peter and John and brought them before the Sanhedrin to find out what they were doing and put them in prison for the night.

The Sanhedrin met the following day and the apostles were asked by what power or by what name had they done these things. Peter, and not John, responded, and Dillon (1990, p737) argues that his first speech before the Sanhedrin (like the second in 5:29–32) is an apologia rather than a sermon. Peter boldly seizes on the moment to defend the gospel by explaining the power behind the miracle. Barclay (1955, p36) notes that by being so confident he was taking his life in his hands, because this was the same court that had condemned Jesus to death.

It is significant that Peter was inspired by the Holy Spirit as he addressed the council. Throughout the book of Acts, the role of the Holy Spirit is referred to many times.

Peter's speech before the Sanhedrin
- Peter is quick to point out that the reason they are gathered is due to a good deed being carried out for someone in need.
- He boldly proclaims that the miracle is to be credited to the power of the name of Jesus Christ of Nazareth.
- The blame for Jesus' death is again put on the Jews and it is emphasised that God raised him from the dead.
- Peter then uses a metaphor by quoting the language of Psalm 118:22 to make his point. Jesus is the *"stone which was rejected"* by the Jews, *"you builders"*. But Jesus has become *"the head of the corner"* or cornerstone/capstone. Guy (1969, p30) explains that when men build a house they place on one side a stone they don't need. Later, however, they find that this is the stone necessary for a cornerstone at the junction of two walls.
- It was Jesus then who saved the lame man and through Jesus they also could be saved.

Dillon (1990, p737) comments that "the little speech" gives a precise answer to the question put by the interrogators (v 7). The members of the Sanhedrin were amazed because the apostles were 'unschooled', meaning that they were not well-read men; they didn't speak with big words but rather in a simple way (Gutzke, 1966, p59). The speech put the Sanhedrin in a dilemma (v 16) and they were content to let Peter and John go with a warning, to which Peter replied that they would proclaim their faith regardless of threats (Lewis, 1960, p32).

> ### TASK
>
> **a) Give an account of the events leading up to Peter's speech before the Sanhedrin, the speech itself and the aftermath.**
>
> - Summary of healing of lame man; the speech:
> - Good deed carried out in name of Jesus.
> - Jesus' death blamed on Jews.
> - They could be saved.
> - Aftermath: reaction of Sanhedrin; let go with a warning.
>
> **b) Assess the view that Peter's words can be described as a defence speech.**
>
> - Answers their question on authority.
> - Defends the gospel through an account of Jesus' death.

Reaction to persecution (Ch 5: 17–42)

Motivated by jealousy, the Sadducees arrest the apostles and throw them into prison. Fernando (1998, p210) comments that this is not surprising given the spectacular ministry of the apostles. No reason is given for the arrest except disobedience of an earlier command not to preach (Lewis, 1960, p33). However, during the night the apostles escape with the help of an angel of the Lord. Neil (1973, pp96–97) speculates that this was "a sympathetic warder" who came later to be seen as "an angel in disguise". As God's spokesman, the angel tells the apostles to go and preach in the Temple.

Meanwhile, the council's officers were sent to the prison, where they realised the prisoners had gone, even though all the doors were secure. Marshall (1980, p118) comments that the guards must have been unconscious during the escape and the doors were re-locked. Therefore they did not realise that anyone had escaped until they checked inside. It is no wonder the council was confused about what was going on. It is at this moment that the news comes of the apostles preaching in the Temple area.

A peaceful arrest followed. Fernando (1998, p211) comments that it is ironic that those who probably had wanted to stone the apostles for blasphemy were now afraid that they themselves would be stoned by the people. The apostles were reminded by the High Priest that they were already forbidden to preach about Jesus. However, they had ignored him. Not only that but they had tried to put the blame of Jesus' death on the Jewish authorities. The role of Peter as a strong and fearless leader is evident in his direct reply to the council (v 29). He was the spokesman for the group, with the others in some way indicating their agreement (Longenecker, 1981, p320). The response is not really a defence speech as you might expect. Rather Peter points out that God's commands have priority over human commands. He then steps into his evangelist's shoes as he takes the opportunity to briefly preach the gospel. He agrees that yes, the Jews had killed Jesus, describing him as "prince and saviour". For them to have done this was "to act against the God whom they claimed to worship" (Marshall, 1980, p119). This Jesus who was crucified was the one that God had exalted to sit at his right hand. He was the Saviour through whom the Jews would have the chance to repent and receive forgiveness.

The Sadducees were furious and even thought about having the apostles put to death. However, just in time, Gamaliel, a leading Pharisee, "rose with quiet dignity" (Packer, 1966, p47) and intervened with a speech, which is renowned "for its sound sense and friendliness" (Lewis, 1960, p34). He warned against such extreme action and advised the court to go into closed session to discuss the matter. Fernando (1998, p213) suggests that the apostles' miracles and escape from prison presumably made him suspect that God might indeed be blessing this new movement.

Gamaliel has been described as "a respected teacher and a firm upholder of the Law" (Marshall, 1980, p117). He was a tutor of Paul (Packer, 1966, p47) (Ch 22:3) and, as a Pharisee, would have exhibited a more tolerant spirit than the rival party of the Sadducees[1] (Stott, 1990, p116). Gamaliel used reason in his advice to the Sanhedrin. Using two examples, he argued that movements that were human in origin would die out themselves, so they should waste no time on it. (There is some confusion over the two examples used by Gamaliel. According to Josephus (*Antiquities*, book XX 5.1), the rebellion of Theudas took place later, about AD44–45). However, movements inspired by God needed to be approached with caution, as there is a danger of opposing

---

[1] The Sadducees accepted only the written Law of Moses and not many of the doctrines accepted by the Pharisees or Jesus. For example, they did not believe in the resurrection of the body.

God. In any case, mass movements often lose momentum once the leader is dead. As Jesus was dead, they should wait to see what happened.

Gamaliel's words managed to calm down the Sadducees. When the apostles were brought back in they were again warned not to speak in the name of Jesus and were released following a beating. Ironically, this punishment filled them with joy. Perhaps they felt that they had been regarded by God as worthy to take their share of suffering for the sake of the gospel (Marshall, 1980, p124).

"We should not be too ready to credit Gamaliel with having uttered an invariable principle" (Stott, 1990, p118). In other words, should we always follow the rule that if a religious group of people succeeds in the long run, then the group must be from God? What do you think?

OTHER ASPECTS OF HUMAN EXPERIENCE

The debate about the relevance of miracles in strengthening religious faith

The healing of the sick has had renewed emphasis in recent years among Christians. For a long time, many people believed that the power to heal had died out with the apostles, but today some churches still have a healing ministry. This theme considers whether miracles still happen today and their link to faith in the life of the religious believer. These examples of human experience are relevant to other sections on the specification, such as the role of miracles in aiding the spread of the gospel.

Read the following examples of healings that lie outside your course of study:

1. Introduction to Lourdes

It is reported that in 1858, in the grotto of Massabielle, near Lourdes, France, the Blessed Virgin Mary appeared eighteen times to Bernadette Soubirous, a 14-year-old peasant girl. She told Bernadette to "Pray and do penance for the conversion of the world". The Catholic Church investigated Bernadette's claims for four years before approving devotion to 'Our Lady of Lourdes'. Lourdes has since become one of the most famous shrines, attracting many millions of pilgrims each year. There have been thousands of miraculous cures at this shrine.

A Medical Bureau was established in 1882 to test the authenticity of the cures. The doctors include unbelievers as well as believers, and any doctor is welcome to take part in the examination of the alleged cures. As many as 500 medical men of all faiths or no faith have taken advantage of the invitation each year. Many books and movies tell the story of Lourdes. In the 1940s, a film depicting the remarkable event, called The Song of Bernadette, was made in Hollywood, and won six academy awards. Many believe that moral and spiritual cures are more amazing than physical cures. Those who are not cured of bodily pain receive an increase of faith and resignation – true peace of soul.

The story of two outstanding miracles that occurred at Lourdes are the stories of Gabriel Gargam and John Traynor. Find out what you can about their experiences.

2. Lourdes 'miracle' officially recognized (14 Nov 2005)

The Catholic Church has recognized as 'miraculous' the case of Italian woman Anna Santaniello, who was cured of a rheumatic illness following a pilgrimage to Lourdes in 1952. It is the 67th 'miracle cure' attributed to the Lourdes sanctuary, which is located in south-west France and is the second most visited Christian pilgrimage site after Rome. It is believed by Catholics that the Virgin Mary appeared to a young woman in a cave at the site in 1858. Six million people visit Lourdes each year, many seeking a miraculous cure from illness and to experience the site's spring water.

Ms Santaniello had been suffering from Bouillaud's disease which affected her ability to walk, her speech, triggered asthma attacks and caused cyanosis of the face. In 1961, nine years after her visit to Lourdes, the international medical committee at Lourdes described her recovery as "extraordinary". She subsequently returned to Lourdes a number of times as a nurse and is now aged 94.

3. Do miracles happen today?

It was every parent's worst nightmare. At just six days old, little Tanya Marlow was admitted to Great Ormond Street Hospital in London with a brain haemorrhage. The doctors ran tests and then told her parents that the news was not good. Not only was there nothing they could do to stop the bleeding, but even if they were able to stop it, she would be severely disabled and have significant learning difficulties. One of the doctors suggested that they might want to pray.

Her parents were not Christians, but a nurse was willing to pray with them. The following day the doctors did another scan and, to their amazement, there was no sign of any bleeding. In fact, the brain was completely healthy. One doctor said "This is what is known in the trade as a miracle".

Tanya Marlow recovered fully and went on to earn an English literature degree and now lives in Devon, working as a writer. Her parents were affected by the experience and embarked on a search for the God who they believed had healed their daughter. Both of them became Christians six months later. It had a profound impact on Marlow growing up. She says "When I was growing up, I always had this awareness that God was real, that He did answer prayer and that He had intervened in my life to save me".

Reference: Relevant Magazine, Issue 74, Mar/Apr 2015

TASK

Answer the following questions:

1. Are miracles a feature of a pre-scientific age? Is there always a rational explanation for any 'miraculous' events?
2. Do miracles still happen today?
3. Is faith necessary for a miracle to happen? Is there any evidence that witnessing a miracle can lead to a religious faith or do miracles strengthen an already existing faith?
4. What do other world religions believe about miracles?

If you have access to the internet, you may wish to find examples to support your ideas.

BY THE END OF THIS CHAPTER YOU SHOULD BE ABLE TO:

- demonstrate knowledge and understanding of, and critically evaluate early events in Jerusalem, including:
  - Jesus' initiation of the church's mission and the significance of the Ascension (1:1–11);
  - the events on the Day of Pentecost and the role of the Holy Spirit in the emerging church (2:1–13); and
  - the significance of these events for the Early Church;
- demonstrate knowledge and understanding of, and critically evaluate the missionary activity of Peter and John, including:
  - Peter's speech on the Day of Pentecost and reaction (2:14–41);
  - focus on teaching and miracles (3:1–26, 4:1–22, 5:12–42); and
  - the apostles' attitude towards opposition;

The Growth and Expansion of the Church

Section 1:
The Role of Stephen and Philip

BACKGROUND TO STEPHEN AND PHILIP

Up until now, the church has been made up only of Jewish Christians and has been limited to Jerusalem. With the introduction of Stephen and Philip onto the scene, Luke turns a page in the book of Acts. Through the next few chapters, he describes how the foundations of the Gentile mission are laid by them.

The choosing of the Seven (Ch 6:1–7)

As the church in Jerusalem grew to include Greek-speaking Jews (Hellenists), a practical issue arose that needed to be sorted out as soon as possible. Following the example of Jewish society, the care of poor widows was an important aspect of church life. The Greek-speaking Christians, however, felt hard done by, in that their widows were not receiving the same help as the Judeans (Hebrews). They were particularly needy as, unlike the native Judean widows, they did not have relatives to care for them (Fernando, 1998, p225). Barclay (1955, p51) suggests there was a deeper problem in that the Hebrews looked down upon the Hellenists.

> **Hebrews and Hellenists**
>
> The name 'Hebrew' refers to Jews. It describes someone who was totally Jewish in all aspects of life – someone who observed the Law of Moses and lived according to Jewish traditions.
>
> The 'Hellenists' were Jews who came out of the Dispersion. They were much more accepting of Greek ideas. Hellenists may not have totally observed ceremonial law and there may have been cultural differences between them and the Hebrews.
>
> The Hebrew Christians probably refused to have full table fellowship with the Hellenists. A result may have been the inequality in the distribution of food to the poor Hellenist widows. This may have caused more division in the fellowship.

Up until now the administration of aid had been part of the responsibility of the twelve apostles, but they were overworked and such a practical issue was taking them away from their main job of evangelising. Therefore, seven men were appointed to take charge of the distribution of food. Even with what some might consider being low order responsibilities, spiritual qualifications were vital (v 3). They were to possess wisdom and the Holy Spirit. Stott emphasises that "there is no hint whatever that the apostles regarded social work as inferior to pastoral work, or beneath their dignity" (1990, p121).

The appointment of the Seven was a huge step forward in terms of church organisation, which was to develop significantly in the first three centuries.

Marshall (1980, p125) believes that the Seven may have been chosen from the Greek-speaking part of the church that had raised the original complaint. The seven names were all Greek. However, Stott (1990, p122) sees this as speculative, agreeing with Lenski that "some of both classes of Jews were elected" (1934, p246). Some scholars would even go so far as to say that the Seven were appointed as leaders of the Greek-speaking part of the church, separate to the rest of the church. Two of the Seven, Stephen and Philip, emerge as having the same evangelistic ability as the Twelve. Marshall (1980, p127) points out that Stephen is given a fuller description as a man full of faith and the Holy Spirit, which prepares us for the next section. The Seven received the laying on of hands by the apostles, which indicates that authority has been passed on to them.

The effect of the appointment of the Seven was positive, as there was an increase in the preaching of the gospel and subsequently more converts.

TASK

Church issues

1. It seems the Twelve realised their own limitations in that they recognised that the task of teaching and administering poor relief was too great for them. They were probably not able to do either task properly.
   Discuss how the church today could learn from their attitude.

2. God calls different people to different roles in the church. Some are called to preach, while others are called to do pastoral or social work. Neither work is superior to the other.
   Do you agree or disagree?

3. Clearly the Early Church had problems of disunity. A good example to follow is how they dealt with such problems immediately.
   Discuss the sort of problems the church might face today – where it would be wise to follow the example of the early Christians.

4. The Early Church did not divide into two separate churches – one for the Hellenists and one for the Hebrews. Rather they made sure the Hellenists were cared for.
   Discuss the difficulties of having one Christian Church today.

Stephen seized (Ch 6:8–15)

Stephen is described as being full of God's grace and power, which reminds us of the apostles (Ch 4:33). His ability to preach and heal was obviously due to being filled with the Holy Spirit. However, his ministry provoked opposition from members of various synagogues. The Freedmen, who, as was mentioned in Chapter 2, were Jews who had been taken prisoner by the Romans and later given their freedom, argued with Stephen, but were unable to get the better of him. So they persuaded some people to publicly complain that they had heard Stephen blaspheme against Moses and God. Stott describes this as "a smear campaign against him" (1990, p127). The people were furious and, along with the religious leaders, they arrested Stephen and brought him before the Sanhedrin. False witnesses were set up to testify against Stephen, saying that he was always attacking the Temple and the Law. In particular, they claimed that he said Jesus would destroy the Temple and change the customs handed down by Moses.

Customs handed down by Moses were the oral traditions that interpreted the Law of Moses. An attack on the oral Law would have been considered to be just as serious as an attack on the whole Law.

What were the accusations against Stephen?

The formal charges against Stephen were twofold:
1. Speaking against "this holy place" (6:13) seems to be summed up by "Jesus will destroy this holy place".
2. Speaking against "the Law" (6:13) is equivalent to "altering the customs which Moses handed down to us" (6:14).

When the Sanhedrin looked at Stephen for a response, they realised that he seemed to have the face of an angel. Marshall (1980, p131) explains that this describes someone who is close to God and reflects some of God's glory as a result of being in his presence. Stott explains that the same thing happened to Moses' face when he came down from Mount Sinai with the Law (Ex 34:29ff): "Was it not God's deliberate purpose to give the same radiant face to Stephen when he was accused of opposing the Law as he had given Moses when he received the Law? In this way God was showing that both Moses' ministry of the Law and Stephen's interpretation of it had his approval" (1990, p129).

Stephen's speech to the Sanhedrin (Ch 7:1–53)

Stephen's speech is the longest speech in Acts. It is not a defence in the sense of an explanation or apology calculated to win an acquittal (Fernando, 1998, p246). Rather, it is mainly a recital of Old Testament history and can be described as a tedious read, with many seemingly irrelevant points. As good debaters do, Stephen avoided the question and did not directly address the charge that he had blasphemed against Moses and God.

Neil, however, calls it "a subtle and skilful proclamation of the gospel" (1973, p107). The detail of Israel's history that Stephen recited was completely familiar to his listeners. His approach would not have been regarded as unusual because it was common practice among Jewish rabbis to recite elements of the history of Israel. Lenski explains that through telling the story of the Old Testament Stephen "first refutes the charge that he blasphemed God; secondly, he blasphemed Moses and the Law; thirdly, that he blasphemed the Temple. In fact, he proves that he does the very opposite" (1934, p256).

Before discussing the purpose of the speech, it is worth taking a detailed look at its content. Stephen retells the Old Testament story "in such a way as to draw lessons from it which they had never learned or even noticed" (Stott, 1990, p130)

Overview of Speech:

Throughout history, God sent deliverers to his people, but the Jews rejected them and broke God's Law.	The Call of Abraham and promises made to him (v 2–8). Joseph, rejected by his brothers but rescued by God (v 9–16). Moses, sent to deliver his own people from Egypt but rejected by them (v 25, 39–43).	Stephen had not spoken against the Law. The truth is that in the past the Jews themselves had rejected Moses, worshipped idols, killed prophets and failed to keep the Law.
The Jews had the tabernacle in the desert and then Solomon's Temple.	They committed idolatry (v 39–43) and came to believe that God actually lived in the Temple (v 44–50).	While the Jews had the tabernacle and the Temple, God was not restricted to them but was everywhere.

Abraham: v 2–8

Stephen responded immediately to the invitation from the High Priest to speak. His speech lacks an introduction, as he launches straight into an account of how God called Abraham to be the father of the nation. It is significant that he mentions how God appeared to Abraham in Mesopotamia (the land now covered by modern Iraq and north-eastern Syria), outside the land of the Jews.

Stephen's main focus is God (7:2), and God's actions dominate this section. God appears (7:3), speaks (7:3, 6), moves (7:4), gives an inheritance (7:5), promises (7:5), judges (7:7) and gives a covenant (7:8). Luke does not even mention Abraham's faith. Abraham merely goes and dwells (7:4) and circumcises (7:8). The focus is on God's promise and the way it will be fulfilled in a time beyond Abraham (Johnson, 1991, p121).

Abraham leaves his home only because he is promised a land of his own (7:3). Although he possessed none of it, the same land was promised to his descendants (7:5). Abraham went on to settle in Haran, but his destination was "this land where you are now living" (7:4). God's promise that Abraham's descendants would live in the Promised Land was fulfilled. The point is that long before there was a holy place, there was a holy people, to whom God had pledged himself (Stott, 1990, p132).

Stephen next describes the giving of the covenant of circumcision to Abraham. Abraham was told that before his descendants received the Promised Land they would be slaves in a foreign land for 400 years. The covenant was a symbol of the promise given to them.

Joseph: v 9–16

In this section, Stephen begins to show the pattern of opposition to God's leaders. Here Stephen is showing how the prophecy in v 6 has been fulfilled. Stephen showed Joseph to be a man of faith. Joseph's brothers were jealous of his dreams, which showed his future role (Gen 37:5–11). Stephen relates how they rejected Joseph (which corresponds to the attitude of the leaders towards Jesus during his ministry) and sold him as a slave, but how God was with him and saved him from any trouble, even enabling him to become ruler over Egypt. Then Joseph's family came to Egypt because of the famine, hoping to buy corn. Once introduced to Pharaoh, they became acquainted with him and were invited to settle in Egypt, where they ended their days.

In the previous section concerning Abraham, Stephen had shown God acting outside of the Holy Land, in Haran. Now he points out that God was with Joseph and his brothers in Egypt, again outside the Promised Land.

When Joseph's family died, they were buried in Abraham's tomb. Stephen may have deliberately singled out the fact that Shechem was the burial place because it was located in despised Samaritan territory. His audience held their land in great esteem. If the respected patriarchs of Israel had been buried in Shechem (and proper burial was important to Jews), this implies again that God can work anywhere.

> A type of Jesus can be seen in the story of Joseph:
> - Joseph was rejected by his brothers, just as Jesus was rejected by his own people (John 1:11).
> - Joseph was thrown into a pit, but God rescues him out of it. Jesus was buried in a tomb and rose from the dead.
> - Though Joseph was rejected by his own, strangers received him. Jesus was accepted by the Gentiles.
> - Finally, Joseph was raised up to be the ruler of Egypt, just as Jesus has been glorified by God.

Moses: v 17–43

It has been suggested that Stephen's handling of Moses' career is longer and fuller than his account of the others, because he had been accused of speaking against Moses (Stott, 1990, p134). In the speech, Stephen turned the accusation of speaking against Moses towards those who had accused him. It was not Stephen but the nation of Israel that had rebelled against Moses (7:9, 35, 39, 51, 52). He discusses Moses' life *in three parts*, each one totalling forty years (7:17–29; 30–35; 36–43):

The first forty year period (Ch 7:17–29):

First, Stephen describes Moses' early life in Egypt, dealing with his birth, upbringing and education. Having been rescued from the Nile, Moses was brought up by Pharaoh's daughter. When Moses was around forty, he attacked and killed an Egyptian who was ill-treating an Israelite. Moses hoped that the Israelites would realise that he could be trusted. When he came upon two Israelites arguing, he attempted to intervene. However, this backfired on him and the perpetrator asked him who he thought he was by setting himself up as ruler and judge over them. Moses realised that they knew he had killed an Egyptian, so he fled to Midian, where he married and had a family.

The second forty year period (Ch 7:30–35):
After another forty years, Moses had a vision of an angel at Mount Sinai in a burning bush. God spoke to him, commanding him to treat the place as holy ground. Stott (1990, p137) highlights that as Mount Sinai was not in the Promised Land this statement shows that there was holy ground outside the Holy Land; that the presence of God is not confined to Palestine. Through Moses, God promised to save his people from their suffering in Egypt. God was sending Moses back to save the very people who had rejected him.

The third forty year period (Ch 7:36–43):
Moses led the Israelites out of Egypt and received the Law as a sign of the covenant God had made with his people. By obeying the Law, the Israelites would continue to be his people. There is now a turning point in Stephen's speech. He describes Israel's reaction to Moses' teaching and Law: "Our fathers refused to obey him" (7:39), which was really a rejection of God himself. Stephen then outlines a series of disobedient acts by the nation in the wilderness:
- They rejected Moses and refused to obey him following their departure from Egypt.
- In their hearts they turned back to Egypt.
- They forced Aaron to make gods and had committed idolatry by worshipping a golden calf. Stephen quotes Amos 5:25–27 to support his firm belief that this despicable form of idolatry caused God to hide himself from Israel.

Stephen's audience claimed he had spoken against the Law, saying it would be removed by Jesus. Ironically, Stephen points out that it seemed his audience belonged to a nation who had rejected the Law right from the start. "So far from speaking against Moses, Stephen accuses his hearers of failing to obey the laws which God gave through him to Israel" (Marshall, 1980, p147).

To sum up, the Jews might offer sacrifices and offerings at the temple, considering it to be the place of God's presence. They might hold the Law in the highest regard and be quite fanatical about it. But Stephen seems to be suggesting that the Jews are not really God's people after all.

God's presence
Throughout the Moses section, Stephen emphasises that God was present outside of Palestine. Here he stresses this point by echoing a number of locations outside the Holy Land where God interacted with Moses:
- God raised up the deliverer Moses in Egypt (7:17–22).
- He provided for the rejected Moses in Midian (7:29).
- He commissioned Moses in the desert near Mount Sinai (7:30–34).
- God pronounced Mount Sinai to be 'holy ground'.
- Moses was sent back to Egypt, not Israel, to do God's will. God delivered his people from this pagan nation, as well as at the Red Sea and in the wilderness (7:35–36).

As in the case of Joseph, Moses can be compared to Christ in Stephen's account:
- Just as Moses narrowly escaped death at the hands of Pharaoh (7:21), so the infant Jesus was saved from King Herod.
- Moses was described as being "no ordinary child" (7:20). The same can be said of Jesus (Luke 2:52).
- Moses grew in wisdom and stature (7:22), as did Jesus (Luke 2:52).
- Moses was mighty in word and deed. Luke describes Jesus in a similar way (Luke 24:19).
- Stephen said that Moses thought that his own people would realise that God was using him to rescue them, but they did not (7:25–28). Like Moses, Jesus was sent to save his own people, but they rejected him.

Solomon: v 44–50
The 'tabernacle of the Testimony' was a moveable place of worship carried by the Israelites in the desert. The tabernacle had been the focus of national worship in Israel from the beginning of the wilderness wandering until David's reign. It was passed on to the next generation under the leadership of Joshua and then until the time of David. David wanted to find a more permanent dwelling place for God, but this privilege was given to Solomon.

The point of Stephen's discussion on the tabernacle seems to be to discourage the institutionalising of worship by saying that God was better served when his presence was focused upon a moveable structure: "The Most High does not live in houses made by men" (7:48).

Barclay (1955, p61) points out that the Temple, which should have become their greatest blessing, was in fact their greatest curse; they had come to worship it instead of worshipping God. Stott agrees: "they conceived of Yahweh (God) as so completely identified with the temple that its existence guaranteed his protection of them, while its destruction would mean that he had abandoned them" (1990, p130). The Jews had made the Temple their safeguard. They were left with a Jewish God who lived in Jerusalem rather than a God of all men whose dwelling was the whole universe. Scott agrees, commenting that the Judaism of Stephen's day had become increasingly "place-conscious, provincial and localised in its view of God" (1978, p133). Palestine in general, and Jerusalem in particular, had come to be looked upon as the only places where God could be found. With God being limited to Jerusalem and its institutions, the implication was that the only way to be saved was to become a Jew first.

Stephen, however, "was striking at the very roots of Jewish nationalism. He was saying, in effect, that God could get along without either the Temple or Judea (the Holy Land), and from now on the world was God's parish. Here we have universalism" (Hewitt, 1964, p70).

Conclusion: v 51–53

Stephen suddenly seems to break off from his recital of Israel's history. He begins a scorching attack on his audience for having the same attitudes as their ancestors. He portrays them as stubborn people. "Uncircumcised hearts and ears" refers to the fact that they have failed to 'cut away' pride and sin from their lives and are deaf to the truth. They always resist the Holy Spirit, who spoke to them through the Old Testament prophets, through Jesus, and now through the new Christian community. Stephen insists that the Sanhedrin's refusal to acknowledge Jesus as Messiah, and to have him killed, reflects their negative attitude towards God's messengers in general throughout Israel's history.

His audience resist the Holy Spirit. They betrayed and murdered "the Righteous One" (Jesus). Finally, they had failed to keep the divine Law. Stephen had now put the blame of Jesus' death on the shoulders of the Sanhedrin, the spiritual leaders of the nation (Luke 24:20; Acts 4:10; 5:30).

The Stoning of Stephen (Ch 7:54–8:1)

Not surprisingly, the Sanhedrin's response to Stephen's speech was one of absolute fury (7:54). The term "gnashed their teeth" was a sign of rage. Claiming to have a vision of Jesus standing at the right hand of God made matters worse, and violence broke out among the council. Some scholars suggest that Christ stood up to welcome his first martyr (Stott, 1990, p141). Stephen was dragged out of the town and stoned to death. His final words were a prayer for himself and for those killing him. Then he "fell asleep". Bruce regards this as "an unexpectedly beautiful and peaceful description of so brutal a death" (1988, p160). They are similar to the words spoken by Jesus before his death (Luke 23:34).

There appears to have been no formal trial. Even if there had been, the Sanhedrin had no legal right to put anyone to death, and was supposed to liaise with the Romans regarding cases of capital punishment (John 18:31). However, a Roman form of execution was not used, as Stephen was stoned. This stresses the intense anger of the Sanhedrin. As Stephen lay dying, he asked the risen Jesus to receive his spirit, and that his killers be forgiven. It has been stressed that Stephen was following Jesus' example, as he also wanted forgiveness for his executioners (Luke 23:34).

Saul, who belonged to the group of Stephen's enemies, was there. While he did not actually take part in the murder, he did approve of what was done and seemed unmoved by the horror of it all. This is in striking contrast to the man he was to become following his conversion. Perhaps Luke includes this comment here to demonstrate how amazing the conversion of Saul was in the Early Church.

Stephen as "a type of Christ"

The way Luke moulds the story, Stephen emerges as "a type of Christ" (Johnson, 1992, p413). Various parts of Stephen's speech and details of his death remind us of the last days of Jesus:

- Like Jesus, Stephen has grace and power, and works wonders and signs among the people (6:8).
- Both enter into debate with those who challenge them (6:9; Luke 20:1–7), including those who are sent as spies (6:11; Luke 20:20).
- Both are arrested (6:12; see Luke 22:54) and brought to trial before the Sanhedrin (6:12–15; see Luke 22:66–71).
- Stephen has false witnesses accuse him (6:13); while this is left out of Luke's passion narrative, it can be found in the Synoptic parallels of Mark 14:56 and Matthew 26:59.
- Both are taken out of the city to be executed (7:58; Luke 23:32).
- At his death, Stephen prays that his spirit be accepted (7:59), as did Jesus (Luke 23:46).
- Stephen asks that his murderers be forgiven (7:60), as did Jesus (23:34).
- Stephen is buried by pious people (8:2), as was Jesus (Luke 23:50–55).

Significance of Stephen's speech and martyrdom

1. In the book of Acts, Stephen's speech and martyrdom stand between the spread of the gospel in Jerusalem (Acts 1–5) and its spread to the rest of the Roman world (Acts 8–14). It was a timely event. If Stephen's martyrdom takes place around AD35, then Peter's vision in Joppa would be around six years later, in AD41, with the Council of Jerusalem occurring in another eight years or so, in AD49.

2. His speech led to a rejection of the Law and the Temple.

3. It resulted in a move away from the Jewish people and Jerusalem. The persecution that led to the spread of the gospel outside of Jerusalem is a direct result of the events in Acts 7.

4. The death of Stephen provided Luke with an important literary transition. Luke has shown how the apostles and others were witnesses in Jerusalem. But the story of the Jerusalem Church was complete. Now it was time for Luke to show the gospel spreading out to "Judea and Samaria, and to the ends of the earth" (1:8).

TASK

Stephen was a Hellenist Jew who came out of the dispersion. There was some tension between Hebrews and Hellenists, with the Hebrews – whose ancestors had always lived in the Promised Land and had access to the Temple – feeling superior. Stephen's speech is not a straightforward defence of the charges made against him. Stephen is attempting to show that God is everywhere and does not just dwell in the Temple in Jerusalem. This is how a Hellenist might present a defence to a Hebrew Jew; yet in doing so, Stephen is also preparing the way for the worldwide mission of the church.

- Study Stephen's speech (Acts 7:1–53) and find examples used by Stephen to show that God's presence is not limited to the Promised Land.
- Present your findings as a spider diagram or list of bullet points.

TASK

a) **Describe what is known from Acts about Stephen and the charges brought against him.**

- Stephen's career as recorded in Acts.
- Institution of the Seven, Stephen's arrest and charges (6:8–15), Stephen's speech and the stoning of Stephen.

b) **Explain the relevance of Stephen's speech in light of the charges brought against him.**

- The charges brought against Stephen (6:8–15).
- Stephen's speech in response to these charges (7:1–54). Either tell the speech in chronological order or pick out Stephen's response in relation to the charges that he spoke against the Law, Moses and the Temple.

c) **With reference to other aspects of human experience, comment on the claim that it is important that Stephen is remembered as a significant Christian martyr. Justify your answer.**

- Stephen is known to be the first Christian martyr.
- His death serves as an example of the ultimate devotion to God.
- While his death was horrific, others suffered worse fates and are not well known in the Christian Church, for example Blandina.
- Many are martyred today in China and other places and they are not remembered the way Stephen is.

The evangelising activity of Philip

After the burial of Stephen, persecution broke out against the church in Jerusalem, and many Christians were scattered to the countryside of Judea and Samaria. On a positive note, this led to widespread evangelism.

The gospel spreads to Samaria (Ch 8:4–25)

As the Christians moved to new areas, they found a welcoming response to the gospel (Marshall, 1980, p152). An example of this is the reaction of the Samaritans to Philip's preaching and miracles. Philip was another member of the Seven (6:5), who took the brave step of taking the gospel to Samaria.

Stott (1990, p147) points out that hostility between the Jews and Samaritans had lasted a thousand years. In the eighth century BC, Samaria was destroyed by the Assyrians and most of the people were deported to parts of the Assyrian empire (2 Kings 17:5–6). The area of Samaria was resettled by a mixed group of peoples from other parts of the empire. The resentment between Samaritans and Jews was centuries old, and may have dated back to this time. It was deepened when the Samaritans opposed the rebuilding of the Jerusalem Temple in the fifth century BC. This led to bitter hatred between Jews and Samaritans, which grew worse through the passage of time. However, in 63 BC the Romans occupied Palestine and the Jewish republic. The Samaritans were freed from Judean domination, but the bitterness between the Jews and Samaritans continued. For Jews to evangelise the people of Samaria and bring them into fellowship with Jewish Christians was a very brave step.

On the surface, it looks as if the mission to Samaria was the first step in the evangelisation of Gentiles. However, the Samaritans were considered by Jews more as schismatics (those who split away from the main group) than Gentiles. Peter, for example, had no problem visiting the Samaritans, but he needed a life-changing vision before visiting the Gentile Cornelius. You could say that the Jews considered Samaritans to be 'half-Jews' or 'half-breeds', both religiously and racially. However, they were regarded more as heretics from the faith rather than outright pagans.

The Samaritans were also hostile towards the Jews. In his Gospel, Luke describes an incident that shows their hostility when a small village of them refused to welcome Jesus and his disciples, because it was known that they were travelling to Jerusalem (Luke 9:52–56).

Yet the Jews and Samaritans did have a lot in common. Philip's preaching would have been particularly attractive to them, as the belief in a coming 'restorer' was part of their theology. Philip, as a Hellenistic Jew, also found himself on common ground with the Samaritans because he too was an outcast from Jerusalem. By now the news of the persecution suffered by the Christian Hellenistic Jews may have reached Samaria, making the Samaritans more willing to receive the missionaries.

Many were in awe of Philip as they heard his message. Like Jesus (Luke 4:33, 36; 6:18; 7:21; 8:2, 29; 9:42; 11:24) and the apostles, he also had the ability to exorcise evil spirits and heal people. It was God's power that got the attention of people so that some might become receptive to the gospel message. Johnson comments that as Philip evangelised the Samaritans he continued "the work of Jesus in reaching out to the marginal and outcast among the people and inviting them to a full participation in the restored people of God" (1992, p151).

Luke combined his story of the Samaritan mission with that of a notorious local religious personality named Simon Magus or Simon the Sorcerer (Magician). Simon features in the writings of second-century Christian writers as the first heretic (false teacher) of the church, and founder of gnostic Christianity. The early Christian theologian, Irenaeus (AD120–202), bishop of Lyons, France, refers to Simon as the originator of a number of heresies (written circa 175–185, *Against Heresies*, 1:23, repr 2015).

Before the arrival of Philip in Samaria, Simon had astounded the people by his magic powers. The people were taken in by him, even calling him the 'Great Power'. It seems that Simon claimed to be divine (from God), but Luke simply presents him as a magician who deceived the people by his tricks.

Philip's preaching, however, was so powerful that the people listened to him instead of Simon. Many, both men and women, went on to believe and be baptised, as did Simon, who stuck by Philip's side from then on. However, whether or not his conversion was real is questionable, because he was preoccupied by Philip's ability to perform miracles and longed to be able to do the same. Luke does not say what exactly these miracles were, but it seems that when people were converted to Christ the Holy Spirit was given to them in such a way that greatly impressed Simon. Hewitt (1964, p77) suggests that they may have engaged in Glossolalia, although this is not stated.

The apostles at Jerusalem sent two delegates, Peter and John, to assess what was happening at Samaria. The spread of the gospel to the Samaritans represented such a dramatic step that the apostles were bound to be intrigued by what was going on. The Jerusalem Church also needed to satisfy itself of the genuineness of the Samaritan conversions. Once they did so, there would be no question of the mother church accepting these new converts. By going to Samaria, Peter and John were also confirming the validity of the Hellenistic Christians' ministry of evangelisation. (During the early years of the church, the apostles seemed to exercise supervision over the progress of the gospel in general. See Acts 11:22.) It was a mission of goodwill by the Jerusalem Church, showing that the church was one body, and demonstrating their brotherly bond with the Samaritan converts.

Peter and John were satisfied that the gospel had been received favourably, but discovered that the new converts had not yet received the Spirit. This seems strange, as Luke did not hint at any deficiency in the Samaritan believers' faith. So they prayed for them, laying hands on them. Up until this point they had only been baptised in the name of Jesus. Many wonder why they had not received the Spirit following baptism. Lampe (1967, p70) suggests God withheld the Spirit until this point so that the Samaritans would be seen to be fully part of the community of Jerusalem Christians, and not only the Hellenistic branch of the church. (This is not to say that the converts could receive the Holy Spirit only through the apostles. Ananias, who had no known ministerial role and was certainly not an apostle, was the instrument through which the Holy Spirit was given to Paul. See 9:17.) Others argue that the conversion of the Samaritans was not real, and that was why they had not received the Spirit (Dunn, 1973, pp63–68). However, Luke tells us none of this.

Simon keenly observed the apostles' ability to bestow the Spirit on people and longed to be able to do the same. (Some speculate that the original Pentecost charismatic gifts were in evidence, such as speaking in other languages. Perhaps the Samaritan converts outwardly exhibited a sense of spiritual joy, which is a gift of the Holy Spirit. See Galatians 5:22.) However, Simon's desire to bestow the Spirit was clearly for the wrong reasons, for he offered to pay for the gift. Here we see again the role of Peter as a disciplinarian. Peter gave Simon a scathing rebuke about his spiritual blindness. The Phillips' translation (www.ccel.org/bible/phillips/CP05Acts08.htm) of Peter's reply catches the sense of his grim reprimand of Simon: "To hell with you and your money!" (8:20). It is a curse against Simon or a warning that he must change his ways. It shows how seriously the church took Simon's misunderstanding of the gifts of God. Unlike Ananias and Sapphira, he was given the chance to repent and seek forgiveness because he was "full of bitterness and captive to sin" (8:23). However, Simon lacked understanding and had his mind only on physical consequences. Stott (1990, p151) comments that instead of praying for forgiveness, Simon asked Peter to pray for him that none of these awful things would happen to him (8:24). He argues that he was more concerned with God's judgement than with receiving forgiveness.

Simon then disappeared from the story, and that is the last we hear of him in Acts, or anywhere else in the New Testament.

TASK

The term 'simony' originates from this story.
Find out why.

Significance of the story:
1. It gives an account of the conversion of the Samaritans, people whom the Jews hated. The story hints at the overcoming of the resentment between the Jews and Samaritans through a common Christian faith.
2. It shows an early indication of bringing Jews and Gentiles together.
3. It suggests that there is the possibility of forgiveness, even for serious sin committed by a baptised person.

Philip and the Ethiopian (Ch 8: 26–40)

A second story in Acts highlighting the missionary activity of Philip is that of the conversion of the Ethiopian. It begins with Philip receiving a divine command from an angel to go to a remote place. This might have seemed strange, considering the extent of Philip's involvement in evangelism in Samaria. This, however, was obviously God's intention, so he obeyed the command to go south and found himself on a desert road. It was also the last community before a traveller encountered the desert waste stretching to Egypt.

It would have been highly unusual to meet anyone on such a remote road, so it is surprising that he met the Ethiopian at all (Marshall, 1980, p161). Luke's narrative is formed in such a way to stress this. The man was a eunuch (meaning he was castrated), and employed as the royal treasurer by the queen mother, who was the ruler of Ethiopia (not to be confused with the modern state of Ethiopia; it was then the Upper Nile region). Stott (1990, p160) suggests that he may have actually been Jewish, either by birth or conversion, for the Jewish dispersion had reached Egypt and beyond. Other scholars disagree, however, believing him to be a Gentile. He had been in Jerusalem 'to worship', probably at one of the pilgrim festivals, so he was most likely a God-fearer. As he travelled home, he put the journey in by reading from the Jewish Scriptures. Some scholars believe it would have been difficult for a non-Jew to get a copy of the Isaiah scroll.

Philip received a second divine command, telling him to stay close to the Ethiopian's chariot. As he went near it, he heard someone reading and recognised the words. He asked the Ethiopian if he understood what he was reading. He admitted that he was having difficulty and asked Philip to interpret the passage for him. "The passage that the eunuch was reading provided a golden opportunity for an evangelist" (Marshall, 1980, p163). Isaiah 53 is a prophecy describing a Servant of God who suffers and bears the consequences of the sins of others. Jesus had quoted from Isaiah 53, saying it had been fulfilled in his death (Luke 22:37). Now, Philip was preaching the same message. The eunuch was concerned with discovering whom the prophet was describing. Philip uses this as an opportunity to show that Jesus was the one who fulfilled the prophecy.

When the two men reached a stream, the eunuch asked for baptism. At this point, the eunuch must have given Philip some indication of his new faith in Jesus, for Philip agreed to baptise him in a nearby stream. The phrase "went down into" implies that baptism was done by immersion, not sprinkling. Jesus himself was baptised this way, setting the example (Mark 1:9-10).

The story ends abruptly with a description of how the Spirit took Philip away as the two men came out of the water. The eunuch returned home rejoicing, which suggests that he had also received the Holy Spirit (8:39). Africa had now been penetrated by the gospel in the person of the Ethiopian eunuch. This signified another small step in the advance of the gospel from its Jewish confines to a wider Gentile world.

However, the church was still far from engaging in a direct effort to bring the gospel to purely pagan Gentiles. While this event may describe the conversion of a Gentile, the fact that he returned to his own country means that the church was not at this point forced to consider its views on the acceptance of Gentiles. Johnson concludes that "as with the Samaritans, the conversion of the Ethiopian does not yet represent a formal opening to the Gentiles, but rather to those who were marginalised within the people of God" (1992, p160).

Meanwhile, Philip turned up in Azotus, preaching as he made his way to Caesarea, his hometown. He probably spent considerable time in each of the towns. Luke, however, passes over the details of what may have been a number of months' work in a sentence.

Philip's final destination was Caesarea, which was either where he then lived or later settled. After arriving in Caesarea, he disappeared from Luke's account. However, Philip made a sudden reappearance about 20 years later, as Paul's host (21:8-9). By this time he was the father of four unmarried daughters, who were all prophetesses.

Significance of the story:
1. This incident is a further advance towards the evangelisation of Gentiles. Philip is breaking new ground both geographically (by preaching in Samaria) and culturally (by witnessing to a eunuch, most likely excluded from full Jewish membership). Peterson comments that "Luke progressively exposes the way God made it possible for the Gospel to move out from Jerusalem, thus fulfilling the promise in 1:8" (2009, p292).

2. Philip was led by the Spirit, so it is obviously God's intention to include Gentiles in the church. The Holy Spirit is active throughout this incident, sending Philip into the desert, making him approach the chariot and taking him away once the mission was completed.
3. The Ethiopian "went on his way rejoicing" (Acts 8:39), no doubt full of the Holy Spirit and inspired to spread the word to others. It is likely that he had success, as the Coptic Church in Ethiopia was in existence by the first century AD, with Christianity the official religion by the fourth century.
4. Baptism, by immersion in water, is now seen as a visible sign of entry into the church.
5. Philip, a Hellenist, is taking the lead in bringing the gospel to the Gentiles. In contrast to his work in Samaria, Philip is now witnessing on a one-to-one basis, rather than being involved in mass conversions. In this incident, he has converted a high-ranking civil servant as opposed to ordinary people.

TASK

a) Describe the role of Philip in the Acts of the Apostles.

- One of the Seven (6:5).
- Mission with Samaritans.
- Conversion of Ethiopian.
- Evangelist (8:40).

b) Give an account of the story of the encounter between the Ethiopian and Philip as recorded in Acts.

- Divine command.
- Discussion of religious outlook of Ethiopian.
- Interaction with Philip.
- Results.
- Implications.

c) Describe Philip's activity in Samaria.

- History of relationship between Jews and Gentiles.
- Significance of Philip's step in taking the gospel there.
- Religious outlook of Samaritans.

- Reaction to Philip's ministry.
- Simon the magician – a genuine conversion?
- Visit by Peter and John – reasons.

d) Comment on the claim that Philip was a forerunner of Paul in accepting Gentiles into the church.
- Explore the consequences of Philip's opening out of the church's mission to non-Jews.
- Philip's activity eventually led to the Council of Jerusalem (chapter 15) and the acceptance of Gentiles into the church.

e) Explore the claim that Philip was a successful preacher. Justify your answer.
- Examples of his ministry – preaching and miraculous signs.
- Evidence from Samaria.
- Ethiopian eunuch.
- Fact that he was still an evangelist 20 years later and had a positive influence on his daughters.

f) Evaluate the claim that from the beginning baptism was essential for entry into the Christian community.
- Peter's call for baptism of the believers (Acts 2).
- Philip, Peter and John and the Samaritans.
- The conversion of the Ethiopian (Acts 8).
- The Gentile Pentecost (Acts 10).
- Peter's report to the church at Jerusalem (Acts 11).
- An exploration of the link between baptism and the reception of the Holy Spirit.

g) Comment on the view that it is easy to overlook the importance of the role of Philip in the spreading of the Good News. Justify your answer.
- Space taken up by Philip in Acts compared to that of Peter and Paul.
- Silence of Philip's activity from Acts 8 until chapter 21.
- Luke's focus on Paul's missionary journeys and stay in Rome dominate the book of Acts.
- On the other hand, Philip laid the groundwork for Peter and Paul and has not been forgotten for this.

OTHER ASPECTS OF HUMAN EXPERIENCE
Defending religious belief and practice in a hostile world

This theme for human experience examines some of the challenges involved in defending religious belief. When Stephen was stoned by the angry crowd, he became the first Christian martyr. His death, and the persecution that followed, were unfortunately only the beginning for the Christian Church. Paul also had to face stoning, beating, imprisonment and other hardships as a result of his attempts to preach the gospel.

Persecution

In the first three centuries in particular, the church suffered much persecution in the Roman Empire.

The following are brief statements about what happened. Find out more using Banks' book, *The Early Church: 3rd Edition* (2017):

- Nero: Christians were imprisoned and executed. Peter and Paul were probably martyrs.
- Domitian: demanded that Christians worship him. Those who refused were oppressed.
- Marcus Aurelius: allowed outbreaks of violence to take place against Christians.
- Decius: thousands died.
- Diocletian: issued four edicts to try to destroy Christianity.

In making connections with these other aspects of human experience, it would be helpful to explore the 'attitude' of the Christians to persecution and compare it to that of the apostles in Acts. For example, compare the attitude of Ignatius of Antioch to martyrdom with that of the apostles following their beating in Acts 5:40–42.

'Open Doors'

'Open Doors' is a Christian Persecution Charity that has been providing Bibles, Christian literature, training and practical support to the Persecuted Church worldwide since 1955. You can access up-to-date information on the work of Open Doors from their website: www.opendoorsuk.org.

Fernando (1998, p401) comments that there are many similarities between the way people opposed the gospel and its proclaimers at the time of Paul and the way they oppose it now. Below are some of the stories of Christians who have been persecuted throughout different parts of the world. As you read through them, take note of any similarities or differences you find between them and Paul's missionary activity in Acts. Focus in particular on similar types of persecution and the response to persecution.

1. Persecuted Christians in the Middle East

Christians in the Middle East are often discriminated against because of their faith in Christ. By providing training, counselling and Scripture resources, Open Doors' teams are helping to strengthen believers across the region.

In June 2000, Shaiboub from Egypt was framed and convicted of murdering his cousin, also a Christian, and another young Christian in a village in Egypt. He was made the scapegoat in a blatant police cover-up, and was sentenced to 15 years' hard labour – the maximum penalty for manslaughter under Egyptian law. His wife and children were left bereft.

Shaiboub is imprisoned in a high-security prison in Cairo. His family live 330 miles away and are allowed to visit him only once a month, for just 30 minutes.

2. Persecuted Christians in South East Asia

Four of the world's five remaining communist states are located in East Asia. In these countries, and across the region, Christians are suffering for their faith. Open Doors' teams support believers through delivering Bibles, Scripture resources and training.

Sister Mei from China pastors a house church of over 300 people. Her story is one of faithfulness and resilience. Now over 80 years old, Mei is as determined as ever to serve God in any way she can. The desire of Mei's heart is to see the church in China grow in size and maturity, despite the pressures and opposition it faces from the authorities.

'Pilot' Jemy from the Philippines is often threatened with death by his Islamic neighbours. He travels far across seas, which are often stormy, to attend Christian training courses. Living in the Muslim-dominated region of Mindanao, southern Philippines, Jemy's life is often threatened because of his faith in the Lord Jesus. Having enrolled in Open Doors' lay leader training programme, his enthusiasm to learn more about God is unquenchable. Jemy loves to serve the Lord through serving his people. He often pilots a small '*ëbanca*' (boat), bringing believers from remote islands together for fellowship.

Pastor Victor from Vietnam was pressured by his parents, who object to his faith. He spent time in prison, shackled and tormented, for his active ministry. Since Victor decided to follow Jesus, his life has been very hard. His parents are staunch Communists, and they violently object to Victor's allegiance to Christ. The same is true for Theresa. When Victor asked her to marry him, he knew their wedding would be bitter-sweet. Although they shared the joy of knowing the Lord, they had to come to terms with the fact that neither set of parents would attend their wedding.

Pastor SK Daniel from India is a convert from Hinduism and, along with his wife, runs an orphanage for 'untouchable' caste children. He has been threatened, assaulted, arrested and his house attacked. Along with their own four children, they care for 20 Dalit ('untouchable') children, their ministry motivated by the love of Christ.

He has experienced severe persecution from fundamentalist groups opposed to his Christian activities. Since 1995, he has been severely beaten and left for dead, and his house stoned by violent mobs who once besieged his home for 15 days. To date, the police have failed to arrest those responsible and in fact arrested Pastor Daniel once, on trumped-up charges. Hindu extremists have ordered him to leave the region or they will burn him alive.

Santosh from India was beaten and threatened by extremists who attacked an evangelistic meeting that he was leading. Along with six other evangelists, Brother Santosh had travelled to Tasra in Gujarat state to show The Jesus Film to a large group of villagers. Suddenly, in the middle of the film, a mob of Hindu extremists descended on the gathering. They smashed the film projector and then turned their wrath on Santosh and his friends. When Santosh refused to pledge allegiance to the Hindu deity Ram, the assailants began to boil water to pour over him. Santosh was thankfully released without serious injury.

"I thought I was going to die," admits Santosh. "I was terrified. But I am glad to suffer for the Lord" (Fernando, 1998, p401).

Aid to the Church in Need

Aid to the Church in Need is an international organization that began at the instigation of Pope Pius XII in 1947. The initial concern was the appalling situation facing post-war refugees and Norbertine priest, Father

Werenfried van Straaten responded to this appeal. Since then, Aid to the Church in Need has reached out to people who are persecuted, oppressed or in need around the world. Aid to the Church in Need has become one of the most important Catholic charities, working in more than 130 countries around the world. Each year, this organization helps to fund around 5,000 projects, mainly in the following areas:
- Emergency aid to refugees
- Help with church buildings
- Grants for priests and support for training
- Transport (such as cars, bicycles and even mules) so priests can reach remote parishes
- Providing Bibles and other religious literature

TASK

1. **Use the internet to research other incidences of religious persecution and intolerance in the world today. Save your examples for possible use in answering part (b) of an AS essay.**
2. **Read the news item that follows. Do you think Ashers bakery was justified in standing up for their Christian Principles?**

Bakery to appeal discrimination ruling over 'gay cake' case.
Ashers Bakery, which lost a discrimination case in 2015, has decided to appeal the ruling. The bakery had refused to make a cake with a slogan supporting gay marriage. The court found that the customer, Gareth Lee, had been discriminated against on the grounds of his sexual orientation and political beliefs, and ordered Ashers to pay £500. Mr Lee's case was supported by the Equality Commission, who paid £39,000 in legal fees.

The judge said that Ashers was a business, and hence was not exempt from discrimination law despite the religious or political beliefs of its owners. The judge acknowledged that Ashers had "genuinely and deeply held" views, but that this was not sufficient to overturn equality legislation.

In announcing their appeal, the McArthur family, who own Ashers, said: "After much careful and prayerful consideration given to legal advice, we have decided to appeal the judgement handed down last Tuesday.

> We continue to insist that we have done nothing wrong as we have discriminated against no individual, but rather acted according to what the Bible teaches regarding marriage."

PRACTICE ESSAY QUESTION

Question from CCEA's Specimen Assessment Materials

(a) Examine the content and significance of Stephen's speech in Acts. [25 marks]

Your answer could make reference to the following points:
- Abraham in Mesopotamia, God's covenant with Abraham, Joseph in Egypt, guided and protected by God.
- A discussion of Stephen's reference to the role of Moses as deliverer and lawgiver.
- The rite of circumcision and the importance of worship in the Temple.
- The significance of Stephen's speech – Stephen's response in relation to the charges that he spoke against the Law, Moses and the Temple.

(b) Comment on the claim that Stephen prepared the way for the worldwide mission of the church, but Philip put the idea into practice. Justify your answer. [25 marks]

Your answer could make reference to the following points:
- Stephen emphasised that God is everywhere, not limited to the Promised Land or Temple in Jerusalem, seeking to prove this with numerous examples from the Old Testament.
- As God is not limited to one land or race of people, the implication from this is that the message of salvation is for all people in all places.
- Acts shows Philip furthering the spread of the gospel by taking the Christian message to Samaria.
- Philip played a key role in the conversion of the Ethiopian with the potential for the gospel to reach Africa.

Section 2:

The Role of Peter

PETER AS AN EVANGELIST TO THE GENTILES

The Conversion of Cornelius

It is at this stage that events in the Early Church turn a corner, which eventually leads to the entry of Gentiles into the church. As Marshall comments, "the church did not simply stumble upon the idea of evangelizing Gentiles; it did so in accordance with God's deliberate purpose" (1980, p161).

The key event is the conversion of Cornelius, a Roman centurion, the first Gentile to become a believer. Marshall comments that "the sheer length of this story and the way in which it is told twice over indicate the very great importance which Luke attaches to it in the context of Acts as a whole" (1980, p181). The story may have been of particular interest to Theophilus. Its length adds to the argument that Luke was writing to try to convince Theophilus of the validity of the Christian faith.

To simplify such a long story, it is probably best to divide it up into the following four sections:

- 10:1–8: Cornelius' vision.
- 10:9–23a: Peter's vision.
- 10:23b–48: Peter's speech and results.
- 11:1–18: Effects of the conversion of Cornelius and his family.

Ch 10:1–8 Cornelius' vision

Caesarea was a Roman government centre for the administration of Judea. A centurion (soldier) named Cornelius lived there with his family. He belonged to a body of troops known as the Italian Regiment, so called because they had been recruited in Italy. Hewitt comments that "the captain of such a regiment would be a man of importance and some standing" (1964, p94). More important than his career is Cornelius' religious outlook. Like many other Romans, he had become interested in local religions. However, he was not a Jew or even a proselyte. Instead, he had attached himself to the group called 'God-fearers'. The strength of his respect for the Jewish faith is evident from his actions (v 2, 4).

At around 3.00 pm, Cornelius had a vision. This was the hour of prayer in Jerusalem, so Cornelius was probably praying. In the vision an angel spoke to Cornelius, addressing him by name. Naturally, he was terrified, but the angel assured him that his prayers and gifts to the poor had been acknowledged by God. He was then told to send to Joppa for a man called Simon (Peter's Jewish name). As would be expected of a man with such great faith, he responded immediately by sending a group of three messengers to find Peter.

Ch 10: 9–23a Peter's vision

In Joppa Peter had gone up on the roof at noon to pray in private. Peter was hungry and his thoughts may have been drifting from his prayers (Marshall, 1980, p185). He fell into a trance and had a strange vision of a sheet containing living creatures. Peter then heard a voice telling him to kill and eat. But the sheet carried animals that would have been considered unclean in the Jewish religion. Peter protested strongly that he had never eaten anything unclean. However, the voice told him that if God had cleansed something people should no longer consider it unclean. Stott (1990, p187) comments that although the vision was challenging the basic distinction between clean and unclean foods, which Peter had been brought up to make, the Spirit was relating this to the distinction between clean and unclean people, and telling Peter to stop making it. After the vision was repeated twice, the sheet disappeared.

As Peter was coming to terms with what had happened, Cornelius' messengers arrived at the door to find him. What seems to be an inward prompting by the Holy Spirit led Peter to go down to these messengers and introduce himself. They repeated their message in such a way as to impress him about Cornelius' faith. As it was late, Peter invited them to spend the night.

Ch 10:23b–48 Peter's speech and results

The next day, Peter and a number of Christians set off for Caesarea. Cornelius and his family were waiting for them, and when he first saw Peter he knelt before him as a sign of reverence. Peter believed that such respect should only be given to God, and told him to get up. Peter and Cornelius went into the house "as equals" (Marshall, 1980, p188). Peter announced to those gathered his new willingness to meet with Gentiles (v 28), and asked why he had been called there.

Cornelius' reply (v 30–33) is a repeat of the events that occurred the previous day. There are some differences between this account and that of verses 1–8, but Marshall (1980, pp188–189) argues that this is more to do with the fact that New Testament writers were not concerned to give a word-for-word account of conversations and speeches. Cornelius thanked Peter for coming and invited him to speak to those gathered.

Peter's speech is significant for the spread of the gospel:

- He explains how he has realised that "there is no racial barrier to Christian salvation" (Haenchen, 1971, p351). In other words, God doesn't have favourites and will accept anyone who worships him regardless of their race or background. Peter continues by preaching the gospel.
- Peter adds some extra material about Jesus' ministry, perhaps because he was speaking to non-Jews.
- The death of Jesus at the hands of the Jews is briefly mentioned, but it is quite unlike his addresses to the Jews themselves.
- Jesus was raised from the dead on the third day.
- God allowed him to be seen by a select group of people.
- Jesus commanded his apostles to preach to the people, that is, the Jews.
- Finally, Peter proclaims that everyone who believes in Jesus can receive forgiveness.

Before Peter had a chance to finish his speech, the Holy Spirit came upon all those who were listening. This implies that they all had faith and that God had accepted them – the proof being the gift of the Holy Spirit.

There was no doubt that these Gentiles had received the gift of the Holy Spirit – the same gift that had been given to the apostles on the Day of Pentecost. Marshall (1980, p194) comments that their receiving of the gift of the Spirit on this occasion stressed the reality of the conversion of the Gentiles "over against all possible doubt". The next step for these new Christians was baptism, the outward sign of acceptance into the church. Peter stressed the need for them to be baptised, and no one objected.

Important note!
The story does not suggest that Cornelius and his family were circumcised. In fact, Ch 11:3 rules circumcision out. It can be concluded that God himself was saying that circumcision was not necessary to becoming a Christian. Hewitt comments that the church was not to be a sect within the narrow limits of the Jewish race, but a worldwide fellowship of believers.

Ch 11:1–18 Effects of the conversion of Cornelius and his family
This final section describes the effects of the conversion of Cornelius and his family. "The apostles and the brothers throughout Judea" refers to the Jewish Christians, and it is their reaction to the events concerning the conversion

of these Gentiles that is now all-important for the spread of the gospel. Not surprisingly, it was the circumcision party who questioned Peter about what had happened. These Christians would have originally been strict Jews who had strongly upheld Jewish laws and traditions. Guy (1969, p44) argues that the objection seems to have been that Peter stayed with Gentiles and ate with them rather than that he had preached to them and baptised them (v 3). Bound by Jewish food laws, they would have believed it wrong to eat with Gentiles unless the Gentiles were circumcised and also kept the food laws.

Peter explained the whole story to them, beginning with his own experience of the vision of the sheet. He had come to realise that the sheet was the church, which would contain all races and classes without any distinction at all (Rackham, 1909, p153). Peter's finishing comments (v 16–17) stress that the Gentiles had the same experience as those in the upper room on the day of Pentecost. If they had been baptised with the Holy Spirit, then they should also receive water baptism. His argument convinced those listening. In fact, the audience praised God that he had allowed the Gentiles the opportunity to be saved.

TASK

a) Give an account of the Peter-Cornelius story.

- Cornelius' call for Peter.
- Peter's vision.
- Peter at Cornelius' house.
- Peter's explanation.

b) Comment on the claim that 'God does not have favourites'. Justify your answer.

- Luke's universalism.
- Ongoing activity of the Holy Spirit in accepting all sorts of people.
- Peter's steep learning curve.
- Gospel preached to all.

c) With reference to other aspects of human experience, comment on the claim that this story is not only of historical interest, but also has long-lasting significance for the Christian Church.

- Lessons to be learned about accepting all into the Christian Church, regardless of background.
- Examples of religious and racial prejudice throughout churches in the world, for example Northern Ireland, Africa.
- Cultural prejudice within some Christian communities.

Peter's escape from prison (Ch 12:1–19)

Herod tried to please the Jews by murdering James, the son of Zebedee, and trying to kill Peter. It is possible that he was plotting with the Sanhedrin, who were also in strong opposition to the church. However, as we shall see, his plan was stopped by "the direct intervention of God" (Marshall, 1980, p206).

Peter was arrested just after the Passover. He was well guarded, with four groups of soldiers working in shifts. The Christians, however, strong in their faith, continued to pray for his release.

The night before Herod's planned execution, Peter was asleep, handcuffed between two guards, and the door was also guarded by soldiers. However, during the night an angel of the Lord entered the prison and a light shone in the cell. The fact that Peter was asleep shows that he was not too worried about the events that lay ahead. The angel had to wake him up to tell him to get ready to leave the prison. Peter, not sure whether he was dreaming or not, followed the angel past the guards and out the three doors of the prison. Presumably the guards were asleep. Immediately after, the angel disappeared and Peter realised he was free. Marshall believes this story to be "miraculous at every point" (1980, p209).

Peter moved quickly to tell his friends what had happened. He went to the home of Mary, the mother of John Mark, where he knew he would find them. Although late, many were gathered in prayer, and when Peter knocked on the door a servant girl was sent to see who it was. She was so excited when she realised that it was Peter that she ran back into the house to tell the others without letting Peter in. They thought she was mad, and when Peter eventually did get in, he explained how the miracle had happened and asked them to inform James and the rest of the believers. Peter then left and went to a secret hiding place.

Chapter 12:24 shows us the tremendous spread of the gospel at this point, which is not hindered by the imprisonment or death of the apostles.

Significance of the story:
1. This is the second of three incidents in Acts where apostles have been imprisoned for preaching, yet are released through God's intervention. This action on God's part shows his care for those who are preaching the message of Christianity and can be taken as encouragement for Christians suffering persecution. Stott comments that "The dramatic details Luke includes all seem to emphasise the intervention of God and the passivity of Peter" (Stott, 1990, p211).
2. While Peter was in prison, "the church was earnestly praying to God for him" (Acts 12:5). According to Peterson, "God acts in response to the prayers of his people, even though they are shown to be doubters at the very moment when Peter is returned to them, safe and sound" (2009, p363).
3. After Peter had described how God had rescued him, he instructed those present to "tell James and the brothers about this" (Acts 12:17). This shows the importance of James in the leadership of the Jerusalem Church. Paul mentions in his letters that this James is the brother of Jesus, who, along with Peter and John, is one of the "pillars" of the Early Church (Gal 2:9).

TASK

Overview questions on the role of Peter in Acts
(You will also need to refer to material covered previously in Chapter 2.)

a) **Explore the claim that Peter's activity caused great excitement in Jerusalem. Justify your answer.**

b) **Describe the evangelising activity of Peter as found in Acts.**
- The miracles of Peter.
- Speeches.
- The Cornelius incident.

c) **Give an account of one of Peter's speeches as recorded in Acts.**
- Solomon's Colonnade.
- First speech before Sanhedrin.

d) **Describe the main features of Peter's speeches as presented in the early chapters of Acts, commenting on his understanding of the Person of Christ.**
   - Apostolic *kerygma*, the dawn of the Messianic age, the death and resurrection of Jesus, call to repentance, baptism and gift of the Holy Spirit.

e) **Explore the view that Luke portrays Peter as a strong leader. Justify your answer.**
   - This question is an opportunity to consider the role of Peter as leader, miracle worker, evangelist and disciplinarian, and to highlight Peter's strengths using different examples.

f) **Explore the statement that during the years covered by the early chapters of Acts, Peter fulfils the prophecy that he will be the 'Rock' on which the church will be built.**
   - Refer to Matt 16:13–20.
   - Evaluate the role of Peter in light of Jesus' statement.
   - Would the church have survived without Peter?
   - Were others just as significant?

PRACTICE ESSAY QUESTION

Question from CCEA's Specimen Assessment Materials

(a) Examine the importance of Peter's missionary activity in spreading the Christian message. [25 marks]

Your answer could make reference to the following points:
- Peter's speech on the day of Pentecost: the first proclamation of the gospel since receiving the gift of the Holy Spirit.
- Discussion of Peter's speech following the healing of the lame man.
- Peter before the Sanhedrin showing a determination to witness in the face of opposition.
- Peter's encounter with Cornelius, leading to the expansion of Christianity beyond Jewish boundaries.

(b) With reference to other aspects of human experience, investigate the claim that without the Holy Spirit there would not be a church today. Justify your answer. [25 marks]

Your answer could make reference to the following points:
- A consideration of evidence from religious movements that are concerned with the Holy Spirit, such as the charismatic and Pentecostal movements.
- A discussion of religious revivals and their impact on society and the church.
- Prominence given to factors other than the Holy Spirit that are essential to the life of the church.
- A contrary argument might be that religious institutions have a tendency to survive with or without the Holy Spirit.

OTHER ASPECTS OF HUMAN EXPERIENCE

Evangelism in a multi-cultural, multi-religious, pluralistic and secular age

This theme arises from Peter's encounter with the Roman centurion, Cornelius. However, it is also relevant to the work of Stephen, Philip and Paul, all of whom played a significant role in taking Christianity beyond the confines of Judaism. The example of the apostles in witnessing to people from different religions, nationalities and cultures gives guidelines for evangelists today.

Northern Ireland today

Northern Ireland has seen significant changes in population between the census of 2001 and that of 2011, with more than double the number of people belonging to ethnic minority groups. (www.nisra.gov.uk/Census/key_stats_bulletin_2011.pdf)

It is therefore appropriate to describe our society as increasingly multi-cultural, multi-religious, pluralistic and secular. But what exactly do these terms mean?

A **multi-cultural** society is one in which anyone is free to express their identity through language, dress, food and customs without fear of persecution. This also includes the freedom to practise the religion of your choice, so a multi-cultural society is also **multi-religious**. If something is **pluralistic**, then this implies diversity, so a pluralistic society is one in which many different cultures exist alongside each other. Such a society also recognises that while some people choose to follow a religion, others choose not to practise any faith. The term **secular** is used to describe something that is completely non-religious. Many people feel Northern Ireland is becoming increasingly secular, as there is a general decline in church attendance, with fewer people showing religious commitment. (https://en.wikipedia.org/wiki/Religion_in_Northern_Ireland)

Read the two articles that follow. How do they highlight the issues facing evangelism in a multi-cultural, multi-religious and pluralistic society?

The Whitewell Metropolitan Tabernacle
Pastor James McConnell founded Whitewell Metropolitan Tabernacle in 1957 at the age of 19, and served as its Senior Pastor for 57 years until his retirement in 2014. The initial membership in 1957 was just ten people and they met in a rented Orange Hall, but has since grown to a large congregation of several thousand people. As well as running the church, where his preaching was known for being hard-hitting, he personally helped and supported many people. Pastor McConnell also engaged in numerous evangelistic outreach events around Northern Ireland. After his retirement responsibility for the church passed to his associated, Pastor David Purse.

Reference: www.metropolitan-tabernacle.org/content/aboutus/pastors

Belfast Pastor James McConnell denounces Islam as "satanic"
Police launched an investigation into a possible hate crime incident after Pastor James McConnell, Senior Pastor at the evangelical Whitewell Metropolitan Tabernacle in north Belfast, described Islam as "satanic" and "a doctrine spawned in hell" while preaching in the church in May 2014.

Raied Al-Wazzan, representing the Belfast Islamic Centre said the remarks were "hurtful" and went on to say "I wonder what knowledge he has about Islam to say all of that. Maybe he has been affected by the media these days because there is a lot of bad reports about Muslims and linking that with terrorism – he is mixing some of the political issues here with religion".

But Pastor McConnell stood over his remarks, telling reporters that the teaching of Islam "is against the holy scriptures" and that "the Bible says there is one God the father and one Lord Jesus Christ and that is what I believe and that is what Christianity is all about." He went on to say that he had "got a lot of comments saying people were pleased that I took a stand and people were pleased that I stood up for the Christian faith."

BY THE END OF THIS CHAPTER YOU SHOULD BE ABLE TO:

- demonstrate knowledge and understanding of, and critically evaluate Stephen and Philip, including:
  - the role of Stephen and Philip in Acts;
  - background to the appointing of the seven helpers (6:1–7);
  - Stephen's speech and martyrdom (6:8–8:1) including interpretation of Stephen's speech as a Hellenist defence;
  - the evangelising activity of Philip (8:4–40); and
  - the significance of Stephen and Philip in furthering the Gospel; an

- demonstrate knowledge and understanding of, and critically evaluate the role of Peter, including:
  - Peter as an evangelist to the Gentiles with contrast to his former missionary activity in Jerusalem (10:1–48);
  - the implications of this incident for the continuing missionary work of the Early Church;
  - Peter's report to the Jerusalem Church (11:1–18);
  - the personal impact of Cornelius' conversion on Peter; and
  - the significance of Peter's miraculous escape from prison (12:1–19).

Paul the Apostle

Section 1:
Paul's Conversion and Missionary Journeys

THE CONVERSION OF SAUL (PAUL) (CH 9:1-19)

Introduction

THE CENTRE OF INTEREST now moves away from Peter and the other disciples of Jesus to one of the most significant conversions in the Early Church, that of Paul the Pharisee (previously called Saul) (Drane, 1986, p247). It could be argued that this conversion on the road to Damascus is the most famous conversion in church history. Luke is so impressed with its importance that he includes the story three times, once in his own narrative (Acts 9) and twice in Paul's speeches. The story is told as part of Paul's speech before a Jerusalem crowd (Acts 22:5-16) and his words before Agrippa and Festus (Acts 26:12-18). Willimon adds that "only an event of greatest importance would merit such repetition by an author whose hallmark is brevity and concision" (1988, p74). In other words, Luke was known not to waste words; he kept his work brief and to the point. So to repeat an event three times shows the importance he attached to it. Johnson (1992, p166) agrees, commenting that the turning of a Pharisaic persecutor into the apostle of the Gentiles is a paradox so profound that it requires multiple retellings.

There are slight variations between the three accounts, mainly concerning what each adds or leaves out from the basic story, with each version bringing out some further nuance of significance (Johnson, 1992, p166). Marshall comments that "Luke is not trying to give us an account of what happened in precise detail but rather the general nature and significance of the event" (1980, p167). It might be useful to refer to a few of these differences in this section. However, it is not necessary to know the exact details of these for your AS examination.

As well as the conversion story being told three times in Acts, Paul mentions three times in his letters that he was "once a blasphemer and a persecutor and a violent man", who "persecuted and tried to destroy" the church of God, and therefore he was "the least of the apostles." In Paul's

Letter to the Galatians, which you will study at A2, Paul highlights the importance of his encounter with the risen Jesus: "God, who set me apart from birth and called me by his grace, was pleased to reveal his Son in me" (Galatians 1:16). Some scholars regard the events on the road to Damascus as a calling rather than a conversion. Stendahl claims it was a call to be a missionary to the Gentiles, not a conversion, and Johnson regards it as the call of a prophet (1992, p167).

Detail of the story

We first read of Saul at the stoning of Stephen, which some scholars feel had a profound influence on him. Perhaps the very fact that he did not himself take part in the stoning of Stephen may suggest that he had an uncertain sympathy with what was being said. However, Lewis (1960, p43) feels we only guess what effect the martyrdom of Stephen must have had on Saul, for when we next meet him, Luke is describing his persecution of the Jerusalem Church, commenting that he "was still breathing out murderous threats against the Lord's disciples" (9:1). Some of the language Luke uses to describe Saul in his pre-conversion state seems deliberately to portray him as "a wild and ferocious beast" (Calvin, 1552, trans 1966, p256). Stott describes Saul's heart as being "filled with hatred and his mind ... poisoned by prejudice" (1990, p169).

Saul also travelled to other towns – Damascus in particular – to round up Christians. For example, he later tells King Agrippa, "I even went to foreign cities to persecute them" (26:10). Saul regarded getting rid of the Christians as part of doing God's will. As far as he was concerned, Christianity was a blasphemous heresy that threatened God's people (the Jews), the sanctity of the Law, and the Temple.

"Damascus was an important town, about 150 miles from Jerusalem, with a considerable Jewish population" (Marshall, 1980, p168). It had been part of the Roman province of Syria since 64 BC. At the time, Damascus was a large and thriving commercial centre and had a large Jewish population. Saul set out towards this city like an avenging prophet, carrying the necessary letters from the High Priest (a Sadducee), with authority to return any Christians he found in the synagogues. The Sadducees were, according to Josephus (Antiquities 20, cited in Sanders, 1985), more heartless in their judgements than the Pharisees, and it may not have been natural for a loyal Pharisee like Saul to go and request letters from the Saducean high priest (v 2). This is an indication of how far he was willing to go to try to stamp out this threat.

Saul would then bring the Christians back to Jerusalem for punishment (9:2). The High Priest would not have had direct authority over the Damascus Christians, as they would not have been part of his jurisdiction (Fernando, 1998, p295). So it is more than likely that those being hunted down were the Hellenistic Christians who had fled Jerusalem, rather than Christians from Damascus.

Luke describes the Christian religion as "the Way" (9:2), which seemed to be a common description for the church. Haenchen (1971, p320) comments that this designation was probably applied to the church by the Christians themselves. The term is used several times in Acts (19:9, 23; 22:4; 24:14, 22), and has parallels with Jesus' words: "I am the way" (John 14:6). Another term used to describe the church, usually by outsiders, was "the sect of the Nazarenes" (24:5, 14; 28:22).

Saul was near Damascus when "without any previous warning he found himself surrounded by an intensely bright light and heard a voice speaking to him" (Marshall, 1980, p169), the shock causing him to fall to the ground. Then he heard a voice saying, "Saul, Saul, why do you persecute me?" (9:4). "The revelation was one given to Saul alone and not shared by his companions" (Conzelmann, 1960, p66), although they were witnesses that something unusual had happened. They stood speechless and saw the light, but did not see the risen Christ (9:7). (Saul's conversion has been given physical and psychological explanations that seek to downplay the idea that a revelation of Jesus caused this huge turnaround – was it an epileptic fit?)

In the other two accounts later in Acts, Paul describes how the bright light flashed, not at night, but at high noon. It was brighter than the sun, which made it all the more amazing (26:13). In Acts 22 Paul says that the men with him did see the light, which is not mentioned in chapter 9. In Acts 22 Paul also says that the men did not hear the sound, presumably meaning that "they did not understand the voice," as the NIV puts it (22:9). What seems to have happened was that the whole group heard a sound, but only Paul understood it as speech.

The voice asked, "Saul, Saul, why do you persecute me?" (9:4). The double name was used for emphasis, and is found in other stories of divine calling, including that of Abraham, Jacob and Moses (Genesis 22:11; 46:2; Exodus 3:4). Chapter 26 tells us that the voice addressed Saul in Aramaic. Scholars have speculated that this is because it was Saul's first language. Saul asked, "Who are you, Lord?", as he did not yet realise it was Jesus. Saul probably discerned a divine quality about the voice as it spoke to him (Bruce, 1988, p182). (The Greek word *Kyrios* can mean both 'Lord' and 'Sir', but the light from heaven and the calling of his name probably made Saul realise that he was in the presence of the Lord.)

Saul must have been considerably shaken when the figure answered, "I am Jesus" (9:5). It does not actually say in this verse that Saul saw the risen Christ, only that he heard a voice. However, it is confirmed afterwards, when Luke introduces Ananias (9:17) and Barnabas (9:27) into the story.

When the risen Christ told Saul that he (Saul) had been persecuting him, he was pointing out that Saul had not only been rejecting people by his actions, but was rejecting Christ himself (Luke 10:16). The followers of Jesus whom Saul hated were the people of God, and were not heretics. The evidence was too compelling to reject any longer (Fernando, 1998, p297). It was now obvious to Saul that the Jesus whose followers he had been persecuting was alive, and associated with the God of Israel. Saul would, therefore, have had to re-evaluate his views on the life, teaching and death of Jesus.

Saul finally struggled to his feet, but he had been blinded by the light (9:8). The men with Saul took him to a house in Damascus. Stott comments that "he who had expected to enter Damascus in the fullness of his pride and prowess, as a self-confident opponent of Christ, was actually led into it, humbled and blinded, a captive of the very Christ he had opposed" (1990, p170). Dillon agrees, describing Saul as "the dreaded persecutor, completely immobilised" (1990, p744).

For the next three days, the blind Saul fasted, no doubt reflecting on the meaning of his encounter with Jesus. There he stayed for three days, taking neither food nor drink. Bruce (1988, p185) believes that there is no need to regard his abstinence as an early instance of fasting before baptism; it was probably the result of shock.

Saul's future commission is not recorded in this account. However, in Acts 22:10 Paul recounts how he was told to get up and go into Damascus. "There you will be told all that you have been assigned to do." This is where Ananias is introduced to the story.

Barclay describes Ananias as "one of the forgotten heroes of the Christian church' (1955, p74). In Acts 9 Ananias reveals to Saul that it was "Jesus ... who appeared to you" (9:17). In the later versions of this event it is clearly stated that Saul saw Christ (26:16; 22:14). Ananias was a believer and "a devout observer of the Law", highly respected by all the Jews living in Damascus (22:12). He was the one through whom God would restore Paul's sight and reveal his future. In a vision from God, Ananias was told to go to the house of a man named Judas, who lived on Straight Street in Damascus (9:11), where he would find Saul praying. He was not keen to meet Saul, for "all that he knew of this man indicated that he was an enemy of the church" (Marshall, 1980, p171). He had not only heard reports about him, but he knew Saul had come to Damascus with authority to arrest Christians.

Note how Ananias referred to the Christians as "saints" (9:13). This is the first time Luke used the term in describing the church community (see also 9:32 and 26:10).

However, the Lord insisted that Ananias visit Saul, even though he had persecuted the saints. Ananias was told: "Go! This man is my chosen instrument to carry my name before the Gentiles and their kings and before the people of Israel" (9:15). Having grasped what was to be involved in Saul's future role, he went to the house of Judas, met Saul, and laid his hands on him. Ananias told Saul that Jesus had sent him so that he might see again and be filled with the Holy Spirit (9:17). However, Saul's calling would be to a life of pain and distress: "I will show him how much he must suffer for my name" (9:16). Dillon comments that "the fierce persecutor is now to become the one fiercely persecuted" (1990, p744).

By placing his hands on Saul and calling him brother, Ananias was welcoming him into the community of believers. Immediately, something like scales fell from Saul's eyes, and he could see again. In Acts 22, a much fuller account of Ananias' role in Saul's conversion is described. Ananias gives Saul his commission, telling him: "The God of our fathers has chosen you to know his will and to see the Righteous One and to hear words from his mouth" (22:14). (The title 'Righteous One' referred to the Messiah.) Ananias also told Saul that he would be a witness to all people of what he had seen and heard. Then he instructed Saul to get up and be baptised (22:16). Saul was obedient and responded immediately to the request to be baptised, and, after taking some food, he regained his strength (9:18–19). Saul had become as convinced a disciple of Christ as he had been an enemy (Boer, 1976, p22).

Marshall (1980, p172) interestingly picks up that as Saul was baptised and received the filling of the Spirit by Ananias, then there was obviously no need of an 'apostle' to perform the task. Bruce agrees, describing Ananias as "an obscure disciple" (1988, p188). This shows that God chooses people for tasks who may not necessarily stand out as obvious candidates. Ananias leaves the story at this point, having played a major part in the conversion of one who was to become one of the greatest missionaries of the Early Church.

DISCUSSION

Was Paul's conversion gradual from the time he witnessed the martyrdom of Stephen or was it really a dramatic conversion?

TASK

a) **Give an account of Paul's conversion as recorded in Acts 9.**
- The context – Paul's pre-conversion outlook.
- Events on the Damascus road.
- Role of Ananias.

b) **Describe the role of Ananias in Paul's conversion.**
- Background to the story.
- Details on Ananias from all three accounts that build up a complete picture.
- Significance of Paul's baptism by such an obscure character.

e) **Assess the claim that even today the more dramatic conversions leave a lasting impression on people.**
- Compare the effects of Paul's conversion with that of a Christian today who experienced a complete turnaround in his or her life.

PAUL'S MISSIONARY ACTIVITY: FIRST JOURNEY (CH 13:1–14:28)

1. Barnabas and Saul sent off (Ch 13:1–3)

The last verse in Acts 12 (12:25) picks up the story of Barnabas and Paul's trip to Jerusalem to deliver the relief fund, which Luke mentioned in 11:30. Luke notes that the relief visit had been made, and that Paul and Barnabas had returned to Antioch, accompanied by John Mark.

Luke introduces us to the leadership of the Antioch Church, commenting that the church was "worshipping the Lord and fasting" (13:2). (This gives us an insight into the workings of the church, which have already been explored in Chapter 1 of this book.) The Holy Spirit spoke to them, saying: "Set apart for me Barnabas and Saul for the work to which I have called them" (13:2). Guy (1969, p51) explains that the message may have come from a prophet speaking in the meeting.

This was to be the first planned overseas mission carried out by representatives of a particular church, initiated by a deliberate church decision (Marshall, 1980, p214). Through the missionary activity of Barnabas and Paul, we see how the gospel spreads around the Roman Empire, particularly to Gentiles. However, as has been emphasised already, it was no mere human initiative, but was guided by the Holy Spirit, who would continue to work throughout the mission.

It was through the Holy Spirit, therefore, that Barnabas and Paul were sent off for the task of evangelising, following the laying on of hands by the leaders (13:3). The laying on of hands showed that the church supported these men as doing God's will, acknowledging that Barnabas and Paul had the authority to act on behalf of the Christian community at Antioch.

2. Cyprus (Ch 13:4–12)

Their destination was Cyprus, an island in the northeast corner of the Mediterranean Sea. As the native land of Barnabas, Cyprus was a sensible place to begin the church's outreach. Barnabas would be acquainted with its ways and its people, and would know his way around. Christian communities also probably existed on the island and could serve as bases (11:19). John Mark accompanied Barnabas and Paul on the journey as an extra helper. He may have been taken because he was related to Barnabas, and was probably familiar with Cyprus.

The first of two cities in Cyprus mentioned by Luke is Salamis, the administrative centre of eastern Cyprus (13:5). Barnabas and Paul "proclaimed the word of God in the Jewish synagogues" of the city (13:5). There was probably a large Jewish population in Salamis, as there were several synagogues in which Barnabas and Paul could preach. Paul would continue this pattern of beginning his missionary work by first preaching in the synagogue (13:14, 44; 14:1, 16:13; 17:1, 10; 18:4, 19; 19:8).

The other city Luke mentions is Paphos, the provincial capital. At Paphos, the island's proconsul, Sergius Paulus, asked for a meeting with Barnabas and Paul. Presumably, they had been preaching in Paphos for some time and had come to his attention. Luke describes Sergius Paulus as "an intelligent man", in the sense that he was curious and open-minded. This is one of the times in Acts where Luke presents the Roman officials as being sympathetic to the gospel. Here he said of the proconsul that he "wanted to hear the word of God" (13:7). However, this probably arose more as an inquiry into the nature of what the missionaries were proclaiming in the synagogues, rather than a desire to be converted (Longenecker, 1995, p240).

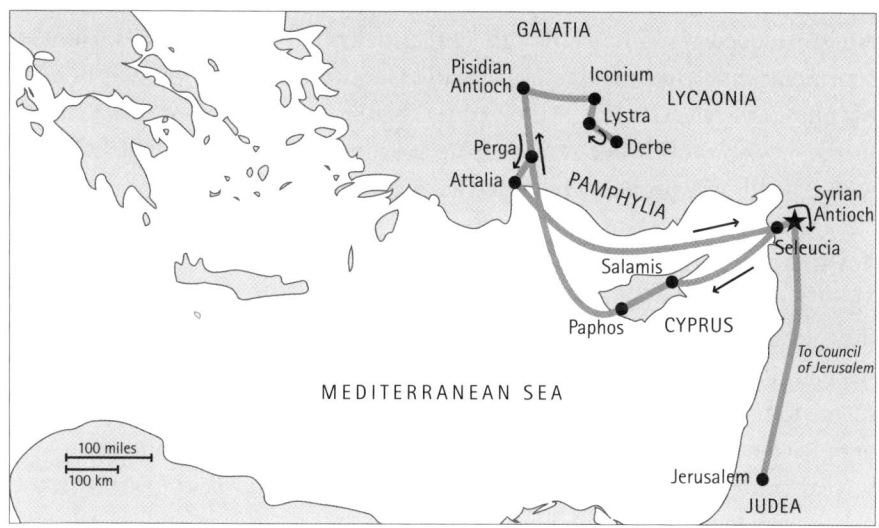

Above: A map of the first missionary journey

There is no indication in Acts that Sergius Paulus became a Christian. Luke's main interest in him was the part he played in the setting for Paul's confrontation with Elymas (or Bar-Jesus) the sorcerer (magician), who was the proconsul's court advisor, and who opposed the preaching of the gospel (13:7–8). Bar-Jesus means 'Son of Jesus', but this name was completely inappropriate for him, as he opposed the missionaries so strongly that Paul finally confronted him.

Filled with the Holy Spirit, Paul told Bar-Jesus: "You are a child of the devil and an enemy of everything that is right! You are full of all kinds of deceit and trickery. Will you never stop perverting the right ways of the Lord?" (13:10). Paul then put a curse on the magician, saying he would be temporarily blinded (13:11). Sergius Paulus was so impressed that "he believed" (13:12). (This does not necessarily mean that he became a Christian. Simon the Magician also "believed" (8:13) and was even baptised, but he was hardly a Christian.)

3. Significance of this story

It can be argued that Luke was interested in telling this, not as the story of a conversion, but to show the superiority of God's power over the magic of the spirit world. Luke wanted to show how Paul used his apostolic authority to stop the evil influence of Bar-Jesus, proving that the power behind the gospel is superior to that of pagan magic.

It is here that Luke tells us for the first time that "Saul was also called Paul" (13:9). Luke had referred to him as 'Saul' from his first appearance in Acts (7:58), but from now on he would call him only 'Paul'. The two names are introduced casually, as though Paul already had the two names. Hanson comments that "the introduction of Saul's Gentile name appropriately heralds his mission to the Gentiles" (1967, p141). 'Saul' was a more appropriate name in the Jewish world, but now that he was moving into the wider Gentile world, 'Paul' was probably regarded as more suitable.

4. Perga (Ch 13:13)

The missionaries sailed from Cyprus to Perga in Pamphylia. While describing these events, Luke, for the first time, no longer speaks of 'Barnabas and Saul'. Instead, Paul is now placed ahead of Barnabas (see 11:30; 12:25; 13:2). This seems to be Luke's way of saying that Paul has taken over the leadership slot or at least the position of prominence (Fernando, 1998, p385). In any case, it is clear from what follows that Paul has become the dominant partner in the missionary team.

John Mark left the evangelising team at Perga and returned to Jerusalem. Whatever the reason for Mark's departure, we later find out that Paul did not like it, referring to it as desertion (15:38). John Mark's departure led to an argument between Barnabas and Paul, and their permanent split (15:39).

5. Pisidian Antioch (Ch 13: 13–52)

Paul and Barnabas travelled to Antioch in Pisidia, about 100 miles north of Perga. It was a difficult and dangerous journey, as the missionaries had to cross the Taurus mountains. The highlands were prone to sudden flooding and there was a danger from attack, as the Romans had not yet fully suppressed the bands of robbers who lived in the mountains.

When they arrived, the missionaries followed the "synagogue formula" (Hewitt, 1964, p113). The Jewish elders invited them to speak, and the rest of Ch 13 is devoted to the preaching of the sermon, which will be studied in detail in the next section.

> ### Summary of speech at Pisidian Antioch
> In the speech, Paul gave a summary of the history of the Hebrews from the Exodus, their stay in Sinai, the entry into Canaan, the period of the judges and the monarchy as far as the reign of David. He reminded the audience of the Jewish hope of a Messiah from the line of David and declared that Jesus was this Messiah. He highlighted the condemnation of Jesus by the rulers at Jerusalem, and his death, burial and resurrection. Finally Paul proclaimed the forgiveness of sins through faith in Jesus, finishing with a warning that his audience should not reject this opportunity (Guy, 1969, pp53–54).

> ### Synagogue
> The synagogue was a place in which the Christian missionaries could find a receptive audience for the gospel message. It played a major role in Jewish life, serving as a meeting place, schoolhouse, library and court. It was a centre of religious education and learning, and the place where all Jews came to worship. Even more significant was the fact that Gentile proselytes and God-fearers attended the synagogue as well as Jews.

Paul's speech aroused a lot of interest, and many who had heard it spoke to Paul and Barnabas after the synagogue service, to discuss the topic of salvation further (13:43). Word must have travelled during the week among the Jews and Gentiles about Paul's message, because "the next Sabbath almost the whole city gathered to hear the word of the Lord" (13:44).

However, conflict with the synagogue leaders was imminent. They were irritated and "filled with jealousy" (13:45) when they saw the large crowd of Gentiles attempting to crowd into the synagogue to hear Paul. They must have refused to allow Paul to speak during the next synagogue service. At some point, he turned to the unbelieving Jews and said: "We had to speak the word of God to you first. Since you reject it and do not consider yourselves worthy of eternal life, we now turn to the Gentiles" (13:46). This began a pattern that was repeated time and time again. Paul would begin his missionary work by preaching in the synagogue. He would be rejected by the leaders and the majority of the Jewish worshippers, and would then preach to the Gentiles.

> ### "I go to the Gentiles"
> Luke records three formal statements by Paul in which he said, "I go to the Gentiles." The first one is here. It is followed by the same statement in Corinth (18:6), and a final one in Rome, which closes the book of Acts (28:28).

Paul and Barnabas must have met with great success in the area around Pisidian Antioch (13:49). When the Gentiles, listening to Paul, heard that God had planned to give them salvation, "They were glad and honoured the word of the Lord" (13:48).

However, the Jewish leaders were furious, and plotted with "the God-fearing women of high standing and the leading men of the city" (13:50). These were probably Gentile women who had become adherents of Judaism with their politically connected husbands.

They were probably convinced to use their husbands' influence in order to have Paul and Barnabas expelled from the area (13:50). Since Paul and Barnabas were not accepted as representing a sect of Judaism, they were regarded as nothing more than troublemakers. As such, they should be expelled, since they were disturbing the Roman peace. Following expulsion, Paul and Barnabas "shook the dust from their feet" in protest (13:51). This was a gesture Jesus had suggested his disciples practise when facing persecution (Luke 9:5; 10:11).

> ### To shake off dust
> It was a custom for Jews to shake off the dust of a pagan town from their feet when they returned to their own land, as a symbol of cleansing themselves from the impurity of sinners who did not worship God. For Jews to do this to their fellow Jews was equivalent to regarding them as pagan Gentiles. In a similar way, the Christians were indicating that Jews who rejected the gospel and drove out the missionaries were no longer truly part of Israel and were no better than unbelievers (Marshall, 1980, p231).

6. Iconium (Ch 14:1–7)

Paul and Barnabas had established a congregation of believers in Pisidian Antioch. However, they were forced to move on to Iconium. Following their usual procedure, they went to the Jewish synagogue to preach to those assembled for services (14:1). Their preaching was so effective that large numbers of both Jews and Gentiles believed the gospel.

As before, the unbelieving Jews caused trouble for the missionaries. They began a smear campaign to poison the minds of the Gentiles "against the brothers" (14:2). In spite of this persecution, Paul and Barnabas "spent considerable time" in Iconium (14:3). This is an example of one of the times where Luke gives few details of events, and condenses the work of several months into a few sentences.

Paul and Barnabas preached effectively in Iconium, and God performed miraculous wonders through them (14:3). However, the city remained divided about them: "Some sided with the Jews, others with the apostles" (14:4). Eventually, the Jews plotted with some Gentiles and political leaders of Iconium to gather a mob, beat up Paul and Barnabas, and stone them to death (14:5). The missionaries were told of the plot, perhaps by sympathetic Jews, so they quickly left Iconium before the plotters could get to them (14:6).

> **"Apostle"**
> Hanson (1967, p147) interestingly comments that Paul and Barnabas are referred to as "apostles" in Acts only in 14:4 and 14. This will be useful information when you are studying Paul's defence of his apostolic authority at A2 level.

7. Lystra and Derbe (Ch 14:8–28)

Paul and Barnabas travelled to "the Lycaonian cities of Lystra and Derbe" (14:6), where they continued to preach the gospel. Luke only reports a single event in Lystra, which began with the healing of a crippled man who was lame from birth (14:8). Paul had been speaking to what was probably a crowd of Gentiles in a public place, and he was somehow drawn to the faith of this crippled man. Suddenly Paul directed his words to the man, demanding him to: "Stand up on your feet!" (14:10). At once the man jumped up and began to walk.

This story depicts Paul as a genuine messenger of God, similar to Peter, who also healed a lame man (3:1–10). In fact, the expressions Luke uses in the two accounts are strikingly similar: "lame from birth"; "looked directly at him"; "jumped up and began to walk". In the same way, both Peter and Paul are shown to be exercising the same power as did Jesus, who also healed a crippled person (Luke 5:17–26).

It should be noted that the people of Lystra were probably acquainted to some extent with three languages:
1. Latin would have been the official language of the Roman Empire.
2. Greek would have been understood to some degree by most of the Lystrans.
3. Their native dialect, the Lycaonian language.

Paul had probably preached in the Greek language, which most people would have understood. It is less likely, however, that he would have understood the Lycaonian language. It seems that following Paul's healing of the crippled man the Lystrans thought that they were experiencing a divine visitation from the gods of Zeus and Hermes. When the beggar jumped up and walked, the crowd began to shout in their own language, "The gods have come down to us in human form!" (14:11). They believed that Barnabas was Zeus, and Paul, as the main speaker, was thought to be Hermes.

> ### Zeus and Hermes
> According to the legend, Zeus and Hermes (to use their Greek names) came to earth in the nearby region of Phrygia disguised as human beings. They looked for somewhere to stay, but no one would show them any hospitality. Finally, an old peasant couple – Philemon and his wife, Baucis – welcomed them into their home, even though they could hardly afford it. The gods were angry and destroyed all the people for their lack of hospitality, except for the gracious Philemon and Baucis. The couple's humble home was transformed into a temple, of which they were given the charge until their death.
>
> This ancient legend was well known in southern Galatia, and it may explain why Paul and Barnabas became the objects of such a wild celebration (Fernando, 1998, p398).

If their ancestors had failed to honour the gods on their previous visit, the Lystrans were determined not to make the same mistake. So the priest at the local temple arranged a sacrifice to honour the presence of Paul and Barnabas (14:13). Fernando (1998, p398) comments that when the apostles found this out "their response was swift and typically Jewish", tearing their clothes, "the usual sign of indignation" (Guy, 1969, p55). They were horrified by the idea that they should be thought of as gods.

The Speech at Lystra

Paul made a moving speech (14–17) in the hope of stopping the attempt of the Lystrans to worship them. It is an example of how the gospel was introduced to purely pagan audiences. The speech differs widely in content from those delivered to Jews and Gentile followers of Judaism. Obviously, when speaking to Jews, the believers had the luxury of drawing upon the Old Testament scriptures. With a purely pagan audience, however, it was necessary to backtrack to first proclaim the existence of the one true God. Therefore, in this speech to the Lystrans, Paul began by explaining that the one God was the creator of all living things (14:15).

Before this, however, Paul and Barnabas were forced to deny that they were gods. When they realised what was about to happen, that is, that the Lystrans were going to make sacrifices to them, they raced into the crowd screaming for them to stop: "We too are only men, human like you" (14:15). Paul was saying that he and Barnabas had no special qualities.

Paul and Barnabas urged the Lystrans to "turn from these worthless things to the living God" (14:15), in other words, to give up their idolatry.

Paul advocated that the one true God is he "who made heaven and earth and sea and everything in them" (14:15). This was a very simple form of 'natural theology'. It means that nature itself bears witness to the existence of a creator God.

Paul and Barnabas went on to insist that the works of creation should lead us to understand that God is kind and merciful (14:17). God is not a vengeful deity who becomes angry over nothing (as Zeus and Hermes were when they destroyed those failing to show them hospitality).

The proof of God's kindness can be seen in his providing rain for crops (14:17). God shows his presence through the good things people enjoy. Since Paul's audience was probably made up of a large number of farmers, they would have appreciated the importance of food, and the fact that they were dependent on God for its supply.

It has been suggested that this speech was incomplete because there was no mention of the death and resurrection of Jesus, and their meaning for the lives of the audience. Perhaps Barnabas and Paul's first concern was to stop the crowd from making sacrifices to them (14:18). Luke implies that the Lystrans failed to grasp Paul's message about God from natural theology. Bruce comments that "they had been made to look foolish, and felt resentful" (1988, p279).

Sometime after this turbulent event, Jews from Pisidian Antioch and Iconium who were opposed to Paul and Barnabas came into Lystra and began to preach against the missionaries. Eventually, they "won the crowd over" (14:19), which shows just how fickle the Lystrans were. At one time they viewed the missionaries as gods. Now they had no respect for them. No doubt they were disappointed that Barnabas and Paul claimed to be no more than ordinary human beings.

As a result, the crowd attacked Paul and stoned him. Thinking he was dead, they dragged his body away and dumped it outside the city (14:19). However, as the disciples gathered around Paul's body, probably to give him a decent burial, "he got up and went back into the city" (14:20). Luke does not list this event as a miracle, although Bruce feels it "has a flavour of a miracle about it" (1988, p279). It may have been that Paul was beaten into unconsciousness, and then revived. Even so, the fact that the stoning did not kill him indicated that Paul was under God's protection.

Once revived, Paul went back into Lystra, and then he and Barnabas left the next day for Derbe. Luke gives no details about the activities of Barnabas and Paul in Derbe. However, their missionary work must have been successful, because their preaching won a large number of disciples (14:21). It also seems that they did not suffer any persecution in Derbe.

Paul and Barnabas prepared to return to Syrian Antioch (the sponsor church) after finishing their missionary activity. They backtracked by returning to Lystra, Iconium and Pisidian Antioch, not to preach the gospel, but for pastoral purposes. Naturally, the threat of harm from Jews and city officials was still a distinct possibility. However, the missionaries probably kept a low profile by avoiding public preaching, for Paul and Barnabas were apparently able to gain entry into the cities without any bother. Bruce sums up their brave determination, commenting that "tribute must be paid to the courage of the two men in returning so soon to Lystra, Iconium, and Pisidian Antioch – cities from which they had so lately been expelled with shameful brutality" (1988, p279).

This was, in a sense, the end of the first missionary journey as far as preaching the gospel to outsiders was concerned, except for a brief mention of it in Perga (14:25).

After arriving in Antioch, Paul and Barnabas gave a full report of their activities to the church. They especially pointed out how God "had opened the door of faith to the Gentiles" (14:27). Luke ends the account by saying that Paul and Barnabas "stayed there a long time with the disciples" (14:28).

TASK

a) Describe the successes Paul experienced during his first missionary journey.
- Extent of ground covered.
- Sergius Paulus in Paphos; power over Elymas.
- Pisidian Antioch.
- Initial preaching in Iconium.
- Appointed elders in every church.

b) Comment on the claim that the spread of the gospel owes much to Paul.
- Use examples from any of the missionary journeys to answer this question if asked in an AS examination.
- For now, however, you have only covered the first journey. You can use the information from the above answer to highlight how Paul's successes helped to spread the gospel. Evaluate the events – did Paul's actions aid the spread of the gospel, or were there times when they did not?
- Compare Paul's work with the missionary work of Philip and Peter

PAUL'S MISSIONARY ACTIVITY: SECOND JOURNEY (15: 36–18: 22)

The purpose of the second missionary journey was to revisit the churches Paul and Barnabas had established, "in order to strengthen and encourage the groups of believers" (Marshall, 1980, p240). They were determined to make sure that the new converts would not fall back into Judaism or paganism (Marshall, 1980, p241). Paul then intended to travel to Ephesus, the great commercial centre on the coast of Asia Minor. This would be a logical step in his goal to evangelise the Roman world. However, the Holy Spirit prevented them from going into the province of Asia (16:6). Luke does not explain the reason for this. Paul instead turned north and went to Mysia. He wanted to circle back to preach in Bithynia, but again the Holy Spirit would not let this happen (Acts 16:7).

1. Troas
Disagreement between Paul and Barnabas (Ch 15:36–41)
There was a strong disagreement between Paul and Barnabas as to whether they should take John Mark along on this journey. He had abandoned the first mission, and Paul did not want to risk the same happening again. Bruce comments that Luke "indicates at a later point in his narrative (15:38) that Paul regarded his departure as desertion" (1988, p251). However, Barnabas wanted to give his cousin another chance to prove himself. In the end, they decided to separate, with Barnabas and Mark going to Cyprus while Paul and Silas went to Galatia. "We hear no more of Barnabas's activities" (Marshall, 1980, p257) as Luke concentrates on the missionary activity of Paul and Silas. Paul may have sent for Silas to join him, as he had connections with the Jerusalem Church. He was also a Roman citizen like Paul, "an asset in an itinerant ministry in the Roman Empire" (Fernando, 1998, p431).

This disagreement reminds us that arguments can arise even between good people, causing separation. Paul and John Mark were unable to work together; therefore, the decision to go their separate ways was probably best for the sake of the spread of the gospel. One positive thing that came out of it, however, was the fact that now there were two missionary teams instead of one. Barnabas and John Mark went to Cyprus, while Paul and Silas went to Syria and Cilicia.

Timothy joins Paul and Silas (Ch 16:1–10)
Paul and Silas began the journey by travelling west through the cities of southern Galatia, preaching and distributing the letter from the Council

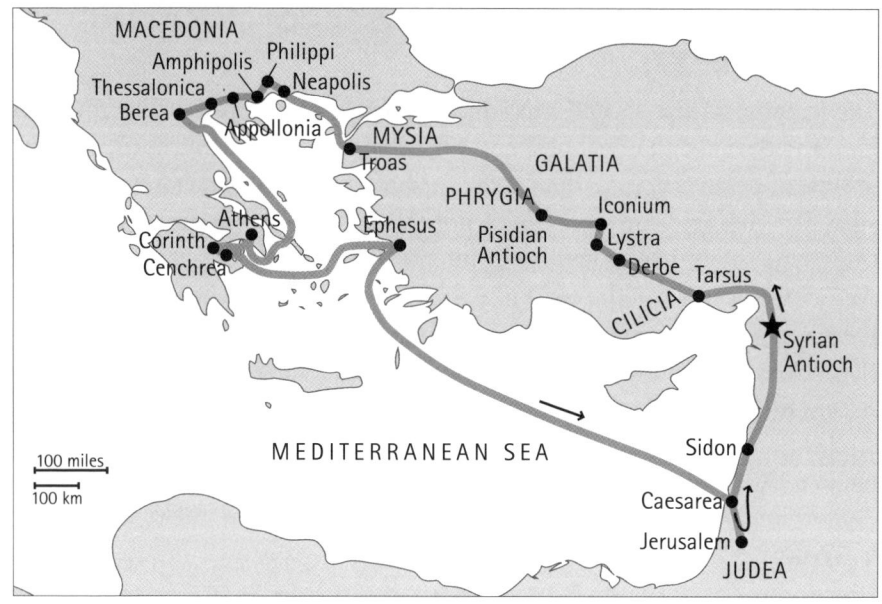

Above: A map of the second missionary journey

of Jerusalem (Acts 16:4). They preached in Derbe and Lystra and, while in Lystra, they met Timothy, who wanted to go with them. As Timothy was half-Jewish, Paul circumcised him in order to help them with their mission among the Jews (16:1–3). As a full Jew, he would be of much greater help to Paul when they went to Jewish synagogues to preach. So Paul, Silas and Timothy worked together during Paul's second missionary journey.

In obedience to the Holy Spirit, they came to the city of Troas, which was a prominent commercial centre. We know that Paul was joined here by Luke the doctor, because a 'we section' begins at this point and continues until they leave Philippi in Macedonia.

While there, Paul had a vision one night of a man from Macedonia who said, "Come over to Macedonia and help us". "Dreams were a recognised means of divine communication in ancient times" (Marshall, 1980, p263). Luke explains how they immediately prepared to go there.

2. Philippi

a. Lydia's Conversion in Philippi (Ch 16:11–15)

Paul, Silas, Timothy (and Luke) travelled to Philippi, "a Roman colony and the leading city of that district of Macedonia" (Acts 16:12). It was an ancient town. There Paul followed his custom to speak first to the Jews. This occurred by the river, as there were not enough Jewish men for a synagogue in Philippi.

The arrival of the missionaries led to successful evangelism, especially among women associated with the Jewish faith. It is interesting that women are mentioned (16:13). Lydia, a prominent dealer in purple, was converted and showed hospitality to the missionaries in her home. (This makes Lydia the first European Christian.) She had been called after the region from which she came. (See Trade, under Archaeological evidence, in Chapter 1 of this book, p41.) "The act of baptism also embraced her household" (Marshall, 1980, p268). It was a common thing for members of a household to embrace Christianity all at one time (see Acts 11:14; 16:31, 33; 18:8).

b. Paul and Silas in Prison (Ch 16:16–40)

Paul and Silas healed a demon-possessed girl, who had the gift of second sight and made money for her owners by telling fortunes. It was not the slave girl who was doing the fortune-telling, but the evil spirit within her. When she met Paul and his companions, she called after them: "These men are servants of the Most High God, who are telling you the way to be saved". (Evil spirits can recognise Christ and his servants. Compare with Mark 1:23–26.) Marshall (1980, p269) points out that this had the effect of giving the missionaries some unexpected publicity, because the slave girl followed them for several days. As it became clear to Paul that she was possessed by an evil spirit, he went on to exorcise the spirit by using the name of Jesus. "The exorcism deprived the girl of her ability or willingness to tell fortunes" (Marshall, 1980, p269), which roused the anger of her pagan owners, who dragged Paul and Silas before the magistrates. It is interesting that when the owners made their charge, their real motive faded into the background and they insisted that they were concerned that the missionaries were causing a public disturbance and promoting non-Roman customs. As a result, Paul and Silas were beaten with rods and thrown into prison. (A Roman citizen should not have been beaten but, at this stage, the authorities were unaware of Paul's Roman citizenship.)

Following a command, the jailor placed them in the most secure part of the prison, taking the extra precaution of fastening their legs securely in wooden stocks, which would have been extremely painful. A sleepless night followed for Paul and Silas, but in the midst of their suffering they sang praises to God. Suddenly, an earthquake erupted, causing the prison doors to open, and loosening the bonds securing the prisoners. Despite the possibility of freedom, the prisoners made no attempt to escape. Many ask why. We are used to thinking of prisons as places that are fairly well kept, clean, and conducive to good treatment. However, prisoners at Paul's time did not have such privileges. As well as being dark, cramped, badly ventilated and sweltering, prisons were breeding pits for disease. If there was any reason why the other inmates did not try to escape, it may be because, unlike Paul and Silas, they were simply too weak to go anywhere. Bruce argues, however, that it may have been "the awed impression which the two missionaries' behaviour produced on the other prisoners that enabled them to dissuade those others from making their escape while the going was good" (1988, p317).

The jailor assumed they had gone and, terrified of receiving the death penalty (see Acts 12:18–19), he decided to kill himself. However, he was stopped in his tracks when he heard the voice of Paul shouting that no one had left the prison. Their joyful outlook influenced the jailor, who became a believer after this miraculous event. Nevertheless, "it took an earthquake and confrontation with death to make him take thought for his salvation" (Bruce, 1988, p315). Just as Lydia had done, the jailor had all of his family baptised.

The following day the magistrates authorised the release of the captives. Before leaving, however, and probably for the sake of the local church, Paul demanded an apology from the city officials, revealing that he and Silas were Roman citizens. The magistrates gave in, knowing that if word reached a higher authority they would be in trouble. After their release, the missionaries visited Lydia and some others and then headed for Thessalonica.

3. Thessalonica (Ch 17:1–9)

It is obvious from the text that Luke did not continue on the journey, as the wording in the text indicates the third person plural (for example, "… they came to Thessalonica …"). Thessalonica, like Philippi, was an ancient city and had a Jewish population. While staying there, Paul supported himself financially (1 Thess 2:9; 2 Thess 3:7–9), which may have taken up valuable preaching time. However, he stayed for at least three weeks, teaching in the synagogues on the Sabbath.

Acts 17:2–3 describes the evangelistic style Paul used with the Jews. His preaching was effective, and some Jews believed, as well as many God-fearers and prominent women. (This may indicate that these women were upper class.) Marshall (1980, p278) points out that many God-fearers, while attracted to the spiritual aspects of Judaism, were unwilling to take the step of circumcision. Christianity, therefore, appealed to them.

Paul's success caused jealousy among the Jewish leaders. As Thessalonica was a free city, it had an assembly before which charges could be brought. The Jews tried to bring Paul and Silas before this assembly by getting a crowd of 'wasters' to start a riot. They could then argue that the missionaries were guilty of disturbing the peace. These wasters gathered outside Jason's house, hoping to find Paul, but none of the missionaries were there. In their frustration, they grabbed Jason and some of the other Christians, and instead of taking them before the assembly, they went even further by taking them before the magistrates (or 'politarchs', as they were known in that part of the world). With gross exaggeration, they argued that the Christians had been causing trouble all over the world and now they had come to Thessalonica. Furthermore, Jason was protecting the missionaries in his own home. As a result, the magistrates "contracted a legal bond" with Jason not to harbour Paul any more (Williams, 1975, p198). As soon as night fell, the local Christians sent Paul and Silas secretly away to Berea, in the south west. Paul was forced to leave behind the young church in Thessalonica, even though it was still in need of teaching and faced the risk of persecution.

4. Berea (Ch 17:10–15)

Paul's ministry in Berea was calmer than in Philippi or Thessalonica. Here the audience in the synagogue "were of more noble character than the Thessalonians, for they received the message with great eagerness and examined the Scriptures every day to see if what Paul said was true" (17:11). Many believed, including, again, some prominent Greek women.

When the Jews in Thessalonica heard of the success of Paul's ministry in Berea, they, too, went to Berea to stir up trouble. They were so successful that Paul was forced to leave and sail to Athens. Once there, he sent for Silas and Timothy to join him.

5. Athens (Ch 17:16–34)
a. Paul and the Philosophers (Ch 17:16–21)
Paul began his ministry in Athens by speaking in the synagogue and the market place. There he confronted philosophers, such as the Epicureans and the Stoics. They regarded Paul as a babbler (one who picks up ideas from various sources and uses them to preach), who was preaching about strange deities and the resurrection. They decided that he should present his views to the Areopagus (the city's council of philosophical leaders). The name 'Areopagus' simply comes from the hill on which this council would often meet. Paul had the opportunity to preach to the educated pagans in Athens.

His speech, which is summarised below, will be studied in detail in the next section.

> **Summary of Paul's speech at Athens (17:22-31)**
> Paul's speech was spoken in an exalted rhetorical style, showing him to be well educated and intelligent. Theologically, the speech follows Paul's normal approach to pagans (for example, at Lystra in Acts 14:14-17):
> - God is the Lord of the world.
> - Man is God's creation and needs him.
> - God and man are related so idolatry is foolish.

b. Aftermath (Ch 17:32-34)

The Greeks mocked the idea of a bodily resurrection as distasteful to their traditions. However, a few people were converted, including one member of the council, Dionysius. Longenecker comments that from Athens Paul "was dismissed with polite contempt rather than being violently driven out" (1995, p475). At this point, Silas and Timothy arrived from Berea to join Paul in Athens. Paul sent Timothy back to strengthen the church in Thessalonica and sent Silas to Macedonia. They were to join him in Corinth (Acts 18:1, 5; 1 Thess 3:1-2).

6. Corinth (Ch 18:1-11)

a. Introduction

Corinth was the capital city of the Roman province of Achaia, with a Jewish minority. Marshall (1980, p292) believes that Corinth was one of the most important cities visited by Paul in the course of his missionary work. Paul stayed in Corinth, a commercial city renowned for its wealth and wickedness, for a year and a half. He probably stayed so long to establish a church that would be capable of evangelising the surrounding areas.

b. Encouragement for Paul

On arrival, he met a pious Jewish couple, Aquila and Priscilla from Rome, with whom he quickly formed "a firm and lifelong friendship" (Bruce, 1988, p346). They may well already have been believers, for there was a flourishing church in Rome (Romans Ch 16). However, they had been expelled from Rome, along with the other Jews, by the emperor Claudius, because of Jewish unrest. As Paul shared the same job of tent making with Aquila and Priscilla, he stayed and worked with them to support himself. Every Sabbath, he would preach in the synagogue to argue the Christian case to the Jews and Gentiles who attended the services.

Further encouragement to Paul came with the arrival of Silas and Timothy.

They brought news about the recently established church in Thessalonica. They probably also brought gifts of money, which enabled Paul to preach full-time rather than having to support himself.

c. Opposition
His preaching, however, was resisted by the Jewish authorities more and more. In the end, Paul felt it best to separate from them, but not before he let them know how he felt. The fact that he shook out his clothes in protest was a sign of breaking off fellowship with them. By rejecting the gospel, the Jews had brought upon themselves the judgement of God. So at Corinth too he would take his saving message to people who knew how to appreciate it (Bruce, 1988, p350). From now on he would turn to the Gentiles. He moved his preaching next door to the house of Titius Justus (18:7). Many were converted, including Crispus, the ruler of the synagogue, and Gaius (Titius Justus).

d. A Vision
At this time, Paul must have felt discouraged about his progress, for the Lord appeared to him in a vision, encouraging him not to be afraid of harm and to keep on speaking, as he had "many people in this city" (Acts 18:9–10). It is clear from Paul's letters to the Corinthians that a large church did in fact develop in Corinth, and spread throughout the region.

e. Gallio (Ch 18:12–17)
An important event that occurred while Paul was in Corinth was his appearance before Gallio, proconsul of Achaia. Gallio had recently arrived in Corinth to carry out his one-year term, and the Jews used the opportunity to attack Paul by bringing him before the proconsul. He would have had the power to prevent Paul from preaching, not only in Achaia, but in every province of the Roman Empire. Judaism was one of the legal religions of the Roman Empire. So the Jews charged Paul with preaching a new illegal religion and persuading the people to worship God in ways contrary to the Law (18:13). Hanson (1967, p186) comments on the vagueness of this charge. It is obvious that they wanted some sort of punishment against Paul. Gallio, however, regarded their dispute as a religious one and had them "ejected from the court".

> **Significance of Gallio's decision**
>
> Marshall comments that "it was probably Gallio's refusal to support Jewish opposition to Paul which encouraged him to stay on in Corinth for some time" (1980, p299). Gallio's decision not to forbid Paul to preach meant that the Christians were able to legally preach throughout the Roman Empire for the next twelve years, "until imperial policy toward Christians underwent a complete reversal" (Bruce, 1988, p354). This freedom ended when the emperor Nero cruelly persecuted the Christians in Rome.

7. Return to Antioch (Ch 18:18–22)

Acts 18:18–22 describes Paul's journey back to his home church at the end of the second missionary journey. He sailed from Cenchrea to Ephesus with Aquila and Priscilla. He only stopped briefly in Ephesus, although he did manage to speak in the synagogue there and promised to come back to Ephesus again. From Ephesus, Paul went to Syria and then "went up and greeted the church" (v 22) in Jerusalem, before returning to Antioch, where he stayed for some months.

We can see that Paul was still willing to keep Jewish customs, for he took a vow in Corinth, and in nearby Cenchrea had his head shaved when the vow was complete (18:18; 21:23–24). Jews made vows to God either in thankfulness for past blessings or as part of a petition for future blessings (Marshall, 1980, p300). This is an example of Paul's determination to do what he could to win the Jews as well as the Gentiles (1 Cor 9:20).

Paul's second missionary journey was complete. To sum up, he had strengthened the churches in Galatia and planted strong churches in Macedonia and Achaia. His next mission was to establish a strong Christian centre in Ephesus.

> **TASK**
>
> a) **Give an account of the main features of Paul's work either in Athens or Corinth.**
>   - This answer really only requires you to recall the main events that occurred in one of these places.

> **b) Describe the struggles Paul faced during his second missionary journey.**
> - Argument with Barnabas over John Mark.
> - Prison at Philippi.
> - Riot in Thessalonica.
> - Jews in Berea.

PAUL'S MISSIONARY ACTIVITY: THIRD JOURNEY (CH 18:23–21:17)

After staying several months in Antioch, Paul set off on his third missionary journey. This transition from the second journey to the third happens very subtly in Acts 18:23, so you should be aware that this is a new journey! This journey was the longest of the three, lasting for almost three years. Paul's companions included Timothy and Titus. We also know that Luke was with him on the return to Jerusalem, as there is another 'we' passage in the text.

1. Revisiting the churches in southern Galatia (Ch 18:23)

At the beginning of the third missionary journey, Paul set out again for Galatia and nearby Phrygia to strengthen and encourage the believers he and Barnabas had established on their first missionary journey.

2. Ephesus

a. Apollos at Ephesus (Ch 18:23–28)

Marshall comments that Luke's account of Paul's activity in Ephesus is "unusually full and vivid" (1980, p308). The third missionary journey begins with an introduction to Apollos, a Jewish scholar and a speaker of great eloquence, who was trained in the Greek Old Testament in Alexandria. (Apollos was to be a central figure in the church at Corinth.) He knew much about Christ and powerfully preached the same message. However, Apollos had only learned about John's baptism, which John had performed in order to prepare people for Jesus (Mark 1:2–4). Bruce explains that "John's baptism was one of preparation rather than one of fulfilment, as Christian baptism now was" (1988, p364). Priscilla and Aquila, having just arrived there with Paul from Corinth, heard Apollos preach and realised that he lacked full understanding of the gospel message. So they instructed him properly about Jesus. As a result, Apollos became "an effective evangelist as well as a pastor to the church" (Marshall, 1980, p304).

After a while, Apollos went to Corinth, where he became a preacher in

Above: A map of the third missionary journey

the Corinthian Church (18:27–19:1). Hanson (1967, p189) comments that it is worth noting that 18:27 implies that Christianity had reached Ephesus before Paul arrived there. Paul mentions Apollos several times in 1 Corinthians.

b. Paul arrives at Ephesus (Ch 19:1–7)

Paul had tried to go to Ephesus during his second journey, but had been prohibited by the Holy Spirit. Finally he was able to spend some time there. On arrival, he found some disciples who, just like Apollos, had only heard about John the Baptist. After Paul preached the gospel to them, they became Christians. They were baptised and Paul laid his hands on them, probably "as a special act of fellowship, incorporating the people concerned into the fellowship of the church" (Marshall, 1980, p308). This is the third place in Acts where Luke describes how the believers spoke in tongues after receiving the Holy Spirit (see 2:4; 10:44–46).

c. Paul's move from preaching in the synagogue (Ch 19:8–10)

About three months later, there was an objection to what Paul was preaching in the synagogue. Therefore, as in Corinth, Paul separated from the synagogue and "moved to neutral ground" (Marshall, 1980, p309), leading the Christians to worship in the hall of Tyrannus, which he used for over two more years.

Tyrannus probably taught only in the mornings, as most people slept in the afternoons due to the intense heat. This would have left the hall free for Paul to preach in the afternoons. Paul wanted everyone to hear the gospel. "This went on for two years, so that all the Jews and Greeks who lived in the province of Asia heard the word of the Lord" (v 10).

d. The Sons of Sceva (Ch 19:11–22)

"Paul's preaching was accompanied by striking healings and exorcisms" (Marshall, 1980, p310). Even pieces of clothing that he touched were taken to the sick in the hope that they could be cured through contact with it. In the first century there were many Jewish sorcerers. When they saw Paul driving out demons in Jesus' name, some of these sorcerers tried to copy him. The seven sons of a priest called Sceva tried to use Jesus' name to cast out a demon, but "with drastic consequences" (Hewitt, 1964, p160). The evil spirit did not recognise them and attacked the seven men, sending them away bruised and naked.

"The effect among a superstitious people was to cause both fear and praise for the name of Jesus" (Marshall, 1980, p312). When the people saw how the demons fled when Paul used the name of Jesus, they were afraid. Many repented and accepted the gospel. They probably realised that no demon could protect them from the power of Jesus' name. All this seemed to set off a campaign against magic. At that time, sorcerers used to recite 'mantras', which were meaningless words written on scrolls. Many believed that by reciting these mantras it was possible to gain great power. When some of the sorcerers themselves were even converted, they piled up their scrolls and burned them, even though they were worth fifty thousand drachmas. (One drachma was the same value as a day's pay for an ordinary working man. So 50,000 drachmas would be a huge amount.)

e. The riot in Ephesus (Ch 19:23–41)

Towards the end of Paul's stay in Ephesus, a riot was caused by Demetrius the metalworker (19:23–41). Fernando comments that the riot "fits in with a theme that Luke considered important: opposition to the gospel" (1998, p518). The Ephesians had built a huge temple in honour of Artemis, the greatest goddess of all in Asia. The silversmiths made little silver images of Artemis and sold them for a huge profit. However, as people became Christians and stopped worshipping Artemis, the sale of these statues fell and the silversmiths lost out financially. Demetrius tried to cover up his real worry about loss of trade with some talk about religious zeal (Hewitt, 1964, p161). "The ordinary people might not be too concerned that Demetrius was going out of business, but they might well take to heart the possibility that the temple of Artemis might lose its position in popular regard" (Marshall, 1980, p318).

A protest meeting followed, "which culminated in a protest march through the streets" (Marshall, 1980, p318). The instigators dragged Gaius and Aristarchus into the theatre. Paul himself wanted to appear to speak to the crowd, but he was advised not to because the crowd was so angry. The meeting was disorganised and some people did not even know what it was for. The Jews present were worried "about trouble coming to them, so they wanted to distance themselves from Paul" (Fernando, 1998, p519), and they probably forced Alexander to come before the crowd to tell them that the Jews had no connection with the Christians. The hysterical crowd, however, realised that Alexander was a Jew, and refused to listen to him.

Ephesus was a free city within the Roman Empire and so it had its own administration. The city clerk, worried that news of the riot might reach the Romans, intervened by trying to get the crowd to calm down. He reminded them that complaints should be brought before the court or legal assembly. He was probably concerned that the Romans would punish the whole city by taking their freedom away. Marshall (1980, p320) comments that the clerk was not an advocate for Christianity, but a defender of law and order, anxious that the city should not get a reputation for disorderliness and illegal action. His appeal was successful, the crowd dispersed and it seems that no further action was taken against the missionaries.

The period of Paul's time in Ephesus drew to a close. Bruce concludes that "it had been a most fruitful and encouraging ministry" (1980, p370).

3. Through Macedonia and Greece (Ch 20:1–6)

Paul spent about a year travelling through Macedonia, and then went to Greece. From there he planned to return by boat to Syria and Jerusalem. Just as he was about to get on the boat, however, he heard that the Jews from Corinth were plotting to kill him, so he changed his plans in order to get away from them. Paul's companions did take the boat, and waited for him in Troas. Meanwhile, Paul went by foot to Philippi, where he met up again with Luke (notice the change of pronoun in v 5).

Eutychus is raised from the dead at Troas (Ch 20:7–12)

The believers at Troas gathered to celebrate the Lord's Supper on the Sunday. (This is the first time it is mentioned in Acts that the believers met on a Sunday rather than on a Saturday.) A young man called Eutychus fell asleep, dropped to the ground from the third storey window and was picked up dead. As Luke the author of Acts was a doctor, he would have known for certain that the young man was dead. Marshall (1980, p326) comments that Luke would not have devoted space in his book for the raising of someone who was merely apparently dead. Paul was able to bring Eutychus back to life. Paul continued talking until daylight, and then Paul's companions boarded a ship to Jerusalem.

4. Paul and the Ephesian Elders (Ch 20:13–38)

Ephesus was about thirty miles from Miletus. As the ship had to stop for several days at Miletus, Paul sent word to the elders of Ephesus to come to meet him there. All the Ephesian elders had become Christians through Paul, and he had baptised most of them. In the verses that follow we have an example of Paul's preaching among Christians.

Paul's Speech at Miletus to the Elders of Ephesus
- Paul had appointed Elders to look after the churches in his absence.
- He reminded the Ephesians of his work among them.
- He defended himself against those who would slander him.
- He predicted that a disaster would come upon him at Jerusalem.
- He encouraged the elders to look after the church and to be on their guard from dangers from within the church (Guy, 1969, p94).

5. Paul departs for Jerusalem (Ch 21:1–17)

After praying with the Ephesian elders, Paul boarded the ship and sailed for Jerusalem, where he had planned to arrive in time for the Jewish feast of Pentecost. Luke describes the final stages of the third missionary journey – which took the missionaries to Cos, Rhodes and then Patara, where they found a ship bound for Phoenicia – in the form of a 'we' passage. This ship brought Paul to Tyre, where the believers pleaded with Paul not to go to Jerusalem. Then the missionaries travelled on to Ptolemais and to Caesarea, where they lodged with Philip the Evangelist. Philip had four unmarried daughters who had the gift of prophecy. While there, a prophet called Agabus (see also 11:28) symbolically informs Paul of the fate that awaits him in Jerusalem, by taking Paul's belt and binding his own hands and feet. However, despite warnings from friends, Paul is determined to go: "I am ready not only to be bound, but also to die in Jerusalem for the name of the Lord Jesus." The believers realised that Paul was not going to take their advice. Paul and his companions then got ready to go to Jerusalem, trusting in God's will. On their arrival in

Jerusalem, the Christian community received them warmly.

Conclusion

This brings us to the end of Paul's missionary activity, although the story of Paul in Acts is far from over. The next sections of Acts, which are not on your specification, describe Paul's arrival in Jerusalem, his transfer to Caesarea, his journey to Rome and his stay there. Paul dominates the rest of the story of Acts.

TASK

a) **Comment on the claim that no matter how important Paul proves himself to be, he is not Luke's main character, but rather is one of a number of people who spread the gospel of Christ.**

b) **Describe what you regard to be the most significant struggles and successes during Paul's third missionary journey.**
   - Struggles: leaving synagogue for hall of Tyrannus; revolt of the silversmiths.
   - Successes: baptism of John's followers; miracles; Sceva's sons; burning of books of magic; foiled a Jewish plot in Greece; Eutychus raised to life in Troas; preaching to Elders of Ephesus.

c) **Describe the events in Ephesus during Paul's third missionary journey.**
   - Apollos.
   - Baptism of John the Baptist's followers.
   - Teaching in synagogue, then move to hall of Tyrannus.
   - Miracles of healing.
   - Sceva's sons.
   - Books of magic.
   - Revolt of the silversmiths.

d) **Explore the claim that mission is essential for the spread of religious belief. Justify your answer.**
   - Reasons of personal integrity and a desire to pass on religious faith to others.

- Types of mission and their purpose.
- Examples from individual missionaries.
- Discussion of the claim that missionary work can sometimes do more harm than good.

OTHER ASPECTS OF HUMAN EXPERIENCE

The importance and relevance of mission for the spread of religious belief

This theme is linked to the extensive missionary activities of Paul, undertaken on his three journeys as described in Acts. In chapter 1:8, Jesus tells his followers:

"You will be my witnesses in Jerusalem, and in all Judea and Samaria, and to the ends of the earth."

So far, Acts has described how the missionary work began in Jerusalem and then spread to Samaria with the work of Stephen and Philip. Paul is seen fulfilling Jesus' command in helping the Christian message to reach the ends of the earth. The importance of missionary work in spreading religious belief can be seen through history to the present day.

The example of Saint Patrick

We know very little for certain about Patrick. According to his own Confession, he was born in Roman Britain – probably near Hadrian's Wall in northern England – the son of a wealthy official. His mother may have come from Gaul [France]. When he was 16, sometime in the early 400s, he was kidnapped by an Irish raiding party and sold into slavery in Ireland. As Roman Britain collapsed, it was increasingly common for Irish, Pict and Saxon raiders to pillage its coastal settlements, and it seems that Patrick fell victim to one of these raids. Patrick tended sheep as a slave for six years. Traditionally, it has been believed that he did this on Slemish Mountain, County Antrim, but it seems possible that he was, in fact, somewhere near the Atlantic Ocean in County Mayo or County Sligo.

Patrick says in his Confession that he discovered God during his time of captivity, and took to praying a hundred times a day. After six years, Patrick managed to escape from captivity, walked the 200 miles to the east coast and managed to negotiate passage aboard a trading ship to Gaul

[France]. There, he probably trained to be a Christian priest and spent time in Auxerre. He then received prophetic dreams in which he heard the people of Ireland near the "western sea" call him to come and walk among them again. He then travelled to Ireland as a missionary, and it seems that he never left. The year traditionally given is 432, but it seems more likely to have been around 460.

Patrick concentrated his work in north-east Ireland, and his first church was at Saul, near present-day Downpatrick. He preached to the Kings and their households and met with varied levels of success. One of his methods was to 'Christianize' the Celtic Pagan festivals. For example, Patrick reputedly lit an Easter bonfire on Slane Hill near the Hill of Tara while the King was having his own Pagan bonfire there. The King was enraged, but Patrick took the opportunity to preach, and managed to make some converts. He is famously said to have used the three-leaved Shamrock to explain the concept of the Trinity: God as the Father, Son and Holy Spirit (although this story is almost certainly a myth). Patrick died in Ireland and is traditionally believed to have been buried on the Hill of Down in Downpatrick, County Down. A stone marking the traditional burial spot was added in 1901 and the site is now a popular tourist attraction.

(www.wesleyjohnston.com/users/ireland/past/pre_norman_history/christianity.html)

TASK

1. **Work in a small group and discuss the following:**

   How important was Patrick's missionary work in bringing the Christian faith to Ireland?

   What parallels are there between the example of Patrick and the missionary work of Paul described in Acts?

2. **Use the internet to find examples of missionaries today who are continuing to follow Jesus' commission.**

TASK

General questions on journeys

a) 'Acts is very concerned with the opposition which surrounds the spread of the gospel'. Explore this claim with reference to the attitude of both the Jewish and Roman authorities.

As preparation for this question it would be useful to complete the following table, highlighting any incidents that reveal the attitude of the Jews or Romans towards the Christians. Look out for opposition in some of the following forms:

- opposition to Paul on economic grounds.
- confrontation with evil.
- jealousy.

Journey	Attitude of Jews	Attitude of Romans
1st		
2nd		
3rd		

b) **Describe the contribution made by the Holy Spirit during Paul's missionary activity.**

To help you with this it might be useful to go through your notes with either a coloured sticker or drawing of a dove in the margin to indicate a mention of the Holy Spirit. Then try to collate the material to answer the question.

c) **Evaluate the claim that Paul was worthy of the title 'Apostle to the Gentiles'.**

- Compare the success that Paul had with the Gentiles compared to the success he had with the Jews.
- Evaluate Paul's attitude to both groups.
- Compare with other preachers, for example, Peter.

> **d) Comment on the claim that the church today has much to learn from how Paul dealt with difficulties during his journeys.**
> - Go through the journeys, making note of how Paul dealt with setbacks and opposition. Try to come up with some suggestions of how the church today could learn from him.
>
> **e) Comment on the claim that Paul's conversion is a turning point in the book.**
> - Evidence of Paul's involvement in the persecution of Christians before his conversion.
> - The drama of his conversion.
> - Paul's missionary activity; missionary to the Gentiles.
>
> **f) Assess the significance of Paul's conversion for the spread of the gospel to Rome.**
> - Paul's determination to reach Rome.
> - Did the gospel reach Rome before Paul did?
> - Comparison with the missionary activity of others.
> - Would the gospel have spread without Paul?

Section 2:

Paul's Speeches

About one third of Acts consists of speeches, debates and dialogues, while the remainder is a description of various events. Out of about 24 speeches in Acts, nine are given by Paul. In this chapter we will look at two of these in more detail, both of which illustrate Paul's message to unbelievers (Pisidian Antioch, 13:16–41; Athens, 17:22–31).

The Audiences

Marshall comments that the variety of speeches in Acts "is no doubt meant to illustrate the different ways in which the gospel was presented to different groups of people, Jews and Greeks, cultured and uncultured" (1980, p33). Longenecker explains that there is enough in each account to suggest that Paul preached the same gospel wherever he went, but that "he altered the form of his message according to the circumstances he encountered" (1995, p424).

Were the speeches made up by Luke?
During the time when Luke was writing, speeches were often invented by the authors. So some scholars argue that the speeches in Acts do not give an exact report of what Peter, Paul, Stephen, James and the others said. For example, Paul's speech at Pisidian Antioch, which is the longest of the three, probably lasted much longer than what is recorded. Luke was not present at this speech, so he would have had to get his information about it from another source. Robertson (1931, p187) suggests that Paul may have written out notes of this sermon afterwards for Luke. Longenecker points out that "each sermon as we have it is only a précis of what was said, for the longest in its present form would take no more than three minutes to deliver and the shortest can be read in thirty seconds or less" (1995, p424). It seems, therefore, that when Luke records Paul's speeches, he provides a careful summary of what was actually said. For example, concerning Paul's speech to the Ephesian elders, Lewis comments that "the speech is from the pen of Luke, but there is little doubt that he has accurately caught the tone and content of what Paul would need to have said to such an audience" (1995, p72).

It is now widely accepted that early Christian preaching followed a common pattern that was based on the models or examples of Jewish rabbis. These models were familiar to Paul, and naturally he adopted this pattern himself.

Paul's synagogue sermon in Antioch of Pisidia (Ch 13:16–41)
Paul's speech at Pisidian Antioch was delivered during his first missionary journey. It is the only speech Paul gave in a synagogue, and the summary Luke gives us is the longest of the three. It provides an example of how Paul preached to people who knew the Hebrew Scriptures and has been compared to the speeches of Peter (especially 2:14–40) in both outline and content (Williams, 1975, p229), and also to the speech of Stephen (7:2–53), as both contain a summary of Israel's history.

The speech contains three parts:
1. Preparation for the coming of the Messiah (v 16–25).
2. The rejection, crucifixion, and resurrection of the Messiah (v 26–37).
3. The application and appeal (v 38–41).

1. Preparation for the coming of the Messiah (Ch 13:16–25)
Fitzmyer describes this section as "a recital of salvation history" (1998, p507). It a summary of selected incidents of Israel's history, and provides an overview of God's unchanging faithfulness, from the election of Israel to the time of Jesus.

Even though teachers in the synagogue in Palestine normally sat to teach, here in Asia Minor, where there was a greater Greek influence, Paul stood up and motioned with his hand to get the audience's attention. Conzelmann says that "according to Luke, Paul opens his speech with the appropriate rhetorical gesture" (1987, p103). He showed immediate respect for his audience by addressing his Jewish hearers as "men of Israel", and the Gentile God-fearers or "Jewish sympathisers" as "you who fear God" (Fitzmyer, 1998, p510).

This first section is clearly designed "to suit an audience with a background of knowledge about the Old Testament" (Fernando, 1998, p386). Paul begins with what Marshall (1980, p223) describes as "a survey of Jewish history", highlighting "God's mighty acts in the election of Israel" (Fitzmyer, 1998, p510). Moyes (1986, p45) points out that Paul clearly understood their pride in their history and their knowledge of Scriptures.

- God was the God of the Israelites (v 17). He chose the patriarchs out of all the nations on earth.
- God had worked with the Jews and made them great while they were in Egypt. God rescued them out of Egypt, led them through the wilderness, put up with their failings in the desert and brought them to the Promised Land (v 7–18).
- God demonstrated his power by driving out seven nations from this Promised Land so that his people could inherit the promise given to Abraham and the nation (Deut 7:1). God then raised up judges to help them in their rebelliousness, until the time of Samuel the prophet.
- The mention of Saul highlighted another point in the history of Israel's failure. God showed them mercy by removing him (this could refer to Saul's deposition or to his death) and raising up a new and faithful king, David (v 20–22). In particular, God regarded David as a man after his own heart.
- David's qualities were also evident in Jesus, his successor. Just as David was raised up at a particular time in Israel's history, so Jesus also came to take his part in history, by rising from the dead. This Jesus was the promised Messiah. (Isaiah 11:1–16 speaks of the Messiah coming from David's descendants.)
- Paul then speaks about John the Baptist's ministry (although John the Baptist is never mentioned in any of Paul's letters), which would have been familiar to most of the Jews of the dispersion (13:24–25). Bock (1994, p93) regards John the Baptist as a "bridge figure", which means he provided a connection. The connection is that John had announced

and prepared for Jesus' coming (cf Mark 1:2–8), making it clear that he, John, was the Messiah's forerunner (Luke 3:15–18).

2. The rejection, crucifixion, and resurrection of the Messiah (Ch 13:26–37)

The second part of the speech begins at verse 26. Before moving on, Paul paused again to personally address his hearers (cf v 16). By calling the Jews "brothers", Paul is bracing himself to talk about the recent events in Jerusalem, and to point to the Old Testament proof that Jesus was the promised Messiah. He wants to try to get his audience on side as much as possible before dealing with these issues.

- Jesus was rejected and crucified by the Jews of Jerusalem (13:27–28).
- These events fulfilled Old Testament prophecies. Most of the Jews living in Jerusalem did not realise this at the time (v 27, 29). It was ironic that the very scriptures that were read in their synagogues each week, which pointed to the death of the Messiah, were fulfilled in their rejection of Jesus. As Marshall comments, "they themselves had unwittingly fulfilled those very prophecies by rejecting Jesus" (1980, p225).
- Jesus was innocent of the charges brought against him (v 28).
- Fitzmyer (1998, p515) points to the contrast between what human beings did to Jesus and "what God has done". Jesus' resurrection shows how God vindicated him (v 30) and prepared him to rule.
- The apostles' personal witness of Jesus' resurrection is highlighted (v 31).
- The promise made to David in 2 Samuel 7:12–16, and referred to by Peter in Acts 13:23 (Williams, 1975, p164), was that seed from David's own body would succeed him and that his kingdom would be established forever. David's promised heir, the Messiah, had come in Jesus (v 33).
- Three Old Testament passages support the fulfilment of this promise: Psalm 2:7 (v 33), Isaiah 55:3 (v 34), and Psalm 16:10 (v 35).

  Psalm 2:7 – Refers to God raising up David as Israel's king and is clearly interpreted in terms of the resurrection of Christ (Fitzmyer, 1998, p517).

  Isaiah 55:3 – Williams refers to this as an "obscure phrase" (1975, p164). The simplest way of attempting an explanation is that since Jesus rose from the dead, God can give people the blessings he promised would come through David. The blessings mentioned in this Old Testament passage are those of the New Covenant.

Psalm 16:10 – Marshall (1980, p227) explains that Psalm 16:10 cannot be applied to David himself because he died an ordinary death that led to corruption (his body rotted). Psalm 16:10 implies that the "holy one" would not die. The fact that Jesus rose from the dead and his body did not decay in the tomb proves that he is the Holy One about whom David spoke.

3. The application and appeal (Ch 13:38–41)

"Having brought Scripture and history together … Paul comes to his appeal" (Stott, 1990, p225). He again refers to all those listening as "brothers", and emphasises that "through Christ come forgiveness of sins and justification, a message not to be spurned" (Fitzmyer, 1998, p508). He also claims that it is for everyone who believes, with the implication that salvation is not for the Jews alone. Jews and Gentiles are on the same level.

This is the only place in Acts in which Paul's teaching about justification by faith is mentioned. This issue dominates Paul's letter to the Galatians.

Paul appeals to Habakkuk 1:5, in which Israel was warned not to be surprised that God was going to use Babylon (a Gentile nation) to discipline his own people for their disobedience. Paul evidently regards his own generation of Jews as being under a similar disciplinary judgement. So he now warns them to be careful not to reject God's work in Christ, even if it was very different to what they had expected (Williams, 1975, p237). The challenge is "to accept or refuse the Gospel message" (Neil, 1973, p160).

The result seems to be favourable, as both Jews and Gentiles wanted to speak further about the matters raised by Paul.

TASK

1. **Discuss the theology and significance of Paul's speech at Pisidian Antioch.**

   - God has revealed his purpose through the saving acts (from Egypt, guiding through the wilderness, in Canaan, giving judges and kings).
   - Culmination in a Saviour from the line of David, who has come, was proclaimed by John the Baptist; Jewish rulers rejected him and condemned him to death.

- Jesus rose from the dead, fulfilled prophecy, proved his Messiahship; David was not the Messiah but died and his body decayed.
- Salvation is offered; sin forgiven; justified by faith and a warning is given.
- Salvation is not just for the Jews but also for the Gentiles.

Paul's speech at Athens (Ch 17:22–34)
Background (Ch 17:16–21)
Although Athens had once been the cultural and intellectual centre of the ancient world, at the time of Paul's visit it was in a period of decline (Marshall, 1980, p283).

It has been said that "there were more statues of the gods in Athens than in all the rest of Greece put together, and that in Athens it was easier to meet a god than a man" (Barclay, 1955, p141). Paul certainly would have seen many temples, statues and shrines, some of which are still found in Athens today. However, as a Christian who had experienced a strict Jewish upbringing, all Paul could see was idolatry, which disturbed him greatly.

Paul continued his preaching to Jews and God-fearing Greeks in the synagogue, but also took part in discussions about the gospel with various people in "the Agora, the market-place used for meetings and discussion" (Guy, 1969, p77). The Agora lay to the west of the Acropolis, and was the centre of community life in Athens. Many philosophers, such as the influential Epicureans and Stoics (Hanson, 1967, p176), would gather there to discuss religious and philosophical views.

Epicureans
Epicureans were followers of Epicurus (341–270 BC) who sought pleasure, believing that it was the most worthy pursuit of man. Guy (1969, p77) explains that some Epicureans interpreted this as promoting the attitude: "Let us eat, drink and be merry for tomorrow we die"; but Epicurus viewed pleasure in a different way than it might be portrayed today. He did not mean sensual pleasures, but those of the mind, such as freedom from pain and fears, especially the fear of death.

The Epicureans' attitude towards the gods was that they were not interested in man and would not punish sinners in the afterlife. Therefore there was no sense in organised religion such as the church as we know it today.

Epicureans also believed that everything happens by chance and that death is final. This philosophy is still popular today.

Rackham suggests that "Epicureanism is most fairly described as the ancient representative of modern utilitarianism" (1909, p304).

Stoicism

Stoicism was "the most popular form of Greek philosophy in Paul's day" (Keener, 1993, p831). The word 'stoic' comes from 'stoa', a porch where Zeno (340–265 BC) taught when he lived in Athens. He placed great importance on living in harmony with nature, and stressed the importance of being rational and self-sufficient.

Stoics were idealists (deSilva, 1995, pp549–564), and had a reputation for being quite arrogant. They "scorned pain and pleasure alike; nothing could make any difference to the upright man". Stoics were pantheists, believing that God is in everything, and everything is God. They were also fatalists, meaning that they accepted everything as it came, without complaint and without enthusiasm (Guy, 1969, p77).

Their teaching is also common today. Henley, a modern poet who followed this philosophy of life, wrote in his poem, 'Invictus', "I am the master of my fate; I am the captain of my soul" (cited in Untermeyer, 1920).

These philosophers called Paul a 'babbler', which, as was mentioned earlier in this chapter, suggests someone who picks up odds and ends of knowledge, as a bird picks up seeds (Guy, 1969, p77). They were implying that Paul had put together his own philosophy by picking up scraps of ideas from various sources.

What was the 'Areopagus'?

There are two suggested meanings for the term 'Areopagus' at the time of the writing of Acts (Barclay, 1955, pp141–142). It could refer to a location on Mars Hill, which was the place where the Council of the Areopagus met. Or it could mean a group of about thirty people who formed the Council of the Areopagus, and who met in the Royal Portico of the Agora. It is difficult to tell from Luke's description if the 'Areopagus' refers to the people or the place.

The Areopagus had a lot of authority over religion, education and morality in Athens. For example, Socrates had earlier been poisoned for teaching strange ideas in Athens. The members of the Areopagus heard that Paul was teaching strange things with which they were not familiar and wanted to know what exactly he was promoting. They were always interested in new ideas, and when Paul was brought before them it provided him with an opportunity to preach the gospel. This would have been an informal appearance because, as Marshall points out, "there is no hint of any legal proceedings" (1980, p285).

Paul's speech (Ch 17:22–31)

This speech is an example of Paul's preaching to intellectual pagans (Zweck, 1987, pp11–12). It is clear to see how he again adapts and uses his message to suit his audience. Paul begins by calling his audience "very religious", although some scholars argue that he was not praising his audience at this point. Fernando (1998, p474) certainly argues that "it was probably not a compliment" for, according to an ancient writer (Lucian), "complimentary exordia [beginnings] to secure the goodwill of the Areopagus court were discouraged". Fitzmyer (1998, p606) explains that the original translation means "rather demon fearing", which could mean superstitious, although Grayston argues that "it is most likely that Paul meant it in a good sense, to provide a way in to his address that would engage the attention of the audience" (1924, repr 1965, pp3–6). Morgan agrees, commenting that "Paul really began with the note of conciliation, and from beginning to end there was nothing calculated to offend, or drive away the men whom he desired to gain" (1924, p327).

Paul began with the Athenians' ignorance about at least one god, and proceeded to explain what Yahweh had revealed about himself. Some scholars feel that Paul probably intended to tell his audience more about a god whom they worshipped but did not know much about. However, Marshall argues that "Paul hardly meant that his audience were unconscious worshippers of the true God" (1980, p286). Rather he may have intended to inform them of the existence of a God whom they did not know.

17:24
- Paul's message does not contain direct quotations or appeals to the Old Testament as he talks to the Jews and God-fearers. Fernando comments that "such appeals would have meant nothing to hearers who did not accept the authority of the Scriptures" (1998, p476). However, Marshall (1980, p286) points out that his language is based

on the Old Testament description of God. The true God is Lord of heaven and earth who created all things. He is everywhere, and human temples cannot contain him. (This would have appealed to the Epicureans, who held the idea of God as above the world.) Some Greek philosophers agreed that temples did not really house their pagan gods, and it has been said that Paul was only repeating what the Stoic philosopher Zeno taught, that one should not build Temples of the Gods (Fitzmyer, 1998, p608).

17:25
- "Such a God has no need of men to supply him with anything" (Marshall, 1980, p287). Rather he sustains all life – human, animal and plant – and participates in human existence. This contradicts the Epicurean belief that God was not interested in human life and the Stoic belief of man being self-sufficient.

17:26–27
- As Greeks, the Athenians would have considered themselves as racially superior to other people. However, Paul proclaimed that the Athenians, like all other people, had descended from one man, Adam. The Greeks also liked to think that they had control over their own destiny. Paul taught that God is ruler over the political world and determines the times, seasons and boundaries of nations.
- God kept this control so that people would seek Him. Fitzmyer (1998, p609) comments that this seeking may mean a philosophical search, or it may involve something less intellectual, a more emotional effort. Marshall explains that "the main point is that seeking should not be difficult since God is not far from each one of us" (1980, p288).

17:28–29
- Paul referred to man's need of God, supporting his arguments by quotations from Greek poets (Guy, 1969, p78). He recited lines from two Greek poets whose ideas were similar to what Paul was preaching. Epimenides (600 BC) had written, "For in thee we live and move and have our being" (from his poem, 'Cretica', cited by Longenecker, 1995, p476); and Aratus (315–240 BC, writer of 'Phaenomena 5') and Cleanthes (331–233 BC, writer of 'Hymn to Zeus') had written, "We are also his offspring" (cited in Longenecker, p476). Paul used these quotations to try to convince his audience that he was speaking the

truth. He concluded that there is no logic in idolatry. God is divine and could not be an image or an idol.

17:30
- Until God revealed himself in Christianity, men lived in ignorance of him and God had been prepared to overlook their ignorance. But now the proclamation of the Christian message had brought this time to an end; they no longer had any excuse for their ignorance and God was calling on men everywhere to repent (Marshall, 1980, p290).

17:31
- Paul stressed that true knowledge of God leads to repentance. It was the audience's responsibility to respond to his message. "The urgency of Paul's appeal for repentance is underlined by his claim that God has appointed a day of judgment of the world" (Marshall, 1980, p290). McGee explains how Paul "has presented God as the Creator in His past work. He shows God as the Redeemer in His present work. Now he shows God as the Judge in His future work" (1983, p.591).

The response to Paul's preaching (Ch 17:32–34)
Jesus was qualified to judge humanity because of his resurrection. Jesus' resurrection vindicated His claim to be the Judge of all humankind (John 5:22, 25–29).

Lewis points out that it is only here, at the end of his speech, that Paul "comes out boldly with distinctively Christian claims, speaking of Jesus and of the resurrection" (1960, p72). Most Greeks rejected the possibility of physical resurrection (Croy, 1997, pp21–39), since the body was increasingly regarded as earthly and evil in comparison with the soul (Marshall, 1980, p291) although many of them, for example Platonists, did believe that after death the soul would finally be free of the body.

Nevertheless, Crowe (1979, p136) describes how this cultured Hellenistic audience dissolved at the mention of the resurrection of the dead. They responded to it in a predictable manner: some mocked, others refused to think about it, and a few believed (for example, Dionysius, a member of the Council of the Areopagus, and Damaris). Fitzmyer sums up the response as a "polite but firm rejection of Paul's message" (1998, p612).

TASK

1. **'Paul realised here that mere academic argument seldom really convinces anyone' (Lewis, 1960, p72).**
   - Do you agree or disagree?
   - How valuable is academic argument in convincing someone of the validity of a religious faith?
   - Find out about Justin Martyrs' dialogue with Trypho. Can you see any similarities between it and Paul's preaching regarding content and outcome?

2. **Outline and examine Paul's speech at Athens as recorded in Acts.**

   An examination may include some of the following, for example:
   - Paul's comments on the religious Athenians; the 'unknown god'.
   - Describes this God as creator; does not require a man-made temple; controls the fate of mankind who are his creation.
   - Repentance is necessary because God will judge the world, the judge is the one who rose from the dead.

3. **Critically evaluate the claim that Paul became all things to all people that he might save some.**

   A critical examination might include, for example:
   - Paul can be seen in various different roles in his attempt to spread the gospel.
   - Paul as a preacher, adapting his message to suit his audience, for example Pisidian Antioch, Lystra, Athens.
   - Paul as a pastor, for example, Miletus.

4. **Critically evaluate the claim that Paul was passionate about preaching the gospel.**

   A critical evaluation of the claim may include:
   - Passion expressed in his commitment and perseverance, in personal suffering; in his speeches; in missionary journeys.
   - Passion expressed in his letters to churches.
   - Passionate about preserving the gospel.
   - Passion was directed in other ways: Gentile inclusion; split with Barnabas; church morality; church unity; church leaders.

PRACTICE ESSAY QUESTION

Question from CCEA's Specimen Assessment Materials

(a) "Paul is an excellent example of a Christian missionary."

Discuss this statement using examples from Paul's missionary journeys. [25 marks]

Your answer could make reference to the following points:

- Paul's ability to relate to different audiences – Jew, Gentile and Christian.
- Paul was always willing to put spreading the gospel before his own needs; examples of the way Paul faced persecution and opposition to his work.
- Reference to the success of Paul's missionary work as seen in the numbers of people coming to faith and from different backgrounds.
- Reference could be made to counter arguments, for example, Paul often caused controversy acting in such a way as to be arrested.

(b) With reference to other aspects of human experience, explore the claim that religious believers often experience suffering and rejection. Justify your answer. [25 marks]

Your answer could make reference to the following points:

- A discussion of possible reasons why religious believers need to defend their religious beliefs and practices.
- A consideration of possible benefits in defending religious faith, for example, community support and strengthening of faith.
- A consideration of the extent to which religious believers invite suffering, for example, seeking martyrdom.
- Examples from individual religious leaders; a consideration of the significance that the suffering and rejection has on the leader.

OTHER ASPECTS OF HUMAN EXPERIENCE

The challenge of religious witness in any age

This challenge of religious witness is linked to the teaching of Paul through his speeches. However, as with all the content for human experience, this theme can also be applied to other sections on the specification. Through his missionary journeys and speeches, Paul faced many challenges in relating to different groups of people and coping with a range of reactions, from indifference to hostility.

The following examples show how two other famous missionaries have faced the challenge of witnessing to their faith:

James Hudson Taylor (1832–1905)

James Hudson Taylor spent more than 50 years in China as an evangelist, doctor and translator. He is credited by some with being the most successful missionary after Saint Paul, in terms of his thorough efforts to bring the Christian faith to a large geographical area. Hudson Taylor was very sympathetic to Chinese culture and faced criticism from other Europeans for wearing traditional Chinese clothes. He believed this practice made people respond to him more favourably when he preached to them. Hudson Taylor was able to speak several varieties and dialects of Chinese, which was a great asset to his preaching and work on translating the Bible.

Hudson Taylor founded the Chinese Inland Mission, which continues today as OMF International, carrying on the work of establishing schools in China and bringing in large numbers of missionaries. Even though Hudson Taylor's work in China was successful, he suffered numerous hardships, including ill-health and persecution.

Eric Liddell (1902–1945)

Eric Liddell is probably best known from the film Chariots of Fire as the Christian athlete who would not run on a Sunday. This led to Liddell withdrawing from the 100 metres race, his strongest event, in the 1924 Paris Olympics. Instead he ran in the 400 metres, in which he was not expected to perform well. Just before the race, a spectator gave him a piece of paper on which was written a quotation from 1 Samuel 2:30, "Those who honour me I will honour". Eric Liddell ran with the piece of paper in his hand, broke the existing world record and won a gold medal.

However, his work in China as a missionary is also very important. Eric Liddell was born in China to missionary parents and returned in 1925 after his education in Scotland. He worked as a school teacher as well as a minister. When the Japanese invaded China in 1940, British nationals were encouraged to leave. However, Eric Liddell stayed to continue his work in China. Even when he was put in a prison camp by the Japanese, he continued to teach children and to preach. He died of a brain tumour whilst in the camp.

TASK

1. Discuss the following questions in small groups:
- How did Hudson Taylor and Eric Liddell show their religious faith?
- What challenges did each of them face?
- How do the experiences of Hudson Taylor and Eric Liddell compare to those of the apostles in the first century? What contrasts and similarities can you find?

2. Use the internet to find other examples of human experience relevant to this theme.

You could consider the following examples:
- Father Damian of Molokai who ministered and died with lepers off Hawaii.
- St John Paul II and his battle with communism.

BY THE END OF THIS CHAPTER YOU SHOULD BE ABLE TO:

- demonstrate knowledge and understanding of, and critically evaluate Paul's missionary journeys, including:
  - Paul's conversion and its significance (9:1–19); and
  - the main events and significance of the three missionary journeys undertaken by Paul (13:1–14:28, 15:36–18:22, 18:23–21:17);
- demonstrate knowledge and understanding of, and critically evaluate Paul's speeches, including an examination of the content, theology and cultural significance of Paul's speeches at Pisidian Antioch and Athens;

5

Paul's Letter to the Galatians

Section 1:
The social and historical context of the letter

INTRODUCTION

ON PAUL'S THREE MISSIONARY journeys, he preached the gospel and set up churches in the provinces of Galatia, Asia, Macedonia and Achaia. Following this, Paul wrote letters to these churches to provide the new Christians with support and encouragement.

One of these letters is the Letter to the Galatians. Many scholars believe this letter to be one of the earliest letters that Paul wrote (around AD48 or 49).

PURPOSE AND MAIN THEMES

Why did Paul write to the Galatians? Stott (1968, p12) explains how, since Paul's visit to Galatia, the churches he had founded had been troubled by false teachers who had launched an attack both on Paul's authority and on his gospel. They argued against Paul's message that people could be saved through faith in Christ alone, arguing that circumcision and obedience to the Law of Moses were also necessary. In other words, anyone wishing to join the ranks of the people of God from the outside must conform to the normal procedure prescribed for proselytes – circumcision and commitment to Israel's Law.

Paul immediately saw the threat that their message would be to the churches he had established and on the spread of the gospel, so he wrote his Letter to the Galatians. Russell (1993, p436) explains that the general purpose of the letter was to persuade the Galatians to reject the Judaisers' non-gospel and to continue in the true gospel Paul had preached to them.

In particular, the purpose of the Letter to the Galatians can be divided into three main themes:

1. **The reasons for Paul writing and the issues which developed in Galatia following the First Missionary Journey (1:1–2:21).** This theme considers of how Paul defends his authority in the face of opposition from the Judaisers.

2. Paul's teaching on justification by faith and the purpose of the Law (3:1–5:6). This theme addresses the theological content of the letter.

3. Life in the Spirit and Christian freedom (5:7–6:10). This theme covers the ethical content of Galatians and importance of codes for living.

These three themes are covered in detail in the rest of this chapter. In the A2 examination, for a question asking for the purpose of Galatians, a summary of these issues is all that is required.

The context of the letter

There has been dispute among scholars over what is meant by the term 'Galatia'. In the main view, referred to as the 'North Galatian' theory, Galatia covers the land in the central parts of Asia, which Paul visited during his second missionary journey, after the Council of Jerusalem. The other view is known as the 'South Galatian' theory. This theory holds that Galatians was written for the Roman province of Galatia, which included towns such as Pisidian Antioch, Iconium, Lystra and Derbe. Paul visited these towns during his first missionary journey, which took place before the Council of Jerusalem. Until the eighteenth century, most scholars thought the North Galatian theory was more likely (Cwiekowski, 1988, p104). However, more recent scholarship favours the South Galatian theory.

Paul had heard that troublemakers were trying to undermine his teaching by claiming it was necessary for Gentile converts to observe Jewish rituals, including circumcision. Paul taught that Christian life began, and continued, through faith in Christ's death on the cross bringing forgiveness of sins. Although Paul spends a considerable amount of the letter defending his authority and his gospel, this is not the main purpose of the letter. In order to convince his readers that they must follow his teachings, he needs to establish his credentials. Stott comments that:

> "Paul's claim then is this: his gospel which was being called into question by the Judaisers and deserted by the Galatians was neither an invention (as if his own brain had fabricated it) or a tradition (as if the church had handed it down) but a revelation, for God had made it known to him." (1968, p30)

The council of Jerusalem is recorded in Acts 15, taking place after the first missionary journey. This meeting of church leaders was called to decide what obligations, if any, should be placed on Gentiles who became Christians. This council is thought to have taken place around AD48, and it is likely that

CHAPTER 5: PAUL'S LETTER TO THE GALATIANS

Above: A map of Galatia.

Galatians was written around this time. Paul probably used the decision of the council as an argument for his defence in the letter.

Tone of the letter

Drane (1986, p289) explains how the Letter to the Galatians "was written hastily in the middle of a raging controversy". Longenecker describes the opening of the letter as "fiery", "like a lion turned loose in the arena of Christianity" (1990, plvii). Paul's message "is personal and polemic, direct and defensive" (Freed, 2005, p92). Paul was so angry because of the seriousness of the issue at stake. Boice (1976, p409) explains that when the gospel was being preached mainly to Jews by Jews, the development of the church progressed smoothly. But as the missionaries pushed out into largely Gentile communities and the gospel began to take root there, questions arose regarding a Christian's relationship to the Law of Moses and to Judaism as a system. Was the church to open her doors wide to everyone, regardless of their relationship to the traditions of Judaism? Were her boundaries to be as wide as the human race? Or was she to be only an extension of Judaism to the Gentiles, as was being promoted by the Judaisers? Paul realised that "the future of Christianity was at stake: was it to become a sect of Judaism or a world-wide movement, embracing all peoples and races?" (Guy, 1969, p66)

TASK

Discuss why Paul wrote the Letter to the Galatians.

The discussion may include some of the following:
- Response to the threat of the Judaisers.
- Preservation of the Galatian churches.
- Defence of the gospel.
- Defence of Paul's apostleship.
- The inadequacy of the Law.
- The adequacy of faith in Christ.
- Explanation of Christian freedom, life in the Spirit, the rule of love.

PAUL'S REASONS FOR WRITING
Overview of chapters 1–2

The Galatians were a group of Christians who had previously been Gentiles. They were converted following Paul's preaching, during his first missionary journey, that all that was needed was faith in Christ.

However, it seems that "certain persons had been working against Paul after he had visited them" (Freed, 2005, p90). Not long after Paul left Galatia, a group of Jewish Christians, called 'Judaisers', arrived in Galatia and began to teach that for these Gentiles to be really saved they needed to be circumcised and keep the Law of Moses. Much has been written on the identity of these men and their theology. Freed (2005, p91) argues that they were probably fellow Jewish believers from Jerusalem. Fitzmyer agrees, adding that they were "of an even stricter Jewish background than Peter, Paul or James" (1989, p781). And Cwiekowski describes them as "Jewish converts to Christianity who sought to harmonise their former faith with belief in Jesus" (1988, p104). Whoever they were, it is clear that they regarded themselves as Jewish Christians.

The main thrust of the Judaisers' message was a critique of Paul. Drane explains that "the first thing the Judaisers had said was that Paul was not a proper apostle … he had no right to give directions to new Christians, nor ought they to pay attention to what he said" (1986, p290). They argued that Paul was inferior to the original apostles of Jesus and that his message had not come from God. Gorman explains that they "seem to have found his apostleship dubious, his message deficient, and his ministry dangerous" (2004, p192). They likely claimed that his message and ministry originated in himself and had the sanction of neither Jerusalem nor heaven. In other words, they were arguing that Paul had no authority to promote his message, a message in which he was "watering down the requirements of the gospel for the sake of Gentile converts" (Fitzmyer, 1989, p781).

In chapters 1–2 of Galatians, Paul defends both his apostleship and his message. The two chapters can be split into four sections:
1. Paul's gospel had been revealed to him by Christ himself (1:11–17).
2. Paul only met the original apostles three years after his conversion (1:18–24).
3. Fourteen years later they endorsed his message (2:1–10).
4. Paul was not inferior to the other apostles; in fact, he had once had to rebuke Peter (2:11–21).

Greetings to the Galatians (Ch 1:1–5)
Letters in ancient times opened in a particular way, with the sender's name, the name of the recipients and greetings. Paul's Letter to the Galatians opens in a similar way (v 1–3); however, it differs from his other letters in two distinct ways:
1. Paul has no praise for the Galatians. Guthrie comments that "in place of the usual thanksgiving, which is entirely lacking, Paul denounces the perverters of the gospel who are, in fact, preaching another gospel" (1981, p486).
2. Paul adds some comments, which hint at the issues he plans to deal with in the rest of the letter. These comments are related to Paul's authority as an apostle of Jesus.

The Trouble in Galatia (Ch 1:6–10)
"Instead of the usual thanksgiving, Paul expresses his indignant astonishment that the Galatians are so quickly forsaking their original teaching for another gospel" (Freed, 2005, pp91–92). The Greek word used for 'astonished' is *thaumazo*, which translates as 'I am amazed'. This was a conventional expression in Greek letters that signalled astonishment, rebuke, disapproval and disappointment (Longenecker, 1990, p11). Fitzmyer describes the action of the Galatians as "fickleness" (1989, p782), which means they were inconsistent or easily persuaded. Ryken argues that Paul "practically splutters with indignation. And rightly so ... As far as Paul was able to tell, the Galatians were guilty of sheer spiritual stupidity" (2005, pp81–82).

MacArthur explains that their stupidity "refers not to lack of intelligence, but to lack of obedience" (2005, p41). The Judaisers had arrived in Galatia, preaching a message that was different to the message Paul had preached, and the Galatians immediately agreed with them. Freed comments that the different message was "a demand that Gentiles be circumcised and obey the Jewish Law" (2005, p91). Paul regarded this message as a perversion of the true gospel. It was not a true gospel. Not only was he stunned at how quickly the Galatians were accepting this other gospel, but he was so outraged that he proclaimed the Judaisers were now under a curse (v 8–9). Stott (1968, p24) explains that this means that Paul hopes that God's judgement will fall upon them.

Paul shows that he is not trying to win favour for himself by placing himself under such a curse (v 10). The Judaisers accused Paul of wanting to please human beings. They intended to undermine Paul's authority to give support to their 'different gospel'. However, they could not attack Paul's gospel without first attacking him. They alleged that Paul's message was motivated by a desire to win human approval rather than the approval of God (v 10).

Some might argue that there is an element of truth in the accusation of the Judaisers against Paul. Paul admits to changing his behaviour depending on the cultural preferences of his audience. He did this to avoid undue offence to the gospel. Freed describes how Paul:

> "Found it convenient to become all things to all persons that he might win some. To the Jew he became a Jew to win Jews. Although not himself under the law, he became as one under the law to win those observing the law. To those without the law, he became like one of them to win some of them, though not himself without law toward God yet under the law of Christ." (2005, p93, based on 1 Cor 9:19–23)

In other words, while Paul was willing to make cultural concessions, he stood firm with regard to the gospel that he preached.

Paul was certainly not motivated by a desire to please humans. The charge that Paul had changed his message in order to do this implied that those he most wanted to please were the other apostles. However, Paul was rarely in Jerusalem, and when he did go there he did not seek the approval of the apostles, but rather sought the advancement of the gospel. The expression, "those who were of reputation" (2:2 and 6), is not meant to be disrespectful to the other apostles, but to show that Paul had no undue sense of awe, since he also was an apostle.

CHAPTER 5: PAUL'S LETTER TO THE GALATIANS

TASK

Morris argues that "there have always been preachers who have sought popular acclaim above all else and there are some still. It is part of fallen human nature that even those charged with the responsibility of proclaiming the gospel can fall into the trap of trying to be popular rather than faithful" (1996, p46).
   a) Explain what is meant by this statement.
   b) In groups try to think of some examples of the truth of the statement in contemporary society.

The origin of Paul's message (Ch 1:11–24)

Paul delves in detail into his own past as a fanatical supporter of the same views as the Judaisers. He wants to stress how his call to be an apostle was a dramatic change in his life, which can only be attributed to God himself (v 13–14). Paul was an unusually promising young man in Judaism before his conversion, exceeding his peers. Morris explains that "this probably does not mean that he became more pious than they, but rather that he was more highly esteemed by those in positions of influence, which would have resulted in his being entrusted with more important assignments, such as the trip to Damascus during which he was converted" (1996, p46).

Drane stresses that Paul "had a face-to-face encounter with Jesus" (1986, p290). As well as his call to be an apostle, Paul also received his gospel message from God. After his conversion, he went straight to Arabia and had no contact with other Christians (v 15–17). It was not until three years after his conversion that Paul met Peter and James, two of the original apostles (that is, those whom Jesus had appointed). Fitzmyer comments that when Paul writes *"to see those who were apostles before I was"* he is deliberately assuming the title apostle "to emphasise his equality with them, for his authoritative commission comes from the risen Lord" (1989, p782).

He went to Jerusalem "to get personally acquainted with" them, not to get information from them or to make inquiry of them (Hofius, 1984, p290). As he only stayed there for a fortnight, he could not have got his gospel message from them. Afterwards, he returned to Cilicia and had no further contact with any of the original apostles (v 18–24). Campbell concludes that "Paul had emphasized that he did not receive his message from men before or at the time of his conversion. Now he affirmed that he was free from human influences afterward as well" (1983, p592).

Paul's message approved (Ch 2:1-10)

Campbell comments that while chapter 2 continues Paul's defence of his apostolic authority and the gospel he preached, he focuses "not on the source of his message but on its content" (1983, p593). First of all, he seeks to show how 'his gospel was precisely the same as that of the other apostles" (Stott, 1968, p40). "He maintains that he had begun his missionary work before meeting the authorities in the church at Jerusalem" (Freed, 2005, p92). "Fourteen years later" (which most scholars take to mean fourteen years after his conversion), Paul met the apostles. He went to Jerusalem because God told him to, and not due to any request by the apostles. With him he took Titus, a Gentile Christian, a fact of some significance given that Jerusalem was the Judaisers' stronghold (v 1-2). As Titus was not circumcised, his presence forced the Christian leadership to take a stand concerning the necessity of circumcision for Gentile converts to Christianity.

However, some of the Judaisers managed to gain access to this meeting between Paul and the other apostles (v 3-5). Even so, Titus was not forced to be circumcised, and Paul's gospel "was not contradicted or even modified in any way" (Stott, 1968, p42). The other apostles "acknowledged his successful work among Gentiles and glorified God because of it" (Freed, 2005, p92). In other words, Paul's view that Gentiles do not need to keep the Law of Moses or submit to circumcision was approved by the original apostles. They also encouraged him to continue such work in the future (v 6-10). Guthrie concludes that "his apostleship was unquestioned" (1981, p486).

Paul rebukes Peter (Ch 2:11-21)

The incident in Antioch shows how many Jewish Christians saw themselves as simply a renewal movement within Judaism, and regarded newly converted Gentiles as proselytes who needed to be circumcised and to submit to the Jewish Law if they were to become fully certified as members of the covenant community. Fitzmyer (1989, p784) explains that such an attitude would affect the unity of the church itself.

Peter had paid a visit to Antioch and enjoyed 'table fellowship' (eating) with the Gentile Christians there. Even though they were not circumcised or bound by the Law of Moses, Peter had no problem whatsoever in spending time with them, socialising, having meals and sharing in the Lord's Supper. However, it seems that some Judaisers arrived at Antioch and that their influence on Peter was such that he stopped having table fellowship with the Gentile Christians. Fitzmyer explains that such behaviour "gave the impression that only Jewish Christians … were the real Christians" (1989, p784). Suddenly, it was as if the Gentile Christians were no longer good enough for his company. Paul was outraged at such shameful behaviour, and told Peter what he thought of him in front of the whole congregation. Paul's equal standing in relation to the other apostles is evident in this verbal attack on Peter (v 15–16). Guthrie argues that "this was an active demonstration of his apostolic authority" (1981, p486).

Freed explains that "Paul's reprimand would be pointless if Peter had not at least partly shared his ideas, especially about food laws" (2005, p98). When Peter and Paul had been Jews, they had firmly believed that God would only accept them as righteous if they managed to keep the whole Law of Moses. As Christians, they now rejected that belief, and instead accepted that sinners can only be justified by faith in Jesus. This is known as 'justification by faith' and is one of the major themes of Galatians. If Peter were no longer associating himself with the Gentiles, it would look as if he could no longer accept that they were saved, because they did not keep the Law of Moses. Paul regards this as very serious, because "to submit to the law again would be to become involved again with sin" (Fitzmyer, 1989, p785). Furthermore, "if the law was still in force as a way of salvation and life, the messianic age had not yet dawned, and Jesus accordingly was not the Messiah" (Bruce, 1982, repr 1983, p83).

"It is perhaps curious that nobody seems to have recalled that Jesus ate 'with publicans and sinners', which can scarcely mean that he conformed to strict Jewish practice" [See Mark 7:19] (Morris, 1996, p77).

TASK

With reference to Galatians Chs 1–2, discuss Paul's response to the accusation of the Judaisers that he was not a proper apostle.

A discussion may include the following, for example:
- First to preach in Galatia.
- Conversion and call.
- Met risen Christ.
- Message approved by other apostles.

Section 2:
Paul's Teaching to the Galatians

PAUL'S TEACHING ON JUSTIFICATION BY FAITH AND THE PURPOSE OF THE LAW

Overview of chapters 3–4

In chapters 3–4 Paul seeks to prove that his message of salvation by faith alone is still the only true gospel message. People cannot be saved by keeping the Law of Moses or submitting to circumcision. Paul uses two main methods in presenting his arguments:

- He appeals to the Galatians' own experience.
- He appeals to Old Testament Scripture.

The Galatians' own experience (Ch 3:1–5)

Paul challenges the Galatians with a series of rhetorical questions (a question to which no answer is expected; Paul is being sarcastic), which are obviously challenges against the Galatians and not polite inquiries. He reminds the Galatians of the experience they had when he first preached the gospel and they became Christians. "What they knew of Christ ought to have shown them that they had received the Holy Spirit, not because they had obeyed the Old Testament law, but because they had exercised faith in Jesus" (Drane, 1986, p290).

This in itself should have been enough to prove he was right. The Holy Spirit was a sign that they had been accepted by God. "A return to 'the deeds of the law' would mean that the Spirit was received to no avail" (Fitzmyer, 1989, p785). Guthrie (1981, p487) explains that Paul thought that for the Galatians to "retrogress" or return to the law could only be evidence of "bewitched minds" (that is, that they had been brainwashed).

For Paul, Christ is everything or nothing. Either God has inaugurated the new, eschatological age of the Spirit through Christ, or he has not. Either justification, or life in the Spirit, is received by faith, or not (Gorman, 2004, p216). As Guthrie explains, "the real issue was a choice between Christ and the law" (1981, p487).

The example of Abraham (Ch 3:6–9)

For further proof, Paul uses the Old Testament (Genesis 15:6) and appeals to the example of Abraham. In Jewish history Abraham was a very important man of God. Abraham was the first person who became righteous through faithfulness towards God (Freed, 2005, p101). The Jews had descended from Abraham and, through him, God had promised that the same blessing that he had given to Abraham would be given to all people. Therefore, Abraham's true descendants were those who, like Abraham, trusted in God and were saved by faith alone.

The danger of relying on the Law (Ch 3:10–14)

The importance of observance of the Law for any Jew of Paul's day goes without saying (Barclay, 1988, pp60–72). Therefore it is understandable that "what made the Gentiles sinners in the estimation of the Jews was not only that they did not observe the Law but also that they did not even possess it and consequently lacked the possibility of obtaining righteousness through it" (Fung, 1988, p113).

The Galatians had started to believe what the Judaisers claimed: that the only way to be saved was by keeping the Jewish Law. However, the Judaisers' view that salvation was gained through keeping the Law of Moses was impossible. To break just one commandment (3:10; James 2:10–11) would lead to condemnation. Freed (2005, p92) comments that the Law was ineffective in helping humankind attain righteousness in God's sight. Ryken (2005, p110) explains that since we cannot keep the Law, the Law cannot bless us. "Instead of bringing blessings, the law brings a curse on whoever breaks the law…" (Freed, 2005, p101).

The scriptures taught that clearly no-one is justified before God by the law, because the righteous will live by faith (from Habakkuk 2:4). Therefore, to say there was another way to be saved was to contradict the scriptures. Paul's most basic problem with the Law is that it is obsolete and therefore following it is no longer appropriate. However, the good news is that "Christ had removed this by becoming a curse for us" (Guthrie, 1981, p487). Bruce (1983, pp237–238) explains that for Jews anyone who was crucified was under a curse (1 Cor 1:23). Paul explains that this is the reason why God sent Jesus to die on the cross. Through Jesus' death, people have been set free from the punishment they deserve because of their sins. Through his suffering, Jesus took the punishment for people's sins, becoming a curse for them (3:13). All that people need to do is believe in Jesus. Therefore, the promise God made to Abraham that sinners can be saved even though they have not kept the Law can be fulfilled.

Freed (2005, p94) argues that when Paul talks about the works of the Law he usually means works of the Law in a specific and limited sense, mostly with reference to circumcision and dietary regulations, not the Law as a whole, and not works in the sense of good deeds. De Silva (2004, p505) agrees, commenting that Paul is not arguing against "good works" but "works of the law". He is opposing the continued observance of a code, an entire body of laws given to Israel as a mark of her distinctiveness and separation from the Gentiles.

What is the purpose of the Law? (Ch 3:15–25)

God had promised Abraham that one of his descendants would save the world through faith. Four-hundred-and-thirty years after this, God gave the Law through Moses to prepare his people for this Saviour. Guy (1969, p68) explains that "the Law of Moses came into being centuries after the time of Abraham, as a kind of afterthought". Therefore, it could not possibly alter a direct promise made to him by God (Drane, 1986, p290). So in Galatians Paul argues that the Law of Moses "was always secondary to faithfulness because Abraham believed God before the law was ever given" (Freed, 2005, p92). Morris comments that this is "what endeared Abraham to many Jewish thinkers … his virtues and his deeds. They understood him to have kept the law before it was written" (1996, p98).

If the Law is not needed to be saved, then the Galatians might wonder what the point of having it was (3:19). Paul explains that the Law was given "on account of sin" (3:19). In other words, the Law showed them that they needed to be saved because it was impossible for them to be able to stop sinning. The Law enabled them to work out what was right and what was wrong. With the threat of punishment hanging over them, people were more likely to do what was right.

The purpose of the Law, however, was not to make the Jews feel bad about themselves. It was to make them realise that they needed a Saviour. Morris (1996, p115) explains that "a law can lay down what people ought to do, but it cannot give them the power to overcome the temptations to do evil". Therefore the function of the Law was to point people to Christ (Morris, 1996, p113). Paul clarified that the Law was only a temporary measure designed to function until Christ came (Hays, 2001, pp21–35). When this time came, the people would be ready to turn to Christ in faith (3:19, 21, 24).

The promise had now been kept, because the Saviour (Jesus) had come. So the purpose of the Law had been served. There was no longer any need to try to keep it (3:25). Guthrie argues that "the gist of Paul's argument is to show that … Christianity according to the Law is inferior to the doctrine of faith" (1981, p486).

TASK

The following quotations provide a summary of this argument. In pairs, explain what each quotation means in your own words:

- "For Paul, the Law can be described as weak in respect of justification simply because it was not given by God for the purpose of justification, but rather as an interim provision pointing forward to the Christ, in whom justification would become a reality. To seek justification by the Law, therefore, as the Galatians were mistakenly trying to do, is to attempt to direct the Law towards an end for which it is essentially unsuited by the purpose of God…" (Bayes, 2003, p138).

- "The gospel is the fulfillment of the promise made to Abraham that in him and his offspring all nations would be blessed (cf 3:8, 16). The Law, which was given later, was a parenthetical dispensation introduced by God for a limited purpose; its validity continued only until the promise to Abraham was fulfilled in Christ, and even while it was valid it did not modify the terms of the promise" (Bruce, 1983, p219) (cf 3:17–25)

The true descendants of Abraham (Ch 3:26–29)

Freed explains that "Paul never gave up his belief that the Jews were God's special people. He simply broadened the concept to include all persons who through their faithfulness toward God are children of God in Christ Jesus" (2005, p101). After accepting Christ, the Galatians had been baptised by Paul (3:27), which was an act to show that they belonged to Christ and "were one with him" (3:26). "Putting on clothes is a metaphor for assuming inner moral or spiritual qualities or a different status in life" (Freed, 2005, p102). Because there was now but one way of justification, all who belonged to Christ were equally regarded as God's children. Therefore, there was no difference between Jews and Gentiles (3:28) (Bruce, 1983, p214). "All are one in Christ Jesus so that there is neither Jew nor Greek, slave nor free, male nor female" (Freed, 2005, p104). All are counted as Abraham's descendants and are entitled to everything that God promised to Abraham (3:29).

TASK

The place of women in Christianity

"There is neither Jew nor Greek, there is neither slave nor free, there is neither male nor female; for you are all one in Christ Jesus." (Galatians 3:28)

It has been said that no other verse in Galatians has attracted as much attention during the debate about the role of women in the church as Galatians 3:28. When Paul states that "there is neither … male nor female … in Christ," is he referring to the role of women in the home and in the church? Most scholars agree that the main point of this verse means that all believers are united in Christ. But does the verse go beyond that? Clearly salvation does not eliminate all of our human differences. As Christians, we keep racial, social, and gender distinctions. So what does it mean that in Christ there is neither male nor female? Does Galatians 3:28 do away with gender specific roles? Can women now have equal roles to men, for example, in the church?

In groups, **discuss** the above points and assess what you think Paul means by Galatians 3:28.

God's dealings with the Jews (Ch 4:1–7)

Paul provides further explanation by using an example from everyday life. In Roman society a son would receive his inheritance from his father when he came of age (a bit like reaching the age of 18 in our society). Up until that time, the son would have had to answer to a guardian or tutor whom his father had put in charge of him. Such a tutor might have been "a slave charged to lead a boy to and from school and to watch over his studies and conduct" (Fitzmyer, 1989, p787). Even though the son might have been an heir to a fortune, in reality, until he came of age, he would be no better than a slave.

Paul explains that this is what it was like for the Jews. The Jews were expected to keep the Law of Moses until such time that they would be free of it. Fitzmyer explains that "the termination of such discipline came with Christ, 'the end of the Law'" (1989, p787). Now that Christ had come, the Jews could enjoy their inheritance, that is, their salvation. The guardian or tutor (that is, the Law) was no longer needed. God was treating them like mature sons, the proof of which was in the gift of the Holy Spirit.

Paul's concern for the Galatians (Ch 4:8–20)

Freed asks the obvious question: "'Now that Gentile believers know God and are known by him, how can they think of returning to pagan gods and pagan ways?" (2005, p103). Witherington stresses that if the Law was meant to function only until Christ came, "then it is a mistake, indeed a serious mistake to go back to keeping it, or in the case of Gentiles to begin to submit to it in any form or fashion" (1998, p354). Witherington continues to explain that what bothers Paul the most is that keeping the Law implies that Christ's death did not accomplish what in fact he believes it did accomplish. To submit to the Mosaic Law is to "nullify the grace of God (Gal 2.21) and to deny that justification or righteousness, whether initial or final, comes through the death of Christ" (Fitzmyer, 1989, p788).

Paul states that he cannot understand why the Galatians want to revert back to keeping the Law of Moses, when they had recently enjoyed freedom from the Law. Paul is concerned that his work among them will have been a waste of time.

Paul reminds the Galatians of his friendship towards them. They had treated him like an angel and had looked after him when he was sick. Fitzmyer suggests that this (4:14) may be "an allusion to some repulsive physical ailment …" (1989, p788). However, now it seems that they were regarding him as their enemy, when really he had only had their welfare at heart (4:12–16). Paul was worried. He believed that the Judaisers were only pretending to be their friends. They wanted the Galatians to turn their backs on Paul and to accept their ways (4:17–20).

The true sons of Abraham (Ch 4:21–31)

Paul closes this doctrinal section using the Old Testament scripture to explain the identity of the true sons of Abraham. The Judaisers had argued that the only way to be saved was to become a true descendant of Abraham, which could be achieved by being circumcised and keeping the Law of Moses. Paul, however, disagrees, using scripture to support his argument.

Abraham had two sons, Isaac and Ishmael. Isaac was the son of Abraham's wife, Sarah, a 'free woman'. Ishmael was the son of a slave woman, Hagar. Which of these sons was Abraham's true son and heir? Fitzmyer suggests that "the women represent two covenants: Hagar represents the Sinai covenant, and Sarah represents the one made with Abraham" (1989, p788). As the Sinai covenant is the giving of the Law, which happened after the promise made to Abraham, then the Sinai covenant is the inferior one.

Drane explains that these verses are "an allegory of the superior position of the good news of Christ over against the legalism of the Jewish Law" (1986, p291). God rejected Ishmael, the son of the slave woman, even though he was circumcised. Instead, God accepted Isaac, as he had been born by the power of the Holy Spirit. Paul compares this story with the situation in Galatia. The Galatians had been born again by the power of the Holy Spirit and were free, just like Isaac, who was regarded as Abraham's true descendant. However, the Judaisers were in bondage (to the Law), like Ishmael, the son of the slave woman.

The importance of standing firm (Ch 5:1–6)

In the previous chapter Paul has explained how the true descendants of Abraham are free. He continues the theme of freedom, explaining that the reason Jesus died on the cross was that we might be free from the 'curse of the Law' and from having to keep the Law to win God's approval (5:1). Such freedom was a privilege and one that the Galatians should not give up by being circumcised. If they submitted to circumcision, they would be obligated to keep all the other Jewish laws as well (5:3). If that were the case, then Christ would have died for nothing (5:2, 4). Fitzmyer explains that "the Galatians must choose one or the other: Christ and freedom, or the law and slavery ... but Paul warns: if you accept the 'sign' of a Jew, you oblige yourself to the whole way of life" (1989, p789, see also comment on Ch 3:10–14). Paul concludes that the only thing that matters to God is faith, which shows itself through love (5:6).

TASK

Critically assess the view that Paul's teaching on the Law is still important today.

A critical evaluation of the view might include, for example:

- The context has changed.
- The specific challenge of the Judaisers.
- Justification by faith.
- Issues related to circumcision.
- Contemporary 'laws' that alter or add to the gospel of faith.

PAUL'S TEACHING ON LIFE IN THE SPIRIT AND CHRISTIAN FREEDOM

Overview of chapters 5-6

Having explained what is meant by 'justification by faith', Paul now draws out some practical lessons for the Galatians to learn. He explains how they are to hold tight to the freedom that Jesus has given them. With that freedom, they are to live a life that pleases God and not let their newly found freedom be an excuse for wrong or reckless living.

Paul's hope for the Galatians (Ch 5:7-12)

"Paul often compares Christian effort to that of a runner in a race" (Fitzmyer, 1989, p789). Here he reminds the Galatians that they had made a good start in their Christian lives, but that the Judaisers have been getting in the way and the Galatians have been sidetracked from the true path (5:7). He compares the influence of the Judaisers to yeast in dough; while the number of Judaisers was small, there were enough of them to affect the whole Christian community (5:9). Paul is convinced, however, that God will judge these troublemakers (5:10, 12).

The proper use of freedom (Ch 5:13-25)

By his death, Jesus had set the Galatians free from having to obey the Jewish Law. However, Paul never said that the Law has been abolished in every sense, or that its ethical demands are now irrelevant. Freed argues that Paul "usually means works of the law in a specific and limited sense, mostly with reference to circumcision and dietary regulations, not the law as a whole, and not works in the sense of good deed" (2005, p94). Murder is still murder, adultery is still adultery, and theft is still theft. Guthrie writes that Paul stresses that freedom or liberty "must not be confused with libertinism" (1981, p487). In other words, freedom from the Law did not mean licence to live as the Galatians pleased, for example, by gratifying their sinful desires (5:13a, 19) (Guy, 1969, p69). The Christian is not the person who has become free to sin, but the person, who, by the grace of God, has become free *not to* sin (Barclay, 1988, p50). They were to use the power of the Holy Spirit to live a life of loving service to others (5:13b, 16). The Holy Spirit would enable them to develop a Christ-like character (5:22). Freed explains that "according to Paul, for converts who live as new creations, the differences between right and wrong is quite explicit … Good conduct is the work of God and the fruit of the Spirit; wrong conduct is the works of the flesh" (2005, p105). Bruce agrees, commenting that to "walk by the Spirit" means "let your conduct be directed by the Spirit" (1983, p243). Guthrie explains that "spiritual freedom will lead to an attitude of sympathy for the burdened" (1981, p487). This will result in mutually helping one another through gentleness, not pride, to refrain from wrongdoing (Freed, 2005, p103). The irony is that if the Galatians lived their lives in this way, they would in fact be actually keeping God's laws. Paul explains that the whole purpose of the Law is summed up in the command "love your neighbour as yourself" (5:14).

The Law of Christ: helping others (Ch 5:26–6:5)
While the Galatians did not have to keep the Law of Moses, this did not mean that they were allowed to live as people with no laws. They were in a way under a new law, the law of Christ (6:2b), which meant that just as Jesus had been humble and willing to bear the burdens of others, so should they be towards one another (6:1).

Sowing to please the Spirit (Ch 6:6–10)
These verses are a reminder to the Galatians of the gift of the Holy Spirit that God had given to the Galatians when they first believed in Jesus. If they were willing to give their hearts over to the Holy Spirit, that is, to "sow to please the Spirit", then the Spirit would produce in them a character that God would approve of, and would reward them with eternal life (that is, reap a harvest: 6:7, 8b–10).

Conclusion (Ch 6:11–18)
It is clear that Paul is now physically writing the letter himself (6:11). Up until this point, he had probably been dictating it to a secretary. The size of his handwriting may be an indication of Paul's poor eyesight, which has been hinted at elsewhere (4:15).

The Judaisers are afraid that if they preach the real message of the cross they will be persecuted for it by Jews or other Judaisers. They prefer to put on a good show to others by preaching circumcision (Fitzmyer, 1989, p789). However, even though they insist on circumcision and observance of the Law, they are unable to keep the Law themselves. For Paul, the only thing sinners can boast about in God's presence is what Jesus has done for them through his death on the cross. Circumcision means nothing; all that matters is a new creation.

Paul concludes his letter with words similar to a standard prayer in the Jewish synagogue liturgy: "Peace and mercy to all who follow this rule, even to the Israel of God" (Gal 6:16) (Cwiekowski, 1988, p105). The core issue of Galatians thus boils down to a simple but profound choice – Christ or the Torah' (Hubbard, 2002, pp199–200).

>
> ### TASK
> Create a spider diagram or mind map to show how the message of Galatians was relevant for the Early Church. You could consider the following areas:
> - Religious teaching.
> - Reassurance for Gentile converts.
> - Practical advice on Christian living.
>
> How far is the focus of Galatians Chs 5–6 a plea for the responsible use of freedom? A critical evaluation of the claim could include, for example:
> - Definition of Christian freedom.
> - The law.
> - Freedom not to sin.
> - Holy Spirit.
> - Responsibility to others.

RELEVANCE OF GALATIANS TODAY

Longenecker (1990, p235) argues that Paul's Letter to the Galatians, though directly relevant to the Galatian situation, speaks also to our situation today. Hunter agrees, commenting that "the precise issues of Galatians – 'except you be circumcised you cannot be saved' – are long dead ones; but the message of the letter is not out of date" (1945, p123).

For example, the question addressed in Galatians concerning circumcision can be asked in another way: 'What makes a person a Christian?' Paul's answer is perfectly clear, "For in Christ Jesus neither circumcision nor uncircumcision has any value. The only thing that counts is faith expressing itself through love." Christians in our society obviously don't argue over issues like circumcision, but Christians believe that the principle is still the same. Many ask how a person can get right with God. Consider the following suggestions:
- By going to church.
- By belonging to a certain Christian denomination.
- By being baptised.

- By keeping the Ten Commandments.
- By avoiding alcohol.
- By only having Christian friends.
- By not working on a Sunday.
- By not smoking.
- By giving to the needy.
- By not using bad language.

And so the list goes on. Paul's message is that people can never earn God's favour by obeying laws or conditions. He argues that a true Christian, with the help of the Holy Spirit, will live a moral and upright life without effort. It will just happen.

DISCUSSION

"Even today, to place any burden on a Christian by telling them to behave in a certain way is to deny them their freedom in Christ."

Do you agree with this statement?
What evidence can you use to justify your views?

TASK

1. Critically assess the view that we meet many of the weightiest themes in Paul's Letter to the Galatians.

A critical evaluation may include, for example:
- An assessment of the importance of Paul's defence of his apostleship, of his doctrine of justification by faith, and of Christian freedom.

2. To what extent is the message of Galatians still relevant today?

A critical evaluation may include, for example:
- Issues of religious authority.
- Legalism, false teaching, influence of trends.
- Christian living, freedom, fellowship.
- Different contexts.
- Circumcision.

PRACTICE ESSAY QUESTION
Writing essays for A2 Level

Your course is assessed through writing essays. For each module, you will have an exam requiring three essays to be written in two hours. One of these essays will test synoptic assessment (this is covered in Chapter 8 of this book).

Each essay on your module will be in two parts: for part (a) you must demonstrate knowledge and understanding; for part (b) you will be required to analyse and evaluate aspects of, and approaches to, religion and belief. Part (a) is worth 20 marks and part (b) is worth 30 marks. This is a significant change in the assessment weightings.

For AS Level, you were aiming for both parts of an essay to be of roughly equal length. Now you will need to write a longer answer for part (b), making sure that you:

- **Engage in critical analysis and evaluation** – You will need to write a longer answer, but try not to include too much narrative.

- **Use evidence and reasoning to support your views** – For this module you could use evidence from the Bible text or refer to the views of scholars.

- **Present balanced arguments** – The question will prompt you to either agree or disagree; having done this, then consider opposing or contrasting views.

- **Show evidence of personal insight and independent thought** – This may involve coming to a conclusion regarding the evidence you have presented.

- **Present your answer as clearly and coherently as possible** – Even though you have a lot to do in two hours, it is worth spending a few minutes planning your arguments.

TASK

Question from CCEA's Specimen Assessment Materials

(a) Analyse Paul's teaching on 'justification by faith' in his Letter to the Galatians. [20 marks]

Your answer could include an analysis of the following points:

- Paul's explanation of justification by faith from chapters 3 and 4.
- Paul's argument drawn from the Galatians' own experience of receiving the Holy Spirit.
- Paul's argument drawn from the faith of Abraham and developed with reference to Sarah and Hagar.
- Paul's teaching on the purpose of the Law and his reference to slaves and heirs.

(b) Critically assess the claim that Paul's teaching on salvation through faith is still an important issue for Christians today. [30 marks]

Your answer could include an evaluation of the following points:

- An examination of why some Christian beliefs about the Holy Spirit can be divisive today, including how the Holy Spirit is received, manifestations of the Holy Spirit and how the Spirit guides someone's life.
- Analysis of why different Christian beliefs about freedom might cause division; this could be linked to Paul's teaching on the proper use of freedom.
- A discussion of other areas that might cause disagreements or division within the church today, such as church liturgy, the importance of sacraments and religious rites and the role of faith.
- A consideration of how the central gospel message brings broad agreement, unity and inspiration to the Christian Church.

RELEVANCE FOR TODAY

Use the diagram below for ideas to explore the relevance of Galatians for the 21st century.

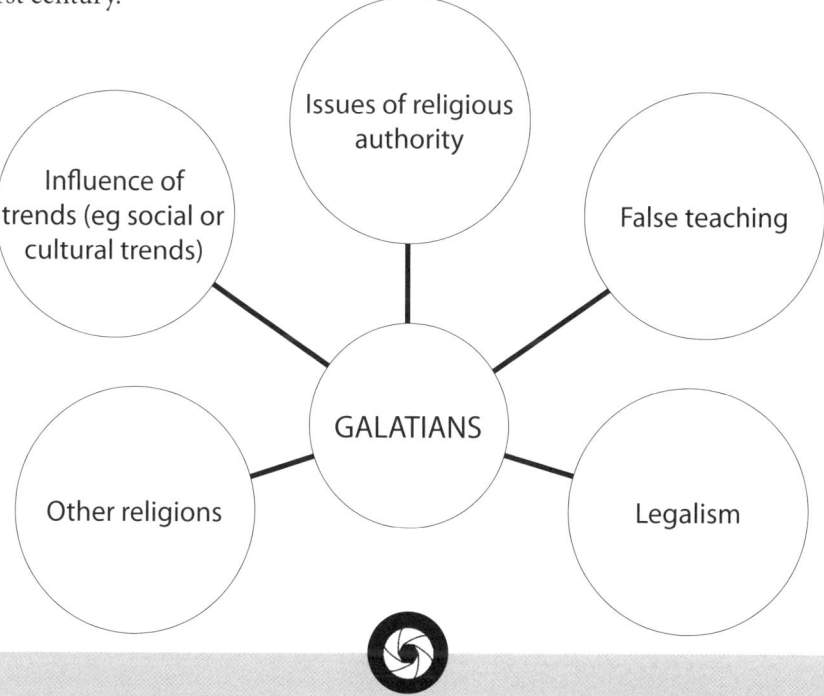

BY THE END OF THIS CHAPTER YOU SHOULD BE ABLE TO:

- demonstrate knowledge and understanding of, and critically evaluate the context of the Letter, including:
  - the social and historical context of Galatians;
  - the reasons for Paul writing and the issues which developed in Galatia following the First Missionary Journey (1:1–2:21); and
  - examination of Paul's main themes in the Letter and how these relate to his intended audience; and
- demonstrate knowledge and understanding of, and critically evaluate Paul's teaching to the Galatians, including:
  - Paul's teaching on justification by faith and the purpose of the Law (3:1–5:6);
  - life in the Spirit and Christian freedom (5:7–6:10);
  - the value of this text for the Early Church; and
  - theological and ethical content and importance of codes for living.

Paul's First Letter to the Corinthians

Section 1:
The Issues Arising in Corinth

PURPOSE

You will recall from the AS course that Acts provides us with information about the founding of the church at Corinth (Acts 18). We learn no more until the Corinthian correspondence, a series of letters, some of which are lost. Therefore, in order to try to work out what happened in Corinth after Paul left, we have to rely upon the information Paul provides as he writes.

Most scholars are agreed that the Corinthian correspondence is something like this:

1. Paul's first letter, which is either completely lost, or else a fragment of it is in 2 Corinthians (6:14–7:1).

2. The Corinthians' own letter to Paul, which is mentioned in 1 Corinthians 7:1, also now lost.

3. 1 Corinthians, written by Paul in answer to their letter, and part of the New Testament.

4. The 'severe' letter mentioned in 2 Corinthians 2:4 and 7:8, and probably preserved in 2 Corinthians 10–13.

5. The 'letter of reconciliation' that forms 2 Corinthians 1–9.

THE CONTEXT OF THE LETTER

After Paul left Corinth, things did not go well there. During Paul's three-year stay at Ephesus, he heard disturbing news about the church at Corinth. He wrote to them immediately, warning them about the dangers of immorality. After this, "Chloe's people" brought more reports to Paul, this time to tell him that the members of the church at Corinth were splitting into opposing parties. (Davies, 1962, p17, tells us that Chloe was a leading lady in the

Above: A map showing the location of Corinth

church at Corinth.) Not only that, but Paul's own authority as an apostle was being questioned. These reports were also confirmed by Stephanas and some others who carried a letter from the Corinthian Church to Paul, asking him for guidance over certain pressing issues (Morris, 1996, p25). 1 Corinthians was probably Paul's reply. A number of the issues that Paul deals with in the letter give an idea of the purpose of 1 Corinthians.

To warn the Corinthians of the danger of divisions

Society in Corinth was varied, in that people came from many different spiritual and intellectual backgrounds. Even so, while in Corinth with the young church, Paul was able to hold the congregation together. However, after he left, the new Christians tried to work out their new faith for themselves, with the result that they began to come up with different answers and ideas.

They had divided into four groups, which reflected the different backgrounds they had come from. Some claimed that they owed their spiritual allegiance to Paul, others to Apollos, others to Peter, and others to Christ. Paul's followers, the 'libertines', encouraged their fellow Christians not to worry about immorality. Those who followed Peter, the 'legalists', asked whether Christians could eat food that had been previously offered to idols. Apollos' followers were convinced that they possessed a wisdom that was superior to anything Paul preached. Finally, the 'mystics', who claimed to follow Christ himself, insisted that they had reached a spiritual level that was superior to the other believers.

One of Paul's purposes in writing to the Corinthians was, therefore, to deal with the confusion that had arisen as a result of these divisions in the church. He knew that the answer could not be found in himself, or Peter, or Apollos, or even the kind of Christ that was being promoted. 1 Corinthians attempts to provide an answer.

Petty arguments were also a cause for division in Corinth. Some Christians were having arguments and then going to pagan courts to sort out their grievances. As well as being upset that arguments were happening at all, Paul was concerned that they were going outside the church for help.

To encourage the believers to avoid immorality

Paul was worried about maintaining morality in the church at Corinth. For example, it emerged that a man was having a sexual relationship with his step-mother. Paul had to warn the Corinthians about the seriousness of this sin. His main argument is that freedom in Christ does not mean freedom to be immoral.

To encourage order in worship

Paul wrote to stress the importance of respect and order in church worship services. For some of the believers at Corinth, the *agape* meal, which took place alongside the Lord's Supper, had been turned into an excuse to have a party and get drunk. This was not appropriate behaviour for the celebration of the Lord's Supper.

Another problem was the Corinthians' desire for the more glamorous spiritual gifts, such as speaking in tongues. The ability to speak in tongues had led to chaos in services, where people were all using their gift at the same time. Paul felt that this was definitely not the way to behave, and wrote to advise the believers about how to bring more order into their worship services.

CHARACTERISTICS AND MAIN THEMES
A personal letter

Paul's First Letter to the Corinthians is a very personal letter, probably because of the deep attachment Paul had to the Corinthians following his long stay with them (Acts 18). Foreman (1961, p62) comments that Paul had good reason to know the Corinthian Church, its members and its problems. He had founded the church himself from nothing at all. The Corinthian letters were written to personal friends in a situation Paul knew very well. Paul felt a strong responsibility for their spiritual development. Prior comments that "because of his deep attachment to the Christians in Corinth, Paul was bound to put pen to paper when strange teachings began to divide the church" (1993, p17).

A pastoral letter

"The letters to the Corinthians are long and reveal a continuing discussion, perhaps over a long period of time, between Paul and the church at Corinth" (Freed, 2005, p64). 1 Corinthians stands out as being a pastoral letter and provides some very practical advice and guidance, particularly on moral issues and issues of public worship. Much of Paul's teaching is still relevant today. Another feature is that, on occasion, Paul gives his own advice if he does not have a direct command from God (for example, 7:25).

Theological guidance

In 1 Corinthians Paul is interested in giving theological guidance, as well as practical advice on certain issues. Hafemann comments that "it is striking that most of the commands throughout 1 Corinthians centre on some aspect of Church unity" (1993, p178). This comes in the form of teaching on divisions (chapters 1–4), lawsuits (chapter 6), the true meaning of the Lord's Supper (chapter 11) and the unity of the Spirit (chapters 12–14).

The Corinthians are both "the temple of the Holy Spirit" (3:16–17; 14:24–25) and the "body of Christ" (6:17; 10:17; 11:29; 12:12–16, 27). While the Kingdom of God has arrived, it is not yet here in all its fullness. Therefore, Paul stresses throughout this letter the importance of Christians having control over their own moral lives.

Warnings

Warnings are another characteristic of 1 Corinthians. Paul warns the Corinthians to stand firm in their faith. He refers to "the present crisis" in chapter 7; he refers to those who oppose him and oppose his teaching; and he ends the letter with a plea to the Corinthians to "be alert, stand firm in your faith".

TASK

Complete the following table explaining the main themes covered in 1 Corinthians.

	Main Themes	List the issues
1 Corinthians 1–6	Chs 1–6 deal with the concerns Paul heard of independently from the Corinthian Church. He heard of these problems from "Chloe's family" (Ch 1:11). It is significant that Paul feels the need to address these issues first before considering the issues in their letter.	
1 Corinthians 7–14	Chs 7–14 deal with issues they wrote to Paul about, seeking advice.	
1 Corinthians 15	Ch 15 is Paul's response to sceptics who denied an important doctrine.	

PROBLEMS ARISING IN THE CORINTHIAN CHURCH
Issues raised by Paul

Paul was concerned with the disturbing news that had come to him from Chloe's people concerning divisions, immorality and lawsuits. Moffat explains that "the Church was in the world, as it had to be, but the world was in the Church, as it ought not to be" (1938, pxv). In the first six chapters of 1 Corinthians Paul deals with this news before moving on to write an answer to the letter from the church at Corinth.

Unity (Chs 1–4)
Divisions in the church (Ch 1:10–17)

Following his greeting to the church at Corinth and his usual thanksgiving, Paul launches into the report received from Chloe's people. No information is given about Chloe, but she was probably a wealthy woman with servants. He warns them that if their quarrelling continues "outright division might be the result" (Bruce, 1992, p32).

Morris (1996, p39) explains that the condition of the Corinthian Church was far from what it should have been. Paul challenges the issue of disunity within the Christian community, which had arisen through preference being shown for different key figures or teachers. "Clearly the trouble was widespread, and cliques had appeared, each attaching itself to a favourite teacher" (Morris, p40). These cliques or groups were refusing to have fellowship with each other and there was clear disagreement between them.

1. The Paul Party

   Many of the Corinthians had become Christians through listening to Paul's preaching and as a result they were very attached to Paul. They clung on to every word he said as the ultimate truth and probably regarded other teachers as second best compared to Paul.

2. The Apollos Party

   As you will remember from your AS study, Apollos came to Corinth during Paul's Third Missionary Journey (Acts 18:24–19:7). He was a very intelligent man and an excellent speaker, which explains why he, too, had a group of devoted followers. Prior (1993, p32) comments that while Apollos probably did not stay that long in Corinth, he was there long enough for some to start comparing him favourably to Paul.

3. The Peter or Cephas Party

   Peter had been a Christian longer than both Paul and Apollos. He had emerged as the leader of the twelve apostles, and in Acts we see that he seems to have been more at home with the Jewish Law than Paul. Barrett argues that it seems to be generally accepted that "the Cephas-group represented Jewish Christianity in some form" (1968, p44). The temptation to return to the Law seems to have been strong among some of the Christians at Corinth. For example, in chapters 8–10, there is a debate about whether or not a Christian should eat food that has previously been offered to idols.

4. The Christ Party

   This group of believers looked upon Christ as their only leader and they were probably opposed to any human leadership in the church. They regarded themselves as super-spiritual and their presence may have made other Christians in Corinth feel spiritually inferior.

Paul was not prepared to ignore the potential divisiveness that these groups might create. Making a strong appeal (1:10), he stresses that unity is essential to the church and develops his argument in three steps:

1. Is Christ divided?
   This is an example of a 'rhetorical' question, because the Corinthians know that the answer is 'no'. Christ is no more divided than a person's body is divided. "Christ is one, and the Church, which is his body, must be one" (Morris, p41).

> **What is a 'rhetorical' question?**
>
> It is question that is not really looking for an answer. For example, your friend might walk into your house on a cold winter's day wearing a jumper, coat and hat. If you say to them, "It's cold outside, isn't it?" you are really stating the obvious rather than looking for an answer. Other rhetorical questions include "Who do they think they are?", "Who cares?" and "Who knows?" We ask them, but we are not really expecting an answer.

2. Was Paul crucified for you?
   Again the answer to this question is a resounding 'no'. Morris explains that "the Corinthians, with their emphasis on wisdom, seem to have overlooked the truth that Christ's cross is absolutely central" (1996, p41). Prior (1993, p36) argues that Paul is challenging the Corinthians to drop their personality cults and to fix their attention on "Jesus Christ and him crucified." It was Jesus who had died to save them, not Paul or Apollos or Peter.

3. Were you baptised in the name of Paul?
   The obvious answer is again 'no'. They had obviously forgotten that they had been baptised into Jesus' name alone. Prior (1993, p37) explains that when a person was baptised in someone's name his life was regarded as being signed over to that person. Paul was simply thankful that he had carried out few baptisms in Corinth, as he was adamant that Christ was central, and no individual man.

Divine and secular wisdom (Ch 1:18–31)

Paul continues his argument by focusing on something that the Corinthians had come to value: wisdom. Morris describes this as "worldly wisdom that they so admired and that was so ineffective" (1996, p43). It seems that by focusing on the importance of individual leaders in the church, the Corinthians were also placing more value on the wisdom of the world rather than on the wisdom of God. Prior argues that to Paul "the wisdom of the world seemed to arise clearly out of man's rebellion against God" (1993, p40).

Paul not only rejected this wisdom but also the way it was proclaimed. For example, Barclay explains that "the Greeks were intoxicated with fine words" (1954, p22).Christians in Corinth were equally becoming impressed with how eloquently a leader could speak. Barrett explains they were "glorying in men and wrongly evaluating their gifts" (1968, p59). Paul valued changed lives, holiness, faith and love, not the ability to take part in vain discussion or eloquent persuasion.

Paul explains how God's wisdom seems to be beneath the sophisticated Corinthians with their worldly wisdom. The worldly-wise despised the message of the cross. The Jews regarded it as a stumbling block and the Greeks saw it as a scandal, because "cursed is everyone who hangs on a tree" (cf Gal 3:13–14). They believed it was unwise to believe that the Messiah could be crucified. Paul, however, insists that through Christ's crucifixion salvation is possible (v 18). Until the worldly-wise stop relying on their own insight, they will never receive God's wisdom in Christ.

Paul illustrates God's power by reminding his readers that many of the people God had chosen were, from a worldly point of view, unimportant (v 26). Prior explains that God is shunning the notion that those who matter most to him are "the wise, the well-bred, the articulate, the gifted, the wealthy, the wielders of power and influence" (1993, p46). There is no room for pride in the Christian Church. God's reason was that no one would have anything to boast about, except in the Lord (v 30).

How Paul preached the gospel (Ch 2:1–5)
Paul reminds his readers of his arrival at Corinth "in weakness and fear and with much trembling" (v 3). Bruce explains that this may have been due to "a sense of complete personal inadequacy in view of the task of evangelizing such a city as Corinth" (1992, p37).

Paul reminds the Corinthians that when he first preached to them he did not use fine and eloquent words or philosophical arguments to try to persuade them. "It had been a plain, unvarnished setting forth of the simple gospel" (Morris, 1996, p50). He simply told them about the crucifixion of Jesus, which he regarded as being at the heart of the gospel. They were convinced by what he said because "he was inspired by God, not because of his own human wisdom" (Thrall, 1965, p23). Prior (1993, p49) comments that in his preaching Paul relied completely on the power of the Spirit. Morris (1996, p52) also notes that Paul's intention had been to make the Corinthians independent of human wisdom.

The ministry of the Spirit (Ch 2:6–13)

Prior (1993, p49) writes that "the work of the Holy Spirit is stressed repeatedly in chapter 2." While Paul rejects human wisdom, he does not reject all wisdom. God's wisdom is superior to worldly wisdom. It is simply that Jesus has been crucified and has been revealed as the Son of God and the Saviour of the world. However, God's wisdom has only been revealed by the Holy Spirit to those who love him. In other words "it is not the learned philosophers but the humble Christians to whom God's truth has been revealed" (Prior, 1993, p56). The fact that the wisdom has been revealed prevents any feelings of superiority or pride among the believers.

Three kinds of men (Ch 2:14–3:4)

Paul speaks to three different kinds of men. At the lowest level is the "natural" or "unspiritual" man (2:14) who refuses to hear the gospel message. Next in line are those who are young in their Christian faith, "infants in Christ" (3:1). At the top of the scale are mature Christians. It is only to these Christians that God's wisdom can be truly revealed. The Christians at Corinth fall into the second category. They had received the Spirit, but they did not live as those who had received him. Splitting into opposing groups to follow 'Paul' or 'Apollos' was not a spiritual activity (Bruce, 1992, p42). Davies (1962, p25) explains that God's wisdom is not revealed to such people who are quarrelsome and jealous "because they have stunted their own growth by their foolishness and selfishness." Whereas Christians should be considerate of others, the Corinthians were asserting themselves and acting like the natural or unspiritual person (Morris, 1996, p62). God's wisdom is a spiritual wisdom that can only be taught by the Holy Spirit. "Maturity comes from growth and development" (Morris, 1996, p61).

Example of planting and watering (Ch 3:5–8)

Apollos and Paul were Christ's servants, performing the tasks assigned to them. Paul uses the example of a plant. Paul planted and Apollos watered, but neither of them made the plant grow. Prior (1993, p57) explains that both activities are vital and each depends on the other. However, only God enabled the plant to grow (Morris, 1996, p63). Both men need to work hard and in the end they will be rewarded. The point of these verses seems to be to play down the importance of individual leaders. Therefore, the implication is that the Corinthian Christians should stop following different individuals but work together.

Example of foundations and buildings (Ch 3:9–15)
Paul asserts his own apostolic authority as the founder of the church at Corinth. God enabled Paul to lay a strong foundation for a church at Corinth by proclaiming the gospel (Thrall, 1965, p31). Paul himself was not the foundation stone, as some thought (Paul party); rather Christ was the foundation of the church at Corinth. Paul warns that all those involved in the life of the church at Corinth were responsible for the quality of their own contribution; he is "warning those who are now teaching and influencing his converts that the worth of what they are doing will eventually be judged" (Thrall, 1965, p32).

Paul looks to the day when every Christian's work will be revealed for all to see. Prior (1993, p59) explains that it will not be a matter of how successful, or effective, or popular or commended they are by men. Will their work be shown to be what God has done through the Holy Spirit or what they have done in their own power and for their own benefit? Those who use "gold, silver and costly stones", that is, quality materials, will be rewarded with profitable work. However, those who resort to using "wood, hay or straw" will achieve nothing.

A personal warning (Ch 3:16–17)
Thrall (1965, pp32–33) argues that Paul probably has the different cliques in Corinth in mind in these verses. Intentional damage to the life of the church can be compared to desecrating a temple. Guilty people will be judged by God himself. Morris agrees, stating that "to engage in making divisions is … to invite God to destroy the sinner" (1996, p67). (The Corinthian Church was a temple that God's Spirit indwelt. Paul was not speaking here of individual believers being temples of God, although he later refers to individual Christians as such.)

The foolishness of worldly wisdom (Ch 3:18–23)
Paul reflects upon the pretentiousness of those in Corinth who claim to have a wisdom superior to others. He reminds them of the inferiority of human wisdom. There is no place for pride in the church, no matter how gifted, successful or eloquent a person might be. It is a mistake to "exaggerate the importance of one or another of the apostles and set him up on a pedestal" (Thrall, 1965, p33). All of the leaders, he argues – Paul, Apollos and Peter – belong to the church at Corinth. Furthermore, all the Corinthian believers belong to Christ, not just those of the 'Christ party' (1:12). They belong to Christ, not to one of his servants. Even Christ belongs to God in the sense of being under his authority and protection (cf. 8:6; 11:3; 15:28).

> **Relevance for today (Ch 1–3)**
>
> - Factions can still be very common in individual churches today. This practice not only hinders Christian growth and development, but can lead to envy and jealousy.
> - Factions are still common in the worldwide church, as seen in the different denominations; the Ecumenical Movement, an initiative that seeks to foster unity between different churches, was formally started in 1910 at the World Missionary Conference.

Servants and stewards (Ch 4:1–7)

"Being man-centred, the Corinthians were giving their allegiance to men, men of God, but only men" (Prior, 1993, p62). Paul regards such men simply as Christ's servants and as such they are expected to be trustworthy. Paul stresses that they are not responsible to anyone but Christ for the quality of their work. Pointing to his own humble attitude regarding his own importance, Paul warns his converts "against the pride and spiritual arrogance which leads them not only to flout (ignore) an apostle of whom they disapprove but also to patronise the one whom they profess to support" (Thrall, 1965, p35). Paul comments that if a man deserves to be commended for his work, then the Lord will commend him.

The Christians in Corinth even saw the gifts of God as grounds for boasting (Prior, 1993, p64). It is ridiculous to take pride in one man over against another because all true ministry in the church is given by God.

The trials endured by the Apostles (Ch 4:8–13)

Paul highlights the trials the apostles have endured and their despised position in society. He condemns the pride and arrogant attitude of the Corinthians. The real consequences of being Christians are suffering and humiliation. This too should be the case for the Corinthians if their faith is genuine.

Fathers and children (Ch 4:14–21)

"Paul writes as a father who is concerned for the welfare of his children" (Thrall, 1965, p37). He did not mean this in a dominant way, but rather that it was through him that they became Christians, and he felt responsible for them. Many of the Christians in Corinth had become arrogant, dismissing Paul and his ministry and causing division in Corinth.

>
>
> ## TASK
> **With reference to 1 Corinthians, critically discuss Paul's teaching on 'Unity in Christ'.**
>
> Your answer may include a critical discussion of some of the following, for example:
> - Reports from Chloe's people about the divisions in the church at Corinth.
> - Paul's own authority as an Apostle was being questioned by some in Corinth and the church had written to Paul for advice on certain issues. 1 Corinthians is Paul's reply to these issues.
> - Reasons for division: Corinth was characterised by people of many different spiritual and intellectual backgrounds. Such people had brought very different concepts and ideas into the church. After Paul's departure, these new Christians began to divide.
> - Divisions over Leadership (Chs 1–4).
> - Paul's frustration over divisions regarding leadership in the church. He encourages the Corinthians to "be completely united, with only one thought and one purpose."(Ch 1 v11).
> - Four different groups: spiritual allegiance to Paul, Apollo, Cephas (Peter) and Christ. Paul knew that the answer to the Corinthian's situation lay in Christ (Ch 1 v13). Paul wanted to show the Corinthians that neither he, nor Cephas, nor Apollos, nor the kind of Christ that was being followed, could actually achieve any lasting result.
> - The foolishness of being impressed by human wisdom.

Section 2:
Christian moral living

PAUL'S TEACHING ON MORAL LIVING FOR CHRISTIANS
Immorality (Chs 5–6)
Sexual Sin (Ch 5:1–5)
Paul turns his attention to the issue of sexual sin. While the Jews had very high standards regarding sexual morality, it was a different case in the rest of society, especially among the Greeks. It seems Paul has just heard a report of

'a particularly scandalous' incident of a sexual sin in the church at Corinth. A member of the congregation was having an affair with his stepmother. This was a form of incest that was not only condemned by the Law of Moses (Leviticus 18:8), but was prohibited by Roman law and even frowned upon by pagans. Not only had the church at Corinth turned a blind eye, but they did not seem bothered about it and were continuing with their superior attitude.

"Since the woman is not mentioned, she was probably not a Christian" (Murphy-O'Connor, 1989, p803). Paul insists that this man should be excommunicated because of his sin. His removal should take the form of a solemn act of excommunication at a special meeting of the church (Bruce, 1992, p54). When Paul says, "hand this man over to Satan, so that the sinful nature may be destroyed" (v 5), he may be implying something similar to the discipline of Ananias and Sapphira. Davies (1962, p50) argues that Paul was not being vindictive here, but was calling for such harsh action for the sinner's own benefit. He explains that the man would realise the consequences of his actions, and would be more likely to repent and be restored to salvation.

Call to clean out all evil (Ch 5:6–8)
Paul warns the Corinthians (v 6) that by allowing this situation to continue there was a danger that the sinner would have a bad influence on the rest of the congregation: "even if only one member of the church is involved his conduct will rapidly influence the rest, just as only a very small amount of yeast is necessary to leaven a large lump of dough" (Thrall, 1965, p41).

Paul continues with the example of baking. He compares the Corinthians to a new batch of dough with no yeast. However, to ensure their complete purity, they must get rid of any old yeast that might still be there. Like yeast having an effect on dough, sin can spread until it affects the whole church. Now that they have become Christians and left behind their pagan ways, the Corinthians must not bring back sinful ways (the old yeast) into the church. Paul refers to Christ as the "Passover lamb" to remind the Corinthians that Christ's death was a sacrifice for them.

A misunderstanding (Ch 5:9–13)
There seems to have been some confusion among the Corinthians concerning whom they were allowed to associate with. Some thought it meant they were not allowed to mix with pagans. However, many of the Christians – for example, slaves in pagan households or workmen – "would lose their jobs if they took absolutely literally the injunction to have nothing to do with people who were leading immoral lives" (Thrall, 1965, pp41–42). Paul explains that he

meant they were to avoid professing Christians who were "sexually immoral or greedy, an idolater or a slanderer, a drunkard or a swindle" (Ch 5:11).

Sexual immorality (Ch 6:12–20)

Some scholars argue that this passage refers to prostitution, which would have been acceptable in secular society at that time. Paul, however, is shocked that Christians would think that they were allowed to be promiscuous or sexually immoral. Using the experience of the Corinthians, Paul outlines four reasons why Christians should not be sexually immoral:

1. It seems the Christians in Corinth were under the impression that being free from the Law meant freedom to do whatever they liked. Paul agrees that a Christian is free, but suggests that a genuine Christian will only act in a way that is beneficial to the Christian life. Freedom should build people up, not destroy.
2. The Corinthians thought that sexual intercourse was a natural function of the body, like eating or drinking. They completely separated sex from the spiritual life. "Since food and stomach alike will pass away, why attach religious importance to either – or, for that matter, to sexual relations?" (Bruce, 1992, p63). Paul argues that natural functions like eating or drinking will come to an end. However, he did not think that sex should be equated with such natural functions because sex 'involved' the body. By the word 'body', Paul included the whole personality, which he argued will continue after the body dies. "But sexual relations were on a completely different footing; they affected the personalities of the parties involved as food did not" (Bruce, 1992, p63). He refers to Christ's resurrection (v 14) and the eventual resurrection of Christians. God's care for the body would be shown by its resurrection. "If our bodies are to be raised, God must attach importance to actions performed in and through the body" (Murphy-O'Connor, p804). Therefore, the Christian should not take part in immorality.
3. Paul stresses that Christians are united with Christ. Therefore, it is outrageous to suggest that it is fine for Christians to also connect their personalities with prostitutes.
4. Finally, Paul makes the point that Christians' bodies and their whole personalities are temples of the Holy Spirit. Christians have given their bodies over to Christ. Their bodies now belong to Christ, not to them, and as such should be treated with respect.

ISSUES RAISED BY THE CORINTHIANS

"In replying to the Corinthian letter (Ch 7:1) Paul deals with a wide variety of questions, but the treatment is not haphazard" (Murphy-O'Connor, 1989, p804). He deals first with problems of social status (7:1–40), then with those arising from contact with the pagan environment (8:1–11:1 not on the A2 course), and finally with those relating to worship services (11:2–14:4). His tone and treatment are modified according to the nature of the problem.

Marriage (Ch 7:1–40)

The transition from chapter 6 to chapter 7 shows how Paul had to deal with two extremes. In chapter 6 he was dealing with the 'libertines' who believed that everything was allowed and had immoral views and potentially damaging views regarding sex. In chapter 7 we see Paul dealing with the 'ascetics', who spoke against every kind of sexual relationship, even that within marriage.

Advice to the married (Ch 7:1–7)

The sexual freedom that was part of the Corinthian way of life, and from which even the church in Corinth was not immune, made some members of the church feel that sex should be avoided altogether (Bruce, 1977, p266). Murphy-O'Connor explains that certain Corinthians even "idealistically believed that married couples should abstain from sexual relations" (1989, p804). They summed up their view in the statement that 'It is good for a man not to marry'. Bruce (1977, p267) explains that some of these Corinthians confidently expected Paul to agree with this. They knew of his preference for the celibate life, and thought that he would applaud this preference in his converts.

It is true that Paul seems to regard the ability to remain single as a gift from God. However, he stresses that if a Christian does not have that gift then it is better to marry. "Monogamy, he says, not celibacy, is the norm for Christians" (Bruce, 1977, p267). So unless a person had a special vocation for celibacy, then any attempt to try to remain celibate was against nature and would expose them to the very kind of sexual temptation they detested.

Paul continued, stressing that within marriage a couple should fulfil each other's sexual needs. It is not fair to deprive the Christian man or wife of sex, except if both have agreed to abstain so that they can devote themselves to prayer. Paul adds that the couple should only agree to this for a time, in case Satan tempts them to go looking elsewhere for sex. Paul is aware that as far as sex is concerned some people may struggle with a lack of self-control. "After the agreed period of abstinence they should resume normal relations: to adopt any other course would be to court disaster" (Bruce, 1977, p267).

Advice to the unmarried (Ch 7:8–9)

Again Paul recommends the single life. However, if a person feels they cannot commit themselves to a life without sex then it is best that he or she looks for a marriage partner.

Murphy-O'Connor explains: "The single have a choice, which must be based on practical consideration. Flaming frustrated passion is a hindrance to Christian living" (1989, p804).

Divorce forbidden (Ch 7:10–11)

In this section Paul refers to Jesus' teaching, not his own. He commands Christians not to get divorced at all: "reconciliation, not estrangement, is the course for Christians" (Bruce, 1977, p268). If it does happen, then remarriage should not take place as long as the divorced partner is still alive.

Mixed marriages (Ch 7:12–16)

In Paul's time it was very common to find a Christian married to a pagan. Some Christians might have wondered if cohabitation with a pagan would pollute the faith of the Christian. Paul argues, however, that if the pagan partner is willing to stay in the marriage then the Christian should not ask for a divorce, because there was the possibility "that the pagan partner might be won for the gospel through the other's witness: such a marriage had missionary potentialities" (Bruce, 1977, p268). So to divorce a pagan partner is to deny them the chance of being saved. Paul also argues that continued cohabitation with a Christian would 'sanctify' the pagan, and the children of such a union would share in that 'sanctification'. What do you think he means by this? It may mean that the pagan husband now belongs to God through the faith of his Christian wife and vice versa. Their children also belong to God. This highlights the importance of the Christian family for Paul.

Calling and status (Ch 7:17–24)

Paul is stressing in these verses that a Christian should not try to change their status in life when he or she becomes a Christian. For example, a slave should not go out of their way to become free, although if freedom is offered they should take it. It is important to realise that Paul is not supporting the system of slavery. He is simply using this as an illustration of how one ought to be content with what one has. Murphy-O'Connor explains that "no change, therefore, will raise one in God's estimation" (1989, p805).

Virgins (Ch 7:25–38)

It should be noted that this passage is dominated by the fact that Paul thought that the end of the world was going to happen within his own lifetime. So he is giving advice with that in mind. Therefore, he advises single people to remain single and married people not to look for a divorce. He is asking Christians to take their minds off worldly matters and to concentrate on Jesus' return. He points out that living in such times a person is at an advantage if he or she is not married. A married man, for example, has the responsibility of looking after his family. The same applies to a married woman. However, the unmarried can devote themselves to God.

Verses 36–38 are quite difficult to understand. It seems that at Paul's time there was a practice in existence where a man would marry a "spiritual bride" (Davies, 1962, p57). Such an arrangement involved getting married but agreeing to abstain from sex altogether, the idea being that it was an act of self-control. Other scholars (for example, Bruce, 1977, p76) view these verses differently, arguing that they probably refer to the practice of 'betrothal'. Should a virgin who was engaged to be married stay as she was, that is, not get married? After all, it was common belief that the end of the world was going to happen very soon. Paul does not pass any judgment one way or the other.

Widows (Ch 7:39–40)

Paul explains that the situation regarding remarriage is slightly different for a widow. She is not forbidden to remarry, although her new husband must also be a Christian.

Relevance for today (Ch 7)

Paul's teaching in this chapter emphasises that the idea of celibacy is not out-dated today. Many people feel that celibacy is a calling from God and a way to devote their whole lives to serving him. This is seen today in the Catholic Church, where priests do not marry and remain celibate, enabling them to serve God without the worry of a wife and family. However, some people today feel it is inappropriate to place celibacy higher in Christian values than marriage, and think both should be complementary.

Paul did recognise benefits in marriage, such as providing the appropriate context for sexual relationships. Many people uphold the value of this teaching today, as moral standards are arguably often low in our society.

With regard to divorce, Paul was not in favour of divorce, and taught that couples should try to remain together if at all possible. However, he did allow divorce if a believer was married to an unbeliever.

TASK

With reference to 1 Corinthians, critically discuss Paul's understanding of marriage and the single life.

Your answer may include a critical discussion of some of the following, for example:

- Paul is replying to a letter he received from them seeking advice on issues relating to marriage.
- Paul makes it clear that he favours the state of celibacy: "A man does well not to marry" (7:1); a man can give his undivided devotion to God without the distraction of a family.
- The influence of ascetics in Corinth, a group who denied themselves physical pleasures, including sexual relations. Paul disagrees, promoting marriage as a means of avoiding sexual immorality.
- Paul accepts that a couple may wish to refrain from sexual activity for a while in order to devote themselves to prayer; this should only be a temporary arrangement and is not a command from him.
- God's intention was that divorce should not occur; accepts that it does and so discourages remarriage; there should always be the hope of reconciliation.
- Advice to those Christians who have become converted whilst married and whose partner is therefore not a Christian; the Christian partner's faith will have a 'holy influence' over their non-Christian partner and any children.
- Paul regards both marriage and singleness as gifts from God.
- Paul's advice to those who believed that because they were now a Christian they had to radically change their circumstances in relation to marriage.

A question of conscience (8:1–13 and 10:14–11:1)
Meat sacrificed to idols (Ch 8: 1–13)

One of the problems brought to Paul by letter, by the three elders Stephanus, Fortunatus and Achaicus, concerned meat that had been offered to idols. The Christians in Corinth wanted to know if it was acceptable for them to eat it. This was an issue for many believers in Greek and Roman cities, and was a particular problem in Corinth, as this was a city full of idols and temples. According to McGrath, "At least twelve pagan temples were known to have been in existence around this time, although not all may have been used for worship of this kind" (1995, p338). The problem of meat that had been sacrificed to idols was one facing all Christians in Corinth, for the following reasons:

- A large number of animals were sacrificed on a daily basis in these temples. Thrall explains that "Priests and worshippers at a sacrifice would ceremonially eat part of the animal and then the rest of the carcass would be disposed of by selling it to the butchers" (1965, p61). Therefore a Christian might unknowingly buy meat from a shop, not knowing whether the animal had been slaughtered in a pagan temple.

- A person might be invited to a social function where the meat might have come from a pagan temple. To avoid any possibility of eating this meat, Christians in Corinth would have to cut themselves off completely from the rest of society.

Paul's initial comments on this issue concern the difference between acting out of knowledge and acting out of love: "Knowledge puffs up, but love builds up" (Ch 8:1). Paul is stating that whereas knowledge can lead to pride, acting out of love towards another Christian can help to give that person confidence.

In verses 4–6 Paul explains what he means. Some Christians look at the problem of meat offered to idols logically and say that there is only one God who made the world and is Father of the Lord Jesus Christ. Therefore, there are no other gods and the meat is the product of a sacrifice to something non-existent. This is the argument based on knowledge, which Paul accepts. It is not a sin to eat meat from an animal that died on a pagan altar.

However, in verses 7–13, Paul gives a warning: not every Christian has this knowledge that an idol is nothing. Fee explains: "Some of the Corinthian believers are among those for whom the 'gods' and 'lords' were a genuine reality while they were pagans" (1987, p379). Christians who are strong in their faith and understand the non-existence of other gods must remember that the meat they eat or abstain from will not be called into question on judgement day. However, no-one is to lead another Christian astray by being seen to eat meat that has been offered in idol worship. Paul says that even if a strong Christian knows they are right, they must stop what they are doing if there is a danger of having a bad influence on a weaker Christian. According to Morris, "love rather than knowledge should be the Christian's determining consideration" (1996, p125). There is a serious implication here, as no-one should lead a person astray whom Christ has died for. Paul says that rather than do this he would "never eat meat again" (8:13).

Idol feasts and the Lord's Supper (Ch 10: 14–22)

After a digression where Paul speaks of his personal experiences, he returns to the topic of pagan sacrifices. Thrall (1965, pp3–4) considers whether Paul contradicts himself, as he appears to take a stricter view than in the previous section. However, there appear to be two main issues:

1. Is it permitted for Christians to eat meat that may have been sourced from a pagan temple? In the previous passage, Paul explains there is nothing wrong with this as long as one person's behaviour does not cause another to be led astray.

2. Are Christians allowed to go to a pagan temple and actually take part in the sacrifices? Paul's response to this question is that Christians are not to do this. He explains his reasons in this passage.

Eating meat from an unknown source is different from taking part in pagan worship, and Paul warns his readers to "flee from idolatry" (v 14). He then uses the examples of the Lord's Supper and Jewish sacrifices to explain why. Morris (1996, p145) comments that the Corinthians prided themselves on their wisdom, to which Paul now appeals with his arguments. When a believer takes part in the Lord's Supper, they share in the body and blood of Christ and are united with the other worshippers. This is similar to the Jewish sacrificial system where those who eat the sacrificed animal share in the offering to God. Paul explains that although an idol is non-existent, actually taking part in the worship can link the participants to demons. This is totally inappropriate for Christians who celebrate the Lord's Supper, as they cannot be linked to both Christ and demons, and Paul states: "You cannot drink the cup of the Lord and the cup of demons too" (v 21). Fee explains that "these words function both as a warning and a prohibition" (1987, pp472–473), as the person who participates in an idol feast is not merely eating with friends at a pagan temple, but taking part in idolatry. Paul's warning is contained in his rhetorical question, "Are we trying to arouse the Lord's jealousy?" (v 22). God will not tolerate idolatry.

Practical advice (Ch 10: 23–11:1)

Paul starts by affirming that Christians have freedom, in the sense that they no longer have to rely on laws as a means of salvation. However, Paul affirms that there is still a need for high standards of behaviour, as not everything is "beneficial" or "constructive" (v 23). In conclusion to the question of meat offered to idols, Paul sums up with the following practical advice:

Any meat that is sold in the market can be bought and eaten "without raising questions of conscience" (v 25).

If a Christian is at an unbeliever's house, the meat that is served may be eaten. However, if someone makes a point of saying that the meat had been offered in a pagan sacrifice, then it should not be eaten. This is to avoid any misunderstanding to those outside the church about what is appropriate behaviour for Christians (v 27–28). Eating the meat will not have an effect on the Christian guest but it may have an effect on the others present.

Whatever a person eats or drinks, they should "do it all for the glory of God" (v 31).

Paul comments that he always puts the needs of others before his own in an attempt to save as many people as possible. Therefore, his readers should be careful not to "cause anyone to stumble" (v 32). McGrath comments that "the Christian life is corporate, and this means that individual believers must pay attention to the scruples and concerns of others" (1995, p339).

Paul's final advice is: "Follow my example as I follow the example of Christ" (11:1).

> ### Relevance for today
>
> These passages emphasise that it is important not to insist on your individual rights if another person will suffer; Christians should consider what effect their behaviour may have on others, even though they may not be doing anything wrong. It is important to try and set a good example.
>
> There is nothing wrong with acting out of knowledge, when a person knows they are not doing anything wrong. However, in some situations it may be better to consider others and act out of love.

GUIDANCE FOR CHURCH LIFE AND WORSHIP
Worship and Lord's Supper (Ch 11:2–26)
The veiling of women (Ch 11:2–16)

While Paul was pleased that the Corinthians had remembered to practise the teachings he had passed on to them, he was concerned, however, about another matter. It seems that a group of women were participating in the church services with their heads uncovered (11:5). In other words, they were not wearing a veil, which was the custom for women when they were in public. Freed (2005, p79) explains that although women were allowed to pray and prophesy in public worship, Paul's Jewish upbringing made it compulsory that they be veiled when doing so. These women may have felt that they were entitled to act like this because, in Christ, distinctions between male and female had been abolished (11:11–12; cf Galatians 3:28). Not only that, but since they had received the same Spirit of prophecy (11:5) as the men, they regarded themselves as equal to them. So prophesying bare headed was an expression of such perceived equality.

The problem with the behaviour of these women was related to wider society in Corinth. Their action could be interpreted by outsiders as an attempt to undermine the conventions or traditions of society, which would present the church in a negative light and bring unwelcome criticism upon it. Davies explains that "it is probably true, although not stated, that for a woman not to wear a cover for her head indicated that her reputation was dubious" (1962, p76). Guy agrees, commenting that "a woman without a veil on her head would arouse suspicion on her moral character" (1969, p104).

The reason for this is that:

> "Women's hair was a prime object of male lust in the ancient Mediterranean world; societies which employed head coverings thus viewed uncovered married women as unfaithful to their husbands, that is, seeking another man (virgins and prostitutes, conversely, were expected not to cover their heads since they were looking for men). Women who covered their heads could thus view uncovered women as a threat." (Keener, 1993, p585)

Paul deals with this issue in three ways:
1. He stresses the divine pattern of relationships. Aside from the fact that in Christ there is no difference between male and female, Paul points to the fact that God is the 'head' of Christ, Christ is the 'head' of man, and man is the 'head' of women. This does not mean that one is superior over the other, but that one chooses to submit to the other.

Prior comments, for example, "as Christ chose to submit himself to his Father, so the wife should choose to submit herself to her husband" (1993, p181). The normal meaning of the word 'head' is origin or source. Man was created directly by God, whereas woman was made from man. Man was created to reflect God's glory (11:7), whereas woman was created for man, to reflect his glory (11:7 and 9).

Paul argues, therefore, that this order of relationships should be reflected in church worship. For a woman to abandon her head dress or veil, the symbol of her status as a woman in society, was regarded as a refusal to respect the position God had given man in creation. Not only would such action invite criticism from pagan society, but it would offend the angels who watched over the church.

2. Paul appeals to the need for respect. There should be no distractions in Christian worship (Prior, 1993, p181). It was not considered to be acceptable behaviour for a woman to "flout these standards and appear in public with her head uncovered" (Bruce, 1977, p107). Christian women were to cover their heads to ensure that there was freedom of worship for all present.

Bruce further stresses that "needless breaches of convention were to be discouraged" (1977, p107). In other words, Christians should not get people's backs up unnecessarily. They were already standing out as being different by following Christ. There was no point in them attracting negative attention. By not wearing a veil and letting her hair hang loose, a woman would be behaving like an adulteress (Prior, 1993, p181).

Some scholars argue that Paul's words are promoting a positive reason for the wearing of the veil. He stresses that people were created to bring glory to God (11:7–10). Bruce explains that in Christ a woman has received equal status with man: "she might pray or prophesy at meetings of the church, and her veil was a sign of this new authority" (1977, p106).

Other scholars, however, feel that the wearing of the veil could be interpreted as implying that a woman must have a sign of the authority her husband exercises over her. Davies (1962, p76) points to the practice at Jewish weddings where the bride keeps her head uncovered, to represent the freedom she still possesses; however, from the moment of marriage she wears a veil to show that her freedom has lessened. The action of wearing the veil is to show respect for her husband. Morris explains that long hair is a glory to a woman; as well as securing her own place of dignity and authority, at the same time "she recognises her subordination" (1996, p76). (Note that Paul in this passage is speaking about veils and not hats.)

3. Paul's third argument is an appeal to nature (11:14–15). In the world at the time it was natural for a man to have shorter hair than a woman. "Generally speaking, men have reflected the distinctions made in nature by using shorter hair styles than those of women" (Morris, 1996, p154). Some people wonder then why art portrays Christ and the disciples as having long hair. For example, look at daVinci's painting of the Last Supper. However, it must have been the case in Corinth, or else Paul would not have used such an argument.

Abuses during the Lord's Supper (Ch 11:17–22)

This passage focuses on abuses that were taking place during the celebration of the Lord's Supper. Foreman describes it as "a shocking and almost incredible picture of a church meeting which, Paul says, actually made the worshippers worse and not better" (1961, p95).

Paul had heard reports that divisions were developing in the congregation at Corinth due to behaviour during the Lord's Supper. In churches today the Lord's Supper or communion (Eucharist) usually takes place as part of a normal worship service. However, in Paul's day, the celebration of the Lord's Supper was divided into two parts. The first part, which only survived for a certain length of time in the Early Church, was called the 'love feast' or 'agape meal' (Jude v 12; 2 Peter 2:13). The idea was that believers coming to worship brought food and drink along with them, which would be pooled together and shared out equally among everyone present. After this meal, the second part of the celebration, the actual Lord's Supper, would take place. However, in Corinth, "when celebrating the Lord's supper some wealthy members of the church brought their own food and went off into a corner by themselves, eating and drinking in a carousing manner and ignoring those who were too poor to bring food" (Freed, 2005, p79).

Murphy-O'Connor explains that "only the wealthier members of the community could afford to arrive early and were concerned exclusively with the gratification of their own desires. Poorer members of the community might have worked all day without eating" (Murphy-O'Connor, 1989, p809). Davies describes how some of the wealthy believers would have eaten and drunk so much that by the time it came to celebrating the Lord's Supper 'they were not in a fit state to do so' (1962, p78).

The result was discrimination and disorder (Guy, 1969, p105), which led to social divisions in the church at Corinth. Paul could not praise them for their actions. Bruce explains that "selfish conduct was an outrage on the sacred occasion; those who participated in such an unworthy spirit, far from deriving any grace from their participation, were eating and drinking judgment upon themselves" (Bruce, 1977, p265). Paul regards the Lord's Supper as a solemn occasion, initiated by Jesus himself in remembrance of him, and it is to be observed accordingly (Freed, 2005, p79).

The true meaning of the Lord's Supper or Eucharist (Ch 11:23-26)

"In order to bring the point most vividly and properly home to his people, Paul reminds them of what happened on the original occasion of the Lord's Supper" (Davies, 1962, p78). Foreman comments that this is "among the most cherished and familiar passages of the entire Bible" (1961, p76). Paul gives the earliest account we have of the institution of the communal meal (Bruce, 1977, p265).

Paul's main point was made "by citing the tradition which he had received concerning the meal and which he had previously passed on to the church by word of mouth" (Marshall, 1993, p572). Paul reminds his readers that this teaching had been given to him from the Lord (11:23), perhaps through a vision. Whatever way it was received, Marshall believes it to have been "an accepted and authoritative tradition" (1993, p572). Therefore, anyone wanting to celebrate the Lord's Supper should observe it in the way that God expected.

The words of this tradition are known as 'the words of the institution'. Some scholars suggest they may in fact have been taken from the actual service used at Corinth. It provides a description of the Last Supper, which most scholars accept was the Passover meal celebrated once a year by Jews to remember the deliverance of their ancestors out of Egypt. For example, during the Passover meal it was normal for thanks to be given for the food (11:24), and Jesus, acting as host, had done this. The bread was then shared among the believers. When Jesus took bread (and wine) and distributed them to his disciples, he added that they were his "body" and "blood". The disciples were also told to repeat the practice in memory of Christ. Marshall suggests that "the meal was thus intended to be a memorial of his death, through which it would be proclaimed" (Marshall, 1993, p572).

In the Catholic church, the celebration of the Eucharist is the focal point of Mass. The *Catechism of the Catholic Church* refers to the Eucharist as "the source and the summit of the Christian life" (#1324) and regard it as a sacramental memorial of the passion and resurrection of Jesus. For Catholics, this passage is important because it indicates that Jesus' body, blood, soul and divinity are all present after the bread and wine are consecrated.

OTHER ASPECTS OF HUMAN EXPERIENCE

The meaning of communion or Eucharist

The words, "this is my body, which is for you", have caused much debate among scholars and theologians over the centuries as to whether Paul's teaching indicates that the Lord himself is present at the supper. Some scholars tend to find a presence of the Lord in the bread and the cup on the basis of "this is my body". This is known as 'transubstantiation', and is a belief held by the Catholic Church. Protestant denominations reject this theory, arguing that the phrase means 'this is a symbol of my body'.

TASK

1. Find out why there are different views on the words of 1 Corinthians 11:24: "and when he had given thanks, he broke it and said, This is my body, which is for you; do this in remembrance of me."
2. Using two columns, explain arguments for and against each view.
3. What is your opinion? Give reasons for your answer.

(Ch 11:27–34)

Paul's anger over the treatment of the poorer members of the congregation at Corinth was therefore justified. Jesus had given freely of himself through his death on the cross; it followed that the believers should follow his example of self-giving. "Paul warns against eating the bread and drinking the cup of the Lord in an unworthy manner" (Foreman, 1961, p96). Murphy-O'Connor believes that "Paul has in mind the lack of loving concern for one another displayed by the Corinthians ... If participants in the eucharist meal are not united in love, they class themselves among those who murdered Jesus" (1989, p810). Paul therefore demands that members of the church think carefully before taking part in communion, to ensure they are not sinning against the body and blood of Christ. Unworthy conduct would bring judgement upon them.

Verse 30 suggests that such judgement could actually involve illness or even death. Morris explains that "spiritual ills may have physical consequences" (1996, p161). Foreman (1961, p97), however, argues that it is best not to take these words literally. An alternative suggestion is to interpret the verse spiritually: "some of the Corinthians are weak in soul and ill in spirit; they have taken communion in a spirit of selfish meanness, and so they have not only profaned what God has given them, they have also denied the very spirit and meaning of it all" (Foreman, 1961, p97).

The right action for the Corinthians, therefore, is to judge themselves before contemplating taking part in the Lord's Supper. Also, Paul stresses the need to treat each other courteously and graciously: "Church members should welcome one another when they came together for their meal ... the rich should welcome the poor" (Marshall, 1993, p572). The rich should eat in the privacy of their own homes if they wanted to have a big meal, and so avoid bringing social divisions into the church.

Spiritual gifts (Chs 12–14)

In this section Paul deals with the division and disorder that was happening in the church at Corinth because of the believers' obsession with the more spectacular gifts such as 'speaking in tongues' or 'glossolalia'. (See Chapter 2 of this book for a discussion on glossolalia, p68.)

Most of the Christians in Corinth had come from a pagan background, where spiritual experiences were not unusual. In their Greek mystery religions, they were well used to being moved by a supernatural force into trances. Therefore, it is perhaps not surprising that when they came to the church their interest in the supernatural continued. Many of them regarded a Christian who had been blessed with the gift of tongues to be a particularly spiritual person. The Corinthians seem to have asked Paul about this (12:1), although we do not know what exactly they wanted to know.

Discerning spiritual utterances (Ch 12:1–3)

Paul reminds the Corinthians that no one can be a Christian without the power of the Holy Spirit. For each individual Christian, the result of the indwelling of the Spirit was evidence of a particular gift, such as the power to heal or to prophesy. Verse 3 is difficult to understand. Thrall (1965, p86) suggests that while some members of the church were in a state of supernatural inspiration, they were in the habit of shouting blasphemous phrases such as 'Jesus be cursed'.

Spiritual gifts (Ch 12:4–11)

It seems that spiritual gifts were the cause of jealousy and envy among the congregation. "The Corinthians wanted to know which were the most important charismata, to find out, if possible, if the one they had was more important than the one that other people had" (Davies, 1962, p30). Bruce explains that "in the eyes of some Corinthian Christians, the most important manifestations of the indwelling of the Spirit were spectacular phenomena like speaking in tongues" (1977, p272). Those who possessed these more supernatural gifts were being viewed by the church members as being more important than those with less striking gifts. People were starting to question their own faith if they had not been given what they thought were the greater gifts.

Speaking in tongues or 'glossolalia' was considered to be "the gift above all other gifts; if you could make that kind of noise you were obviously one of the saints" (Davies, 1962, p32). So the question on everyone's lips was why do all Christians not have the gift of glossolalia, which is the most obvious sign of his presence?

Paul answered this in four ways:

1. Being preoccupied with one particular sign of the Spirit is wrong. The Spirit's presence can be seen in the variety of gifts that he gives.

2. All spiritual gifts come directly from God. The Corinthians had created division, encouraging believers to be proud if they possessed certain gifts. This led to some Christians thinking they were better than others. Paul said this was wrong. He pointed out that while there may be very different gifts, they all came from the same Holy Spirit.

3. God was the one who decided who would receive particular gifts. It was nothing to do with the Corinthians themselves. The Greek word for gifts, *charismata*, means 'gifts of grace', and that perfectly describes how the gifts were given.

4. The purpose of the gifts was for the benefit of the whole Christian community and not for personal advancement.

Gifts of the Holy Spirit

1 Corinthians 12:8–10 and 28 provides a list of the gifts of the Holy Spirit. Paul gives other lists in his letters to the Romans (12:6–8) and to the Ephesians (4:11–12). These lists vary, with the gift of prophecy common to all.

Wisdom/Knowledge	The difference between wisdom and knowledge is unclear
Faith	All Christians have faith; faith here means a special kind of faith, "the kind of faith that, when everybody else is doubting, remains staunch" (Davies, 1962, p31)
Healing	
Miraculous powers	
Prophecy	Inspired speech. Prophets in the Old Testament often predicted the future; so too did those with this gift in the New Testament
Ability to distinguish between spirits	
Ability to speak in different kinds of tongues	Glossolalia, a spiritual or heavenly unintelligible language, which is different from the speaking in foreign languages we read about in Acts Ch 2.
Ability to interpret tongues	This is the gift that makes sense of the gift of tongues. It makes the meaning of a message given in tongues known to the believers.

One body, many parts (Ch 12:12–26)

Paul explains his point using the human body as an illustration. He explains that God made the body with many parts, each part having its own functions to perform. The body needs all parts to work, so no part is regarded as unnecessary, or less important, than another part.

Similarly, Paul argues, the church can be regarded as the body of Christ (12:12), with members representing the different parts. Just as the body does not have one body part, so too, the church is made up of people with a variety of gifts and abilities (12:28). All are necessary, so no Christian should be made to feel inferior because he or she does not have the more spectacular gifts (12:15–17). Foreman (1961, p100) explains that each member of the body is useful to all the rest, but in turn needs the rest. "If one organ suffers, they all suffer together. If one flourishes, they all rejoice together" (Davies, 1962, p33).

The exercise of spiritual gifts (Ch 12:27–31)
Paul describes the different gifts that are evident in the body of Christ (the church). "Many people have taken this to be a list in order of priority" (Davies, 1962, p34). Some had the gift of apostleship, others the gift of prophecy, others teaching and so on (12:28). Clearly not everyone had the same gift. Paul's point is not that one is more important than the other, but that we aren't all apostles or all prophets; we aren't all teachers or miracle workers.

As the Corinthians were keen to receive spiritual gifts, Paul encourages them to seek the "higher gifts", that is, gifts that would build others up in their faith. His final words introduce us to the focus of Ch 13; Paul explains that he will show the Corinthians the best way of all, that of "love".

Love (Ch 13:1–13)
1 Corinthians 13 is one of the most famous chapters of the New Testament. Harnack describes it as "the greatest, strongest, deepest thing Paul ever wrote" (cited in Morris, 1996, p176). You may have heard it recited at a wedding you have attended, as it is a popular choice for couples at their marriage ceremony. The theme of the passage is 'love', and Paul includes it as part of his teaching about spiritual gifts. Bruce argues that it is an essential part of Paul's whole argument (1977, p117).

Love is essential (Ch 13:1–3)
Paul's teaching here implies that for the Christian love "is not a human achievement but a divine gift" (Davies, 1962, p35). He knows that the Corinthians are very keen on gifts, but is also aware that their enthusiasm for such gifts is to draw attention to themselves rather than to edify (improve intellectually/morally) the church as a whole. His opening words of chapter 13 show his concern that the Corinthians are not inspired by love, and that therefore their actions achieve nothing.

What love is (Ch 13:4–7)
Paul's words explain that love is not a feeling, but a deliberate action that is expressed in how Christians treat others. The recent behaviour of the Corinthians stands in clear contrast to Paul's description of the outworking of such love.

TASK

Read the descriptions given below about what love is and what love is not. Complete the table using examples of:
    a. how the list might relate to the situation of the Corinthians concerning spiritual gifts.
    b. where these characteristics of love are needed in the church today.

What Love Is	
Patient	
Kind	
Rejoices with the truth	
Always protects	
Always trusts	
Always hopes	
Always perseveres	
Never fails	

What Love Is Not	
Does not envy	
Does not boast	
Is not proud	
Is not self-seeking	
Is not easily angered	
Keeps no record of wrongs	

Clearly there is nothing that love cannot face; there is no limit to its faith, its hope, and its endurance (Davies, 1962, p36). Paul explains that the Corinthians should be running for love as they would run for a prize. The preoccupation they had for spiritual gifts was childish (13:11), especially because gifts are only temporary and one day will no longer exist (13:8–9). Paul stresses that only faith, hope and love are permanent, and that of these three the greatest is love (13:13).

>
> ### TASK
> **Love**
> Some people regard true Christian love as going further than the love of one person for another. That love should mean that Christian communities should respect other Christian communities – be willing to learn from them, pray for them and seek the best for them.
>
> In light of these comments, find out what you can about inter-church and inter-faith contacts and explain how Paul's principle of love can be seen in their work.

Gifts of prophecy and tongues (Ch 14:1–33)

In Ch14 Paul appears to be playing down the importance of the gift of speaking in tongues. He comments that it is a useful gift to those who possess it, but not of much use to the rest of the church. Paul regards prophecy as a much more important gift. Thrall (1965, p97) explains that prophecy corresponds quite closely to our idea of preaching. A prophet is inspired by the Holy Spirit to deliver a message to the church that should encourage believers or even convince unbelievers of the truth of the gospel.

Gifts of prophecy and tongues (Ch 14:1–12)

Paul compares speaking in tongues to a musical instrument that "makes unrelated and meaningless sounds instead of playing a proper melody" (Thrall, 1965, p99). Paul suggests that those with the gift of tongues should realise that their gift is merely an individual religious experience that would be best practised in private. Prophecy stands poles apart from tongues. It can be described as a direct line of communication between God and his followers.

Tongues must be interpreted (Ch 14:13–19)

Paul's criticism of tongues indicates that the Corinthians attached undue importance to this gift. "The mysterious babble of unintelligible sounds was seen as the clearest sign of possession by the Spirit and so offered enhanced social prestige" (Murphy-O'Connor, 1989, p811). However, Murphy-O'Connor (1989, p811) points out that although audible, glossolalia is intelligible only to God, the author of the gift (and so is different from the foreign languages of Acts 2:2–11). Speaking in tongues is only useful, Paul argues, if there is someone who can interpret what is being said. "Tongues can make a contribution to the community provided they are accompanied by the exercise of the mind, which makes them intelligible" (Murphy-O'Connor, 1989, p811). Furthermore, every church member should be able to feel part of the worship service. Speaking in tongues without interpretation prevents this.

Bruce concludes that "only when an interpreter was available would glossolalia be helpful to an assembled congregation; otherwise its value was confined to private devotion" (1977, p272).

A sign for unbelievers (Ch 14:20–25)
Bruce explains that:

> "…prophecy is a sign for believers in the sense that it produces believers; the unbeliever or outsider who would be put off by an outburst of tongues will be impressed if, on entering a church meeting, he hears all the members speaking words in a language he knows, which pierce direct to his heart and conscience, expose his inmost secrets, and convict him of sin." (1977, p133).

In other words, a Gentile visitor to the church might think someone who is speaking in tongues is completely mad, especially if more than one person is speaking in tongues at the same time. "Prophetic utterance, on the other hand, may move a non-Christian visitor to repentance and belief in God" (Thrall, 1965, p100).

Orderly worship (Ch 14:26–33)
It was foolish for too many members of the church to concentrate on the exercise of speaking in tongues "when so many more gifts, some of them obscure and unspectacular but none the less valuable, were needed for the common good" (Bruce, 1977, p273). However, for those who were determined to speak in tongues, Paul advises that at least it should be in an orderly manner. It seems that up until now Corinthian members of the church were free to contribute to the church service as the spirit moved them. But this freedom was causing chaos and confusion. Paul suggested, therefore, that only two speakers or at most three should take part, and that each should have their own turn. Afterwards, each should be interpreted. If there were no one available to interpret them speaking in tongues, it should be kept for private devotion. All things were to be done to build the people up in their faith.

Paul also argued that prophecy should be carried out in an orderly manner. Only two or three prophets should speak, and there should be time to digest what is being said. If someone sitting in the congregation receives a message from God, then whoever is speaking at the front should graciously step aside and allow them to speak.

The role of women (Ch 14:33–36)
These verses are difficult to follow when they are compared with Ch 11:5, where Paul says "and every woman who prays or prophesies with her head uncovered dishonours her head". The implication here is that it is fine for a woman to pray or prophesy in public worship as long as her head is covered. However, Ch 14:34–35 seems to suggest that women should not speak at all! Some scholars think that Paul is simply warning about needless chatter in the worship service. Thrall, for example, believes that "Paul is referring not to a woman's exercise of the gift of prophecy, which he did not forbid, but to the practice of women joining in congregational discussion of what a prophet or a teacher had said" (1965, p102). Their lack of self-discipline was "causing confusion and disorder in the worship of the church" (1993, p252). Bruce simply sees Paul as "forbidding them to interrupt proceedings by asking questions" (1977, p135). Whatever way you wish to interpret these verses, it is perhaps wise to follow Morris' advice to "take due caution in applying his principle to our own very different situation" (1996, p197).

Summing up (Ch 14:37–40)
Paul claims to have the Lord's authority for what he has written. Again, he encourages the gift of prophecy, although it is important to note that while he is not keen on the gift of speaking in tongues, he does not forbid it.

> ### Relevance for today (Ch 12–14)
> - Paul's teaching in these chapters emphasises the importance of every Christian in the church community. Everyone has a contribution to make and also needs the help and support of others in the congregation. Just as different parts of a body all work together for the common good, so should Christians work together in the church.
> - God gives everyone gifts; these gifts vary but they are all important. No one should feel superior as a result of having a particular gift, as all gifts come from God and all are equally important. Paul taught the Corinthians they should not over-emphasise the importance of one gift at the expense of others, for example, speaking in tongues. This is still relevant today.

TASK

Create a spider diagram or mind map to show how the message of 1 Corinthians was relevant for the Early Church. You could consider the following areas:
- The consequences of allowing divisions in the church.
- Moral living for Christians in a secular society.
- Guidance for church life and worship.

PRACTICE ESSAY QUESTION

1. **Critically discuss Paul's teaching in 1 Corinthians on the use of Spiritual Gifts.**

A critical discussion may include some of the following, for example:
- Importance of these chapters, which provide an insight into church worship in the first century.
- Disorder arising in the Corinthian Church, causing divisions due to the preoccupation with certain gifts.
- The pagan background of the Corinthian Christians; supernatural experiences were the norm; valued such experiences as the sign of true spirituality.
- Paul makes it clear that the possession of a gift is not the true sign of a 'genuine believer' – instead it is the proclamation of the Lordship of Christ.
- Christians were setting one believer against another depending on the possession of this or that gift. Paul denounces this disunity and points out that the preoccupation with supernatural gifts is to restrict the spirit's power and activity.
- The Spirit's power is shown in diversity – there are many gifts. It is God who decides who receives what gift. To question why a believer does not have a gift is therefore to question God.
- Paul outlines the variety of gifts: wisdom, knowledge, faith, healing, miracles, speaking God's message, interpreting between gifts of the spirit and gifts not of the spirit, tongues, interpretation of tongues.

- The purpose of these gifts is to benefit the whole Christian community, not for individual personal advancement.
- The analogy of the human body to show how all the gifts used together can benefit the church and work as God intended.
- Paul concentrates on the two gifts of prophecy and speaking in tongues, and clearly favours prophecy because it can be understood and because it edifies. Paul points out that tongues are useless unless accompanied by the gift of interpretation.
- The Christian life is not merely an emotional exercise – there is a place for enthusiasm, but one should also use one's intellect; the example of singing and prayer – both must be done intelligently with the use of the mind.
- Paul's main principle is that church worship should be orderly.
- He gives practical advice to curb the use of tongues when he suggests that only two or three people should speak in tongues in a service and only if there is an interpreter.

2. Critically evaluate the view that this letter offers guidance for Christians in the modern world.

A critical evaluation of the view may include some of the following, for example:
- In his first century letter, Paul is writing to a particular church in a specific situation and context. Some issues to which Paul refers are cultural and of his time (head covering) and therefore not immediately relevant to today.
- He is replying to queries they have raised with him on a number of issues. Despite this, there are principles that should apply to the church today as much as to the Corinthian Church – important teachings and principles that transcend time and culture, and speak to us today.
- Morality: Paul emphasises the need to guard against sexual immorality. The Christian Church today must not tolerate any immorality from within its membership, but must take appropriate action. Refer to attitudes to many sexual partners/homosexuality/AIDS. The church must not give in or weaken towards more liberal attitudes but must guard against sexual immorality. Give examples.
- Sanctity of marriage: Paul upholds the sanctity of marriage in

this letter; defends the rightful use of the act of sexual intercourse within marriage, and emphasises the dependency of man and wife. Relevant for today's church, where marriage break-ups are on the increase; adultery is common; 'living together' is much more acceptable in today's society. The church must not feel under pressure to give in to pressure from society to lower its standards. Refer to attitudes to marriage today (divorces are common/ gay marriage/attitude to monogamy). Church must promote the sacredness of marriage in light of these attitudes.
- Respect for the body: Paul emphasises that our bodies belong to God and are temples of the Holy Spirit. Relevance for the issues of drugs, abortion, eating disorders.
- Church worship: Paul's advice that everything must be done in a proper and orderly way, especially concerning the more spectacular spiritual gifts. Such gifts are still in use in charismatic churches today, so advice is relevant. Charismatic/Pentecostal churches today can take heed from Paul's teaching regarding gifts. Need to recognise that the over-exaggerated use of the gifts can weaken worship or set believers against each other.
- The principle can be applied to all worship. Give examples.
- Divisions: there are frequently divisions and frictions which affect churches and congregations today, making worship and fellowship difficult. Churches reminded of our unity in Christ and under the one, unifying Spirit.

EXAMINATION PRACTICE

Question from CCEA's Specimen Assessment Materials

(a) With reference to at least two letters you have studied, examine and discuss Paul's teaching on morality. [20 marks]

Your answer could include an analysis of some of the following points:
Galatians
- Discussion of Paul's teaching on freedom: not to indulge the sinful nature but to serve one another in love.
- The implications of Paul's analogies for Christian living: running a good race and the yeast.

- Consideration of Paul's teaching on the fruits of the Spirit and the acts of sinful nature.
- Paul's teaching on reaping and sowing and his advice to carry one another's burdens.

1 Corinthians
- Examination of Paul's teaching on divisions in the church and the need to avoid superior attitudes.
- Discussion of Paul's practical teaching when dealing with a case of sexual immorality.
- Consideration of Paul's teaching on the correct behaviour of Christians towards each other.
- Discussion of Paul's instructions on marriage, divorce and relationships.

Ephesians
- Discussion of the overall theme of chapters 4–6: the need for high conduct in the church.
- Consideration of Paul's practical advice on humility, correct behaviour and attitude towards others.
- Paul's teaching on the Christians as light in the Lord, with the requirement for them to live as children of light, shunning sexual immorality and other wrong-doing.

(Remember you must refer to at least two letters; if you choose to include all three you will not need to include as many points for each letter.)

(b) "In his letters, Paul's pastoral advice to churches always includes theological teaching." Critically assess the validity of this claim. [30 marks]

Your answer could include an evaluation of the following points:
- Discussion of the various roles undertaken by Paul in his missionary work and support for developing churches, for example, pastor, theologian, disciplinarian, teacher.
- Consideration of the link between practical teaching on Christian behaviour and implications for Christian belief.

- In 1 Corinthians: divisions in the church hindering Christian development; the theological implications of union with prostitutes; meat offered to idols and the believers' freedom; the conduct of the Lord's Supper.
- In Galatians: the implications of seeking circumcision once already saved; reference to teaching on freedom in Christ and life by the Spirit.
- In Ephesians: understanding God's plan for salvation leads to the response of believers living a morally acceptable lifestyle.

(In this part (b) you should draw on more than one letter for your arguments.)

BY THE END OF THIS CHAPTER YOU SHOULD BE ABLE TO:

- demonstrate knowledge and understanding of, and critically evaluate issues in Corinth, including:
  - the context of the Letter;
  - problems arising in the Corinthian Church following the Second Missionary Journey;
  - Paul's teaching on unity (1:1–4:21); and
  - how this teaching relates to Paul's intended audience;
- demonstrate knowledge and understanding of, and critically evaluate Christian moral living, including:
  - Paul's teaching on moral living for Christians (5:1–13, 6:12–20, 7:1–8:13, 10:14–11:1);
  - guidance for church life and worship (11:2–14:40, 16:1–4);
  - the value of this text for the Early Church; and
  - relevance of Paul's teaching for today;

Paul's Letter to the Ephesians

Section 1:
The Background to the Letter

INTRODUCTION

The Letter to the Ephesians has received many accolades from scholars and writers. French theologian and church reformer, John Calvin, considered Ephesians to be his favourite letter, preaching 48 sermons based on its teaching. The English poet, Samuel Taylor Coleridge, has called it "the divinest composition of man". More recently, Bruce describes Ephesians as "the quintessence of Paulinism"[1] (1961, p11), while, according to Williamson, "the Epistle to the Ephesians is the most eloquent of the letters attributed to St. Paul" (2009, p13). This letter has had an important impact on the lives of Christians since it was written nearly two centuries ago.

BACKGROUND
The historical context of the text

Ephesus, situated on the south-west coast of Asia Minor, was one of the most important trade centres of the Roman Empire. The remains of the city, in modern day Turkey, show that it was a wealthy commercial centre with a number of significant buildings. Ephesus also has an important Greek heritage and was the centre for worship for the fertility goddess, Artemis.

Ephesus was an important centre for Paul's missionary activity. He visited Ephesus towards the end of his second missionary journey and during this brief visit his preaching aroused interest. Hoehner comments that Paul "was well-received there and, in fact, was asked to stay longer but he declined" (2002, p90). However, although Paul was unable to spend more time with them on this occasion, he promised, "I will come back if it is God's will" (Acts 18:19–21). On his third missionary journey, Paul returned to Ephesus for an extended stay of three years (Acts 19:1, 10; 20:31). The generally accepted date for this journey is AD54–58.

---

1 'The Quintessence of Paulism' is also the title of an important study of Paul's theology by AS Peake.

The length of time spent in Ephesus is an indication of the success of Paul's work. After an initial three months teaching in the synagogue, Paul was forced to leave; however, he was able to continue preaching in the lecture hall of Tyrannus. The book of Acts confirms the success of this missionary work: "This went on for two years, so that all the Jews and Greeks who lived in the province of Asia heard the word of the Lord" (Acts 19:10). Bruce comments that "Paul had established his headquarters in Ephesus … and not only planted a strong church in that city, but with the help of a number of colleagues evangelised the whole province" (1961, p16).

Following his stay in Ephesus, Paul continued his third missionary journey through Macedonia and Greece. On his return to Jerusalem, he stopped at the coastal town of Miletus and sent for the elders from the church at Ephesus. In a tearful parting speech, Paul spoke about the time he had spent with them in Ephesus, giving both warnings and encouragement for their role as leaders in the church (Acts 20:17–38). This speech gives the impression that Paul is speaking to trusted friends with whom he has built a close relationship: "They all wept as they embraced him and kissed him", and were particularly upset by Paul's remark that "they would never see his face again" (Acts 20:37–38).

Authorship

There is both internal and external evidence for attributing authorship of this letter to Paul. In keeping with the style of his day, Paul begins by identifying himself (Ephesians 1:1). According to O'Brien, "we should hold anyone who claims to be the author of any letter coming to us from antiquity to be just that unless there is very strong evidence to the contrary" (1999, p4). Early sources in church history also claim Pauline authorship for this letter, including Irenaeus, Clement of Alexandria and Origen. Paul is given as the author of Ephesians in two of the earliest canons. O'Brien (1999, p4) explains that Marcion considered Ephesians to be a genuine letter of Paul, though written to Laodicea, while it is listed as a Pauline letter in the Muratorian canon.

However, in the early nineteenth century, German theologians from the Tübingen School, notably Baur, challenged the traditional view of Pauline authorship. O'Brien comments that this challenge "had considerable influence on the subsequent course of scholarship, so that today scholarly opinion is divided" (1999, p4).

A detailed knowledge of the arguments concerning authorship is not needed for your course; however, a brief consideration of some of the main objections raised by scholars is given below:

1. The language and style

Many writers draw attention to the distinctive language and style of Ephesians, distinguishing it from other letters where Paul's authorship is certain. Thielman refers to the "high number of long sentences, some of them extraordinarily long" (2010, p6). He also comments that "Ephesians is full of grammatical and lexical ambiguities that affect the meaning of the text." These features have led to some scholars questioning whether Paul wrote this letter. However, Stott argues that variations to Paul's usual style and vocabulary are no reason to doubt his authorship, commenting that "linguistic and stylistic arguments are notoriously precarious" (1979, p1). Hoehner comments that there are difficulties in determining authorship on the basis of language and style and concludes that "certainly Ephesians manifests some differences in vocabulary and style, but not enough to discount authenticity" (2002, pp28–29).

2. The impersonal tone

The account given in Acts of Paul's ministry in Ephesus gives the impression of a close relationship. However, there are no references to people by name in Ephesians and the letter ends with a brief and impersonal farewell, quite unlike that in his speech to the Ephesian elders. Furthermore, the author of Ephesians writes: "I heard about your faith in the Lord Jesus and your love for all the saints" (Ephesians 1:15). Surely this reference would not be appropriate if Paul were writing to a group of Christians with whom he had spent three years. This issue will be addressed further when considering the recipients of the letter.

3. The content of the letter

Some scholars have emphasised that the theological teaching and concepts in Ephesians are different to the other letters of Paul where there is no dispute over authorship. Stott refers to an interest in "the heavenly places" and a lack of reference to 'justification' (1979, p18). Other writers have commented on the references to predestination and spiritual enlightenment as being uncharacteristic of Paul's theology. Thielman argues that "Ephesians is missing the argumentative, fast-paced feel typical of Paul's undisputed letters" (2010, p7).

Some scholars have concluded that Ephesians was written by an unknown author attempting to adopt the style of Paul. According to Stott, theories of this nature are "almost entirely speculative" (1979, p20). Bruce also rejects this idea, writing that "the man who could write Ephesians must have been the apostle's equal, if not his superior, in mental stature and spiritual insight" (1961, p11). Bruce concludes that "of such a second Paul early Christian history has no knowledge" (1961, p12). Thielman argues that Paul "could write in a variety of styles" and "was clearly a versatile writer" (2010, p11), as shown by a study of passages from First and Second Corinthians, Philippians and Romans.

Modern scholarship remains divided on the issue of authorship. However, many feel that the traditional view of Pauline authorship is the most convincing and that "the onus of proof is upon those who must establish that Paul was incapable of this versatility" (O'Brien, 1999, p47). In this chapter the author of Ephesians will be referred to as Paul.

The recipients of the letter

O'Brien notes that "traditionally Paul's letter has been understood to have been written to believers in Ephesus" (1999, p47). At the opening of the letter, Paul writes "to the saints in Ephesus" (Ephesians 1:1). Some scholars regard this as the only solid evidence that Paul intended to write this letter to the church he established on his third missionary journey. However, this reference is problematic, as the words "in Ephesus" are not included in some of the earliest manuscripts. The impersonal tone has led to further doubts that this letter was intended for the Ephesian Church. Bruce suggests that "the most acceptable view, having regard to the general character of the letter, is that it was intended for all the churches in the province of Asia, some of which were personally known to Paul, while others were not" (1961, p13). This is, perhaps, the most plausible suggestion and one that accounts for the lack of personal references in the letter: it was not intended to be read by just one local church. Hoehner suggests that "it is not inconceivable that there were several churches in the area because on his third missionary journey Paul had ministered in Ephesus for around two and a half years" (2002, p79). Bruce comments that the title 'The Epistle to the Ephesians' is justifiable, "provided that we remember that it was sent to other churches in the province of which Ephesus was the capital city" (1961, p13).

Evidence for the letter written from prison in Rome

The book of Acts ends with Paul a prisoner in Rome. Although he is under house arrest, he has a certain amount of liberty to preach and receive visitors (Acts 28:31). The New Testament letters of Ephesians, Philippians, Colossians and Philemon are known as the prison epistles, and are believed to have been written by Paul while under arrest in Rome, most likely around AD 60–62. In Ephesians, there are references to Paul as "the prisoner of Christ Jesus" (Ephesians 3:1) and "a prisoner for the Lord" (Ephesians 4:1). At the end of the letter, Paul asks the Ephesians to pray for him and he goes on to describe himself as "an ambassador in chains" (Ephesians 6:19–20). This is consistent with the narrative in Acts that Paul is in prison in Rome awaiting trial, following his appeal to Caesar (Acts 26:32).

While in Rome under arrest, Paul kept in touch with churches he had founded in Asia, and he preached to local people in Rome. One of his visitors was Epaphras, a Christian preacher who is believed to have established the church at Colossae. He remained with Paul in Rome and is referred to in his letter to Philemon: "Epaphras, my fellow prisoner in Christ Jesus, sends his greetings" (Philemon 1:23). Bruce (1961, p14) comments that Epaphras brought news to Paul of a form of false teaching that was attracting Christians in the area; Colossians was his reply to this heresy. Bruce (1961, p15) maintains that Paul's teaching in Colossians gave rise to important questions that he addressed more fully in his subsequent letter to the Ephesians. Thielman (2010, p8) comments that the literary relationship between Colossians and Ephesians is clearly evident. Both letters were dispatched with Tychicus, "the dear brother and faithful servant in the Lord" (Ephesians 6:21). Tychicus is mentioned in Acts as one of the group that accompanied Paul on the return voyage of this third missionary journey (Acts 20: 4).

In summary, Paul wrote Ephesians during his two-year imprisonment in Rome, at roughly the same time as the other prison letters. Thielman surmises that "he was chained to a Rome Soldier during this period but free to receive visitors. These probably included a secretary who took down the letters at Paul's dictation" (2010, p19). Paul's letters were carried to their destination by Tychicus, "a trusty Christian co-worker from Asia who was also with him [Paul] in Rome" (2010, p19).

The purpose of the letter

According to McGrath, "the letter does not deal directly with any false teaching, which further suggests that the letter was intended to circulate throughout the churches of Asia Minor, rather than deal with the specific problems of any one congregation" (1995, p350).

Since the end of the third missionary journey, Paul has had a long period of captivity and little opportunity to re-visit churches he established. During his imprisonment in Rome, Paul seems to have heard that Christians in Ephesus were "discouraged" by his suffering (Ephesians 3:13). Thielman comments that "he probably also learned that most Christians in the city, whether they knew him or not, were disunified and attempted to assimilate to the culture they had left behind at their conversion" (2010, p28). In response, Paul addresses important themes concerning the church as the body of Christ and the role of individual Christians within the church. Hoehner concludes that the theme of love has a dominant place within the book of Ephesians and that "it seems reasonable to conclude that the purpose of Ephesians is to promote a love for one another that has the love for God and Christ as its basis" (2002, p106).

Paul is therefore writing to:
1. Remind Christians of the grace of God and how they have been blessed by Christ.
2. Explain the important role of the church in bringing all people to faith in Christ.
3. Call Christians to live in a way that reflects what God has done for them.

TASK
Essay practice
1. Explain and discuss the arguments for the authorship of the letter to the Ephesians.

A discussion may include some of the following points:
- Reference to the time Paul spent in Ephesus on his third missionary journey.
- Internal and external evidence supporting Paul as author.
- A summary of the main objections given by scholars.
- Evidence for Ephesians written from prison in Rome.

2. "There is little value in trying to establish authorship of an ancient text. What is important is its relevance for today." Critically evaluate this claim.

A critical evaluation may include some of the following points:
- The previous answer shows scholars are divided on the issue of authorship of Ephesians.
- Reference could be made to other texts studied for this course and the question of authorship.
- Establishing authorship helps to give important background, including date and purpose.
- Identifying the authorship of a religious text can help to establish authenticity.
- To what extent the texts you have studied have relevance for today and whether this is the primary consideration.

Section 2:
The Main Themes of Ephesians

INITIAL GREETINGS (1:1–2)

O'Brien comments that "the prologue of Ephesians follows the regular Pauline pattern with its three elements: the name of the sender, the recipients and a greeting" (1999, p83). Paul's opening, in which he describes himself as "an apostle of Christ Jesus", establishes his credentials and authority at the outset of the letter. Paul describe the recipients of the letter as 'saints', a term often used in the New Testament for Christian believers. However, the words "in Ephesus" are omitted from the earliest manuscripts, leading scholars to debate whether the letter was intended for a wider group of God's people than just those living in Ephesus.

The customary Jewish greeting was 'peace' (*shalom*), while the usual Greek greeting was 'grace' (*charis*). Paul often combines the two when sending greetings to his readers at the start of a letter.

GOD'S PLAN FOR SALVATION THROUGH CHRIST (CH 1:1–3:21)

Spiritual Blessings (1:3–14)

After the initial greetings, Paul often begins his correspondence by referring to the recipients, often giving praise for their faith. In this letter, Paul sets a completely different tone by opening with an outburst of praise to God: "Praise be to the God and father of our Lord Jesus Christ, who has blessed us in the heavenly realm with every spiritual blessing in Christ" (Ephesians 1:3). O'Brien comments that these opening words are "in the typical Old Testament and Jewish style of an extended blessing or berakah" (1999, p93). Hoehner agrees that the roots of this hymn are in the Old Testament, but adds that its content goes beyond them; rather than following a liturgical pattern, "it is more likely to be a spontaneous utterance of praise to God" (2002, p159). Paul's praises to God are the keynote of the whole letter: Paul and his readers are 'in Christ' and can share his eternal life; Bruce explains that "because Christ himself is now exalted in the heavenly realm, those who are 'in him' belong to that heavenly realm ... it is there that they enjoy 'every spiritual blessing' that God has bestowed upon them as the people of Christ" (1961, p27).

Paul continues with his praises to God through the rest of this section. Stott writes that "in the original Greek, these twelve verses constitute a single complex sentence" (1979, p32), and he describes how Paul must have dictated this section without pausing for breath or punctuating his words with full stops. This benediction is much longer than any others at the start of New Testament letters. Thielman concludes that Paul may have written this prayer to remind his readers "of all that God has done for them in Christ and of the important place that they, as the church, occupy in God's historical purposes" (2010, p44).

It is significant that in the opening verse there is reference to the Trinity. In this passage of praise, Paul refers to blessings from the Father, Son and Holy Spirit. Williamson comments that "the extraordinary affirmation made in 1:3 is that God has blessed Christians in every possible way through what Christ has done" (2009, p32). He goes on to explain that this includes giving the Holy Spirit and uniting believers to Jesus, who is enthroned in heaven. This benefit has already begun to be experienced.

Blessings from the Father (v 4–6)

In this section, Paul describes how believers have been chosen by the Father, since the beginning of the world, to be adopted as Sons of God. Thielman comments that "God has made believers his people as a completely free act of grace" (2010, p45). God acted out of love to give believers the means of salvation through Jesus, not because of human merit. This gift from God was accomplished before they even existed, showing it has always been God's intention to provide a means for redemption.

Blessings from the Son (v 7–12)

This section focuses on the redemption and forgiveness of sins that have resulted from Christ's death on the cross. Williamson explains that "'Redemption' means liberation, for instance, of a slave or captive, often by the payment of a ransom" (2009, p37). God has made his purposes known through Jesus, so through him believers can have some understanding of God's plans for salvation. Paul starts by reminding his readers of the blessings that have resulted from Christ's death on the cross, referring to "redemption through his blood" and "the forgiveness of sins" (v 7). Paul's use of 'redemption' implies that God has acted on behalf of sinful humanity so that wrong-doing can be forgiven. In effect, Jesus has paid the ransom price through his death on the cross so that sins can be forgiven. Stott writes of how "God's children enjoy free access to their heavenly father, and their confidence before him is due to the knowledge that they have been redeemed and forgiven" (1979, p40). Redemption and forgiveness therefore go together, both made possible "through his [Jesus'] blood". Paul's reference to blood shows that Christ's death on the cross was a great sacrifice to secure salvation for sinful humanity. According to Thielman, "God's carefully considered willingness to pay such a price for the forgiveness of the sins of his people reveals something about his character: he is not merely a gracious God but an overwhelmingly gracious God" (2010, p68). Paul continues to praise God, as, through Christ and his death on the cross, he has enabled people to understand something of "the mystery of his will" (v 9) and his plans for the unfolding of history. God has carefully planned in advance that his people will have the means of salvation; it is not the result of some accident or anything they have achieved through their own efforts.

Blessings from the Holy Spirit (v 13–14)

The final section describes blessings relating to the Holy Spirit. Paul explains that when believers receive God's Holy Spirit this has a dual significance – they now belong to God, and also have a promise or guarantee of eternal life. McGrath explains that "Paul is thus declaring that the presence of the Spirit in believers' lives is both a sign of God's ownership and sovereignty, and a confirmation of the promise to give more in the future" (1995, p30). Paul concludes this whole section in the way he began, with praise to God for his blessings on his people. Hoehner comments that "though it is Paul's praise of God's goodness to him, it also serves as a model to encourage the Ephesian believers to offer praise to God" (2002, p159).

Thanksgiving and prayer (1:15–23)

This is Paul's first prayer for the Ephesians. He begins this section by giving thanks for their faith, saying that he remembers them continually in his prayers. Paul has two petitions to make on their behalf:

1. **He asks God that they might receive the Spirit's gifts of wisdom and revelation so that they may know him better (v 17)**. The knowledge Paul is speaking of here is not an academic or factual knowledge, but a personal understanding of God. Hoehner writes that "Paul's desire is for the Ephesian believers to deepen their relationship with the God who has enriched them with every spiritual benefit" (2002, p247). McGrath comments that "knowing that they already believe in the Lord Jesus Christ, Paul prays that they might come to the full knowledge of his glory in every respect" (1995, p350).

2. He prays that they will understand there is a great inheritance for them – the gift of eternal life (v 18–19). Before coming to faith, Paul's readers did not have hope in eternal life, but now Paul can pray that they "may know the hope to which he has called you". They have this hope because God has called them to be his people. Williamson comments that "besides imparting a personal knowledge of God, the spirit helps Christians to grasp the value of what God has given in Christ" (2009, p48). Paul continues to explain how God's gifts have been made possible through his "incomparably great power" (v 19) and he prays that the believers will understand something about their future.

Paul is especially concerned that his readers will understand the significance of God's power, so he elaborates on this in the remainder of the section. To summarise, God has shown his power by raising Christ from the dead to a position of honour in heaven (v 20), giving him absolute authority in the present age and the one to come (v 21) and appointing him to be head of the church (v 22). Hoehner comments that "the fullness of God's power and attributes are given to the church by Christ, who in turn is being filled with them completely" (2002, p301).

New Testament writers often refer to the death of Christ as a way of showing God's love for sinful humanity. According to Bruce, if the death of Christ is the chief demonstration of the love of God, the chief demonstration of His power is the resurrection of Christ" (1961, p41). Paul explains how God showed his power by not only raising Jesus from death, but by "seat[ing] him at his right hand" and therefore exalting him to the highest position in heaven. This great power shown by God is the same power at work in the lives of believers. God has also used his power for the church, by giving Christ supreme authority and appointing him head of the church. Thielman explains that "Christ and the church, his body, are one; thus Christ's victory is also the church's victory" (2010, p116).

Stott (1979, p52) refers to the 'Trinitarian' nature of this prayer, which is in parallel with the first half of this chapter. The prayer is addressed to "the God of our Lord Jesus Christ", who through his power has raised Christ from the dead and sent his Spirit so that believers can understand what God has achieved for them. McGrath concludes that "the power of the risen Christ, under whose authority God has placed the present age, is available to believers through faith" (1995, p350).

CHAPTER 7: PAUL'S LETTER TO THE EPHESIANS

TASK

1. List the main points that Paul makes in his opening praise. (Your answer should make reference to 1:3–14.)

2. Give a brief outline of Paul's petitions for his readers. (Your answer should make reference to 1:15–23.)

Made alive in Christ (2:1–10)

Paul presents a contrast in this section:

What it means to be without Christ (v 1–3)

Before becoming Christians, Paul's readers used to live by the standards of the world, not recognising the authority of God. Their lifestyle was typically one of selfish and immoral behaviour, as they attempted to satisfy all their physical cravings. As a result of this constant sin, with no means of redemption, Paul tells them, "you were dead in your transgressions and sins" (v 1). Stott explains that the meaning of 'sin' (from the Greek *hamartia*) means "a missing of the mark, a falling short of a standard" (1979, p71). This has led to spiritual death through alienation from God. Therefore, their former life without Christ was never going to lead them to inherit God's promise of eternal life. Williamson sums this up by commenting that "Paul is saying that before they entered into a relationship with Christ, his Gentile readers were spiritually dead because of their sinful actions" (2009, p58). The condition Paul is describing here is not that of an especially immoral group of people; he is simply stating the implications of living without Christ. As a result, they can expect God's justified wrath against those who disobey him.

What it means to be alive in Christ (v 4–10)

This section presents a dramatic comparison, moving from despair to hope. Stott comments that "what Paul does in this passage is to paint a vivid contrast between what man is by nature and what he can become by grace" (1979, p69). Paul explains how God has provided a way for people to be saved from their sins, so they can be "alive with Christ" (v 5). This has not happened because people deserved it; indeed, Paul stresses that God's plan for salvation was initiated when people were "dead in transgressions" (v 5). Hoehner comments that "the main assertion of this section is that God has made sinners alive, raised them up, and seated them with Christ" (2002, p306). Paul gives two characteristics of God that have led him to save sinful humanity – his love and mercy. In this passage he states twice that "it is by grace you have been saved" (v 5 and v 8), showing that salvation is a gift freely given by God, but not deserved by the recipients. Paul wants his readers to understand that what they can receive from God is truly amazing – they will be raised from death, like Christ, to be with him in heaven (v 6). Thielman explains that "by giving believers life with Christ, raising them with Christ, and seating them with Christ in his place of victory, God has demonstrated the overwhelmingly merciful, loving, and gracious nature of his character" (2010, p139).

Paul says this act further illustrates God's grace, and also his kindness, in sending Christ to die on the cross (v 7). The whole emphasis is on what God has achieved through Jesus; all that is required from people is to recognise what God has already done and accept this gift through faith. O'Brien comments that "if God's grace is the ground of salvation, then faith is the means by which it is appropriated" (1999, p174). No one should think they are more righteous or deserving than anyone else, or that they have secured their salvation by their own efforts (v 9). According to Williamson, "even religious people sometimes believe or act as though their religious and moral exertion is the fundamental way they can gain God's favour" (2009, p66). McGrath comments that "this great hope does not rest on any human achievement, but on the workmanship of God within believers, as he works to refashion them in his service" (1995, p351). God's salvation can be seen as a new creation, where people are not saved by their good works, but saved so they can be made into new people doing God's work.

Paul develops this idea of a new creation in the next passage, where he goes on to explain how God's purpose is to create a new group of people out of both Jews and Gentiles.

One in Christ (2:11–22)

The theme for this passage is the status of Gentiles compared to God's chosen people, the Jews. Paul explains how the death of Jesus has united both groups and given Gentiles equal status to the original covenant community. O'Brien comments that "this paragraph provides one of the most wonderful descriptions of peace and reconciliation within the Pauline letters" (1999, p182), as believers come near to God and to one another (Gentiles and Jews) through the saving death of Christ.

The passage can be divided into the following sections:

The position of the Gentiles without Christ (v 11–12)
Circumcision is an important ritual in Judaism. When God made the original covenant with Abraham, he gave the instruction that all male Jews would be circumcised, thus carrying the mark of this covenant on their bodies. Circumcision was therefore a means of distinguishing Jews and Gentiles both in religion and social life. It was a barrier between them, showing how they were two distinct groups of people. Paul reminds his readers, many of whom were Gentiles before becoming Christians, of how this gave them an inferior status, "excluded from citizenship in Israel … without hope and without God in the world" (Ephesians 2:12). Thielman describes the plight of the Gentiles: "They were alienated from Israel's scriptures, both from the way of life described there and from the promises the scriptures contained of a coming Messiah and of the outpouring of God's Spirit" (2010, p159). Barclay describes Gentile history as "a progress to nowhere"; however, with the coming of Christ, "the Gentile entered into that new view of history in which a man is always on the way to God" (2002, p108).

The position of the Gentiles through the death of Christ (v 13–18)
Paul states that God responded to the bleak situation of the Gentiles by offering salvation to the Gentiles as well as to his chosen people. This has been made possible through the death and resurrection of Jesus. Paul describes Christ as the "peace" of the Christian community, as he has:

- brought reconciliation between the Jews and Gentiles.
- broken down the barrier that kept the Jews separate from other people, but at the same time served to exclude Gentiles.
- brought about the creation of one new humanity out of two formerly opposing groups of people.

At the start of this passage, Paul refers to "the barrier, the dividing wall of hostility" (v 14). According to Williamson, "most scholars believe this 'dividing wall' refers to one or other of the two most important identity markers of first-century Judaism: the temple in Jerusalem and the Law of Moses" (2009, p71). The Temple was constructed as a series of courts, with Gentiles only permitted in the outermost area. Archaeologists have uncovered stone plaques warning Gentiles of death if they proceeded further than their designated area. Williamson comments that "if this is the division

Paul had in mind, the Gentiles' participation in a spiritual temple indicates an immense change of status" (2009, p72).

The Jewish Law was the other barrier in Judaism that excluded Gentiles. This was both a religious barrier and a social one, as Jews were not even permitted to eat with Gentiles. Jesus' death on the cross has given people a new way to approach God and done away with many of the previous rituals that distinguished God's people. At the death of Christ, all barriers have been broken down and everyone has access to God in the same way. Thielman comments that Christ's death "made it possible for him to present to God both Jewish and Gentile believers, now united peacefully with each other as a newly created human being" (2010, p176).

The position of the Gentiles as believers in Christ (v 19–22)

The Gentiles are no longer "foreigners and aliens", but "fellow citizens with God's people" (v 19). Gentile Christians and Jewish Christians now have equal status in God's kingdom. Paul describes how God's work in creating a new community can be compared to the construction of a holy building. The foundations of the building are the teachings given through God's messengers, the prophets and the apostles; however, "Christ Jesus himself is the chief cornerstone" (v 20). The cornerstone is one of the key stones in the construction of a building. Bruce writes that "the cornerstone … not only bonds the structure together but serves as a 'stone of testing' to show whether the building has been carried out to the architect's specifications" (1961, p57). Stott explains the reason for this reference: "Paul has particularly in mind the function of Jesus Christ in holding the growing temple together as a unity" (1979, p108). O'Brien explains that with Jesus as the cornerstone to the building, "the foundation and position of all the other stones in the superstructure were determined by him" (1999, p217). These references therefore emphasise the important role of Jesus.

The Gentile believers are being built as living stones in this new community. Hoehner comments on the relevance of this teaching for the people of Ephesus, explaining that "before their conversion the Jews thought of God as dwelling in the temple made with hands. On the other hand, the Ephesians thought of the goddess Artemis as the one who dwelt in the renowned temple at Ephesus" (2002, p415). Before becoming Christians, Jews and Gentiles had two opposing ideas about where God lived. Now they have been made into a new temple, which is a dwelling place for God's Holy Spirit.

TASK

You should aim to write a detailed paragraph to answer each question.
1. Explain how the lives of Paul's readers have changed now they are Christians.
2. Paul refers to "the dividing wall of hostility" (v 14). Discuss what he might be referring to here. What is Paul explaining to his readers?
3. Discuss Paul's reference to the building. In your answer explain the role of Christ and the role of the Gentile believers.

Paul the preacher to the Gentiles (3:1–13)

Paul begins this passage following the theme from the previous chapter. However, before beginning a prayer for the Gentiles, he breaks off to explain two important points about how God has used his power to give the Gentiles equal status to the Jews:

A hidden mystery is revealed (v 2–6)

Paul explains that God has intended all through history to make salvation available to Gentiles as well as Jews. This was not made known to earlier generations, but God has revealed to Paul that "Gentiles are heirs together with Israel, members of one body and sharers together in the promise of Christ Jesus" (v 6). Thielman comments that "this complete equality between Gentiles and Jews in one new people of God is something that neither Paul nor the other apostles and prophets could have known apart from God's revelation of it to them. It is in this sense a 'mystery'" (2010, p207). Williamson agrees and writes that "when Paul uses the term 'mystery' he is referring to God's previously hidden plan of salvation that has now been revealed through the coming of Christ and the Gospel" (2009, p86).

Paul's role in making this mystery known (v 7–13)

God has given Paul the responsibility of making this mystery, which has been kept hidden for years, known to the Gentiles. Paul refers to himself as "less than the least of all God's people" (v 8), perhaps referring to his former role as persecutor of the church. O'Brien comments that Paul "indicates how deeply conscious he is of his own unworthiness and of Christ's overflowing grace to him" (1999, p240). It is through God's grace that Paul has been chosen, and it is through "the working of his power" (v 7) that Paul is enabled for the task.

Paul has played his role in creating a united church of Jews and Gentiles, but here is further work to be done. The church must proclaim that God's purposes, planned before the beginning of time, have now been fulfilled through the death of Christ. According to Stott, some scholars interpret the reference to "rulers and authorities" (v 10) as "the politico-economic structures of human society" (1979, pp124–125). While Stott does not support this view, he acknowledges that there is an argument for claiming that all worldly institutions will be given a chance to be redeemed.

Paul describes how those who have faith "may approach God with freedom and confidence" (v 12). Thielman comments that "those who believe in him, whether Jews or Gentiles, have the kind of relationship with God that friends have with each other" (2010, p209).

Paul ends this passage by asking his readers not to become discouraged when they hear of how he has had to suffer for preaching the gospel; he is playing his part in God's plan. Hoehner explains that "if Paul had never carried out his ministry of the mystery to the Ephesians, he would not have been in prison and the Ephesians would never have been introduced to Christ" (2002, p470).

Paul's second prayer for the Ephesians (3:14–21)

Paul now continues with the prayer he started at the beginning of the previous passage, describing how he kneels before God to pray on their behalf.

Paul's petition (v 16–19)

Paul asks that God will give his readers inner strength through his spirit, that they can realise important religious truths. Paul prays that they will understand how Christ lives in their hearts through faith, and that they will "grasp how wide and long and high and deep is the love of Christ" (v 18). Understanding these truths will help Paul's readers gain spiritual maturity and make progress towards being the person God intends them to be. Hoehner concludes that "here Paul prays to the father that they may be strengthened by the Spirit with the result that Christ be deeply rooted in the lives of the believers through faith" (2002, p482).

Paul praises God (v 20–21)

Paul's petition on behalf of his readers is no small request; he has asked that they will go from being discouraged to having a spiritual maturity and understanding of important truths. Paul now gives praise to God who can make things happen through his power: "to him who is able to do immeasurably more than all we ask or imagine" (v 20). Thielman comments that "this doxology is a fitting conclusion not only to Paul's intercessory prayer, but also to the entire first half of the letter" (2010, p240). Paul has begun this section by praising God (1:3) and concludes it in a similar way. (A doxology is a hymn or prayer of praise to God.)

TASK
You should aim to write a detailed paragraph to answer each question.
1. Explain what Paul means by the 'mystery' and describe his role in making it known.
   (Your answer should make reference to 3:2–13.)
2. Summarise the main points of Paul's second prayer.
   (Your answer should make reference to 3:14–21.)
3. Explain the significance of both of Paul's prayers within the context of the letter.
   (Your answer should make reference to 1:15–23 and 3:14–23.)

LIVING THE CHRISTIAN LIFE
This chapter marks the beginning of a new section in Paul's letter. He has described previously how Jews and Gentiles have attained unity in the salvation given through Jesus' death on the cross. In recognition of all that Christ has done for them, they should live their lives in keeping with this.

In the local church (Ch 4:1–16)
Unity in the Body of Christ (4:1–6)
An obligation implicit in their calling from God is how Paul's readers should now walk with God. Bruce comments that "those who have been chosen by Christ to sit with God in the heavenly places must remember that the honour of Christ is involved in their daily lives" (1961, p75). Paul refers once again to his status as prisoner, perhaps to reinforce the importance of what he is telling them and to demonstrate how receiving the Christian message has come at a price. The church is now united, so its members must make sure that this unity is maintained. They can do this in the following ways:

1. On a personal level, they should behave in an exemplary manner towards one another: "Be completely humble and gentle; be patient, bearing one another in love" (v 2).

2. They must live in peace with each other, making every effort to remember that the church is now united through the Holy Spirit: "One Lord, one faith, one baptism; one God and father of all, who is over all and through all and in all" (v 5–6).

Paul uses the Greek word *agape* in verse 2, to show that he is referring to the highest form of love, that which involves self-sacrifice. Barclay (2002, p140) explains that to regard a person with *agape* means to seek the highest good for this person, no matter what treatment might be given in return. Thielman comments that "this final affirmation of God's unity prepares the way for Paul's discussion of how he has given 'each one' of his readers a measure of grace to use in aiding the church on its way to unity" (2010, p250).

Maturing in faith (4:7–16)

To develop the idea of God's grace, Paul quotes from Psalm 68:18, a passage that describes God's power in raising Jesus from death. This same power has been given to Paul to help him carry out his responsibilities in preaching the gospel. It is available to every believer, as they also have a role to play in building up the church. The goal is for everyone in the church to be united in faith and become spiritually mature. Bruce comments that "each individual Christian ought to grow up into spiritual maturity, but spiritual maturity in the individual Christian is not enough: there must be spiritual maturity in the corporate personality of the church" (1961, pp86–87).

According to Thielman, "the more mature the church becomes, the more effective it will be at refuting false teaching and maturing into the body of Christ" (2010, p288). For this to happen, each person in the church must make their contribution, recognising that they are all parts of one body: "the whole body grows and builds itself up in love, as each part does its work" (v 16). Hoehner comments that "as each believer functions with the gift given to each, Christ's body, the church, will be built up" (2002, p551).

In conclusion to this teaching on Christian life in the church, it might be useful to note Stott's approach. He writes that "Paul elaborates four truths about the kind of oneness which God intends his new society to enjoy" (1979, p147). They may be stated in the following four propositions:

1. It depends on the **charity** of a person's character and conduct (v 2).
2. It arises from the **unity** of God (v 3–6).
3. It is enriched by the **diversity** of spiritual gifts (v 7–12).
4. It demands the **maturity** of Christian growth (v 13–16).

In the world today (Ch 4:17–5:21)

Living a new way of life (4:17–24)
In this passage, Paul explains to his readers how they are to live as Christians. The teaching can be divided into two parts:

The lifestyle that is no longer appropriate (v 17–19)
Firstly, Paul begins in the negative, instructing his readers not to act as the Gentiles do. Williamson (2009, p126) comments that Paul's use of the word 'Gentiles' is interesting and is an indication that Paul no longer considers his non-Jewish Christian readers to be Gentiles; now they have been brought into the people of God, their conduct needs to change to be consistent with their new identity. Paul describes some of the characteristics of Gentile behaviour and existence – their thinking is futile, they lack understanding and live in ignorance. O'Brien comments that "it is noteworthy that the apostle goes out of his way to emphasize the perceptive and mental dimension in the human estrangement from God" (1999, p320). As a result of being cut off from God, their dissatisfaction has led them to indulge in immoral behaviour. O'Brien describes the Gentiles' sinful condition: "Because of their lack of moral feeling and discernment there were no restraints to their plunging into all kinds of degrading activities" (1999, p322). The behaviour of Paul's readers should stand in stark contrast to this way of life now they have become Christians.

The lifestyle expected now that they know Jesus (v 20–24)
For this section, Paul writes positively about the implications of knowing Jesus and receiving instruction in his teaching. Hodge comments that "hence they are to put off the old self and put on the new self, which is more and more conformed to the image of God" (1994, p148). Paul's readers should know, from the instruction they have received, that they should give up their old way of life characterised by greed and corruption. The attitude of their minds should stand in contrast to the Gentile way of life, where their misguided thinking has left them in darkness (Thielman, 2010, p295). Just as if they were putting on new clothing, Paul urges his readers to put on a new self (v 24). They have recently been recreated in God's image, so their behaviour should reflect this. God created humankind in his likeness or image (Genesis 1:27). Hoehner comments that "what Adam lost in the fall, has been regained by Christ, a new creation in the likeness of God's image" (2002, p611).

Moral behaviour for Christians (4:25–5:2)

In this passage, Paul gives practical advice on how to live as a new creation of God. Stott marvels at how Paul can descend from lofty theological talk "to the nitty-gritty of human behaviour – telling the truth and controlling anger, honesty at work and kindness of speech, forgiveness, love and sexual self-control" (1979, p184).

Paul gives instructions covering:
1. Telling lies (v 25).
2. Anger (v 26–27).
3. Stealing (v 28).
4. Unwholesome speech (v 29).
5. General behaviour, including bitterness, brawling, slander and malice (v 31).

Such immoral behaviour as Paul has described would "grieve the Spirit of God" (v 30). McGrath comments that "Paul stresses that Christian faith must lead to a Christian lifestyle, in which believers stand out from the world in terms of their moral conduct" (1995, p352). After his instructions on the negative behaviour to avoid, Paul characteristically turns to the positive. Hodge comments that "instead of malicious feelings, they should be kind, compassionate and forgiving, just as God forgives them" (1994, p148). Here Paul is stressing the need for believers to try to imitate God, by using his example as a pattern for their lives.

TASK

Read Paul's advice in Ephesians 4:25–32.
Copy and complete the following table.

NEGATIVE BEHAVIOUR	REFERENCE	POSITIVE BEHAVIOUR
Telling lies	v 25	
Anger	v 26–27	
Stealing	v 28	
Unwholesome speech	v 29	
General behaviour, including bitterness, brawling, slander and malice	v 31	

Avoiding sinful behaviour (5:3–7)

Paul spells out very clearly the type of behaviour that is not acceptable for Christians, giving specific examples. Williamson comments that Paul "contrasts the holiness of the Christian way of life to the darkness of the surrounding society" (2009, p138). While immoral or impure behaviour might be common in society, and was perhaps part of their lifestyle before they became Christians, if they continue they will not be part of God's kingdom. They need to set themselves apart and follow a different standard. Paul gives the following examples:

- Sexual immorality and any other impurity.
- Greed.
- Obscenity, foolish talk and coarse joking.

In the previous chapter, Paul has already warned against impurity and unwholesome talk, and now he is reinforcing the importance of correct behaviour. Bruce comments that "fornication and other forms of unclean living were certainly sins against which converts from paganism needed to be put on their guard, as is particularly evident from Paul's Corinthian correspondence" (1961, p102). Paul describes anyone who is "immoral, impure or greedy" (v 5) as an "idolater", no doubt recognising that the person who commits these sins is not putting God first in their lives.

Paul concludes this passage with a warning against those who might try to deceive them with "empty words" (v 6–7). Thielman comments that Paul "is probably talking about anyone, whether an erring believer or an unbeliever, who claims that no harm will come to those who are sexually active outside of marriage or who accumulate wealth for themselves" (2010, p327). Hoehner writes that "because it appears that the unbelievers were not presently suffering the consequences of this lifestyle, believers might easily slide into a similar mode of life" (2002, p663). Paul warns that such behaviour will incur God's anger.

Living as children of light (5:8–14)

A common metaphor in the Bible is the use of darkness to describe the condition of sinful humanity living without God; this is in contrast to the light that comes from God. Williamson comments that "in Paul's letters, 'darkness' usually refers to ignorance and spiritual or moral evil, and 'light' refers to true knowledge and spiritual and moral goodness" (2009, p144). Paul reminds his readers: "For you were once in darkness but now you are light in the Lord" (v 8). As a result, they should live as "children of light" which means showing behaviour such as "goodness, righteousness and truth" (v 9).

This behaviour is in stark contrast to the sexual immorality and greed of the previous passage, as light is to darkness.

However, Paul urges his readers to do more than simply avoid immoral behaviour, now they are living lives of light. They are to be proactive in shining this light in the darkness to make sinful deeds visible. Thielman comments that "they should expose this behaviour for what it is by training the light of the gospel on those who engage in it" (2010, p352). There are differences of opinion in modern scholarship as to whether light is to be shone on those outside or inside the church. Hoehner believes that this passage "is not talking about unbelievers but believers who have become co-partners with the works of unbelievers" (2002, p685); the expectation is that when this wrong-doing is exposed the offending believers might "produce the fruit of light, namely, goodness, righteousness and truth". However, O'Brien disagrees with this interpretation and concludes that "we believe that the passage is describing the process by which darkness is transformed into light. The function of the light is twofold: it exposes the sins of unbelievers and transforms them so that they enter the realm of light" (1999, p374).

Paul concludes with a quotation – possibly from an early Christian baptismal hymn (Williamson, 2009, p147) – to support his argument, urging unbelievers to "wake up" to the truth of the gospel and receive the light of Christ.

Wise behaviour (5:15–21)

Paul has already warned his readers living in a sinful age that it is easy to be led astray by following the wrong example (4:14). In this passage, Paul repeats his warning, urging them to make wise choices about their lifestyle "because the days are evil" (v 16). O'Brien (1999, p383) believes that Paul's language, given his eschatological perspective, means he is not just referring to evil times but to the last days before the end of the world. As Paul's readers await their final redemption, "they are to live wisely, taking advantage of every opportunity in this fallen world to conduct themselves in a manner that is pleasing to God".

The loss of control that results from drunkenness is to be avoided, as it can lead them into sin. Williamson comments that "Paul criticises drunkenness on the basis of what it leads to: debauchery, the ruin that comes from excess or throwing off restraint" (2009, p150). Instead of this form of intoxication, they are to be filled with the Holy Spirit. Hoehner comments that "believers have urgent need of the Holy Spirit's power to live in a manner pleasing to the Lord" (2002, p698). Paul then describes how members of the Christian community can support each other through praising God "with psalms, hymns and spiritual songs" (v 19). Such communal worship can be a great encouragement, but Paul reminds his readers always to give thanks to God for his many blessings.

Paul's final instruction – "submit to one another out of reverence for Christ" (v 21) – provides a link to the following passage, where Paul gives detailed instructions for Christian behaviour in the household.

In the family and household (Ch 5:22–6:9)

This section is sometimes referred to as 'The Household Code', as instruction is given about relationships between husbands and wives, children and parents and slaves and masters. O'Brien notes that "Martin Luther called this scheme a *Haustafel*, which means 'a list of rules for the household'" (1999, p405).

Paul is continuing his advice about the importance of living wisely in a corrupt society. Stott comments that "the divine family ceases to be a credible concept if it is not itself subdivided into human families which display God's love" (1979, p213). According to Bruce, "the graces which ought to flourish in the Christian fellowship might be expected to find a specially congenial environment in the Christian household" (1961, p113).

Paul's practical advice reflects the age in which it was written; he assumes that wives should be obedient to their husbands and he accepts the practice of slavery. However, in his teaching he addresses the subordinate member of each pair first. The focus is not on telling them how to please their husband, parents or master, but how to live in a way that is consistent with their Christian faith. This reinforces the idea that all people are important to God, no matter what their status in society. Stott writes that "in the light of the teaching of Jesus and his apostles, we may confidently and repeatedly affirm at least three relevant truths" (1979, p217). These are:

1. The **dignity** of womanhood, childhood and servanthood.
2. The **equality** before God of all human beings, irrespective of their race, rank, class, culture, sex or age.
3. The **unity** of all Christian believers.

Wives and Husbands (5:22–33)

This section is far longer than the advice given to children and parents or slaves and masters. One reason could be that Paul has emphasised the need to avoid sexual immorality, and Thielman comments that "here Paul provides a positive counterpart to those warnings against sexual perversion" (2010, p370). The other reason is that in this section Paul is giving both practical advice and theological teaching.

Paul begins his teaching to wives with the words, "Wives, submit to your husbands as to the Lord" (v 22). Williamson comments that "these verses are the hardest to understand in the Letter to the Ephesians and cause many people to cringe" (2009, p158). Taking these words as they appear, it might be tempting to dismiss them as following the traditional model of a first century marriage, but inappropriate for our society. Thielman notes that "in the same breath, however, he redefines the traditional expectations about the husband's authority so that his power is used entirely for his wife's benefit, even if loving her in this way should involve laying down his life for her" (2010, p392). To husbands, Paul gives the following instruction: "Husbands, love your wives, just as Christ loved the church and gave himself up for her" (v 25). Wives are being asked to submit voluntarily to a husband who loves them as much as Christ loves the church. Barclay comments that "the basis of the passage is not control; it is love".

Paul makes a number of points about the love between a husband and wife:

1. **It is sacrificial (v 25–27)**

    The ancient Greeks distinguished between different types of love. The word '*eros*' was used for sexual attraction, and '*philos*' conveyed feelings of friendship. Paul does not use either of these words in this passage. "Here, however, the apostle speaks of *agape* ... a love that arises from a choice of the will and that does not depend on the worthiness or response of the person beloved" (Williamson, 2009, p165). *Agape* love involves self-sacrifice; it is the love shown by God for sinful humanity, in sending Jesus to die on the cross. In these verses, Paul describes how Christ's death has cleansed God's people, making them sinless. He compares this to the way a bride is washed and carefully prepared for her wedding day.

2. **It involves caring and respect (v 28–29, 33)**

    Paul instructs husbands to love their wives "as their own bodies" and as much as they love themselves, reasoning that a man will look after himself and respect his body. Bruce comments that "the care which a man bestows upon his body as a matter of course, in feeding and clothing it and generally looking after its care and comfort should equally be bestowed upon his wife" (1961, p118). Therefore a marriage relationship is characterised by care and respect between partners. In this advice about marriage, Paul also includes theological teaching, again referring to the relationship between Christ and the church. Williamson comments that "Jesus likewise looks after the church, because we are members of his body, the physical expression of Christ on earth" (2009, p167).

3. It is permanent and exclusive (v 31)
   Paul quotes from Genesis 2:24, a verse which is also used by Jesus when teaching about marriage. Marriage is a sacred act where a man and woman become one flesh, emphasising the permanence of the union. A further implication of "one flesh" is noted by Hoehner: "Therefore it [marriage] should not be divisive but rather a loving and harmonious relationship" (2002, p784). The love between a husband and wife involves complete fidelity. Paul is, however, giving religious teaching as well as practical advice and he states, "I am talking about Christ and the church" (v 32). The quotation refers to the unity between Christ and the church as well as the unity between a husband and wife; both are permanent relationships requiring total fidelity. According to Thielman, Paul is claiming that when God instituted marriage in Genesis, he intended it to illustrate the union that Christ now has with the church. This is the 'mystery' referred to in v 32, which has been revealed now that the relationship between Christ and the church is apparent. Paul uses this quotation to illustrate both themes in this passage – the relationship between husbands and wives and the relationship between Christ and the church.

The main theme in this passage is the comparison between a husband's love for his wife and the love of Christ for the church. When a wife submits to her husband and when a husband loves, respects and cares for his wife, then this reflects the relationship between Christ and the church. Hoehner concludes that "the primary goal of marriage is not to please oneself but to see the purposes of God work in and through each partner individually and corporately" (2002, p785).

Children and parents (6:1–4)
Paul now gives his attention to another household relationship, that of children and parents. Thielman comments on Paul's approach when he writes that "once again, [Paul] addresses the children and fathers directly, speaking to the subordinate member of the pair first, and probably imagining that both groups are gathered within a house with other believers for worship, listening to his letter as it is read aloud" (2010, p395). O'Brien agrees, writing that "it is obvious from these exhortations that the apostle thinks of local congregations as consisting of whole families who come together not only to praise God but also to hear his word addressed to them" (1999, p440). In this teaching on the relationships between children and parents, Paul focuses on practical advice. Hoehner writes that "there is nothing of the imagery of Christ's authority over the church or the church's

submission to Christ as in the first portion of the household code" (2002, p785).

Paul tells children, "obey your parents", giving the reason that it is the right thing to do. There is another important reason for children to do this. "Honour your father and mother" is one of the Ten Commandments (Exodus 20:12), and Paul explains that this is the first commandment with a promise: anyone who keeps this commandment will live for a long time in the Promised Land. O'Brien notes that "here the text has in view children who are in the process of learning and growing up" (1999, p441). However, the obligation on children to honour their parents extended into adulthood, where the father could maintain authority over the family until death.

When Paul gives advice to parents, he focuses on fathers. Thielman comments that "although children must obey both parents, Paul implicitly recognises that as the dominant person in the household, fathers need special instruction on how to use their positions of authority" (2010, p359). Children should be raised in a positive and supportive environment, ensuring that they receive appropriate religious instruction (v 4). According to Bruce, it is possible for parents "to be so unreasonable in their demands on their children that the children are irritated beyond measure and try to please their parents and do what they say" (1961, p122).

Slaves and Masters (6:5–9)

Slaves and masters are the final set of relationships in Paul's household code, and as with his previous instruction, Paul addresses the subordinate member of the pair first. Slaves are instructed to be obedient and to not win their master's approval only when they are being watched. Paul instructs slaves to "serve wholeheartedly, as if you were serving the Lord, not men" (v 5), as everyone will be rewarded for the good they do, whether a slave or free person. Slaves should therefore do their work with an attitude of goodwill. O'Brien comments that "this kind of inner commitment can occur only as slaves recognise that in serving their masters they are rendering obedience to their heavenly Lord, Christ" (1999, p450).

Paul then instructs masters: "treat your slaves in the same way" (v 9), presumably with respect and not with heavy-handed authority. This teaching would be radical in Paul's day, compared to the treatment usually given to slaves. "In order to deal with their slaves, owners were known to threaten beatings, sexual harassment, or selling male slaves away from the household with the result that they would be parted forever from their loved ones" (O'Brien, 1999, p454). Paul reminds slave owners that they share equal status with their slaves, as both have the same master who is in heaven. Williamson comments that "masters will themselves be judged by their master Christ on the basis of their conduct, and this judge treats masters and slaves the same" (2009, p187).

Bible scholars have often commentated that this passage shows Paul accepting the social convention of his day by accepting slavery. While there is no direct criticism of slavery in this passage, Paul's advice to slave owners suggests a very different type of relationship to that which would be commonplace in the first century between slaves and masters. Thielman comments that "Paul's advice to believing slave owners subtly undermines the whole system of slaveholding … the threat of violence is impossible in such an arrangement, and without the threat of violence, the whole system will theoretically collapse" (2010, p410).

In this passage, Paul is giving practical advice to Christians on how they should live and work. "The issue was not that of an acceptance of an institution sanctioned by law and part of the fabric of Graeco-Roman society; nor was it a question of how to react to demand for its abolition" (O'Brien, 1999, p448).

TASK
Essay practice
1. Discuss Paul's teaching on living the Christian life.
- A discussion may include some of the following points:
- Behaviour towards other Christians in the local church.
- Reference to the sinful lifestyle often lived by Gentiles and how this is no longer appropriate.
- The moral behaviour expected of a new creation.
- Reference to the 'Household Code'.

2. "Even when giving practical advice, Paul always includes theological teaching." Critically evaluate this claim.
- A critical evaluation may include some of the following points:
- Reference to Paul's teaching on behaviour towards other Christians and the church as the body of Christ.
- Paul's advice on maturing in faith includes teaching on God's power.
- Reference to teaching on moral living that involves a discussion of light and darkness.

continued

> - The relationship between wives and husbands is seen as a parallel to Christ and the church.
> - On the other hand, the teaching to parents and children, slaves and masters seems to be mostly practical advice.
> - Reference to Paul's teaching on preparing for spiritual warfare and to what extent this is practical advice or theological teaching.

SPIRITUAL WARFARE (CH 6:10-18)
The Armour of God (6:10-18)
Throughout this letter, Paul has urged his readers to avoid sin and live a life that is pleasing to God. However, he recognises that this is not an easy task and believers need all the resources available to them.

How to be prepared
Paul encourages his readers to "be strong in the Lord" (v 10). Living the Christian life involves conflict, and Paul was no stranger to this, as he often faced hostilities on his missionary journeys. However, there is another conflict facing Christians on a spiritual level "against the powers of this dark world and against the spiritual forces of evil" (v 12). In this well-known passage, Paul urges his readers to "put on the full armour of God so that you can take your stand against the devil's schemes" (v 11). O'Brien comments that "the emphasis here is on donning the 'whole armour' in order to be protected fully in this spiritual warfare" (1999, p462). Paul describes what this involves:

- **The belt of truth:** The first preparation in arming for spiritual warfare is to have the protection of truth – knowing the truth of the gospel and remaining truthful in personal conduct.
- **The breastplate of righteousness:** "To put on the breastplate of righteousness is to conduct oneself justly in a manner consistent with the new self" (Williamson, 2009, p195).
- **Feet fitted with the readiness that comes from the gospel of truth:** A believer can strengthen their own faith by being ready to share the gospel with others; this is an important part of spiritual warfare.
- **The shield of faith:** "Paul is summoning Christians to believe firmly in God and his word, especially when under attack" (Williamson, 2009, p196).
- **The helmet of salvation:** A soldier would feel fully protected after putting on his helmet; "Likewise, believers' possession of salvation gives them confidence of safeness during the assaults of the devil" (Hoehner, 2002, p850).

- **The sword of the Spirit:** "The only offensive weapon is the 'sword of the spirit' which allows the Christian to launch a counter-attack against such spiritual forces, armed with the spirit of the living God" (McGrath, 1995, p353).

Why there is a need to stand firm

Paul is speaking metaphorically in this passage of a well-protected soldier equipped for defence against enemy attack. A Christian, armed with the truth of the gospel and protected by righteousness and faith, has a strong defence against the forces of evil. It is interesting to note that in Paul's list of the armour of God, everything is defensive except the final item, "the sword of the spirit, which is the word of God" (v 17). Paul assures his readers that if they are defended in this way, they will be able to stand firm against the devil and the forces of evil. The Roman Centurion, according to Polybius, was to be the kind of person who could be relied upon, when under pressure, to stand fast and not give way (O'Brien, 1999, referring to Polybius, *Histories*, 6.24). The same determination is needed from Christians as they stand firm against attacks from evil forces. "The devil and his forces must not be allowed to gain new territory in Christ's kingdom or rob believers of their spiritual blessings in Christ" (Hoehner, 2002, p853). A Roman soldier did not fight alone, but as a member of a regiment. In the same way, the church, as a group of believers, must be united in spiritual battle.

Who is the enemy?

In his commentary on this passage, Stott (1979, p270) returns to consider the argument presented on page 259. Stott refers to scholars, notably GB Caird and Markus Barth, who claim that Paul's references to 'rulers' and 'authorities' include the political and judicial authorities of society. Stott concludes that he finds this suggestion "artificial to the point of being contrived" (1979, p272). O'Brien agrees that Paul is not writing about a struggle against secular conventions and authorities, as this view "fails to do justice to the historical context of the New Testament in which belief in the spiritual realm was widespread" (1999, p469). Hoehner comments that "the struggle of believers ultimately is not a human conflict but is a battle against wicked spiritual forces" (2002, p820).

The importance of prayer

However, in addition to putting on the armour of God, Paul stresses the importance of prayer. O'Brien notes that "prayer is given greater prominence within the context of the battle with the powers of darkness than any of the weapons listed" (1999, p483). Believers are to pray "on all occasions with all kinds of prayers and requests", as the struggle with the powers of darkness is never ending. Paul asks his readers to pray for all believers and especially for him, in his calling to preach the gospel. Even though he is in chains, Paul is continuing in his endeavours to preach the gospel.

TASK
You should aim to write a detailed paragraph to answer each question.
1. Explain how Paul uses an analogy of a Roman soldier to give advice and encouragement to Christians.
2. Outline the debate between scholars on the interpretation of "rulers and authorities". Give reasons for which view you think is most likely.
3. What can Paul's readers learn from his example about the importance of prayer?

FINAL GREETINGS (6:21–24)
Paul is sending the letter with Tychicus, whom he commends to his readers as "dear brother and faithful servant in the Lord" (v 21). When he arrives, Tychicus will also bring news of how Paul is doing and give them encouragement. Paul ends in a similar way to that in which he ends his other letters, asking that his readers know peace, love and faith (v 23). Finally, he asks for "grace for all who love our Lord Jesus Christ with an undying love" (v 24).

TASK
Create a spider diagram or mind map to show how the message of Ephesians was relevant for the Early Church. You could consider the following areas:
- Theological teaching.
- Practical advice on Christian living.
- The household code: advice for family life.

RELEVANCE FOR TODAY
Williamson comments that the rich theology in Ephesians makes it an important source of church teaching and adds that "although it contains a few texts that must be applied differently because of cultural changes, Ephesians remains as relevant today as when it was first written" (2009, p21).

Some points that remain relevant for today:

- **Christian conduct:** Williamson writes that "today also, Christians must choose to put off the lifestyle of the old fallen human nature and to … live in union with Christ" (2009, p22). It is important for Christians to give shining testimony in a dark world. The types of behaviour referred to by Paul as inappropriate for his first century readers still apply today, including unwholesome talk, rage, brawling and sexual immorality.

- **The importance of prayer:** This letter contains two passages where Paul prays for his readers. He also asks them to pray for him in his efforts to preach the gospel, even though he is a prisoner. Prayer is therefore an important way of strengthening oneself and others in Christian faith and witness. Paul also refers to prayer as being vital in the spiritual battle against the forces of evil.

- **Relationships at home:** Christian marriages must adhere to the highest standards, with the relationship between husband and wife being like that of Christ and the church. Paul's teaching on relationships within marriage continues to be an important part of church teaching today. Likewise the teaching on family relationships where children show respect for their parents, who in turn honour their obligations and responsibilities towards their children, is still relevant.

- **Relationships in the workplace:** Hoehner discusses how some principles from Paul's teaching on slaves and masters can be applied to employee/employer relationships, although he warns that "the application of this passage to contemporary times must be done with caution" (2002, p816). Employees should work with diligence and integrity, while employers should treat employees with similar respect. The behaviour of both employees and employers should be a good witness in the workplace to non-Christian employees. Hoehner comments that "both Christian employees and Christian employers need also to realise that they have a heavenly master to whom they are accountable for their attitudes and conduct" (2002, p816).

- **Spiritual warfare:** The teaching about putting on the armour of God continues to be relevant today, as there is still a spiritual battle being fought. In summary, Paul's teaching about spiritual armour involves being truthful, behaving appropriately, reading the gospel and having an attitude of faith and hope. All of these are still an important part of Christian life today.

TASK

1. Work with a partner. Review the text of Ephesians and see what other examples you can find for relevance today.
2. Read the following quotation and discuss the questions that follow:

"It is all too easy for believers to be influenced by the surrounding world and to succumb to its ways of thinking and behaving. The result is that what is acceptable to the culture of the day becomes acceptable in the church. This is particularly true in contemporary Western society in the area of sexual morality" (O'Brien, 1999, p364).

- What points is the writer making?
- Do you think Christian standards should reflect contemporary values in society or should they remain separate?
- Is there a danger that church teaching can become outdated and therefore ignored completely?

EXAMINATION PRACTICE

Question adapted from CCEA's Specimen Assessment Materials

(a) Analyse Paul's teaching on Christian theology in his Letter to the Ephesians. [20 marks]

Your answer could include an analysis of the following points:
- Paul's teaching about God's kingdom on earth; marriage as a mirror of Jesus' relationship with the church.
- Consideration of Paul's teaching on salvation as God's plan from eternity to show the glory of his grace.
- Salvation as the work of a gracious and loving God; the blessings available to those who accept salvation.
- Discussion of Paul's teaching on the power of the Holy Spirit sealing the redemption and forgiveness from God.

> **(b) "Paul's advice on Christian living has no relevance for life in the twenty first century." To what extent do you agree with this statement? [30 marks]**
>
> Your answer could include an evaluation of the following points:
> - Examination of different ways of interpreting and applying scripture: literalist and more liberal.
> - Consideration of the belief that these letters are the word of God, are timeless and always relevant.
> - The relevance or otherwise of teaching on immorality: the variety of attitudes to sexual morality, differing attitudes to the role of the church in administering discipline.
> - Consideration of the relevance or otherwise of the church settling its own disputes, how the church has been influenced by society in relation to use of the law.
> - Discussion of the relevance or otherwise of Paul's teaching on marriage, singleness, separation, divorce; the role of wives in marriage and Paul's advice to slaves.
> - The context of each letter and the issues which were found in each community.
> - Possible reasons why the letters might seem problematic, unhelpful or less relevant: the first century contexts, ancient documents, the expectation of an imminent *Parousia*.
>
> (Note that this part (b) does not refer specifically to Ephesians; this means you can include relevant material from any of the letters you have studied.)

PAUL AS TEACHER, PASTOR AND THEOLOGIAN
Teacher
This role involves both evangelism and support for those who are already Christians. Paul spends much of his time teaching non-Christians about the message of the gospel, with the aim of gaining as many converts as possible. Another aspect of this role is giving further teaching and advice to those who are already Christians.

In chapter 3 of Ephesians, Paul shows courage and determination in proclaiming the gospel. At the start of this chapter, Paul refers to his current status as a prisoner. Although he has often faced suffering as a result of preaching the gospel, Paul accepts this as part of his call from God. He is thankful for any opportunity to share the gospel, whatever the cost to himself. The 'Household Code' in Ephesians chapters 5–6 is an example of Paul teaching Christians how to live their lives in a way that is pleasing to God.

Pastor

The term 'pastor' is sometimes used for a minister responsible for a congregation; it also implies care and support.

In chapter 6 of Ephesians, Paul can be seen in a pastoral role, giving advice about spiritual warfare and standing firm against the devil and forces of evil. Paul shows great concern that his converts do not underestimate the difficulty involved in maintaining their faith in a hostile world. Through his letters, he tries to give as much help and support as he can to churches and individuals.

Theologian

Theology is a study of the nature and attributes of God. For your AS course, you had an introduction to Paul's theology, reported by Luke in his speeches given at Pisidian Antioch and Athens. Paul undoubtedly had great intellect, which before his conversion was spent studying under the Jewish scholar, Gamaliel (Acts 22:3). In his letters, Paul shows his ability as a theologian, explaining complex religious truths.

The first part of Ephesians is mostly theological teaching. In chapter 1, Paul deals with some weighty theological teaching as he gives details of God's plan for salvation through Christ. This continues in the next chapter, as Paul explains how God's plan for salvation was always to unite Jews and Gentiles. In the second part of the letter, the emphasis is more on practical teaching about Christian living. However, even when giving practical advice on marriage relationships, Paul uses this as an opportunity for theological teaching about the role of Christ and the church.

TASK

The consideration of Paul's different roles is also valid for the other letters you have studied. Copy and complete a table like the one below, finding relevant references for Galatians and 1 Corinthians, plus any additional examples for Ephesians.

PAUL'S ROLE	GALATIANS	1 CORINTHIANS	EPHESIANS
Teacher			
Pastor			
Theologian			

Remember that there will be overlap between these different roles and you may have a different opinion to other students in your class about what role is shown by a particular reference. Decide where you think is the most appropriate place to write your example.

BY THE END OF THIS CHAPTER YOU SHOULD BE ABLE TO:

- demonstrate knowledge and understanding of, and critically evaluate the background to the Letter, including:
  - the historical context of the text: establishing the church in Ephesus during the Third Missionary Journey;
  - evidence for the writing of the Letter; and
  - Paul as teacher, pastor and theologian giving both religious teaching and practical advice; and
- demonstrate knowledge and understanding of, and critically evaluate the main themes of Ephesians, including:
  - Ptheological teaching on God's plan for Salvation through Christ (1:1–3:21);
  - living the Christian life: in the local church (4:1–16), in the world today (4:17–5:20), in the family and household (5:21–6:9);
  - spiritual warfare: the armour of God (6:10–18);
  - the value of this text for the Early Church; and
  - relevance for today.

Synoptic Assessment

Theme: Controversy, division and reconciliation

Synoptic assessment continues to be a compulsory part of the assessment for A2, but in a different form from the previous specification. CCEA have given three areas of study for each synoptic theme. Students will be expected to answer a specific question on this prescribed content. This chapter contains material relevant to the prescribed theme for this module with suggestions for study and other aspects of human experience. However, it is important to remember that there are many other relevant examples as well as those suggested here.

Part (a) will assess knowledge and understanding and will be awarded 40% of the marks for the answer. Students will use the specified content to identify, investigate and analyse issues asked for by the question and also to look for connections, comparisons and contrasts with their other area of study. These links with the different units of study are not expected to be exhaustive, but they are required.

Part (b) of the synoptic assessment will be an examination of other aspects of human experience, which will also assess the skill of critical evaluation. It will be necessary for students to discuss varying points of view. This part of the answer will be awarded 60% of the marks.

THE PROBLEM OF CONTROVERSY WITHIN RELIGION
Introduction

The term 'controversy' originated in c1384 from the Latin '*controversia*', as a composite of controversus, meaning 'turned in an opposite direction', from *contra* (Latin for 'against') and *vertere* (Latin for 'to turn') (www.wikipedia.org). A controversy can be described as an argument, debate or disagreement between people or groups of people. Religious controversy can take place between different faiths, or within the same faith. For centuries, there have been conflicts of a religious or theological nature. These conflicts have occurred within faith groups, sometimes leading to denominational schisms; other conflicts have occurred between orthodox and liberal groups within the same religion. Controversy can be related to both religious belief and practice. Religious controversy can arise due to intolerance, or a lack of understanding or acceptance of others religious ideas, beliefs or practices.

Controversies in church history

For many centuries, there has been controversy in the Christian Church regarding the date of Easter. These disputes are known as paschal controversies. The Gospels of Matthew, Mark and Luke describe Jesus' death and resurrection as taking place at the same time as the Jewish Passover festival, which was always celebrated on 14 Nisan. Easter was originally celebrated on this date, but dispute soon arose about whether Easter should always be celebrated on a Sunday, the day of the resurrection. This meant a fixed date would not be possible. Churches in and around Rome adopted the practice of celebrating Easter on the Sunday following Passover, calling it 'The day of the resurrection of our Saviour'. The Eastern Christians continued to celebrate Easter on Passover, a practice officially condemned by the Council of Nicaea in AD325. This leads to the question of whether greater efforts could have been made at this stage to breach the division.

However, the controversy between Eastern and Western churches ran deeper than the dispute about the date of Easter. There were other issues concerning leadership and theology. To add to the division, there were barriers with language, as the Eastern Church used Greek, while those in the West adopted Latin. As a result, there was a break between the churches in AD1054, known as the East-West Schism, resulting in the formation of the Eastern Orthodox Church and the Roman Catholic Church. There have been two formal attempts at reconciliation, in 1274 at the Second Council of Lyon and in 1438/1439 at the Council of Florence. Some agreements were reached by church leaders, but in practical terms, the schism was never going to be healed. The reunion of East and West was seen to be an unattainable goal. It could be argued that this controversy could never reach a satisfactory conclusion, as there were political, social and cultural differences as well as religious issues.

The controversy regarding the date of Easter had repercussions for the church in Britain and Ireland in the sixth and seventh centuries. There was serious disunity in Northumbria, which had been converted by Celtic missionaries who followed the Eastern tradition for dating Easter. However, by 662 there was also a Roman influence in this area, which included Queen Eanfled, Bishop Wilfrid and other influential people. As Bede explains:

"It is said that the confusion in those days was such that Easter was sometimes kept twice in one year, so that when the King had ended Lent and was keeping Easter, the Queen and her attendants were still fasting and keeping Palm Sunday … This dispute rightly began to trouble the minds and consciences of many people, who feared that they might have received the name of Christian in vain." (*Ecclesiastical History of the English People*, 731, available on http://sourcebooks.fordham.edu/basis/bede-book1.asp)

The Synod of Whitby was held in 663/664 to decide whether the Kingdom of Northumbria would follow the Celtic or Roman tradition. King Oswiu decided that his kingdom would calculate Easter according to the custom of Rome. This Synod marked an important turning point in the history of the Celtic church in the British Isles and showed a successful attempt to bring unity.

TASKS

Research

There are opportunities for further research into these issues. Find out more about:
- The dating of Easter and the system used today.
- The reasons for the East-West Schism.
- The fundamental issues underlying the Synod of Whitby.

For discussion
- What do these historical examples show about reasons for controversy within religion?
- How effective is the response of the church to conflict and controversy?
- To what extent was the division between the Eastern and Western churches inevitable?

The split between the Eastern and Western churches was the first major schism in the church. However, the Reformation brought further division. McGrath comments that "the Reformation initially led to the formation of a cluster of Protestant churches in Europe, subsequently to the renewal and reformation of the Catholic Church in the same region, and inevitably to the conflict between Protestants and Catholics on the one hand and between the various Protestant churches on the other" (2011, p43).

One of the great leaders in the Reformation was Martin Luther, who began his protest by nailing his 95 theses on the door of the Castle Church in Wittenberg in 1517. Although he had been a monk and later a priest, Luther had for many years been troubled by some of the teachings and practices in the church, particularly concerning the forgiveness of sin. Luther believed that God's gift of salvation through faith should not depend on good works or the purchase of indulgences. Luther's list of theses was an attack on the indulgence system and the authority of the Pope. However, by choosing to write in Latin, Luther showed he did not intend to initiate a break with the Catholic Church, but to have dialogue with church leaders. However, this was not to happen and a confrontation with the Pope led to Luther being excommunicated; he publically burned the Papal Bull[1] and became an outlaw. According to Shelley, "those flames in early December, 1520, were a fit symbol of the defiance of the Pope raging throughout Germany" (1982, p237). The Reformation had begun.

What had started as an attempt at reform had led to a split in Western Christianity. The response of the Catholic Church was to react to criticism and initiate self-reform. The resulting Council of Trent was held in three parts from 1545 to 1563, and clarified every doctrine disputed by the Protestants. Shelley comments that "the Council of Trent guaranteed that modern Catholicism would be governed by the collaboration between God and man. The Pope remained, the seven sacraments remained, the sacrifice of the mass remained" (1982, p278). The Council played an important part in Catholic history and revitalised the church in many parts of Europe.

> ### DISCUSSION
> Was Luther right to make his protest in such a public way? It could be argued that Luther should have sought a way to bring about reform without causing such a serious split in the church, which remains to this day. Or, as with the schism of 1054, where there are significant differences of doctrine and practice, is it inevitable that controversy will lead to division?

The question of authority

Many of the controversies surrounding the Reformation involved the question of authority: What is the position of the Pope and what authority

---

1 A Papal Bull was a letter or charter issued by the Pope, so named because of the lead seal (Latin bulla) that authenticated it (www.wikipedia.org/wiki/Papal_bull). In this case, Luther was ordered to retract his views or be excommunicated.

does he hold? If the ultimate authority comes from God's Word, then should people have a right to read the Bible for themselves?

The Catholic Church today teaches that Christ created the church so that his mission in the world could continue through his living presence in the form of the Holy Spirit. Therefore, the authority of the church comes from Christ. The Apostles appointed successors to make sure the gospel would continue to be preached faithfully as "the lasting source of all life from the church" (Vatican II, *Lumen Gentium*, 20. Also *Catechism of the Catholic Church*, #860[2]). This idea of apostolic succession began when Jesus said to Peter that "on this rock I will build my church ... I will give you the keys of the Kingdom of Heaven; whatever you bind on earth will be bound in heaven, and whatever you loose on earth will be loosed in heaven" (Matthew 16:18–19).

The authority Jesus gave to Peter is the source of Papal supremacy, the doctrine that the Pope has full and universal power over the whole church. The Catholic Church teaches that "the Pope enjoys, by divine institution, supreme, full, immediate and universal power in the care of souls" (*Catechism*, #937). The Pope has the power to act as supreme pastor, and he is the only spokesperson for the entire Catholic Church. Papal infallibility is a teaching of the Catholic Church that states that the Pope is preserved from the possibility of error when he defines a doctrine to be held by the whole church. However Papal infallibility is only on matters of faith and morals (and has been used twice in Church history). Bishops have the role of teacher within their individual diocese. Their teaching is understood to be authentic doctrine, as they teach in communion with the Pope. It is not considered a possibility that there will be a conflict.

For Protestant churches, the direct source of authority is not the church, but the Bible. Martin Luther, as an educated university professor, was able to read the Bible in Latin and study it for himself. He came to his famous doctrine that the way to salvation was by faith alone. Shelley explains how "Luther saw it clearly now. Man is saved only by his faith in the merit of Christ's sacrifice. The cross alone can remove man's sin and save him from the grasp of the devil" (1982, p239).

Preaching and Bible study, with an emphasis on people having access to the Bible in a language they could understand, became important features of reformed churches. McGrath comments on how "a new emphasis came to be placed upon the public status of scripture within the church. The expository

---

2   For *Lumen Gentium*, see www.ewtn.com/library/councils/v2church.htm. For the *Catechism*, see www.vatican.va/archive/ENG0015/_INDEX.HTM.

sermon, the Biblical commentary and works of biblical theology came to be characteristic of the reformation" (2011, p59).

Protestants believe that the Bible alone has absolute authority and is the source of God's revelation regarding salvation: "All scripture is God-breathed and is useful for teaching, rebuking, correcting and training in righteousness" (2 Timothy 3:16). Catholics believe that the Bible and church tradition are equally binding on believers, whereas Protestants do not accept the supremacy and infallibility of the Pope as God's representative on Earth. There have been attempts in recent years to encourage inter-church dialogue and find common ground; however, there are differences between the Catholic and Protestant churches that are as significant today as they were at the start of the Reformation.

OTHER ASPECTS OF HUMAN EXPERIENCE
Ecumenism

The ecumenical movement is made up of people who seek unity in diversity within the Christian church. It confronts what it sees are the frustrations, difficulties and ironies of the modern world of pluralism. Its ideas are founded in the teachings and prayers of Jesus as recorded in the Bible, which ecumenists believe indicate that Jesus wanted "one, holy, catholic [universal] and apostolic church". The word 'ecumenism' is ultimately derived from the Greek word *oikoumenē* which means 'the inhabited world'.

Within the Protestant tradition, the term 'ecumenism' came to be used, following the International Missionary Conference of 1910 in Edinburgh, to refer to the gathering together and cooperation between various missionary and evangelistic Christians. In the Catholic tradition, the term came to be used after the Second Vatican Council of 1962-65 to refer to the renewal of the whole life of the church and in particular its attempt to be more responsive to non-Catholic ('separated') Christian denominations.

Contemporary church practices

Today, churches have different opinions about the role of women. In the Catholic Church, while the role of women is not generally restricted, a woman cannot be a priest. In some Protestant churches women can be ordained, but in others they can only assist in worship, but not preach. This is clearly an area of controversy, and some people would accuse the churches of being sexist in denying women the same rights as men. This controversy is seen by some to have a negative impact on the church, in a society where there is both legislation and public awareness to ensure the rights of women. On the other hand, some Christians would argue that as the Bible is God's word; Christians have to accept Paul's teaching that "women should remain silent in the churches. They are not allowed to speak, but must be in submission, as the Law says" (1 Corinthians 14:34). Some denominations hold the view that women can serve as worship leaders or youth ministers, but may not be in a role where they have spiritual authority over adult men.

OTHER ASPECTS OF HUMAN EXPERIENCE
Attitudes to women in leadership

As part of a major survey of the views of evangelicals in the UK by the Evangelical Alliance, 17,000 Christians were asked to comment on the statement that:

"Women should be eligible for all roles within the church in the same way that men are."

- 51% agreed strongly with the statement.
- 20% agreed a little with the statement.
- 9% were unsure.
- 10% disagreed a little with the statement.
- 10% disagreed strongly with the statement.

(www.eauk.org/church/research-and-statistics/women-in-ministry.cfm)

The issue of spiritual gifts is also controversial within Christianity today. Paul teaches at length about spiritual gifts in 1 Corinthians Ch 12–14, considering them to be important in the life of the church. Every believer had at least one gift to be used for the good of others and the church. As God decides who receives each gift, Paul stressed that there should be no feelings of superiority over who has a particular gift. The issue of speaking in tongues was divisive in Corinth and continues to be so today. Some Christians do not accept that spiritual gifts happen today in the way they are described in the Bible, particularly speaking in tongues. They argue that Paul teaches that tongues are temporary and inadequate: "Now these three remain: faith hope and love. But the greatest of these is love" (1 Cor 13:13). Once the Bible was written down, there was no longer any need for this form of revelation from God. However, there are millions of Christians who speak in tongues today, across many different denominations, particularly Elim and Pentecostal churches. Tongues are a way for a believer to communicate with God, sometimes with a message for the whole congregation. Nevertheless, the issue of speaking in tongues remains controversial, as some doubt their authenticity.

> ### DISCUSSION
>
> Is there a way for this problem to be resolved or will it continue to be an issue that divides Christians?

Healing Miracles

A further problem involving spiritual gifts relates to healing miracles. During his ministry, the Gospel writers record Jesus healing, exorcising demons and raising people from the dead. In Acts, the apostles are described as performing similar miracles through the power of Jesus. Miracles of healing cause division among Christians, with some maintaining that dramatic healings, like speaking tongues, are not signs of God at work today. To further add to the controversy, some people who call themselves "faith healers" have been proved not to be genuine. However, there is general agreement among many Christians that God works miracles today, but at the time and in the manner of his choosing. Many churches have a healing ministry where people's needs are brought to God in prayer. The emphasis is not on a sudden healing but more on asking God to bring relief to the whole person, in body, mind and spirit.

Baptism

The issue of baptism has long been problematic for the church. Some churches practice infant baptism as a symbol that the child is a member of God's family. Promises are made by parents and godparents, with water sprinkled or poured on the baby's head as a symbol of new life and being washed from sin. However, for other Christians it is clearly more than a symbol, as baptism is a sign of sharing in new life received through sacramental grace. However, some Christians believe that infant baptism is not consistent with Bible teaching. In Acts, most of the baptisms described were of adult believers who had already come to faith. In addition, baptism should be performed by full immersion under water, as Paul taught that baptism was a symbol of Christ's death and resurrection (Romans 6:4). McGrath comments that the rise of Baptist churches in England during the seventeenth century shows a rejection of the traditional practice of baptising infants, and that "baptism was to be administered only when an individual showed signs of grace, repentance, or faith" (2011, p423).

These issues show how diverse the Christian Church has become over the last two centuries. An important question concerns the extent to which these differences matter, as not every variation in church practice is a cause for controversy. However, many Christians believe that efforts should be made to bring greater unity between churches.

TASK
For discussion
- What other issues are there on which different Christian denominations are divided today?
- Do you think there is any possibility that controversies within the church could be reconciled? Explain your reasons.
- Use the internet for further research into the work of the Ecumenical Movement. Assess its contribution in attempting to bring unity to the church.

MORAL CONFLICT BETWEEN RELIGION AND SECULAR SOCIETY

Introduction

Religious controversy and division do not just take place within religious groups. Throughout history, and especially in contemporary society, religious values and ideas often clash with secular views. The word 'moral' is concerned with what is right and wrong. A person's morals relate to their beliefs and values as well as their actions. Moral standards are determined by a number of factors, including religion, upbringing and personal experience, so it is arguably impossible to have one moral code that applies to all people everywhere. Therefore, some degree of conflict is inevitable, particularly in the relationship between religion and secular society.

Sometimes secular society promotes values that are compatible with religious teaching and such policies can have a positive impact. However, as human experience has shown, the state can often promote policies that are totally contrary to religious teaching and therefore unacceptable for religious believers.

Sex and relationships

The issue of sexual behaviour is the cause of much controversy between the church and secular society and illustrates the tension that can exist. There are practices regarded as highly immoral by some Christians, yet which are legislated for by the state, making them legal and widely accepted.

Sex and Marriage

Sexual behaviour continues to be an area of controversy in society today. Many Christians would take a conservative view that the only place for a sexual relationship is within marriage. Conservative Christians, perhaps influenced either by Scripture or the theory of Natural Moral Law, would condemn any form of sexual activity outside marriage and view cohabitation as being immoral. Wilcockson comments that "in the past, as today, the most important institution through which men and women could express themselves sexually was through marriage" (2000, p76).

However, some Christians today would take a more liberal stance on sex outside marriage. For example, Catholic theologian Jack Dominion, disagreeing with official Catholic teaching, claimed that where a relationship is "committed, loving and permanent" then high moral standards are realised regardless of whether the couple are married or not (Bowie, 2001, p180). However, when Christian views as a whole are compared to standards of secular society today, there is often controversy and division. Many people feel the church is out-dated with its teaching on marriage for life and no sex outside marriage.

OTHER ASPECTS OF HUMAN EXPERIENCE
Contraception

Contraception is an issue where secular society may promote practices that are not in harmony with religious teaching. The Catholic Church believes that contraception goes against one of the main purposes of marriage, which is to have children. Wilcockson explains that "having a child reminds us that in Catholic theology sex must always be considered in the purpose or 'goods' of marriage" (2000, p135).

However, in many societies in the world today, contraception is legal, freely available and actively promoted in an attempt to limit the spread of HIV/AIDS.

It is estimated that nearly 40 million people around the world are living with HIV/AIDS, with nearly two thirds of them in Sub-Saharan Africa. It is widely accepted that the use of condoms can prevent the spread of this disease. The Catholic Church, following Natural Law, remains officially opposed to artificial contraception, even though some within the church would condone its use to restrict the spread of HIV/AIDS.

More recently, speaking in February 2016 in response to the Zika crisis, Pope Francis suggested pastoral approaches to this difficult situation. Zika, a disease carried by mosquitoes, is thought to be a risk factor in a condition that can lead to babies being born with unnaturally small heads. However, Pope Francis completely ruled out abortion for women carrying babies affected by the virus. (www.inquisitr.com/2847486/avoiding-pregnancy-is-not-an-absolute-evil-pope-francis-approves-the-use-of-birth-control-in-some-instances)

Discussion

It could be argued that these cases are examples of where religion should have to accept the authority of the state, with government schemes to promote the use of contraception having the support of the church. On the other hand, is moral conflict inevitable in cases such as these?

Divorce

Questions of divorce and remarriage continue to cause controversy between religion and society. From a secular point of view, divorce is legal and socially acceptable in most cases. The British Humanist Association claims that divorce is "sometimes the best solution, putting an end to conflict, improving the quality of life for everyone in the family". (www.humanismforschools.org.uk/pdfs/Family%20Matters.pdf)

However, there are many different opinions among Christians. The Catholic Church teaches that marriage is a sacrament and an indissoluble bond. Wilcockson explains Catholic teaching by writing that "there are no grounds for divorce, although it is possible to separate or to declare that a marriage never occurred and that it was null from the start" (2000, p81). Many Protestant churches, such as the Anglican Church and Methodist Church, would disagree with this teaching and believe that divorce should be available as a last resort.

Homosexuality and same sex marriage

Homosexuality is another source of religious controversy. Wilcockson writes that "homosexuality, more than any other area of sexual ethics at present, challenges theology to consider just what it means to be a sexual person living a full life in God's image" (2000, p61). Many Christians today take an absolutist approach to acts of homosexual sex. Basing their views on biblical teaching, they believe homosexual sex is a sin and should therefore not take place. The main Bible references to support this view are from Leviticus and Paul's letters. Paul wrote:

> *"Do you not know that the wicked will not inherit the kingdom of God? Do not be deceived: Neither the sexually immoral, nor idolaters nor adulterers nor male prostitutes nor homosexual offenders nor thieves nor the greedy nor drunkards nor slanderers nor swindlers will inherit the kingdom of God."* (1 Cor 6:9).

This issue raises the question of whether moral conflict and controversy are inevitable. If a religious text prohibits an action, then surely believers can be expected to uphold this, despite the changing views of secular society. Historically, homosexuals have suffered greatly as a result of both religious attitudes and discriminatory treatment by the state. However, many state authorities now have legislation in place making it unlawful to discriminate against a person because of their sexual orientation. This is in direct contrast to the official opinion of the main churches in Northern Ireland, who would not condone homosexual acts. While the Catholic Church makes a distinction between the inclination and the act, the *Catechism of the Catholic Church* states that "homosexual acts are intrinsically disordered" (#2357), where the term "disordered" means being in contrast to the natural "order" of creation. However, the rest of the *Catechism* teaches about the need to treat homosexual people with love, respect and sensitivity. These views are shared by many Protestant Christians.

In conclusion, ethics writer Bowie argues that "to produce a Christian ethic that regards homosexual lifestyles as positive and good requires a considerable re-evaluation of scripture and a change in the assumptions about natural law" (2001, p187).

The issue of same sex marriage is a significant area of moral conflict between religion and secular society, particularly in Northern Ireland. Many Christians refer to Bible teaching to support the view that marriage, as instituted by God, should be between a man and a woman.

OTHER ASPECTS OF HUMAN EXPERIENCE

Since 29 March 2014, same sex marriages has been permitted in England and Wales. It became legal in Scotland in December 2014, and on 22 May 2015 a majority in the Republic of Ireland voted in a referendum in favour of same sex marriage. Some people regard the introduction of same sex marriage as an important human rights issue; for others it is a source of controversy, possibly as a result of religious views, which see the traditional definition of marriage being redefined. Same sex marriage is not at this time being introduced in Northern Ireland, which is a further cause of controversy for some, as this is another issue where Northern Ireland has separate legislation to the rest of the UK.

The divisions highlighted by this issue show that religious controversy can have a negative impact on society. Many people are angry with the decision taken by the Assembly at Stormont. On the other hand, people in England and Wales are concerned that same sex weddings may be carried out in their church. Nevertheless, some might argue that this issue has helped to highlight the rights of same sex couples, and that this is a positive outcome to controversy. A further consideration is whether, given the divisive nature of this issue, some form of conflict and controversy is inevitable.

The state and religious issues

For many religious believers, the wearing of religious dress and symbols is not just a question of faith but also of human rights. Religious symbols are part of every religion and a way for believers to show their faith and devotion. These symbols can include a Christian wearing a cross, perhaps as a piece of jewellery, a Sikh man wearing a turban or a Muslim woman choosing to cover her hair, face or whole body. This is an area of conflict between religion and secular society. Some people would claim that in the workplace such symbols should be banned as they can cause unnecessary tension. On the other hand, it can be argued that wearing religious clothing is part of the right to practise your religion.

OTHER ASPECTS OF HUMAN EXPERIENCE
Religious dress in France
France has a secular constitution providing the grounds for excluding religion from schools. In 2004 a law came into force banning Islamic headscarves and other religious symbols from schools. There are now calls for these to be banned in universities as well.

In October 2010 a law was introduced preventing full-faced veils from being worn in public places. The penalty for this offence is a fine of up to €150 and participation in a citizenship course. This controversial ruling has been described by some people as religious bigotry and prejudice against Muslims. However, the French government argues that wearing a full-face veil is inconsistent with French secular values and can also constitute a security risk, as the face cannot be seen.

An important question is whether these examples of religious controversy show that it is religious practice rather than belief that is the cause of controversy. In the examples given, most of the objections would involve the expression of religion rather than the faith itself. Another consideration is whether such controversy is to be expected and is unavoidable. On the other hand, perhaps a secular society should be able to accept expressions of religious identity as a human right rather than seeing them as a threat. Perhaps the authorities should be more lenient on religious symbols that are a religious requirement rather than a matter of choice.

Consumerism and altruism
A potential area of moral conflict concerns the idea of spiritual values and consumerism. Many religions, for example, Christianity, Islam and Sikhism, place value on limiting personal spending and consumption to benefit others. Walker comments that "the altruist would want to alleviate poverty for the benefit of others. Also, the altruist would be prepared to make any necessary self-sacrifice in order to bring this about" (2000, p105). This raises the question of whether such practice is a particularly religious perspective. However, the issue of aid for the developing world shows that conflict between religion and secular society need not be inevitable. In the UK, the government's

Department for International Development aims to raise people's incomes and reduce poverty in the developing world (www.gov.uk).

In the church of the New Testament, caring for the needy was an important obligation, and this continues to be a priority for the church today. Christian organisations are actively involved in the fight against poverty in the developing world. Christian Aid works globally to eradicate the causes of poverty, striving to achieve equality, dignity and freedom for all people. Trócaire works to bring about positive and lasting change in some of the world's poorest places. From a secular point of view, ethicist Peter Singer (2009) emphasises the need for social responsibility in the developing world, giving examples of how he gives charitable support. A question for consideration is why religious and secular values are similar on this issue. Is the motivation the same for both, however?

The example of Islam and Sharia law shows that in some parts of the world, the authority of the state comes from religion, so there is no conflict between religion and society. Sharia law is the moral law and religious code of Islam and is contained in the Qu'ran. Sharia law deals with many topics, such as justice and punishment, economics and politics. One example is the legal system of Saudi Arabia, which depends on Sharia law. Criminal law punishments in Saudi Arabia include public beheading, stoning, amputation and lashing. Serious criminal offences include not only internationally recognised crimes such as murder, rape, theft and robbery, but also apostasy, adultery, witchcraft and sorcery. Punishments for these offenses are based on Sharia law, so in this example religion provides the ultimate moral guide for society. An important question is whether religion should be able to dictate the laws of the state. What issues could arise if not everyone in the state is a member of that religion?

Respect for life

Issues concerning the sanctity of human life are often the source of religious controversy. While all Christians will place emphasis on the value and uniqueness of human life as being made in the image of God, there are differences between churches. The Catholic Church, following Natural Law, does not allow abortion or euthanasia. However, not all Protestant Christians take such an absolutist stance, although all the main denominations are officially not in favour of either practice. This is a further example that raises the question of whether moral conflict is inevitable between religion and secular society. Nevertheless, perhaps religious believers need to be more willing to focus on what they have in common, rather than concentrating on their differences. The issue of abortion raises the questions about the value of a human life, which is one of the reasons why it is controversial. A secular society that legislates for abortion is acknowledging that the woman has more right to life than that of the foetus. However, this can lead to moral conflict with religious groups opposed to abortion. Bowie comments that "religious arguments against abortion stress the limits of human authority over the taking of human life" (2001, p193).

OTHER ASPECTS OF HUMAN EXPERIENCE

Abortion
The opening of the Marie Stopes clinic in Belfast in October 2012 raised important questions concerning the relation between religion and state. Abortion is legal in Britain and Marie Stopes is one of the largest providers of private abortions. The Abortion Act of 1967 was not introduced in Northern Ireland. In this situation it can be seen that religion provided the ultimate moral authority, as the laws of the state reflect religious views. Despite many protests, the clinic can carry out some abortion procedures in a very limited range of circumstances. In March 2013 the Northern Ireland Assembly attempted to have all abortions banned at this clinic. However, the attempt failed, as the proposal did not have enough support.

Discussion
There are some important questions raised by this area of moral conflict. To what extent should religious views be taken into account by politicians when making laws that affect the whole community? Is it right that MLAs should let their own religious views influence their decisions?

Euthanasia
The issue of euthanasia raises the question of whether the state should put legislation in place to ensure personal autonomy, even though religious opinion would challenge this. Although euthanasia is currently illegal in the UK, there have been recent attempts to introduce an Assisted Dying Bill, which could bring legislation a significant step closer. Opinion polls have shown a high level of public support for a change in the law, while churches and other religious groups have voiced their opposition. Who should make

the final decision – religious groups or the government? Many people fear that the introduction of assisted suicide legislation could be the start of a 'slippery slope' towards involuntary euthanasia. Christians are concerned that the state is introducing policies that can lead to a negative experience for many people. Some argue that hospice care should be more widely available, as it is a better response to terminal illness than assisted dying. On the other hand, the new laws proposed for the UK could give people the freedom to decide for themselves when they wish to die, without being forced to travel abroad to a euthanasia clinic. Bowie comments that:

> "The ethical arena of voluntary euthanasia is divided between those who tend to feel that it's right and merciful for us to have the freedom to decide the time and nature of our deaths, and those who claim that such an autonomy would have harmful side-effects on society, or that it goes against religious belief." (2001, p216)

OTHER ASPECTS OF HUMAN EXPERIENCE
Calls to change UK law on assisted dying

Campaigners who support the right of people to choose to end their own lives have called for a change in UK law, which currently prohibits people from helping someone to kill themselves, known as assisted dying. Swiss organization Dignitas, which assists terminally ill patients in ending their own lives, has said that almost 300 people from the UK went to Dignitas between 2002 and 2015 for this purpose. Dignitas was founded in 1998 by Ludwig Minelli, a Swiss lawyer who believes that people of sound mind should have the right to have an assisted death if they so wish.

Opponents of changing the law say that the current ban is there to prevent vulnerable people from exploitation and abuse, and that any change would leave the disabled and elderly particularly unprotected.

Belgium legalized assisted dying in 2002, and in 2014 extended the practice to terminally-ill children of any age, provided they are suffering a lot of pain. In the Netherlands, children over the age of 12 can be assisted to die provided they have parental consent. In both countries, the decision is discussed in detail between the parents, doctors and psychiatrists before proceeding.

TASKS

Activity

1. Working in a small group, discuss other relevant issues for this theme. You could consider further ideas concerning relationships, respect for life issues and the conflict between religious belief and secular society.
2. Look at the other module you are studying. What examples from this area of study connect to the issue of moral conflict between religion and secular society?
3. List the points resulting from your discussion. You may be asked to share your ideas with others in your class.
4. Working individually, use the internet to research some of these issues and find specific examples for other aspects of human experience.

For discussion

These questions can be discussed in groups or treated as written exercises. Your ideas should be supported with examples from this theme, the modules you are studying and other aspects of human experience. It is also valid to include your own personal insight and independent thought.

- Is moral conflict more concerned with ideas or practices? Give examples of both and assess which has the potential to result in the greatest controversy.
- To what extent do moral conflicts with secular society cause negative consequences for religions? Try to balance your answer with reference to positive consequences.
- Are conflicts and divisions between religion and secular society largely due to misunderstanding and intolerance? Give examples to support your view.
- If there is a disagreement in society between religion and the state (secular) authorities, who should have the right to make the final decision? Consider a potential problem with the group you have chosen having the ultimate authority.
- When considering issues of morality, is it more important to be willing to accept change or to maintain continuity with past tradition? Give reasons for your answer.

THE ROLE OF RELIGION IN FOSTERING RECONCILIATION

Introduction

Reconciliation involves the restoring of relationships after a disagreement or following a lack of communication. Reconciliation can involve individuals or groups of people; it can also be the action of making different views or beliefs compatible with each other. Reconciliation is therefore a healing process following controversy and division, although it assumes different forms in different contexts. In the aftermath of an armed conflict or a human rights abuse, reconciliation can involve a search for truth, justice and forgiveness. In these situations, a truth and reconciliation commission might be given the task of uncovering past wrongdoing by a government and formalising the process of apology and forgiveness. Following genocide or war crimes, initiatives are often focused on bringing about reconciliation with the past, in an attempt to prevent similar atrocities from happening again. At a more personal and individual level, the reconciliation process can involve workshops, face-to-face meetings and opportunities for dialogue through mediation. Peace education also plays a vital role, by promoting the values of non-violence and social justice.

Reconciliation programmes can operate at different levels, each with their own role to play in the peacebuilding process. 'Top down' approaches to reconciliation tend to be high-profile and situated at the national level, and involve mechanisms attempting to create reconciliation by bringing atrocities to public awareness through truth telling, confession, apology, retribution and the rule of law, and making recommendations regarding the prevention of further abuses. However, meaningful reconciliation in post-conflict environments also requires 'bottom-up' approaches that focus on the past trauma of individuals and communities so as not to pass on intergenerational anger and cause violent recurrences. (www.insightonconflict.org/themes/reconciliation)

Reconciliation programmes are not a quick solution, but a slow and often difficult process that can take many years to bring results. However, there is a growing realisation that reconciliation is an essential step in helping to create a safe and just society where individuals' rights and freedoms are respected. For this reason, many reconciliation programmes have a religious basis. This final area for synoptic assessment involves an analysis of the role played by religion in reconciliation initiatives, past and present.

Reconciliation at the heart of Christianity

Reconciliation does not have to have a church or religious basis, as many initiatives are entirely secular. However, reconciliation plays a very important part in Christianity. Reconciliation is about mending a relationship that has become estranged. According to Genesis, God created a world with which he was pleased. However, human disobedience soon spoiled this paradise and the relationship between God and humankind. As a result, people were alienated from God, due to sin. Christianity teaches that God's plan was to reconcile sinful humanity to himself by sending Jesus to die on the cross; God was the only one who could initiate this reconciliation by providing his son as the perfect sacrifice for sin. Paul writes that *"God was reconciling the world to himself through Christ, not counting men's sins against them. And he has committed to us the message of reconciliation"* (2 Corinthians 19). John Calvin (1536, II.16.2) describes reconciliation as the peace between God and humanity from the atonement of sin and the placation of God's anger. Ryken describes reconciliation as "part of the message of salvation that brings us back together with God … God is the author, Christ is the agent and we are the ambassadors of reconciliation" (2001, pp118–119).

The Bible also teaches that reconciliation between people is a priority. Jesus taught in the Sermon on the Mount that an unresolved disagreement should be settled before making an offering in the temple: *"Leave your gift there in front of the altar. First go and be reconciled to your brother; then come and offer your gift"* (Matthew 5:24). The right approach is needed for reconciliation: a humble attitude and a desire to resolve a problem without making the other person feel inferior. This is reinforced by Paul who wrote: *"Brothers, if someone is caught in a sin, you who are spiritual should restore him gently"* (Galatians 6:1). Finally, reconciliation in the Bible involves being willing to ask for forgiveness and to forgive others. This is summed up by Jesus' teaching on prayer: *"Forgive us our debts, as we have also forgiven our debtors"* (Matthew 6: 12).

Confession of sins and asking for God's forgiveness is an important part of Christian life and worship, although the nature of this confession varies between churches. In the New Testament, John prepared people for Jesus' ministry by baptism, which was preceded by a public confession of sin (Matthew 3:6). By the third century, lapses into sin required penitential actions as well as a public confession. These included dressing in sack cloth, covering oneself in ashes and fasting. By the fifth century, there was the practice of a detailed confession to a priest or bishop. The confession was made at the start of Lent and the penitent sinners were reconciled on Holy Thursday. Gradually, the practice was introduced for reconciling sinners immediately after confession, except for the most serious sins. By 1215, the Fourth Lateran Council made it obligatory for every Christian to confess to a priest at least once a year.

Today, the Catholic Church teaches that penance is a sacrament, an obligation instituted by Christ, although Protestant churches do not share this view and consider private confessions to be unbiblical. However, public confessions through corporate prayer are an important part of a service of worship. For Catholics, in the sacrament of Reconciliation, the priest acts as the agent of God, hearing a confession and forgiving the sins committed. This is usually performed through individual and private confession, although the Rite of Reconciliation can include several penitents and a general absolution.

Historical examples of reconciliation

The process of reconciliation does not just refer to people, whether individuals or groups. *Vergangenheitsbewältigung* is a German word that means coming to terms with the past. It is an attempt to learn to live with the past as well as to learn lessons for the future, so it is a process of reconciling the past to the present. This can be summed up in the words of Spanish philosopher, George Santayana, who observed that "those who forget the past are condemned to repeat it". The German churches are currently playing a significant role in this process. However, at the time of the Holocaust, there was very little church resistance to the Nazi regime, which is another factor that has led to the need for reconciliation concerning past events. In West Germany, both Catholic and Protestant churches are working to develop a 'theology of repentance'. Much of this work is carried out in schools, through lessons teaching about the Holocaust, trips to former Nazi camps and inviting Holocaust survivors as guest speakers. The official church positions changed radically in the fifty years or so following the Holocaust, with admissions of guilt about silence during the Holocaust. The process of *Vergangenheitsbewältigung* started to gain momentum, with the two main driving forces being the churches and Socialist student associations. This process is still ongoing today. (www.quora.com/How-did-Germans-deal-with-antisemitism-after-WWII-ended)

The Holocaust Reconciliation Project is an example of an initiative seeking to foster a better understanding and relationship between German and Jewish communities, largely through workshops that take place in German schools. Dr Geoffrey S Cahn, creator of the project explains:

> "The mission of The Holocaust Reconciliation Project is to empower the current generation of Germans to transcend the guilt and shame of previous generations, while being ever mindful of the past. Through educational workshops presented in gymnasiums and other secondary schools in Germany, a new sense of responsibility can help eradicate anti-Semitism and other forms of prejudice." (www.holocaust-reconciliation.org)

Dr Cahn is an accomplished historian with a specialisation in Germany from 1918 to 1945; he is also Jewish and the child of Holocaust survivors. His personal story is one that resonates with students and helps them to confront their feelings about the burdens of the past.

The churches' involvement in reconciliation can also be seen in the example of South Africa. In 1948, the all-white National Party gained power and started policies of racial segregation (Apartheid), which meant the majority black population were treated as second-class citizens. For many years, these policies were supported by the Dutch Reformed Church in South Africa. Desmond Tutu, however, was a member of the Anglican Church and he became an outspoken critic of Apartheid. When this regime collapsed, the Truth and Reconciliation Commission was established by the new South African government in 1995. This Commission was set up to hear about the human rights abuses that had taken place during Apartheid and to help bring reconciliation. The main focus of the work was gathering evidence and hearing accounts from both victims and perpetrators. Desmond Tutu was the chair of the commission. His example shows that although there was some church support for the Apartheid regime, there was Christian involvement at the forefront of the process of rebuilding and reconciliation.

OTHER ASPECTS OF HUMAN EXPERIENCE

Desmond Tutu is a South African Anglican cleric who is known for his role in the opposition to Apartheid in South Africa. In 1978 Desmond Tutu was appointed general secretary of the South African Council of Churches and became a leading spokesperson for the rights of black South Africans. During the 1980s he played an unrivaled role in drawing national and international attention to the iniquities of apartheid, and in 1984 he won the Nobel Prize for Peace for his efforts. In no small part due to Tutu's eloquent advocacy and brave leadership, in 1993 South African apartheid finally came to an end, and in 1994 South Africans elected Nelson Mandela as their first black president. The honor of introducing the new president to the nation fell to Tutu.

President Mandela appointed Tutu to head a Truth and Reconciliation Commission tasked with investigating and reporting on the atrocities committed by both sides in the struggle over apartheid. Perhaps what makes Tutu so inspirational and universal a figure is his unshakable optimism in the face of overwhelming odds and his limitless faith in the ability of human beings to do good. "Despite all of the ghastliness in the world, human beings are made for goodness," he once said. "The ones that are held in high regard are not militarily powerful, nor even economically prosperous. They have a commitment to try and make the world a better place." (Information taken from www.biography.com/people/desmond-tutu-9512516#personal-life)

The capacity of religion to promote reconciliation can also be seen in the work of the Compassionate Listening Project. This initiative was started in 1990, in the Middle East, and has led to talks between Syrian and Lebanese people, and between Palestinians and Israelis. The concept aims to break down barriers and bring reconciliation through non-judgmental listening. Gene Knudsen Hoffman, international peacemaker and the founder of the project, comments that "an enemy is one whose story we have not heard." (www.compassionatelistening.org)

A Brief History of the Compassionate Listening Project – by Leah Green

As an American-Jewish woman who had lived in Israel and worked in the West Bank, my original vision was to strengthen US support for Middle East peace by connecting Americans to Israeli and Palestinian reconciliation leaders and providing them with a firsthand experience of the complexities on the ground.

It became clear over time that my greatest interest was in Israeli-Palestinian reconciliation and healing. In 1996, after leading nine delegations, I sought out Gene Knudsen Hoffman (1919–2010), who became my trusted mentor. I adopted Gene's framework for compassionate listening as an overarching framework for the delegations and Gene and I travelled together to launch the Compassionate Listening Project in Israel and Palestine.

Buddhist monk, Thich Nhat Hanh, was one of Gene's teachers, and the essence of Compassionate Listening comes from his teachings: a call for peacemakers to initiate humanising contact and cultivate compassion for those on all sides of a conflict.

In 1997, after experiencing the powerful nature of this work, and with the encouragement of Gene and Israeli and Palestinian NGOs, The Compassionate Listening Project (TCLP) was established as a non-profit organization. (www.compassionatelistening.org/about/history)

Initiatives in our society

The 'troubles', the sectarian violence lasting for over twenty years at the end of the last century, prompted many initiatives for reconciliation in Northern Ireland. Many of these are church projects or enterprises prompted by Christian belief.

Corrymeela is a well-known example of an organisation working to promote reconciliation in Northern Ireland through the healing of religious, social and political divisions. Corrymeela was founded in 1965 by Ray Davey, a Presbyterian minister. Ray Davey was a chaplain during World War II, experienced imprisonment as a prisoner of war in Dresden and witnessed the bombing of that city. These experiences had a deep impact on him and, on his return to Belfast, he became increasingly concerned about tensions between people of different backgrounds. Corrymeela was the initiative that resulted from this concern. It began before the 'troubles' and continues on after the 'troubles', promoting tolerance and reconciliation between people of differing beliefs and backgrounds.

Corrymeela has a centre at Ballycastle on the North Antrim coast and residential programmes are an important part of their work. Some of Corrymeela's other activities include a schools' programme to address community relations issues and giving support to individuals and church communities in building relationships with other faiths. Corrymeela is an organisation with a Christian foundation, working with people from a wide variety of differing backgrounds to encourage tolerance and healing in an often divided society. This is a positive and relevant example of the capacity of religion to foster reconciliation.

The following information is taken from the website of Corrymeela:

"We have fifty years of experience working alongside fractured communities and groups who are finding their relationships difficult, as well as addressing relational, societal, structural and power dynamics. Corrymeela has a residential centre on the north coast of Ireland that hosts over 11,000 people a year, as well as a lived community of volunteers and staff.

Corrymeela also has a dispersed community of over 150 members who commit to living out Corrymeela's principles of reconciliation in their own communities. Corrymeela's programme staff travel to work with school and community groups throughout Northern Ireland, as well as hosting groups on site.

We work alongside people from youth and school groups, family and community organisations, faith communities and political parties. We run group sessions using dialogue, experiential play, art, storytelling, meal times and shared community to help groups embrace difference and learn how to have difficult conversations. We work alongside visiting university groups as well as groups from other parts of the world who wish to learn from our experience, and learn how to apply the Corrymeela lens to fractures in their own societies.

All of this work helps us learn how to live well together. It helps groups learn how to work well together. Corrymeela believes in the power of people telling their stories, of shared hospitality, of telling the truth about the present, of turning towards each other and finding strength, life and hope in each other. Ultimately, the work of Corrymeela helps groups learn how to be well together."
(For more information visit www.corrymeela.org/about)

Youth Link NI is an inter-church youth service that was founded in 1991 and exists to provide support and training for youth workers and community relations experiences for young people. Churches work together to develop excellence in youth work and ministry and promote diversity and interdependence. It was originally the vision of the Presbyterian, Church of Ireland, Methodist and Catholic churches, who were later joined by the Religious Society of Friends and the Non-Subscribing Presbyterian Church. There is an important emphasis on reconciliation. Young people are encouraged to become involved in activities that help to heal divisions in society. One example is the Kairos Project.

'Kairos' is the Greek word for 'time', which Youth Link has adopted to suggest God's time, a particular moment of opportunity that must be seized. The Kairos Project is built on the idea that the 21st century is such a moment, with new challenges and opportunities to enable young people to be creative peacemakers of the future. It is aimed at young people aged between 16 and 18 and works across communities.

The initiative shows that different churches can work together to achieve a shared vision of hope for the future through an emphasis on youth work. It shows how young people can be instrumental in bringing healing and reconciliation within a diverse community.

According to Youth Link's web site, their central focus is the Christian faith, which commits them to:

- The personal, social and spiritual development of young people.
- Encourage and support leaders in their personal and professional development.
- Developing effective and strategic partnerships.
- Building relationships that enable healing in the lives of individuals and communities within a diverse society.
- Fairness in provision of service.
- Integrity and accountability in all aspects of our work.

(For more information visit www.youthlink.org.uk)

The Redemptorists are a community of Catholic Priests and lay brothers. It was founded by St Alphonsus Liguori at Scala in Italy, a small town near Naples, in 1732. By the early 1970s, the community was established throughout the world. There are currently more than 5,300 Redemptorists working in 78 countries (www.redemptorists.ie/about/who-we-are-2).

One of the main activities of the Redemptorist community is preaching the word of God, particularly to those who are poor and needy. There have been Redemptorists in Ireland since 1851 and they are currently involved in all areas of pastoral need, with ministry to young people being an important part of their work. There is a Redemptorist community at Clonard Monastery in West Belfast. Together with co-workers at Clonard, they have established a long tradition of healing division through their Peace and Reconciliation Ministries. The main focus of this work is on preaching the gospel through leading parish missions and retreats. The Redemptorist monastery at Clonard, particularly the work of two key figures, Father Alec Reid (1931–2013) and Father Gerry Reynolds (1935–2015), has played a vital role in the Northern Ireland peace process. For over 30 years, they were actively involved in reconciliation work in the local community.

The following information is taken from the website of Clonard Monastery:

"The Clonard Peace and Reconciliation Mission is an expression of the fullness of Redemption announced by Jesus Christ in the gospel to gather in all God's people from every language, race and colour. We want to awaken the Church and the world to the call of God to bring peace to the Earth, respecting the dignity of each person, enabling them to contribute to the common good and enhancing in our society the longed for culture of encounter, bonding and partnership.

The location of Clonard Monastery on the 'border line' between the Catholic Falls and the Protestant Shankill placed it at the centre of the deep-seated historical conflict.

Over the past 100 years, the Redemptorist Community and the people of Clonard have responded in creative ways to the challenges it has faced. Many of these responses have contributed significantly to the development of Clonard's Peace and Reconciliation Ministry.

The Clonard Peace and Reconciliation Mission continues to work and pray for the reconciliation and unity of all Christ's disciples."

(For more information visit www.clonard.com/peace-and-reconciliation)

TASK

Use the internet to research other examples of reconciliation projects that have a religious basis or are the result of a church initiative. Here are examples you may wish to research and include in your synoptic planning:

- Irish Churches Peace project

The Irish Churches Peace Project (ICPP) is an initiative of the island's four largest churches, Catholic, Presbyterian, Church of Ireland, Methodist and the Irish Council of Churches.
(www.irishchurches.org/about/irish-churches-peace-project)

- The Columba Community

The Columba Community of Prayer and Reconciliation was founded in Derry in 1981. The organisation is dedicated to the service of the marginalised and committed to working for peace, reconciliation and healing. (www.columbacommunity.com)

- The Dock Café in the Titanic Quarter, Belfast

The Chaplain to the Titanic Quarter, working with other church leaders, sought to provide something different – a shared gathering point – a boat on neutral waters, in which all traditions could share the excitement of

building community together. This venture stresses the importance of:
- living in community with other people.
- living in relationship with God.
- living together with people from all backgrounds.

(www.the-dock.org)

EXAMINATION PRACTICE

Question adapted from CCEA's Specimen Assessment Materials

(a) "Controversies involving religion never seem to reach a satisfactory conclusion."

Analyse this statement. You should support your answer with reference to different areas of study.

- Reference to examples of conflict and controversy in the New Testament church, for example the challenge to Paul's gospel from the Judaisers, the party spirit of the Corinthians.
- Challenges from outside the church; the reaction to heresy.
- Consideration of controversial issues today involving religion and secular society, for example same sex marriage, assisted dying.
- Reference to areas of conflict within churches, for example the equality of women, attitudes towards sex and relationships.
- The answer should be supported by reference to different units of study.

(b) Critically evaluate the view that in a pluralist society, religion needs to find more common ground for agreement. You should refer to other aspects of human experience in your answer.

- Examination of the changing nature of society, with the rise in atheism and secularisation challenging the value and position of religious faith.
- Consideration of some of the contemporary differences in religion

today, such as the role of women and attitudes to other World Faiths.
- The contribution of Ecumenism and inter-faith movements; consideration of other attempts to deal with difference.
- Consideration of some of the common ground between religions, such as response to moral issues, the authority of sacred texts and teaching about the afterlife.
- Evaluation of the view that diversity is inevitable and does not need to result in conflict; differences should be treated with tolerance instead of suspicion or criticism.
- Reference should be made to other aspects of human experience, either historical or contemporary.

BY THE END OF THIS CHAPTER YOU SHOULD BE ABLE TO:

- demonstrate knowledge and understanding of, and critically evaluate the problem of controversy in religion, including the response of the church to conflict and controversy;
- demonstrate knowledge and understanding of, and critically evaluate the potential areas of moral conflict between religion and secular society; and
- demonstrate knowledge and understanding of, and critically evaluate the role of religion in fostering reconciliation.

Bibliography

Banks, R (2017). *The Early Church: 3rd Edition*. Newtownards: Colourpoint.

Banks, R (2006). *The Gospel of Luke: Introduction and Theology*. Newtownards: Colourpoint.

Barclay, JMG (1988). *Obeying the Truth: A Study of Paul's Ethics in Galatians*. Edinburgh: Clark.

Barclay, W (1954). *The Letters to the Corinthians*. The Daily Study Bible. Edinburgh: The Saint Andrew Press.

Barclay, W (1955). *The Acts of the Apostles*. The Daily Study Bible. Edinburgh: The Saint Andrew Press.

Barclay, W (2002). *The Letters to the Galatians and the Ephesians*. The New Daily Study Bible. Westminster: John Knox Press.

Barrett, KC (1961). *Luke the Historian in Recent Study*. London: Epworth.

Barrett, KC (1968). *A Commentary on the First Epistle to the Corinthians*. London: A & C Black.

Bayes, JF (2003). *The Weakness of the Law: God's Law and the Christian in the New Testament Perspective*. London: Paternoster Press.

Bengel, JA (1742). *Gnoman Nom Testamenti*. 3rd edn. Repr 1862. London: Williams and Norgate.

Bock, DL (1994). A Theology of Luke-Acts. In DL Bock & RB Zuck (eds), *A Biblical Theology of the New Testament*. Chicago, IL: Moody Press.

Boer, HR (1976). *A Short History of the Early Church*. Grand Rapids, MI: William B Eerdmans Publishing Company.

Boice, JM (1976). Galatians. In FE Gaebelein (ed), *The Expositor's Bible Commentary: Romans through Galatians*. Vol 10. Grand Rapids, MI: Zondervan Publishing House.

Bowie, R (2001). *Ethical Studies*. Cheltenham: Nelson Thornes.

Brown, RE (1977). *Introduction to the New Testament*. New York: Anchor Bible.

Browne, LE (1925). *The Acts of the Apostles*. Indian Church Commentaries. London: SPCK.

Bruce, FF (1943). *Are the New Testament Documents Reliable?* Leicester: IVP.

Bruce, FF (1958). *The Spreading Flame*. Exeter: The Paternoster Press.

Bruce, FF (1961). *The Epistle to the Ephesians*. Basingstoke: Pickering Paperbacks.

Bruce, FF (1977). *Paul: Apostle of the Free Spirit*. Exeter: The Paternoster Press.

Bruce, FF (1982). *The Epistle to the Galatians*. New International Greek Testament Commentary Series. Exeter: Paternoster Press. Repr 1983, Grand Rapids, MI: Eerdmans.

Bruce, FF (1988). *The Book of Acts*. The New International Commentary on the New Testament. Revised. Grand Rapids, MI: William B Eerdmans Publishing Company.

Bruce, FF (1989). *New Bible Commentary*. 3rd edn. Leicester: IVP.

Bruce, FF (1992). *Corinthians I and II*. The New Century Bible Commentary. Grand Rapids, MI: Eerdmans.

Bruner, FD (1970). *A Theology of the Holy Spirit*. London: Hodder.

Cadbury, HJ (1924). *The Making of Luke-Acts*. London: SPCK.

Calvin, J (1536). *Institutes of the Christian Religion*. Revised edn 1986. Grand Rapids, MI: Eerdmans.

Calvin, J (1552). *The Acts of the Apostles, an exposition in 2 volumes: vol.1, Ch1–13*. DW & TF Torrance (eds). English Translation 1966. Edinburgh: Oliver and Boyd.

Campbell, DK (1983). Galatians. In JF Walvoord and RB Zuck (eds), *The Bible Knowledge Commentary: An Exposition of the Scriptures by Dallas Seminary Faculty*. Dallas, TX: Chariot Victor Publications.

Carson, DA, Moo, DJ, & Morris, L (1992). *An Introduction to the New Testament*. Leicester: Apollos.

Catholic Church (1992). *Catechism of the Catholic Church*. www.vatican.va/archive/ENG0015/_INDEX.HTM.

Collins, RF (2004). *1 & 2 Timothy and Titus: A Commentary*. Louisville, KY: John Knox Press.

Conzelmann, H (1960). *The Theology of Luke*. Trans G Buswell. London: Faber and Faber.

Conzelmann, H (1987). *The Acts of the Apostles: A Commentary on the Acts of the Apostles*. Minneapolis, MN: Fortress Press.

Crowe, J (1979). *The Acts*. New Testament Message 8. Dublin: Veritas.

Croy, NC (1997). Hellenistic Philosophies and the Preaching of the Resurrection (Acts17:18, 32). *Novum Testamentum*, 39(1), pp21–39.

Cwiekowski, FJ (1988). *The Beginnings of the Church*. Dublin: Gill and Macmillan Ltd.

Davies, RE (1962). *Studies in 1 Corinthians*. London: The Epworth Press.

deSilva, DA (1995). Paul and the Stoa: A Comparison. *Journal of Evangelical Theological Society*, 38(4), pp549–564.

deSilva, DA (2004). *An Introduction to the New Testament: Contexts, Methods and Ministry Formation*. Leicester: IVP.

Dibelius, M (1956). *Studies in the Acts of the Apostles*. Eng Tr. London: SCM.

Dillon, RJ (1990). Acts of the Apostles. RE Brown, JA Fitzmyer, & RE Murphy (eds), *The New Jerome Biblical Commentary.* London: Chapman.

Dodd, CH (1936). *The Apostolic Preaching and its Development.* London: Hodder and Stoughton.

Drane, J (1986). *Introducing the New Testament.* Oxford: Lion Publishing.

Dunn, JDG (1973). *Baptism in the Holy Spirit.* London: SCM.

Dunn, JDG (1975). *Jesus and the Spirit.* NLT. London: SCM.

Du Plessis, IJ (1998). *Guide to the New Testament IV.* AB du Toit (ed). Halfway House (South Africa): Perskor Publishers.

Ehrhardt, A (1969). *The Acts of the Apostles.* Manchester: Manchester University Press.

Ehrhardt, A (1953). *New Testament Studies.* Manchester: Manchester University Press.

Fee, GD (1987). *The First Epistle to the Corinthians.* The New International Commentary on the New Testament. Grand Rapids, MI: Eerdmans Publishing Company.

Fernando, A (1998). *Acts.* The NIV Application Commentary to Contemporary Life. Grand Rapids, MI: Zondervan.

Fitzmeyer, JA (1998). *The Acts of the Apostles: A New Translation with Introduction and Commentary.* New York, NY: The Anchor Bible.

Fitzmeyer, JA (1989). The Letter to the Galatians. In RE Brown, JA Fitzmyer, & RE Murphy (eds), *The New Jerome Biblical Commentary.* London: Geoffrey Chapman.

Foreman, KJ (1961). *1 Corinthians, 2 Corinthians.* Layman's Bible Commentaries. Vol 21. London: SCM Press Ltd.

Freed, ED (2005). *The Apostle Paul and his Letters.* London: Equinox.

Fuller, RH (1966). *A Critical Introduction to the New Testament.* London: Duckworth.

Fung, RYK (1988). *The Epistle to the Galatians.* New International Commentary on the New Testament Series. Grand Rapids, IL: Eerdmans.

Gasque, WW (1975). Translation of FC Baur, *A History of the Criticism of the Acts of the Apostles.* Tübingen: Mohr.

Gasque, WW (1988). *Luke.* The New International Bible Encyclopaedia. Volume 4. GW Bromiley (ed). Grand Rapids, MI: Eerdmans.

Gorman, MJ (2004). *Apostle of the Crucified Lord: a Theological Introduction to Paul and his Letters.* Grand Rapids, IL: Eerdmans.

Grayston, K (1966). *Theology as Exploration.* London: Epworth Press.

Green, M (1975). *I believe in the Holy Spirit.* Grand Rapids, MI: Eerdmans.

Green, M (1993, 2002). *30 Years that changed the world: A fresh look at the book of Acts.* Leicester, IVP.

Guthrie, D (1961). *New Testament Introduction.* Leicester: IVP.

Guy, HA (1969). *The Church in the New Testament.* London: Macmillan Educational.
Gutzke, MG (1966). *Plain Talk on Acts.* Grand Rapids, MI: Zondervan.
Haenchen, E (1971). *The Acts of the Apostles.* Philadelphia, PA: Westminster Press.
Hafemann, SJ (1993). Letters to the Corinthians. In GF Hawthorne, RP Martin, & DG Reid (eds), *Dictionary of Paul and His Letters.* Leicester: IVP.
Hanson, RPC (1967). *The Acts.* New Clarendon Bible. Oxford: Clarendon Press.
Harnack, A (1907). *Luke the Physician.* London: ET.
Harnack, A (1911). *The Date of Acts and the Synoptic Gospels.* Eng. Tr RJ Wilkinson. Eugene, OR: Wipf and Stock Publishers.
Hays, JD (2001). Applying the Old Testament Law Today. *Bibliotheca Sacra,* 158(629), pp21–35.
Henley, WE (1920). Invictus. In L Untermeyer (ed), *Modern British Poetry.* New York, NY: Harcourt, Brace & Howe.
Hewitt, FS (1964). *Genesis of the Christian Church.* London: Edward Arnold.
Hodge, C (1994). *Ephesians.* The Crossway Classic Commentaries. A McGrath, & JI Packer (eds). Wheaton, IL: Crossway Books.
Hoehner, HW (2002). *Ephesians: an Exegetical Commentary.* Ada, MI: Baker Academic.
Hofius, O (1984). Gal 1:18: historesai Kephan. *Zeitschrift für die Neutestamentliche Wissenschaft* 75, pp73–84.
Hubbard, MV (2002). *New Creation in Paul's Letters and Thoughts.* Society for New Testament Studies Monograph Series, 119. Cambridge: Cambridge University Press.
Hull, JHE (1967). *The Holy Spirit in the Act of the Apostles.* London: Lutterworth.
Hunter, AM (1945). *Introducing the New Testament.* Revised Edition. London: SCM Press.
Johnson LT (1992). *The Acts of the Apostles.* DJ Harrington (ed). Collegeville, MN: Liturgical Press.
Keener, CS (1993). Man and Woman. In GF Hawthorne, RP Martin, & DG Reid (eds). *Dictionary of Paul and His Letters.* Leicester: IVP.
Keener, CS (1993). *The IVP Bible Background Commentary: New Testament.* Downers Grove, IL: IVP.
Kirk, JA (1975). Apostleship since Rengstorf: Towards a Synthesis. *New Testament Studies* (21).
Knox, WL (1971). *The Acts of the Apostles: A Commentary.* Oxford: Blackwell.
Lake, K, & Lake, S (1938). *An Introduction to the New Testament.* London: Christophers.
Lampe, GWH (1951). *The Seal of the Spirit.* London: Longmans.
Lenski, RCH (1934). *The Interpretation of the Acts of the Apostles.* Minneapolis, MN: Augsburg.

Lewis, ER (1960). *The Acts of the Apostles and the Letters of St Paul*. London: James Clarke & Co Limited.

Lietzman, H (1950). *The Founding of the Church Universal*. London: E.T.

Longenecker, RN (1990). *Galatians*. World Biblical Commentary Series. Dallas, TX: Word Books.

Longenecker, RN (1995). The Acts of the Apostles. In *The Expositor's Bible Commentary*. Volume 9. Grand Rapids, MI: Zondervan Publishing House; London: Hodder & Stoughton.

MacArthur, J (2005). *The MacArthur Bible Commentary*. Nashville, TN: Thomas Nelson, Inc.

Marshall, IH (1978). *The Gospel of Luke*. Exeter: Paternoster Press.

Marshall, IH (1980) *Acts*. Tyndale New Testament Commentaries. Leicester: IVP.

Marshall, IH (1993). Lord's Supper. In GF Hawthorne, RP Martin, & DG Reid (eds), *Dictionary of Paul and His Letters*. Leicester: IVP.

McCann, V (2003). The Historical Reliability of the Acts of the Apostles. Spotlight Ministries. www.spotlightministries.co.uk.

McDowell, J (1991). *Christianity: A Ready Defence*. San Bernardino, CA: Here's Life Publishers Inc.

McGee, JV (1983). *Through the Bible with J Vernon McGee*. 5 vols. Pasadena, CA: Thru the Bible Radio.

McGrath, A (1995). *NIV Bible Commentary*. London: Hodder and Stoughton, Ltd.

McGrath, A (2011). *Christian Theology: An Introduction*. Chichester: Wiley-Blackwell.

Moffat, J (1938). *The First Epistle of Paul to the Corinthians*. London: Hodder and Stoughton.

Morgan, GC (1965). *The Acts of the Apostles*. Tyndale New Testament Commentary Series. Repr London: Pickering and Inglis.

Morris, L (1996). *1 Corinthians*. Revised Edition. Leicester: IVP.

Morris, L (1996). *Galatians: Paul's Charter of Christian Freedom*. Leicester, IVP.

Moyes, G (1986). *Discovering Paul*. Sutherland, NSW (Australia): Albatross Books Pty Ltd.

Munck, J (1986). *The Acts of the Apostles*. The Anchor Bible. New York, NY: Doubleday & Co, Inc.

Murphy-O'Connor, J (1989). The First Letter to the Corinthians. In RE Brown, JA Fitzmyer, & RE Murphy (eds), *The New Jerome Biblical Commentary*. London: Geoffrey Chapman.

Neil, W (1973). *The Acts of the Apostles*. London: Oliphants.

O'Brien, PT (1999). *The Letter to the Ephesians*. The Pillar New Testament Commentary. Leicester: Apollos; Grand Rapids, MI: WB Eerdmans.

Packer, JW (1966). *The Cambridge Bible Commentary: The Acts of the Apostles.* London: Cambridge University Press.

Peake, AS (1917/18). The Quintessence of Paulinism. *The Bulletin of the John Rylands Library*, 4, pp285–311.

Peterson, DG (2009). *The Acts of the Apostles.* The Pillar New Testament Commentary. Grand Rapids, MI: WB Eerdmans.

Phillips, JB (1958). *The New Testament in Modern English.* Online version, JB Phillips' Translation of the New Testament, (2014, Gordon Smith), available at www.ccel.org/bible/phillips/CP05Acts08.htm

Polhill, JB (1992). *Acts: An Exegetical and Theological Exposition of Holy Scripture.* The New American Commentary. Nashville, TN: Broadman and Holman Publishers.

Pope Paul VI (1964). *Lumen Gentium.* www.ewtn.com/library/councils/v2church.htm.

Porter, SE (2001). *Paul in Acts.* Library of Pauline Studies. Peabody, MA: Hendrickson Publishers.

Powell, MA (1991). *What are they saying about Acts?* New York, NY: Paulist Press.

Prior, D (1993). *The Message of 1 Corinthians.* The Bible Speaks Today. Leicester: IVP.

Rackham, RB (1909). *The Acts of the Apostles: An Exposition.* 4th edn. The Westminster Commentaries. London: Methuen.

Ramsey, W (1915). *The Bearing of Recent Discovery on the Trustworthiness of the New Testament.* London: Hodder and Stoughton.

Robertson, AT (1931). *Word Pictures in the New Testament.* 6 Vols. Nashville: Broadman Press.

Russell, WB III (1993). Rhetorical Analysis of the Book of Galatians, Part 2. *Bibliotheca Sacra* 150(600).

Ryken, PG (2001). *The Message of Salvation.* Leicester: Inter-Varsity Press.

Ryken, PG (2005). *Galatians.* Reformed Expository Commentary. Phillipsburg, NJ: P & R Publishing.

Saint Irenaeus of Lyons (c 175–185). *Against Heresies.* (Repr 2015). South Bank, IN: Ex Fontibus.

Sanders, EP (1985). *Jesus and Judaism.* London: SCM.

Scott, EF (1932). *The Literature of the New Testament.* New York, NY: Columbia University Press.

Scott, JJ (1978). Stephen's Defence and the World Mission of the People of God. *Journal of the Evangelical Theological Society* (21).

Shelley, BL (1982). *Church History in Plain Language.* Nashville, TN: Thomas Nelson Publishers.

Singer, P (2009). *The Life You Can Save.* New York, NY: Random House.

Smith, M (1988). *Acts*. Educational Pack. London: Edward Arnold.

Streeter, BH (1924). *The Four Gospels: A study of origins, treating of the manuscript, tradition, sources, authorship and date*. London: Macmillan.

Stott, JRW (1968). *The Message of Galatians*. The Bible Speaks Today. Leicester: IVP.

Stott, JRW (1979). *The Message of Ephesians*. The Bible Speaks Today. Downers Grove, IL: InterVarsity Press.

Stott, JRW (1990). *The Message of Acts*. The Bible Speaks Today. Leicester: IVP.

Stott, JRW (1990). *The Spirit, the Church, and the World*. Downers Grove, IL: InterVarsity.

Tannehill, RC (1994). *The Narrative Unity of Luke-Acts: A Literary Interpretation*. Vol 2. Minneapolis, MN: Fortress.

Thielman, F (2010). *Ephesians*. Baker Exegetical Commentary on the New Testament. Ada, MI: Baker Academic.

Thompson, JA (1962). *The Bible and Archaeology*. Exeter: The Paternoster Press; Grand Rapids, MI: Eerdmans.

Thrall, ME (1965). *I and II Corinthians*. The Cambridge Bible Commentary. Cambridge: The Cambridge University Press.

Unger, MF (1982). *Archaeology and the New Testament*. Grand Rapids, MI: Zondervan.

van der Horst, PW (1977). Peter's Shadow: the Religio-Historical Background of Acts 5:15. *New Testament Studies*, 23(2), pp204–212.

Wainright, W (1965). *A Guide to the New Testament*. London: Epworth Press.

Walker, J (2000). *Access to Philosophy: Environmental Ethics*. London: Hodder and Stoughton.

Wilcockson, M (2000). *Access to Philosophy: Sex and Relationships*. London: Hodder Murray.

Williams, CSC (1975). *The Acts of the Apostles*. Black's New Testament Commentaries. London: Adam and Charles Black.

Williamson, PS (2009). *Ephesians*. Catholic Commentary on Sacred Scripture. Ada, MI: Baker Academic.

Willimon, WH (1988). *Interpretation: Acts*. Westminster: John Knox Press.

Witherington, B (1998). *Grace in Galatia: A commentary of Paul's Letter to the Galatians*. Grand Rapids, MI: Eerdmans Publishing.

Witherington, B (2001). *The Acts of the Apostles: A Socio-Rhetorical Commentary*. Grand Rapids, MI: WB Eerdmans Publishing.

Zweck, DW (1987). The Areopagus Speech of Acts 17. *Lutheran Theological Journal*, 21(3), pp11–12.

Internet sources

Ashers Bakery: www.bbc.co.uk/news/uk-northern-ireland-32913283
Assisted dying: www.theguardian.com/society/2015/aug/15/assisted-dying-britons-dignitas-rises-campaigners-change-law
Attitudes towards ethnic minority groups: www.belfasttelegraph.co.uk/news/northern-ireland/video-belfast-pastor-james-mcconnell-denounces-islam-as-the-devils-doctrine-at-whitewell-metropolitan-tabernacle-church-sermon-30291041.html
Attitudes towards women in leadership in the church: www.eauk.org/church/research-and-statistics/women-in-ministry.cfm
Consumerism/altruism: www.gov.uk
Definitions (for example, *Miracle*): www.wikipedia.org
Divorce/humanism: www.humanismforschools.org.uk/pdfs/Family%20Matters.pdf
Do miracles still happen? www.relevantmagazine.com/god/worldview/do-miracles-still-happen
Ecumenism: www.britannica.com/topic/ecumenism
Evangelism: www.metropolitan-tabernacle.org/content/aboutus/pastors
Lourdes: www.news24.com/World/News/Lourdes-miracle-is-official-20051114
Mission/St Patrick: www.wesleyjohnston.com/users/ireland/past/pre_norman_history/christianity.html
Pope Francis on Abortion in response to Zika: www.inquisitr.com/2847486/avoiding-pregnancy-is-not-an-absolute-evil-pope-francis-approves-the-use-of-birth-control-in-some-instances/
NI Census (ethnic minorities): www.nisra.gov.uk/Census/key_stats_bulletin_2011.pdf
Open Doors Charity: www.opendoorsuk.org
Pentecostal churches: www.bbc.co.uk/news/uk-northern-ireland-23092787

Reconciliation:

www.columbacommunity.com
www.compassionatelistening.org
www.corrymeela.org/about
www.the-dock.org
www.biography.com/people/desmond-tutu-9512516#personal-life
www.holocaust-reconciliation.org
www.insightonconflict.org/themes/reconciliation
www.irishchurches.org/about/irish-churches-peace-project
www.quora.com/How-did-Germans-deal-with-antisemitism-after-WWII-ended
www.redemptorists.ie/about/who-we-are-2
www.youthlink.org.uk/about/values-vision-mission

Glossary

Abrupt ending of Acts – the fact that the book of Acts appears to end in the middle of the story

Anti-Marcionite prologue – a preface to the third Gospel

Antonia – a military barracks built by Herod the Great in Jerusalem

Apology – a justification or defence of beliefs

Areopagus – the word 'Areopagus' simply comes from the hill on which this council would often meet

Aramaic – language of the Old Testament

Ascension – the return of Jesus to heaven after his resurrection

Baptism – the sacramental act of cleansing in water that admits a person as a full member of the Church

Blasphemy – irreverence towards God; false claims to be God

Colony – a territory under the political control of a state

Controversy – a dispute or argument

Conversion – in Acts it refers to becoming a believer in Christ

Court of the Gentiles – the outer court of the Temple in Jerusalem

Court of women – beyond the Court of the Gentiles; women were not allowed any further into the Temple

Day of Atonement – the most solemn and important of Jewish holidays, which centres on repentance, fasting and prayer

Deacon – derived from the Greek word *diakonos*, which is translated as servant. Deacons helped with the charitable work of the early church

Dead Sea scrolls – around 1000 documents, including texts from the Hebrew Bible, discovered between 1947 and 1979 in eleven caves in and around the Wadi Qumran in the West Bank

Elder – a person who holds an office of responsibility in the church

Eunuch – a castrated man

Evangelism – the Christian practice of trying to make converts

External evidence – evidence found outside the New Testament, usually in connection with the date or authorship of Acts

Exorcism – the practice of casting out demons or evil spirits

The Fall of Jerusalem – a decisive event in the First Jewish-Roman War. The city and its Temple were completely destroyed

Forerunner – someone who lays the groundwork for another

Gentile – someone who is not a Jew

Glossolalia – commonly called 'speaking in tongues'; unintelligible utterances

God-fearer – someone who respected the Jewish religion, worshipped the same God and held high morals. They were still regarded as pagans by the Jews in Palestine. However, there seems to have been a more liberal attitude held by Dispersion Jews

Hebrews – Jews. It describes someone who is totally Jewish in all aspects of life; someone who observed the Law of Moses and lived according to Jewish traditions

Hellenists – Jews who came out of the Dispersion. They were much more accepting of Greek ideas

Heretic – a person who expresses an opinion considered to be heresy

Historical reliability – the notion of how trustworthy a source can be

Idol – false god

Idolatry – worshipping false gods

Internal evidence – evidence found inside the New Testament, usually in connection with the date or authorship of Acts

Jew – a member of Judaism

Justification by faith – the idea that faith alone is needed to be justified before God

kerygma – early Christian preaching

Laying on of hands – a symbolic and formal method of invoking the Holy Spirit

Law of Moses – law given by God to Moses in the Old Testament

Liberation theology – the theology of using sociology and economics to understand poverty, focuses on Jesus as the liberator of the oppressed

Lourdes – a place of pilgrimage in France, renowned as a place of healing

Mass – worship service in the Catholic Church

Messiah – the redeemer

Miracle – an act of wonder which cannot be explained logically, eg a healing

Montanism – a Christian movement of the mid second century, named after its founder

Montanus – focused on the Holy Spirit, prophecy and spiritual gifts. Was favourable towards women in leadership

Muratorian fragment/canon – a compilation of New Testament collated around AD170

Nazarite vow – a vow described in Numbers 6:1–21

The sect of the Nazarenes – the term given to the early Christians

Neronian persecution – the period of persecution carried out by the Roman Emperor Nero

Oral traditions – laws and traditions passed on by word of mouth

Paradox – an apparently true statement that leads to a contradiction

Penance – repentance of sins/sacrament of reconciliation

Pharisees – comes from the Hebrew word meaning 'separated'; refers to a Jewish religious party at the time of Jesus

Predestination – the belief that before creation God determined the fate of mankind

Primitive church – the very first church

Proconsul – governor of a Roman province

Prologue – an introduction to a piece of work

Prophecy – a religious prediction

Proselyte – a Gentile who had fully accepted the Jewish religion by being circumcised

Purpose – the reason suggested for the writing of a book

Relic – an object or a personal item of religious significance, carefully preserved with an air of veneration

Religio licita – a lawful religion

Repentance – expressing sorrow for sin

Romans – the people who occupied Palestine at the time of Jesus

Sadducees – members of a Jewish sect at the time of Christ

Sanhedrin – the Jewish Council

Schismatic – a person who splits away from the faith

Second Coming – the belief that Jesus will return again to the earth

To shake off dust – a custom for Jews to shake off the dust of a pagan town from their feet when they returned to their own land, as a symbol of cleansing themselves from the impurity of sinners who did not worship God

Simony – the crime of paying for offices or positions in the hierarchy of the church, named after Simon Magus

The Seven – the deacons chosen in the early church

Sorcery – magic or witchcraft

Synagogue – a Jewish place of worship, which played a major role in Jewish life serving as a meeting place, schoolhouse, library and court. It was a centre of religious education and learning and the place where all Jews came to worship.

Tabernacle – a moveable place of worship carried by the Israelites in the desert

Team ministry – a group of Christians working together to spread the gospel

Two volume work – the term given to the work of Luke-Acts

Universalism – the idea that Christianity is open to everyone, Jews and Gentiles

Vision – a spiritual experience or message believed to have come from God

'We' passages – passages in Acts that are written in the first person, like a diary

Index

Abraham, 89, 102, 103, 104, 122, 136, 168, 190, 191, 192, 193, 195, 196, 202, 255
Acts of the Apostles,
　Authorship, 10–15
　Characteristics of, 29–33
　Context of, 5–7
　Date, 16–20
　Historical reliability of, 37–41, 44
　Purpose of, 21–27
　Structure of, 7–10
　'We' passages, 34–36, 318
Admission of the Gentiles, 18. (*see also* Gentile mission)
Aeneas, 56
Agabus, 40, 77, 161
Agape, 266
Agrippa, 23, 26, 134, 135
Ananias (Saul's conversion), 73, 113, 137–38, 139
Ananias and Sapphira, 8, 10, 30, 32, 50, 54–56, 59, 60, 78, 91, 113, 216
Angels, 30, 46, 66, 93, 105, 114, 123, 127, 195, 226
Anglican church, 288, 299
Anti-Marcionite Prologue, 11, 315
Antioch in Pisidia, 8, 10, 78, 142–44, 147, 148, 166, 167, 182, 276
Antioch, Syria, 6, 8, 9, 10, 32, 34, 47, 61, 76, 77, 118, 139, 140, 148, 156, 157, 188
Antonia, 315
Apology, 16, 24–26, 102, 315
Apollos, 157, 158, 162, 205, 206, 209, 210, 212, 213, 215, 308, 311
Apostle, 3, 51, 53, 134, 135, 137, 139, 141, 143, 145, 147, 149, 151, 153, 155, 157, 159, 161, 163, 165, 167, 169, 171, 173, 175, 177, 179, 215, 308, 309
Aramaic, 11, 69, 136, 315
Archaeology, 28, 41
Areopagus, 153, 172, 173, 175, 313, 315
Aristarchus, 13, 160
Armour of God, 270–71, 273, 277
Artemis, 40, 159, 160, 243, 256
Ascension, 22, 64, 65, 66, 67, 72, 98, 315
Asiarchs, 26
Athens, 10, 31, 40, 153, 154, 156, 166, 171, 172, 173, 176, 180, 276
Azotus, 115

Baptism, 24, 32, 47, 51, 65, 67, 68, 72–74, 83, 87, 113, 115, 116, 117, 125, 126, 129, 137, 139, 151, 157, 162, 210, 260, 264, 285–86, 297, 315
Bar-Jesus, 141
Barnabas, 23, 51, 52, 54, 76, 77, 137, 139, 140, 142, 143, 144, 145, 146, 147, 148, 149, 157, 176
Barsabbas, 319
Baucis, 146
Beautiful Gate, 56
Begging/beggars, 88, 90, 145
Believers, 9, 30, 47, 48, 49, 50, 52, 54, 57, 58, 62, 63, 71, 72, 73, 74, 75, 77, 84, 91, 96, 112, 117, 119, 120, 125, 127, 138, 144, 146, 149, 154, 157, 158, 160, 161, 177, 184, 194, 195, 206, 209, 212, 213, 222, 224, 227, 228, 229, 230, 231, 232, 235, 236, 240, 242, 246, 249, 250, 251, 252, 254, 256, 257, 262, 263, 264, 265, 267, 270, 271, 272, 274, 283, 285, 287, 289, 290, 292

Berea, 10, 153, 154, 157
Bernadette Soubirous, 95–96
Bernice, 319
Bishop, 279
Blasphemy, 315
Boldness, 10, 79, 81, 92, 175
Breaking of bread, 48–49, 50, 53
British Humanist Association, 288

Caesarea, 8, 10, 34, 74, 79, 115, 123, 124, 161, 162
Catholic Church, 45, 60, 62, 83, 95, 96, 220, 228, 229, 279, 280, 281, 282, 283, 287, 288, 289, 292, 297, 298, 302, 303, 304, 316
  Catechism of, 45, 228, 282, 289
Catholic Charismatic Renewal, 83
Charismatic 43, 62, 82, 84, 85, 113, 130, 240
Chloe's people, 204, 208, 215
Christ, 5, 18, 30, 31, 37, 47, 49, 50, 55, 56, 61, 65, 66, 67, 72, 74, 75, 86, 89, 90, 92, 106, 108, 112, 119, 120, 129, 131, 132, 136, 137, 138, 151, 157, 162, 169, 170, 181, 182, 184, 185, 186, 189, 190, 191, 192, 193, 194, 195, 196, 197, 198, 199, 200, 205, 206, 207, 209, 210, 211, 212, 213, 214, 215, 216, 217, 222, 223, 224, 225, 226, 227, 228, 230, 232, 233, 238, 240, 242, 246, 247, 248, 249, 250, 251, 252, 253, 254, 255, 256, 257, 258, 259, 260, 261, 264, 265, 266, 267, 268, 269, 270, 271, 272, 273, 276, 277, 282, 283, 286, 297, 304, 315, 317
Christian, 3, 11, 19, 21, 24, 25, 27, 30, 31, 32, 33, 42, 47, 48, 49, 50, 51, 52, 53, 59, 60, 62, 63, 64, 65, 67, 75, 77, 78, 82, 83, 84, 101, 107, 110, 111, 112, 114, 117, 118, 119, 120, 121, 122, 123, 125, 127, 129, 132, 136, 137, 139, 140, 141, 143, 151, 154, 156, 157, 162, 163, 164, 167, 171, 175, 177, 178, 182, 183, 184, 188, 197, 199, 200, 202, 203, 209, 211, 212, 213, 214, 215, 216, 217, 218, 219, 220, 221, 222, 223, 224, 226, 228, 230, 231, 232, 233, 235, 236, 237, 239, 240, 241, 242, 245, 247, 249, 255, 259, 260, 261, 262, 263, 264, 265, 269, 270, 271, 272, 273, 274, 275, 276, 277, 279, 280, 286, 287, 289, 290, 292, 297, 299, 301, 303, 307, 308, 310, 311, 315, 316
Christian Aid, 292
Christian living, 199, 200, 219, 240, 272, 275, 276
Christology, 30
Church life, 30, 47–50, 53, 61, 62, 63, 99, 225, 238, 242
Circumcision, 103, 122, 125, 126, 152, 181, 182, 188, 190, 191, 196, 197, 198, 199, 200, 242, 255
Claudius Lysias, 320
Clement of Alexandria, 11, 16, 61, 244
Commission, 65–66, 137, 138, 164, 187
Communion, 65, 227, 229, 230
Confirmation, Sacrament of, 83
Corinth, 3, 10, 50, 69, 70, 143, 154, 155, 156, 157, 158, 160, 204, 205, 206, 207, 208, 209, 210, 211, 212, 213, 214, 215, 216, 217, 218, 221, 222, 225, 227, 228, 229, 230, 242, 284
Corinthians, First Letter to the, 14, 45, 68, 69–70, 71, 158, 241, 242, 246, 276–77, 284
  Characteristics and main themes, 206–08
  Context of, 204–06
  Guidance for church life, 225–37
  Issues raised by, 218–24
  Problems arising in the church, 208–215
  Purpose, 204
Cornelius, 10, 26, 74, 111, 123, 124, 125, 126, 128, 129, 130, 133
Consumerism, 291–92

Conversion, 6, 31, 73, 74, 82, 83, 84, 87, 95, 100, 112, 141, 154, 164, 182, 184, 247, 256, 275, 315
  Cornelius. (see Cornelius)
  Ethiopian, 76, 114–16
  Lydia, 150–51
  Paul, 10, 14, 33, 38, 47, 73, 108, 134–139, 180, 185, 187, 188, 276
  Samaritan, 73, 112–13, 114
Corrymeela, 301, 302
Council of Florence, 279
Council of Jerusalem, 25, 29, 35, 38, 48, 77, 109, 117, 149, 182
Council of Lyon, 279
Council of Trent, 281
Court of the Gentiles, 315
Crete, 40
Crispus, 155
Crucifixion, 86, 167, 169, 211
Customs, 40, 101, 144, 156, 225, 317
Cyprus, 8, 10, 41, 140, 142, 149
Cyrene, 320

Damaris, 175
Damascus, 8, 14, 134, 135, 136, 137, 138, 139, 187
David, King, 79, 87, 88, 106, 142, 168, 169, 170, 171
Day of Atonement, 315
Deacons, 50, 51–52, 61, 315, 317
Dead Sea Scrolls, 320
Decius, 118
Demetrius, 159, 160
Demons, 151, 159, 173, 223, 285, 315
Derbe, 10, 31, 145, 147, 150, 182
Diocletian, 118
Dionysius, 154, 175
Disciples, 13, 18, 31, 32, 51, 52, 65, 66, 67, 68, 69, 72, 73, 75, 79, 88, 111, 134, 135, 138, 144, 147, 148, 158, 227, 228
Discipline, 52, 54–55, 59, 63, 78, 170, 194, 216, 275
Divisions, 70, 99, 205–06, 207, 208–210, 213, 214, 227, 228, 230, 231, 241, 255, 278, 279, 280, 285, 286, 287, 290, 296, 301, 302, 303
Divorce, 219, 220, 221, 241, 288
Domitian, 64, 118
Dorcas, 8
Drusilla, 320

Easter, 164, 279, 280
Eating together (table fellowship), 15, 49, 99, 126, 188, 227, 228, 229–30, 256
Egypt, 102, 103, 104, 105, 106, 114, 119, 122, 168, 170, 228
Elders, 161, 162
Elisha, 320
Elymas, 8, 57, 78, 141, 148
Ephesus, 10, 19, 23, 26, 40, 73, 149, 156, 157, 158, 159, 160, 161, 162, 204, 243, 244, 245, 246, 247, 248, 249, 256, 277
Ephesians, Letter to the, 241, 243, 266, 275, 276
  Background, 243–48
  Main themes, 249–59
  Paul's teaching to, 259–272
  Relevance for today, 272–74
Epicureans, 153, 171, 172, 174
Eros, 320
Eschatology, 190, 264
Ethiopian Eunuch, 76, 114–16
Eucharist, 227, 228, 229
Euthanasia, 292, 293–94
Eutychus, 8, 57, 160, 161, 162
Exorcism, 41, 80, 111, 151, 159, 173, 285, 315

Fair Havens, 40
False teaching, 112, 181, 203, 247, 260
Fasting, 137, 139, 280, 297, 315
Feast of Weeks, 67
Felix, 26
Fellowship, 48, 75, 111, 125, 155, 158, 209, 240
Festus, 26, 134
Food laws, 18, 126, 189

Fortune telling, 151
Freedmen, 80, 101

Gaius, 13, 155, 160
Galatia, 146, 149, 156, 157, 181, 182, 183, 184, 185, 186, 189, 196, 203, 313
Galatians, Letter to the, 6, 14, 15, 38, 135, 170, 276
   Paul's teaching to, 190–199
   Purpose and main themes, 181–84
   Reason for writing, 184–89
   Relevance for today, 199–200, 203
Galilee, 5, 6, 32, 66
Gallio, 26, 39, 155, 156
Gamaliel, 38, 94, 95, 276
Gentile mission, 10, 99
Glossolalia, 68, 112, 232, 316
Gnostic, 321
God-fearers, 7, 114, 123, 143, 152, 168, 171, 173, 316
Grace, 6, 65, 82, 101, 108, 135, 195, 197, 228, 231, 248, 249, 250, 253, 254, 257, 260, 265, 272, 285, 286
Greece, 6, 8, 19, 22, 39, 40, 160, 162, 171, 244
Greek, 5, 6, 7, 11, 23, 24, 39, 48, 50, 51, 68, 69, 82, 84, 99, 100, 136, 145, 146, 153, 157, 168, 172, 174, 185, 193, 194, 222, 230, 231, 243, 249, 253, 260, 279, 283, 302, 308, 315, 316

Healing, 8, 10, 32, 33, 53, 56, 57, 58, 80, 82, 83, 84, 88–91, 95, 101, 111, 145, 151, 159, 230, 232, 279, 285, 316. (see also Miracles)
Hebrews, 50, 55, 99, 101, 109, 142, 316
Hellenists, 50, 99, 101, 109, 316
Hermes, 145, 146, 147
Herod, King, 106, 127, 315
High Priest, 94, 103, 135, 136
HIV/AIDS, 288
Holocaust, 298, 299
Holy Spirit, 13, 24, 26, 29, 30, 32, 33, 42, 47, 48, 50, 51, 53, 54, 57, 58, 62, 65, 66, 67, 68, 69, 70, 71, 72, 73, 74, 75, 76, 77, 78, 79, 80, 81, 82, 83, 84, 85, 86, 87, 88, 91, 92, 98, 100, 101, 107, 112, 113, 115, 116, 117, 124, 125, 126, 129, 130, 138, 139, 140, 141, 149, 150, 158, 164, 165, 190, 194, 196, 197, 198, 199, 200, 202, 207, 212, 213, 217, 230, 231, 232, 235, 240, 250, 251, 256, 260, 264, 274, 282, 308, 309, 310, 316
Homosexuality, 289
Hospitality, 321
Hypocrisy, 321

Iconium, 10, 144, 147, 148, 182
Idols/idolatry, 40, 102, 105, 146, 154, 171, 175, 206, 209, 217, 222–24, 263, 289, 316
Ignatius of Antioch, 61, 118
Immorality, 204, 205, 206, 208, 215–17, 241, 263, 264, 265, 273
Incest, 216
Interpreter, 236
Irenaeus, 11, 16, 112, 244, 312
Isaiah, 78, 114, 168, 169
Italy, 123, 303

James, 13, 19, 20, 25, 27, 47, 52, 65, 127, 128, 131, 167, 178, 184, 187, 191, 311
Jason, 153
Jenkins, David, 321
Jerusalem, 3, 5, 6, 7, 8, 9, 11, 14, 18, 19, 22, 24, 25, 27, 28, 29, 32, 34, 35, 38, 42, 47, 48, 50, 51, 52, 64, 65, 66, 67, 70, 72, 74, 77, 79, 80, 86, 98, 99, 107, 109, 110, 111, 112, 113, 114, 115, 117, 122, 123, 128, 133, 134, 135, 136, 139, 142, 149, 150, 156, 157, 160, 161, 162, 163, 169, 182, 184, 185, 186, 187, 188, 244, 255, 315, 316
Jews, 5, 6, 8, 11, 20, 22, 23, 24, 25, 27,

29, 30, 32, 45, 47, 48, 51, 69, 72, 78, 79, 80, 86, 87, 88, 89, 90, 91, 92, 93, 94, 99, 100, 101, 102, 103, 104, 105, 107, 111, 114, 116, 117, 125, 126, 127, 135, 137, 143, 144, 146, 147, 148, 150, 152, 153, 154, 155, 156, 157, 159, 160, 165, 166, 168, 169, 170, 171, 173, 183, 186, 189, 191, 192, 193, 194, 198, 211, 215, 228, 244, 254, 255, 256, 257, 258, 259, 276, 316, 317, 318
Joel, 70, 86, 88
John the Baptist, 65, 68, 72, 74, 158, 162, 168, 170
John Mark, 127, 139, 140, 142, 149
Joppa, 322
Joseph, 102, 103, 104, 106, 122
Josephus of Alexandria, 20, 94, 135
Judas, 55, 64, 65, 67, 137, 138
Judea, 6, 7, 19, 47, 79, 107, 109, 110, 123, 125, 163
Julius, 322
Justification by faith, 170, 182, 189, 190–96, 203, 245, 316

Kember, Norman, 322
Kerygma, 31, 32, 33
Kingdom of God, 65, 67, 72, 207
Koran, 292
Kyrios, 136

Law of Moses, 6, 29, 45, 67, 86, 94, 99, 101, 102, 105, 107, 109, 110, 122, 135, 137, 155, 181, 182, 183, 184, 186, 188, 189, 190, 191, 192, 193, 194, 195, 196, 197, 198, 202, 203, 209, 216, 217, 255, 256, 284, 287, 288, 292, 307, 310, 316
Laying on of hands, 47, 51, 73, 74–75, 100, 112, 140, 266, 316
Leaders, 50, 52, 73, 77, 91, 100, 101, 103, 107, 128, 139, 140, 142, 143, 152, 182, 188, 209, 210, 213, 215, 279, 281, 284, 299
Legalists, 205
Libertines, 205, 218

Liberation Theology, 316
Life in the Spirit, 182, 190, 197–99
Lord's Supper, 49, 160, 188, 206, 207, 223, 225, 227, 228, 230, 242, 311
Lourdes, 59, 95, 96, 314, 316
Love, 233, 234, 235
Luke's Gospel, 5, 8, 10, 11, 12, 14, 15, 18, 19, 21, 22, 23, 34, 37, 66, 111, 279
Luther, Martin, 265, 281, 282
Lycaonia, 322
Lycia, 322
Lydda, 56
Lydia, 41, 50, 150, 151, 152
Lystra, 10, 23, 40, 57, 145, 146, 147, 148, 150, 154, 176, 182

Macedonia, 8, 10, 22, 40, 150, 154, 156, 160, 181, 244
Magic, 322
Malta, 39, 40, 57
Marcus Aurelius, 118
Mark's Gospel, 18, 279
Marriage, 121, 218–20, 226, 233, 241, 263, 265–67, 273, 276, 287–90
Mars Hill, 172
Martyr/martyrdom, 10, 17, 19, 20, 23, 47, 61, 108, 109, 188, 133, 135
Matthew's Gospel, 18, 279
Matthias, 64
Mesopotamia, 103, 122
Messiah, 6, 31, 32, 65, 86, 87, 88, 90, 107, 138, 142, 167, 168, 169, 171, 189, 211, 255, 316
Methodist Church, 2, 288, 302, 304
Miletus, 10, 161, 176, 244
Miracles, 10, 32, 56–58, 80, 86, 88–91, 94, 95–97, 110, 112, 285
Mixed marriages, 219
Mnason, 13
Montanism, 53, 62, 316
Moses, 29, 45, 89, 90, 94, 99, 101, 102, 104, 105, 106, 110, 122, 136, 181, 183, 184, 188, 189, 190, 191, 192, 194, 195, 198, 216, 255, 316

323

Muratorian Canon/Fragment, 11, 244, 317
Myra, 322
Mysia, 322
Mystics, 206

Nazarenes, 5, 6, 136, 317
Nazareth, 5, 90, 92
Nazarite vow, 317
Nero, 16, 17, 19, 20, 26, 118, 156, 317
Nicanor Gate, 88

Open Doors, 118, 119, 314
Oral tradition, 101, 317

Palestine, 5, 8, 22, 105, 106, 107, 111, 168, 300, 316, 317
Pamphylia, 40, 142
Paphos, 57, 140, 148
Parousia, 22, 50, 61, 67, 90, 275
Passover, 67, 127, 216, 228, 279
Paul
  Athens speech, 153–54, 171–75
  Circumcision, 152, 181, 182, 188, 190, 196, 198, 199, 255
  Conversion, 10, 14, 33, 47, 73, 108, 134–38, 187, 188, 276
  First Missionary Journey, 139–48
  Miletus speech, 161, 244
  Pastor, 276
  Pisidian Antioch speech, 167–70
  Rebukes Peter, 188–89
  Second Missionary Journey, 149–56
  Teacher, 275–76
  Third Missionary Journey, 157–62
  Theologian, 276
Penance, 60, 297, 317
Pentecost, 8, 10, 32, 47, 52, 64, 67, 68, 69, 70, 71, 72, 73, 74, 79, 82, 83, 88, 89, 98, 113, 117, 125, 126, 129, 161
Perga, 40, 142, 148
Persecution, 17, 19, 20, 25, 93–95, 109, 110, 111, 118–21, 128, 135, 144, 147, 153, 317

Peter,
  and Ananias and Sapphira, 32, 54–55, 78
  and Cornelius, 74, 123–26
  escape from prison, 93–94, 127–28
  in Joppa, 109
  and Lame man, 32, 57, 80, 88–89, 145
  miracle worker, 80, 91
  and Paul's rebuke, 188–89
  preaching at Caesarea, 79
  in Samaria, 111, 112
  before Sanhedrin, 32, 57, 92–93
  speech at Pentecost, 72, 86–88
  speech in Solomon's Colonnade, 89–90
Pharisees, 6, 38, 94, 135, 317
Philemon, 10, 13, 146, 246, 247
Philip, 3, 5, 10, 13, 24, 51, 57, 71, 73, 76, 77, 99, 100, 110, 111, 112, 114, 115, 116, 117, 122, 130, 133, 148, 161, 163
Philippi, 23, 26, 39, 41, 50, 57, 58, 150, 152, 153, 157, 160
Philos, 266
Phoenix, 40
Pope, 60, 83, 120, 281, 282, 283, 288, 312, 314
Possessions, sharing of, 47, 49–50
Presbyterian church, 60, 61, 301, 302, 304
Priscilla and Aquila, 47, 62, 154, 156, 157
Prophecy, 30, 77, 232, 235, 317
Prophets, 30, 52–53, 77, 78, 79, 90, 107, 115, 135, 139, 233, 235, 236–37, 256, 257
Proselyte, 317
Publius, 39, 57

Qumran, 315
Qu'ran community, 292

Redemptorists, 303
Reformation, 280, 281, 283

324

Repentance, 47, 54, 55, 72–73, 78, 87–88, 175, 236, 286, 298, 315, 317
Resurrection, 65, 86, 308
Revival, 82
Roman Catholic Church. (*see Catholic Church*)
Rome, 5, 6, 7, 8, 13, 16, 17, 19, 20, 22, 23, 24, 27, 28, 33, 40, 42, 47, 60, 61, 64, 71, 81, 96, 117, 143, 154, 156, 162, 166, 246, 247, 248, 279, 280

Sadducees, 6, 91, 92, 93, 94, 95, 135, 317
Salamis, 140
Salvation, 171, 274, 277, 312
Samaria, 6, 7, 8, 32, 40, 73, 74, 79, 109, 110, 111, 112, 114, 115, 116, 117, 122, 163
Samaritans, 73, 110, 111, 112, 113, 114, 115, 116, 117
Sanhedrin, 6, 32, 57, 80, 92, 93, 94, 101, 102, 107, 108, 127, 128, 129, 317
Saul of Tarsus, 38, 47, 52, 73, 77, 108, 134, 135, 136, 137, 138, 139, 141, 142, 164, 168
Sceva, sons of, 159, 162
Seven, the, 9, 10, 47, 50, 51–52, 80, 99–100, 110, 317
Secundus, 13
Sergius Paulus, 26, 39, 140, 141, 148
Sexual immorality, 206, 215–216, 217, 263, 264, 265, 273
Shake off dust, 144, 317
Sharia law, 292
Shipwreck, 39, 23
Sicily, 324
Sidon, 324
Silas, 23, 149, 150, 151, 152, 153, 154
Simon Magus/the Sorcerer/Magician, 73, 112, 317
Single life, 218, 219, 220
Solomon's Colonnade, 89, 91, 128

Son of God, 212
Spain, 324
Spiritual gifts, 62, 68, 69, 206, 230–33, 234, 260, 284, 285, 316
Stephen, 3, 5, 6, 10, 23, 24, 33, 47, 51, 57, 71, 75, 78, 80, 81, 99, 100, 101, 102, 103, 104, 105, 106, 107, 108, 109, 110, 118, 122, 130, 133, 135, 139, 163, 167, 312
Stoics, 153, 171, 172
Stoning, 107–08, 118, 135, 147, 292
Straight Street, 137
Suetonius, 40
Synagogue of the Freedmen, 80
Synagogue, 80, 143, 318
Synod of Whitby, 280
Syracuse, 324
Syria, 8, 47, 76, 77, 103, 135, 149, 156, 160

Tabernacle, 131, 132, 318
Tabitha, 56, 58
Tacitus, 40
Tarsus, 73
Teachers, 52, 233
Temple, 15, 32, 48, 49, 50, 88, 91, 93, 101, 102, 107, 109, 110, 111, 122, 135, 255, 315, 316
Tertullian, 11, 16
Theology, 29, 30, 276, 307, 308, 309, 311
Theophilus, 12, 21, 23, 26, 28, 64, 123
Thessalonica, 10, 39, 152, 153, 154, 155, 157
Theudas, 94
Thyatira, 41
Timothy, 13, 14, 25, 44, 52, 61, 89, 149, 150, 153, 154, 157, 283, 308
Titius Justus, 155
Tongues, 84, 235, 285
Travel diaries, 9, 12, 35, 36, 318
Troas, 49, 57, 149, 150, 160, 162
Trócaire, 292
Trophimus, 13
Tutu, Desmond, 299, 300

325

Twelve, the, 51, 64, 65, 100, 209
Tychicus, 13, 247, 272
Tyrannus, 158, 159, 162, 244
Tyre, 161

Universalism, 23–24, 29, 318

Veiling of women, 225–27, 291
Virgins, 220
Visions, 86, 105, 107, 109, 111, 123–24, 126, 137, 150, 155, 228, 318

Vow, 15, 25, 156

'We' passages, 34–36, 318
Widows, 50, 51, 99, 220

Yahweh, 107, 173
Youth Link NI, 302, 303

Zeus, 145, 146, 147, 174

INDEX